Deliberative Democracy Now

While millions feel politically marginalized, there is evidence that democracy is evolving into a conversation-based, public-centered practice called deliberative democracy. In this new form of democracy, public discussion, conscious reflection, and collective choice drive democratic governance and have the power to override democratic dysfunction. Illustrating this emerging possibility with examples from twenty-eight years of US public engagement on LGBT equality, this book offers a practical model for the growth of deliberative democracy in which everyone can take part. It identifies the necessary social catalysts, the role of social networks and technology, and key pathways to addressing unconscious bias, hidden fears, and identity based polarization as they were overcome in the LGBT case. It demonstrates how each person can gain voice and influence in a deliberative democracy in which people once again become the true source of political power. This book will interest anyone who cares about the future of democracy.

EDWINA BARVOSA is an associate professor at UC Santa Barbara who holds a PhD in Government from Harvard University and an MA from Cambridge University. An interdisciplinary social scientist and applied theorist, she focuses on democracy, social change, and resolving the influence of implicit bias in organizations and governance, especially of socially inherited biases stored as contradictions within the self. She is the author of *Wealth of Selves: Multiple Identities, Mestiza Consciousness, and the Subject of Politics* (2008) and articles in journals such as *Perspectives on Politics* and the *Journal of Political Philosophy*.

THEORIES OF INSTITUTIONAL DESIGN

Series Editor
Robert E. Goodin
Research School of Social Sciences
Australian National University

Advisory Editors
Carole Pateman, Barry Weingast, Claus Offe,
Susan Rose-Ackerman, Keith Dowding, Jeremy Waldron

Social scientists have rediscovered institutions. They have been increasingly concerned with the myriad ways in which social and political institutions shape the patterns of individual interactions that produce social phenomena. They are equally concerned with the ways in which those institutions emerge from such interactions.

This series is devoted to the exploration of the more normative aspects of these issues. What makes one set of institutions better than another? How, if at all, might we move from the less desirable set of institutions to a more desirable set? Alongside the questions of what institutions we would design, if we were designing them afresh, are pragmatic questions of how we can best get from here to there: from our present institutions to new revitalized ones.

Theories of Institutional Design is insistently multidisciplinary and interdisciplinary, both in the institutions on which it focuses, and in the methodologies used to study them. There are interesting sociological questions to be asked about legal institutions, interesting legal questions to be asked about economic institutions, and interesting social, economic, and legal questions to be asked about political institutions. By juxtaposing these approaches in print, this series aims to enrich normative discourse surrounding important issues of designing and redesigning, shaping and reshaping the social, political, and economic institutions of contemporary society.

Deliberative Democracy Now

LGBT Equality and the Emergence of Large-Scale Deliberative Systems

EDWINA BARVOSA
University of California, Santa Barbara

CAMBRIDGE
UNIVERSITY PRESS

CAMBRIDGE
UNIVERSITY PRESS

University Printing House, Cambridge CB2 8BS, United Kingdom

One Liberty Plaza, 20th Floor, New York, NY 10006, USA

477 Williamstown Road, Port Melbourne, VIC 3207, Australia

314–321, 3rd Floor, Plot 3, Splendor Forum, Jasola District Centre, New Delhi – 110025, India

79 Anson Road, #06–04/06, Singapore 079906

Cambridge University Press is part of the University of Cambridge.

It furthers the University's mission by disseminating knowledge in the pursuit of education, learning, and research at the highest international levels of excellence.

www.cambridge.org
Information on this title: www.cambridge.org/9781108425186
DOI: 10.1017/9781108688079

© Edwina Barvosa 2018

First published 2018

Printed in the United Kingdom by Clays, St Ives plc

A catalogue record for this publication is available from the British Library.

Library of Congress Cataloging-in-Publication Data
Names: Barvosa, Edwina, author.
Title: Deliberative democracy now : LGBT equality and the emergence of large-scale deliberative systems / Edwina Barvosa.
Description: Cambridge, United Kingdom ; New York, NY : Cambridge University Press, [2018] | Series: Theories of institutional design | Includes bibliographical references and index.
Identifiers: LCCN 2017053781 | ISBN 9781108425186
Subjects: LCSH: Deliberative democracy – United States. | Political participation – United States. | Sexual minorities – Civil rights – United States
Classification: LCC JK1726 .B29 2018 | DDC 323.3/260973–dc23
LC record available at https://lccn.loc.gov/2017053781

ISBN 978-1-108-42518-6 Hardback

Dedico esta obra a mis seres queridos y al legado de mis
antepasados al cual he intentado ser fiel/
I dedicate this work to my loved ones and to the legacy of my
ancestors, to which I have tried to be faithful
and
to the students of democracy everywhere–
you are the future.

Contents

Acknowledgments

I am indebted to the many scholars and other specialists who have written on deliberative democracy over the decades, together building a literature that unites scholarship and hope for a better world. As a theorist, my observations of social life are ongoing, but my understanding always evolves from my interactions with others. In this project, I have benefitted from transformative interactions in a diversity of settings. I received invaluable intellectual feedback as well as financial support as an affiliate researcher at the National Science Foundation Center for Nanotechnology and Society at the University of California at Santa Barbara. This collaborative research center gathered an international network of scholars studying many topics, including processes of public deliberation related to science and technology governance. My work in this book and other writings on the democratization of science governance has been greatly influenced by scholars from this group, including center Director Barbara Herr Harthorn, Nick Pidgeon, Terre Satterfield, Robin Gregory, Karen Henwood, Tristan Partridge, Merryn Thomas, and Christina Demski. Thanks especially to Merryn Thomas for organizing group comments on an earlier draft. My thanks also go to members of the Understanding Risk Research Group at the University of Cardiff who kindly offered feedback on this work in June of 2014. I am also grateful to the CNS staff members who supported my participation in the research team including Val Kuan, Shawn Barcelona, and Bonnie Molitor. Overall, this text is based on research supported by the US National Science Foundation (NSF) under Cooperative Agreement # SES-0938099. The opinions, findings, and conclusions offered herein are mine and do not necessarily reflect the views of the NSF.

In addition, a team of seven undergraduate students contributed to this project as research assistants helping to gather the original data for this study. They include Kimberly Bolanos, Danielle Cizek, Andrew

Farkash, Briahn McClarty, Ryan Orihood, Evan Tambini, and Riane Torres. Guadalupe Perez and Diana Solano also provided subsequent research assistance. My thanks go to the entire team and to then graduate student Chloe Diamond-Lenow who collaborated with me in overseeing the working group and also provided technological expertise. I am especially grateful to Chloe whose contributions to organizing the data were crucial to completing this project. My special thanks also go to Rosie Bermudez who provided expert research assistance throughout the writing and production of this manuscript; her insights into the material deepened my own reflections. I am grateful for inspiring student engagement in my courses *Democratizing Gender* and *Democracy and Diversity*, especially to the 2011 cohort, and for conversations on this topic with former graduate student and now colleague Kathleen Cole. Thanks also to Amy Foss and Ana Barba for sharing their insights on social media as part of youth organizing and social change.

Much about the formation of deliberative democracy described in this book hinges on understanding how implicit bias – the product in part of social inheritances – influences everyday life, and how the willingness to courageously respond to it might best be found. In my effort to observe implicit bias in organizations and in governance, and to reflect on mitigation options, I have benefitted enormously from conversations with attorneys working in diverse capacities in Southern California, including insights gathered from working as an expert witness and as a continuing legal education instructor on implicit bias. My thanks go to all those who took the time to share their diverse perspectives on bias with me during the period of this project, including Mark Saatjian, Michael Hanley, Tara Haaland Ford, Steve Dunkle, Ann Richardson, and participants in my continuing legal education trainings on the mitigation of bias.

Among the many scholars for whose influence I am grateful, I especially thank John Garcia and Valerie Martínez-Ebers for their careful guidance over time. I am thankful also to the members of the APSA Latino Caucus for community, encouragement, and friendship. I am also especially grateful to CUP series editor Robert Goodin – a renowned scholar of deliberative democracy. His encouragement and critical feedback on this project has been invaluable. Likewise, I offer my special thanks to the three anonymous reviewers for CUP who provided extremely valuable feedback that helped me to improve and refine this offering. I also thank the team at Cambridge University Press who guided me expertly through the review and production process, especially John Haslam and Julie Hrischeva, who supported me unwaveringly throughout, including during the final editing of this book, which took place during historic wildfires and landslides in my location.

Lastly, it gives me joy to thank my family and friends who gave me loving encouragement and support as I completed this project, including all who sustained my health and wellness. Many thanks go to my brother Eduardo Barvosa II, Natalie Schonfeld, Jana Renner, Ben Flores, Allan Walters, John Lubina, Lance Todd, Dave Malinowski, Wendy Bowers, Lara Kelly, Dee Langford, Amanda Crowell, Lisa West, Lissa McGraw, Cheryl G, David Hallegua, and my mother Pamela – who all cheered and eased my path. Lastly, in remembrance I thank my father Eduardo Barvosa, Sr. who passed away in 2015. My dad encouraged me in this project at every opportunity and he inspires it still. I am grateful for the bountiful love and intellectual support that I have been given during this project. Any and all errors or omissions remain my own.

Introduction

Deliberative Systems and the Problem of Scale

> Even the decentered society cannot do without the reference point provided by the projected unity of an inter-subjectively formed common will.[1]
>
> —*Jürgen Habermas*

Dysfunction in American democracy has become a source of concern to people across the political spectrum in the US and around the globe. While this disquiet is well founded, it is also worthwhile to remember that democracy itself is evolving. As with other forms of social self-organization, democracy shifts and transforms in and over time as societies themselves change in unforeseen ways.[2] For several decades numerous scholars have held that one potential next stage in the evolution of democracy is the emergence of "deliberative democracy." In this vision, deliberative democracy is democratic self-governance in which a society chooses how to live in common through a conversation-based process of collective reflection and discussion. This deliberative democracy has been described often – frequently following the philosopher Jürgen Habermas – as involving an exchange of reasons among people who are engaged in meaningful communication and consideration on

---

[1] Habermas, Jürgen. 1992. "The Unity of Reason in the Diversity of Its Voices," in *Postmetaphysical Thinking: Philosophical Essays*, trans. William Mark Hohengarten. Cambridge: MIT Press, 141.

[2] R. J. Reinhart, "More in US Say Government is the Most Important Problem," *Gallup*, June 15, 2017, www.gallup.com/poll/212426/say-government-important-problem.aspx?utm_source=alert&utm_medium=email&utm_content=morelink&utm_campaign=syndication. For a detailed discussion of how American democracy has already evolved and become more democratic over time, see Robert Dahl, *How Democratic is the American Constitution?* (New Haven: Yale University Press, 2001). In this book, I follow established convention in using the terms *America* and *American* in reference to the United States of America, thus eclipsing their larger reference to the Americas as a whole. I acknowledge, however, that for some readers, especially those attuned to colonial and postcolonial history, this narrow application is problematic from a long-term hemispheric perspective.

a matter of common concern. In this democratic ideal, the common will is created and influentially expressed through a process of collective reflection, discussion, and choice.

This idea of deliberative democracy, including its many scholarly variations, has taken a central place in democratic theory in what is often called the "deliberative turn." Predominant as this idea has become, however, the concept of deliberative democracy has also gained as many critics as advocates. Those who reject the idea of deliberative democracy have often done so on the grounds that it is too idealistic, vague, and abstract. Many critics thus dismiss deliberative democracy as impossible to realize, considering it a theoretical fantasy that ignores, or leaves in place, the brutal and unjust social hierarchies and inequities of power that have infected the heart of politics around the globe for thousands of years.[3] Critics have likewise emphasized, with good reason, that most representative democracies today seem to be *less,* rather than more, attentive to the voices of their publics. To many, this increasing irrelevance of public voice signals a democratic malaise that appears intractable because it is sustained by inequities of power and access for which there is no end in sight.[4]

The scholarly debate over deliberative democracy has long ago moved beyond the domain of political theory to the work of empirical researchers. The deliberative turn has sparked extensive scholarly experimentation with deliberative practices. These experiments yielded useful institutional designs intended to help implement deliberative democracy (Nabatchi et al. 2012; Smith 2009; Parkinson 2006). Yet experimentation with deliberative practices has also remained primarily small-scale. To date this has left scholars searching fruitlessly for ways to institutionalize deliberation on a large national or international scale. Political

---

[3] The literature encompassing the deliberative democracy debate is voluminous and widely known. For a narrative of the full extent of the discussion see Nabatchi et al. *Democracy in Motion: Evaluating the Practice and Impact of Deliberative Civic Engagement* (Oxford: Oxford University Press, 2012).

[4] The literature on democratic malaise includes many scholarly works, including Jacob S. Hacker and Paul Pierson, *Winner-Take-All-Politics: How Washington Made the Rich Richer and Turned Its Back on the Middle Class* (New York: Simon & Schuster, 2010) and Larry M. Bartels, *Unequal Democracy: The Political Economy of the New Gilded Age* (New York: Russell Sage Foundation, 2008). Many contributions have arisen in domains beyond the academy. See for example, Parker Palmer, *Healing the Heart of Democracy: The Courage to Create a Politics Worthy of the Human Spirit* (San Francisco: Jossey-Bass, 2011).

scientist Robert Goodin has stated the remaining task simply: "Deliberative democrats need to find ways of linking the virtues of small-scale deliberation with decision-making for larger-scale societies" (Goodin 2008, 3). One theoretical response to this challenge has been the emergence of the idea of deliberative systems that potentially span and include many diverse parts of a society in deliberative practice.[5] Yet so far, for many reasons – including the size, diversity, and persistent internal social divisions in the United States and other democracies – the establishment of large-scale deliberative democracy has remained beyond reach.

But perhaps the goal of realizing deliberative democracy is much closer than we think. In this work, I explore the possibility that the practical creation of deliberative democracy on a large scale – particularly in the form of a publicly self-organized deliberative system – is much closer to fruition than we realize. Specifically, I propose that without our full awareness, at least one large-scale deliberative system has already emerged in the US in the form of a publicly self-assembled, national-scale, public engagement on a topic of key public concern. In this process, members of the public themselves created the deliberative system that they needed, aided in part by new communication technologies and existing social networks that together facilitated public self-organization through tools and experiences available today to nearly all members of US society.[6] If so, then the shape of this deliberative system largely followed the pattern theorized by a team of democratic theorists led by Jane Mansbridge (2012). In addition, in practice deliberative system formation also required a number of additional features and mechanisms as yet unexamined. I propose in this work that these additional features included three specific social catalysts, several underlying mechanisms, and the overcoming of particular

[5] As discussed later in this chapter this possibility has been theorized by Jane Mansbridge with a team of democratic theorists, see Mansbridge et al., "A Systemic Approach to Deliberative Democracy," in *Deliberative Systems: Deliberative Democracy at the Large Scale*, ed. John Parkinson and Jane Mansbridge (Cambridge: Cambridge University Press, 2012), 24–26.

[6] Most of the literature on deliberative democracy employs the term *citizen*; however, I have used other more inclusive terms in this work to include the many millions of non-citizen member of the US who are contributing members of the political landscape, including an estimated 12 million unauthorized residents, the majority of whom are Latina/o immigrants. For further discussion see, Raymond Rocco, *Transforming Citizenship: Democracy, Membership, and Belonging in Latino Communities* (East Lansing: Michigan State University Press, 2014).

cognitive obstacles, elements that all together enabled the practical formation and growth of a large-scale deliberative system.

To investigate this possibility, I offer in the chapters that follow an empirical, data-driven, exploratory, and theoretically grounded inquiry into the prospect that the US public – a highly diverse democratic people – has *already begun* to informally implement the long elusive practice of deliberative democracy. In so doing, I ask in this study two interrelated questions: *Are the practical processes for the implementation of deliberative democracy emerging as new social practices in the US public domain? And if so, what underlying mechanisms are at work in these nascent processes?* My overall answer to the first of these questions is yes. There is reason to believe that there is at least one – and potentially only one – example of the formation of a deliberative system in the United States on an issue of common concern. I propose that this example can be seen in the extended US public discussion of the issue of social and legal equality for the US lesbian, gay, bisexual, and transgender (LGBT) minority. This discussion, I suggest, grew into an informal, large-scale, deliberative system that formed and grew in the US until reaching a national scale over time during the years from 1987 to 2015, with rapid acceleration from the introduction of new communication technologies after 2006. This large-scale deliberative system, in turn, served as the vehicle for a relatively rapid and seismic shift in US public opinion, including a new consensus favoring full equality for LGBT people. This new consensus overcame longstanding anti-gay bias, thereby producing an unexpected transformation in societal practice that occurred most visibly in the United States between 2002 and mid-2015.[7]

If this observation is accurate, then this development raises the possibility that large-scale deliberative practices can also arise on other topics. If so, then a practical path is emerging by which it is possible to render public voice and will as the guiding mainstays of democratic decision-making. If deliberative democracy is increasingly viable as a form of

---

[7] This case study focuses primarily on the US context, but other discussions have taking place in other nations around the globe. Ireland, for example, approved same-sex marriage by a wide margin of 62.07 percent to 37.93 percent in national referendum on May 22, 2015, www.irishtimes.com/news/politics/marriage-referendum/results. Thus while it is beyond the scope of this study to attend to the international examples of public engagement on LGBT civil rights, some international developments may parallel the developments discussed here.

large-scale democracy, then it remains to be understood, however, exactly how such a transformation has unfolded, and by extension, what other practical steps might still be needed to advance deliberative systems on other issues of common concern. This book offers an empirical exploration of these unfolding possibilities. In it, I focus on the prospects for implementing deliberative democracy now as a practice of democratic self-governance centered on public choice that is exercised through public engagement and deliberative practice.

In the remainder of this introduction, I describe the scholarly context and trajectory of this study. I also situate the concept of deliberative democracy in its broader historical context by briefly describing its larger philosophical and practical purpose within its intellectual history. I then sketch the current state of scholarly knowledge on deliberative democracy, focusing on one major challenge in the study of deliberative democracy: the problem of scale. Finally, I identify the methodological approach used in this project, as well as provide a brief roadmap for the chapters that follow.

Deliberative Democracy in Context: Habermasian Origins and Contemporary Conundrums

The potential implementation of deliberative democracy is intertwined today with the emergence of the information age, networked societies, and a development in knowledge and awareness known as the "linguistic turn." As noted by philosopher Jürgen Habermas in the epigraph to this introduction, the linguistic turn has significantly shifted how we understand the processes of human reason, but it has left public reason and collective will as significant as ever. The linguistic turn is the understanding that all societal norms, practices, and human identities are socially constructed in an ever-ongoing manner through language-mediated processes.[8] As detailed in later chapters, these language-

---

[8] The insights of the linguistic turn have emerged across many disciplines, yet as discussed in later chapters, the implications of the linguistic turn are not always consistently or fully taken into account in democratic theory. As elaborated in this work, the possibility of deliberative democracy via deliberative systems depends to a large extent on processes of social construction. For classic scholarship across disciplines, see in ordinary language philosophy, Ludwig Wittgenstein, *Philosophical Investigations* (New York: Macmillan, 1968); in continental social theory see Michel Foucault, *History of Sexuality, Volume One* (New York: Vintage Books, 1980); in anthropology, Fredrik Barth,

based processes of social making and remaking – combined also with factors of communication technology, and social networks within existing social domains – together play a constitutive role in the emergence of large-scale deliberative systems. To situate these diverse elements in the narrative to follow, it is helpful at the outset to briefly review and contextualize the idea of deliberative democracy itself as Critical Theorist Jürgen Habermas originally theorized it. Doing so also positions deliberative democracy in its broader historical context and original purpose. The backstory of the idea of deliberative democracy begins with the Age of Reason.

The Age of Reason in Europe (1620s–1780), also known as the Enlightenment, arose from the turmoil and hardship of the Wars of Religion (c. 1524–1648). While not all of the conflicts of the period were religiously based, the rigid unreason of religion at that time fostered incalculable losses and bloodshed across Europe. The Age of Reason, which also coincided with the rise of Newtonian physics, sought to cast aside religion in favor of reason, objectivity, and science. Secular reason and science were thought at that time to be untouched, and therefore untainted, by emotion, metaphysics, religious fanaticism, and related social influences and fervors. It was therefore thought that the project of privileging Enlightenment reason and science would solve the problem of humanity's persistent engagement in war, thievery, and other self-destructive activities (Muthu 2003).

This Enlightenment project, however, did not produce the hoped for peace and justice. Instead, the claims of reason and the tools of science were soon put to use to justify renewed rounds of destruction, including the atrocities of colonization, empire-building, war, and bigotry in its many forms, including racism, sexism, and the imperialist erasure of sexual, gender, religious, and cultural diversity (e.g. racial and ethnic eugenics).[9] By World War II, science and reason had not only permitted

---

Ethnic Groups and Boundaries: The Social Organization of Culture Difference (Boston: Little, Brown and Company, 1969); in sociology Anthony Cohen, *The Symbolic Construction of Community* (Chichester: Tavistock Publications, 1985); and in psychology Kenneth Gergen, *Invitation to Social Construction* (London: Sage, 1999).

[9] These facts are generally well known, but for anuanced treatment see Sankar Muthu, *Enlightenment Against Empire* (Princeton: Princeton University Press, 2003). For these forms of bigotry in the US context, see Michael Omi and Howard Winant, *Racial Formation in the United States: From the 1960s to the 1990s* (New York: Routledge, 1994) and Michael Bronski, *A Queer History of*

violence, but both were heavily implicated in the genocide of the Holocaust and in the creation of the greatest threat to humanity – the atomic bomb.[10] The grand failure of the Enlightenment project to produce peace and justice thus posed a conundrum: Why had reason failed to produce peace? The scholars of the Frankfurt School, particularly Max Horkheimer and Theodor Adorno, sought to understand and resolve this conundrum through their scholarly work in the tradition of Critical Theory (Wiggershaus 1994).

Philosopher Jürgen Habermas – a key originator of the concepts of public reasoning now central to the theory deliberative democracy – is the principle intellectual heir to the Frankfurt School tradition. As Horkheimer and Adorno reached the end of their productive years, they thus looked to Habermas to undertake their concern with the failure of the Enlightenment project to realize peace and justice.[11] Having assumed the intellectual mantle of the Frankfurt School from its founders, Habermas then proceeded to guide the living tradition of Critical Theory. Discourse ethics – or more precisely the theory of communicative reason – theorized by Habermas was his response to the conundrum that concerned his predecessors (1990d). Over time, other scholars also embraced the project of developing discourse as a mode of collective reasoning that could help humanity overcome conflict and live in peace. These various developments eventually led to the conception of deliberative democracy (Bessette 1978, 1994; Dryzek 1990, 2000; Dryzek and Niemeyer 2010; Ackerman and Fishkin 2004). Yet a deliberation-based answer to the shortfalls of

the United States (Boston: Bacon Press, 2011); with regard to the colonial suppression of gender diversity see also, Will Roscoe, *Changing Ones: Third and Fourth Genders in Native North America* (New York: St. Martin's Griffin, 2000).

[10] Or at least the *appearance* of reason, see Kai Erikson, "Hiroshima: Of Accidental Judgments and Casual Slaughters," In A *New Species of Trouble: The Human Experience of Modern Disasters* (New York: W.W. Norton & Co., 1994), 185–202; For artistic representation of the scale, the use, and testing of nuclear weapons see also aConcernedHuman, "A Time-Lapse Map of Every Nuclear Explosion Since 1945 – by Isao Hashimoto," *YouTube*, Video, 14:24, posted on October 24, 2010, www.youtube.com/watch?v=LLCF7vPanrY.

[11] The work of the early Frankfurt School was broad and varied and many other concerns were also addressed. The tradition continues today having produced many students over time. I am trained in part in this tradition by two of Habermas's students and later colleagues, Seyla Benhabib and John B. Thompson.

the Enlightenment project was not the response that Habermas's mentors expected or desired of him. Rather, Horkheimer and Adorno felt that the key to understanding the failure of Enlightenment reason – and thus to redeeming and transforming the Enlightenment project – lay in transcending the false understanding of the self as unitary.

More specifically, in several of their later works Horkheimer and Adorno argued that the presumption that the self (i.e. defined here as the embodied consciousness of human subjectivity) is unitary is a deceptive and destructive error. This error contributes to the subjugation of nature and to a false image of human beings as impenetrably separate from each other, rather than mutually influencing and fluidly interconnected.[12] They observed (like Hume, William James, and others) that the self, and thus the subjectivity of political agents, is not unitary (Barvosa 2008, 2–5). Rather, the self is decentered, internally diverse, and multiple. Horkheimer and Adorno came to believe that insistence on this factual error was somehow linked to – and in part responsible for – a great deal of the violence, conflict, and failed democratic practice that marred post-Enlightenment human history. Together Horkheimer and Adorno gestured that the way forward to resolve this conundrum and to increasingly produce peace was to consider how the actual inner diversity of the self could be better understood both on its own terms and also in relationship to the projects of anti-fascism and greater social justice. Their expectation was that their protégé, Habermas, would undertake this next step, explore the multiplicity of the self, and thus solve the conundrum.

Conversely, however, Habermas held that the kind of "subject-centered" philosophical approach to the issues of fascism, failed democracy, and large-scale violence that he was expected to pursue

---

[12] In an extended account of the project of Enlightenment and its distortions, including the humanity's destruction of nature, Horkheimer and Adorno stated (albeit in esoteric terms) how human subjectivity is perceived falsely as shorn of its inner diversity: "It is the identity of the spirit and its correlate, the unity of nature to which the multiplicity of qualities falls victim. Disqualified nature becomes the chaotic matter of mere classification, and the all-powerful self becomes mere possession – abstract identity." Max Horkheimer and Theodor W. Adorno, *Dialectic of Enlightenment* (New York: Continuum Publishing Company, 1991), 10. For further discussion in the context of a longer tradition of seeing the self as a multiplicity, see Edwina Barvosa, *Wealth of Selves: Multiple Identities, Mestiza Consciousness, and the Subject of Politics* (College Station: Texas A&M University Press, 2008), especially 2–9.

had reached the end of its usefulness (1990b). Habermas contended alternatively, that what was needed was to rethink reason itself as a collective communicative exercise that took place in an uncontrolled public sphere. To him, this kind of collective public reason could be self-correcting and thus, to Habermas, was a far more promising path to democratization and also to peace and justice. This path, he argued, would bring new philosophical and practical understanding that would be useful in resistance to fascism, social hierarchies, and other forms of injustice. Habermas thus shifted focus from intersubjectivity to discourse and public reason (Habermas 1984, 1984a, 1989, 1990b). As these ideas of centering collective reasoning in the pursuit of justice were taken up and developed by others, the multidisciplinary study of deliberative democracy was born.[13]

In Habermas's departure from the course of his mentors, he significantly redirected the focus of the Frankfurt School tradition.[14] Habermas's initial arguments regarding the public sphere, and communicative and discourse ethics sparked key debates and have, over time, founded an enormous and still growing field of scholarship dedicated to debating the theory and practice of deliberative democracy. Thus for over thirty years, Habermas's work has led scholars on an inspiring and ongoing intellectual journey to reimagine public reason. More specifically, Habermasian deliberative theory conceives of public reason as a process of deliberative rationality in which public reasoning involves an exchange of mutually intelligible reasons toward the formation of mutual public understanding and agreement. But Habermas described this ideal of deliberation less as a specific procedure, and more as a philosophically complex vision. In that vision, public reason was reconceived in the form of a free, full, and

---

[13] Some narratives also credit Rawls, but for reasons articulated by Simone Chambers, it is arguably more accurate to trace the origins of deliberative democracy primarily to Habermas. See Simone Chambers, "Deliberative Democratic Theory," *Annual Review of Political Science* 6 (1) (2003), 308.

[14] Some scholars, such as Paul Apostolidis, have argued that returning to the concerns, cultural focus, and methods of the early Frankfurt School is productive for understanding continued political challenges to justice and peace, especially the continued problem of religion-related intolerance; see Paul Apostolidis, *Stations of the Cross: Adorno and Christian Right Radio* (Durham: Duke University Press, 2000). In undertaking a cultural focus in this inquiry, I likewise strive to echo the approaches of the early Frankfurt School.

equal public exchange and deliberation that is not controlled, determined, or otherwise undermined by coercion or hierarchies of power (Habermas 1992, 1993, 1990d). Moreover, this view was not based on an existing empirical reality, but rather theorized in an anticipatory manner from the pressing needs and problems of existing democratic practice.

As compelling and inspiring to many as this philosophical vision of deliberative democracy has been, however, the implementation of this ideal has often been seen as impossibly utopian and frustratingly elusive. As such, despite its appeal, the theory of deliberative democracy has often seemed perplexingly out of sync with the contrary realities of everyday democracy – democracy marked by inequities of power, inattention to public voice, intolerance, violence, and widespread human inclinations toward mutual disregard and miscommunication within and among large and deeply diverse societies. These persistent problems – which caused the failure of the Enlightenment project in the first instance – also appear to many to plague the seemingly ideal solution of deliberative democracy (Hagendijk and Irwin 2006, 169). As detailed in the next section of this chapter, among scholars working in various intellectual traditions today, the deliberative turn is widely embraced and prolifically discussed. Yet it has been also a point of ongoing frustration that deliberative democracy has not yet been put into practice on a large scale even as people worldwide have increasingly clamored for increased democratic voice of the kind promised by the ideal of deliberative democracy. Moreover, the serious consequences of unwise governance – involving for example extreme economic inequality, climate change, and decaying infrastructure – have continued to mount. In this context, arguably the most significant problem of the study of deliberative democracy has been the problem of how deliberative democracy can be realized on a large scale.

A Primary Challenge to Deliberative Democracy: The Problem of Scale

Many scholars of democracy generally share with the American public, and many observers worldwide, a concern with deep dysfunctions in American democracy. This concern often extends to hope for productive change not only in the US, but also in less-than-fully democratic nations around the globe.[15] Scholarly production on deliberative democracy alone has been extensive. Stacks of recent books speak to a need for democratic innovation, while an array of other writing counts the ways that American democracy currently fails to meet its own articulated ideals.[16] Nor have scholars restricted their activities to academic contexts.[17] A significant number of scholars of deliberative democracy have studied, and themselves worked, as public practitioners of democratic engagement, some founding longstanding centers and institutions dedicated to implementing public deliberations.[18]

Thus the scholarly literature related to deliberative democracy theory and practice is large and diverse, and as some scholars have pointed out, it is also significantly fragmented (Nabatachi et al. 2012, 4). Taken as a whole, however, and as already alluded to, many scholars regard the most pressing and intractable problem to be the problem of scale.[19] The question behind this challenge is: *How, if at all, can deliberative practice take place on a national level?* The scholarly effort to resolve the problem of scale is potentially undermined by frequent disconnection between work in deliberative theory and the study of

---

[15] This is true among scholars specifically addressing deliberative democracy (see Goodin, *Innovating Democracy: Democratic Theory and Practice After the Deliberative Turn* [Oxford: Oxford University Press, 2008]), but also among scholars of democracy more generally such as Ian Shapiro, *The Real World of Democratic Theory* (Princeton: Princeton University Press, 2011) and Mark Bevir, *Democratic Governance* (Princeton: Princeton University Press, 2010).

[16] Sheldon S. Wolin, *Democracy Incorporated: Managed Democracy and the Specter of Inverted Totalitarianism* (Princeton: Princeton University Press, 2008); Thomas E. Mann and Norman J. Ornstein, *It's Even Worse Than It Looks: How The American Constitutional System Collided with the New Politics of Extremism* (New York: Basic Books, 2012).

[17] For a list of public centers and institutes dedicated to deliberative democratic practice, see Matt Leighninger, "Mapping Deliberative Civic Engagement: Pictures from a (R)evolution," in Nabatchi et al. *Democracy in Motion*, 32–37.

[18] For example, Stanford Professor James Fishkin has for 20 years conducted experimental research in deliberative democracy through the Center for Deliberative Democracy at Stanford University and he has advocated for public deliberation to general audiences as means to solve collective problems. See Joe Klein, "How Can a Democracy Solve Tough Problems?" *TIME*, September 2, 2010, accessed July 23, 2012, content.time.com/time/magazine/article/0,9171,2015790,00.html.

[19] For a list of other open questions see, Nabatchi et al., *Democracy in Motion*, 264–265.

empirical public deliberation in practice. In other words, many scholars have tackled the question of whether deliberative democracy can be realized on a large-scale (or in culturally diverse democracies) from divergent vantage points that are only infrequently bridged. With few exceptions, for example, nearly all empirical studies of public deliberation focus on relatively small-scale exercises using established techniques such as deliberative polling, study circles, mini-publics, World Café–style small group discussions, deliberative workshops, online deliberations, citizen juries, consensus conferences, initiative forums, among other protocols (Smith 2009; Kahane et al. 2010; Nabatchi 2012). Yet these important empirical explorations often set aside theoretical insights regarding how small-scale, face-to-face, deliberative practices might function best in diverse social contexts (Nabatchi 2012). Nonetheless, enormous scholarly effort has been put into addressing the question of scale over time, and three possible answers to this problem are currently pending.

One possible solution to the problem of scale is that among the various small-scale forms of deliberative practice being studied (e.g. deliberative workshops, study circles, citizen juries, etc.) one or more may be redesigned to include millions of participants at once.[20] Alternatively, the use of small-scale deliberation practices might become practiced so widely that public deliberation would begin to constitute a major factor in democratic life at large. Either way, this first approach addresses the problem of not only including all members of a democratic society, but also incorporating its diversity. As one scholar has put it, "there is no realistic chance of capturing the full range of diversity within any modest-sized deliberative body" (Goodin 2008, 4). If so, then large-scale deliberation remains crucial for

---

[20] The discussions are innumerable and diverse. For examples see on performative deliberation Arabella Lyon, *Deliberative Acts: Democracy, Rhetoric, and Rights* (University Park: The Pennsylvania State University, 2013); on deliberative elections, John Gastil, *By Popular Demand: Revitalizing Representative Democracy Through Deliberative Elections* (Berkeley: University of California Press, 2000); on deliberative polling and other approaches see *Approaching Deliberative Democracy: Theory and Practice*, ed. Robert Cavalier (Pittsburgh: Carnegie Mellon University Press, 2011); and on deliberative public planning, see John Forester, *The Deliberative Practitioner: Encouraging Participatory Planning Processes* (Cambridge: MIT Press, 1999).

meaningful democratic inclusion. The institutional design for implementing this first possibility, however, remains unclear.[21]

A second possibility in response to the problem of scale is to reimagine public deliberation as something that does not occur face-to-face, but rather in the minds and hearts of people as they reflect individually on matters of collective concern. Robert Goodin has proposed this form of "democratic deliberation within" in his book *Reflective Democracy* (2003). The advantage of this approach is that it does away with logistical constraints of physical co-presence and draws attention to practices of reflection. This move is realistic, for even when people are co-present in face-to-face deliberation, much of the cognitive work that is taking place occurs as reflection in the minds of deliberators. Internal reflection while in engagement with others, in turn, results in analysis and thought that then may be conveyed to others for further consideration. Moreover, in this approach, the reasons why people choose as they do – i.e. the underlying values that they employ – are as important as the answers that deliberators reach. Here too, however, the institutional design that would render deliberation within as a practical protocol is not yet available (Goodin 2003, 18–19). The empirical research offered later in this book, however, sheds light on the possibility that emerging deliberative systems rely in large part on deliberation within the self.

The third potential option is that large-scale deliberative democracy might take the form of a large-scale deliberative system that is made up of many diverse sites and forms of public deliberation that distribute deliberative work and functions throughout a society in ways that "form a complex whole" (Mansbridge et al. 2012, 2). Although scholarship focused on small-scale deliberative practice is comparatively more visible in the intellectual history of deliberative democracy, theories of deliberative systems also go back to early scholarship on deliberative democracy, including Habermas's early account of the

---

[21] Nabatchi et al., for example, emphasize seeking ways to better understand those who use deliberative techniques in local settings, and stress developing appeals to others who may potentially adopt them, see Nabatchi et al., *Democracy in Motion*; for examples of use of deliberative practices in discrete localities see, Clark and Teachout, *Slow Democracy: Rediscovering Community, Bringing Decision Making Back Home* (White River Junction: Chelsea Green Publishing, 2012).

public sphere.[22] More recently, however, the deliberative systems approach to deliberative democracy has gained renewed support and attention.

The most comprehensive recent contribution regarding deliberative systems is a collaborative effort led by political theorist Jane Mansbridge, who worked in concert with a number of prominent theorists to synthesize and advance current theoretical approaches to the idea of deliberative systems. The results of this collaborative effort were published in 2012 in *Deliberative Systems: Deliberative Democracy at the Large Scale*, co-edited by Mansbridge with John Parkinson. In their book, Mansbridge and her collaborators have offered the most definitive theoretical account of deliberative systems to date, including an account of the system's shape, rationale, and three main functions. They identified these functions as *epistemic, moral, and democratic* – or stated in more general language: (1) increasing public knowledge, (2) generating mutual respect, and (3) fostering inclusive democratic practice (10–13).

Mansbridge and her colleagues theorized a deliberative system as a large, diverse, and decentered talk-based system through which questions of common life are discussed in the form "What is to be done?" In their account, deliberative systems may be bounded by institutional forms or by issues. Any and all institutions, e.g. churches, schools, diverse social groups, organizations, and individuals, may play a deliberative role. The arms of the state facilitate elements of the system, but the state does not have an all-pervasive or determining influence. Particular elements or moments of the system may or may not be democratic in and of themselves, but taken *as a whole* the system serves to foster and sustain its three overall functions. In this process, partisan conflict, social movements, and the contributions of experts may all play roles in the formation of a deliberative system. Mansbridge and her colleagues have also anticipated extensive redundancy in the

---

[22] Jürgen Habermas, *Between Facts and Norms: Contributions to a Discourse Theory of Law and Democracy* (Cambridge: MIT Press, 1996);
Jürgen Habermas, "Further Reflections on the Public Sphere" in *Habermas and the Public Sphere*, Ed. Craig Calhoun (Cambridge: MIT Press, 1993), 421–461. For a recent discussion further relating Habermas's contributions to mediated communication in deliberative systems, see Rousiley C. M. Maia, *Deliberation, the Media, and Political Talk* (New York: Hampton Press, 2012).

system as a diverse public deliberates questions through many means and moments scattered throughout the overall system (1–12).

In offering their account, Mansbridge and her team have further noted that there remains a need to develop a template by which to empirically assess when a deliberative system exists, how healthfully it might be functioning, and what practical supports and conditions an effective system requires. As Mansbridge et al. have stated:

> The question becomes more complex when we try to specify the conditions more concretely ... Therefore in addition to the three larger functions [i.e. epistemic, moral, and democratic] we would also *need a template to evaluate the conditions that support the various functions of good deliberation. This is, however, not a project that we will take up here.* (Mansbridge et al. 2012, 13, emphasis added)

Here Mansbridge and her colleagues pinpoint a remaining task of identifying and evaluating the underlying mechanisms required to support a large-scale deliberative system. Mansbridge and her collaborators of necessity set this task aside as beyond their endeavor.

In this book, I respond to this call for a more empirically grounded template of deliberative system formation, including a sketch of the underlying conditions necessary for a large-scale deliberative system to form and to serve as a vehicle for public deliberation. I focus in this work on developing an empirically grounded theoretical model of the underlying mechanisms needed to support deliberative system growth, including the mechanisms by which it comes into being, and how an informal deliberative system achieves implementation power in the democratic process. As described further below, I undertake this task through the production of a theoretical model that is illustrated through the analysis of empirical evidence from a case study of American public engagement on the issue of LGBT equality over a 28-year period.[23]

Overall, this study of the underlying mechanisms at work in the practical formation of a large-scale deliberative system ultimately suggests that, in practice, such a deliberative system would draw elements from all three of the pending possibilities for realizing deliberative democracy on a large scale. This case study of US public engagement on LGBT equality illustrates the pivotal importance of widespread

---

[23] Here and throughout this work I use public engagement, public reflection, and public deliberation interchangeably to reduce repetition of terms.

individual reflection – i.e. Goodin's deliberation within – in deliberative system formation. Moreover, small-scale deliberations were also sometimes deployed in the LGBT case and played a role that helped to create large-scale deliberation. Consequently, in this study I suggest that there is no need to choose only one of the three major options for implementing large-scale public deliberation. All three possibilities form part of the solution to the problem of scale in the realization of deliberative democracy.

Scholarship and the Problem of Scale: Bridging Empirical and Theoretical Research

As noted above, the deliberative turn is influential in political science, especially in democratic theory. But it also has a central place across a number of other social science disciplines and domains (Habermas 1990; Davies 2006, 424–428). For example, deliberative democracy has become a major focus in the study of science governance in the field of science and technology studies (STS). Yet scholarly engagement across disciplinary lines and between theorists and practitioners has often remained limited. Addressing this factor in their book *Democracy in Motion*, Tina Nabatchi, John Gastil, and their colleagues offer a comprehensive survey of the extensive and far-flung literature on empirical deliberative practice (2012). They attend to the different forms of deliberative practice that have been developed in the last few decades, including study circles, deliberative polling, and other protocols. Nabatchi's team, like other scholars, has found that while the literature on deliberative democracy is vast and varied, it is also significantly fragmented. Nabatchi et al. have noted that scholarship on deliberative practice features significant divides between theoretical work and empirically oriented efforts. In addition, they note that relevant scholarship is divided by different terminologies, disciplinary traditions, assumptions, and theoretical or practical orientations. As such, clusters of scholars are working in relative disengagement from many others who are on a similar path (2012, 3–6).

For example, STS scholar Sheila Jasanoff (2005, 272–291) and democratic theorist Dennis Thompson (2008) have separately called for more dialogue between STS scholars and political scientists, and especially between democratic theorists and researchers of empirical practice. In this vein, Jasanoff has underscored a "need for new theoretical resources to bring the missing public back into studies of science and democracy" (2005, 248). In different ways Thompson and Jasanoff thus have contended that more interdisciplinary engagement would reveal that political theorists and STS scholars are often tackling interrelated questions, encountering related problems, and often pointing out similar ways forward from their respective disciplines. Among these disciplinary convergences, scholars in both political theory and STS have encountered significant gaps between theories of public deliberation (i.e. theories of deliberative democracy) and empirical practices among deliberation researchers. Some STS scholars have declared that these gaps between theory and practice are so extensive that they warrant a full-scale mapping of all current disjunctures (Delgado et al. 2011, 826–827).

Relatedly in political theory, scholars of public deliberation have noted that theorists and empirical researchers often "talk past each other" as empirical deliberations often fail to generate the advantages that theorists had anticipated (Neblo 2005; Thompson 2008). Conversely, relevant available theory is not always considered or incorporated into research designs in experimental studies of deliberation. As such, as Dennis Thompson notes, many small-scale deliberation protocols have remained unreliable – succeeding only variably, and often for reasons that are not understood theoretically (Thompson 2008). Together these observations call for scholars to better theorize the disjunctures between the expectations of deliberative theory and the practical outcomes of empirical public deliberation research. Moreover, relevant empirical research is also conducted in scholarly traditions and disciplines beyond STS and political science, such as risk perception research, that are seldom considered by democratic theorists (Pidgeon 1998; Butler, Parkhill, and Pidgeon 2013; Pidgeon et al. 2014; Gregory, Satterfield, and Hasell 2016). Consequently, Thompson in particular has urged political theorists to look more carefully at the empirical realities that deliberation presents and to engage with empirical research findings more fully (2008, 498).

In the research presented in this book, I contribute to the project of bridging theoretical contributions and empirical research by answering the call to attend to empirical deliberative practices. I work here to generate theory that not only suggests how large-scale deliberative systems may be publicly self-assembled, but in so doing, I also consider how some specific cognitive obstacles to public deliberation may sometimes disrupt some small-scale deliberative practices. Theory building in this book is based on and illustrated with data and information collected regarding observable events that have occurred in the public domain. But it also draws on existing theoretical literatures in various disciplines, including constructivist theory and social network theory as further described in the methods section of this chapter. As a social and political theorist working in this study toward an applied theoretical analysis, I have also undertaken to collect and analyze empirical data needed to develop a grounded theoretical account of a deliberative system. In addition to shedding light on the immediate prospects for deliberative democracy, my hope is that this form of inquiry can also help to bridge the common divide between empirical research on public deliberation and the work of democratic theorists.

Methods and Approach: An Exploratory Study in Applied Social and Political Theory

Like many research projects in the social sciences, this study began with simple curiosity about the significance of an event. In this case, the event was the levying of a $50,000 fine to an NBA player named Joakim Noah for his use of a homophobic slur during a basketball game televised in the US in the spring of 2011. The event occurred near the time when majority public opinion in the US turned in favor of endorsing same-sex marriage. Teaching on democracy at the time, it struck me that the shifting terrain of US public opinion featured increasingly diverse occasions in which members of US society could consciously think about their unexamined views and attitudes toward LGBT equality. It occurred to me also that in levying this heavy fine, the NBA had not only taken a strong stand on player conduct, but also potentially opened up an informal forum in which sports fans who might not otherwise reflect on the issue of equality rights for LGBT people might now do so as part of viewing their favorite sporting event. The curiosity roused by my observation combined with an awareness of the concept of deliberative systems (Mansbridge et al. 2012) to shape my intuition that public engagement on LGBT civil rights might be taking the form of a deliberative system of some significant scale and diversity.

The hunch that a deliberative system might be emerging on LGBT issues led to a formal research study centered in political theory, but one with an interdisciplinary sensibility. In practice, political theory itself has been described as "an unapologetically mongrel-subfield" of political science (Dryzek, Honig, and Phillips 2009, 63). Its diverse traditions and wide purview include, but are not limited to, normative theory, intellectual history, and a wide range of specific theoretical traditions including Critical Theory, poststructuralism, postcolonial theory, and feminist theory, all of which influence this work. Moreover, despite occasional rumors to the contrary, there are methods to the diverse subfield of political theory. Rather than gravitate to a formulaic norm, however, political theorists have generally chosen from among a wide array of theoretical frameworks often situating their contributions heavily toward humanistic study. Many political theorists thus privilege interpretive methods over more empirical (some would say allegedly empirical) enterprises.

I share this interpretive-humanistic approach to political theory to an extent and I honor it fully. But I also see the diverse facets of political theory – especially when combined with social theory – to be a productive toolkit that can be usefully applied in scholarly inquiries that might also contribute to practical problem solving. If specific practical problems warrant it, therefore, I also consider it worthwhile as an applied theorist to pursue empirically oriented theory building and analysis. In the case of the present inquiry, the problem of scale in deliberative democratic theory is both a theorist's puzzle and a practical conundrum. As a result, I have taken an applied theory approach.

More specifically, the scholarly context of this study includes, (a) widespread scholarly doubt as to the practical feasibility of deliberative democracy, (b) the highly abstract quality of much deliberative theory, and (c) the call by Mansbridge et al. (2012) and others (Dryzek 2007) for an empirically grounded template or blueprint of a deliberative system in action. This state of scholarly inquiry on deliberative systems pointed to a need to bridge theory and practice and to inquire more empirically into the unlikely and elusive, if hopefully not impossible, phenomenon of deliberative systems. To pursue the factual potential on the ground, methodologically, I opted to undertake a data-driven study in the form of an exploratory data analysis (EDA). EDA has a long tradition in statistics and across the social sciences (Mosteller and Tukey 1977; Hoaglin, Mosteller, and Tukey 1983; Behrens and Smith 1996; Behrens and Rowe 1997; Cramer 2003; Stebbins 2001).

In contrast to conformational data analysis (CDA), EDA generally seeks to corroborate and verify quantifiable relationships in existing numerical data. Exploratory data analysis is a companion method used to forward the explanation of phenomena that are not yet fully understood. In this case, the unknown phenomenon is the empirical possibility that a large-scale deliberative system might have formed and functioned in the US on the issue of LGBT equality.

In his classic works, statistician John Tukey (1986) as well as Stebbins (2001) and others have argued that exploratory data collection and analysis is not a preliminary phase of empirical research to be quickly transcended for more empirically valid study. As Turkey once put it: "Exploratory data analysis is an attitude, flexibility, a reliance on display, NOT a bundle of techniques, and should be so taught."[24] Thus for various purposes, EDA is a key form of study useful in the exploration of complex or new phenomena. It helps to identify the properties of the unfamiliar through a data-driven analysis to locate characteristic concepts, categories, relationships, and patterns. Exploratory data analysis is used here as the best approach to the present task of exploring the empirical possibility that a large-scale deliberative system can form, and that one might have emerged in the US on the issue of LGBT civil rights.

In general, exploratory data analysis can be undertaken on either quantitative or qualitative data. In this case, I chose qualitative data collection over quantitative study. I made this choice because, in general, quantitative statistical analysis reveals the measurable size of observed relationships found in a phenomenon and "the likelihood that such a relationship occur[ed] by chance" (Cramer 2003, 5). But in the LGBT case, the phenomenon of shifting public opinion and social practices regarding LGBT equality was already known to be largely based on majority public opinion polling and other evidence. Moreover, while chance occurrence in the LGBT case was and is a possibility, the significant and fairly rapid change in public opinion appeared to have been fostered by the concerted efforts of many. With this in view, quantitative investigation of the magnitude of these changes and their relative probability logically needed to await

---

[24] John W. Tukey, "We Need Both Exploratory and Confirmatory," in
     The Collected Works of John W. Tukey, Lyle V. Jones, ed. Vol. 4 (Belmont, CA:
     Wadsworth, 1986), 811, emphasis in original.

greater clarity as to whether public deliberation in the form of a deliberative system had truly emerged in the LGBT case, and if so by what means.

What remained uncertain at the outset of this study then – and what Mansbridge et al. (2012) had urged as a point of further theorizing – was a basic sense of what a deliberative system might look like in practice, and also what underlying mechanisms may have been at work in the major shift in public opinion in the LGBT case. Was shifting public opinion a sign of public deliberation and democratizing? Was it instead a function of trendsetting and social following, or something else? If the phenomenon was deliberative then, what mechanisms fostered that deliberation, how did it spread, and how had new public attitudes and shifting norms applied pressure on governmental institutions for legal and procedural change? Quantitative analysis of numerical data – if it were available – could not answer these questions in the first instance. I thus opted instead therefore for a qualitative approach to better meet the needs of the inquiry. In qualitative study the data is, of course, comprised primarily of "words and sometimes visual representations" but content is not the distinguishing factor. Rather "what distinguishes qualitative research is its quest to understand the qualities ... of a phenomenon *by focusing on the meanings of events and phenomena* and the social events that transform these meanings" (Behrens and Smith 1996, 978, emphasis added). In addition, qualitative data analysis is widely viewed across disciplines as exhibiting a number of properties including:

(a) a focus on understanding "participant meaning and action" and identifying clusters and patterns of meaning that define the phenomenon under consideration; (b) the primary influence of – and unavoidably situated quality of – the researcher; (c) the related obligation to produce not objective, but interpretively "coherent, credible accounts [of a phenomena] that have authenticity and verisimilitude"; (d) use of a reflexive approach to data collection and analysis; (e) the foregoing of hypothesis testing in favor of "constructing meaning from [qualitative] data" as a means to characterize a phenomenon; (f) rigorous contextual sensitivity; (g) avoidance of reductionism; (h) cognitive engagement with and effective management of an internally diverse and often "vast and cumbersome" dataset(s); (i) focus on units of analysis relevant to the specific object domain of study; (j) the provision of robust and detailed description that as fully as possible reflects the phenomena that the data represent; and finally (k) validity derived findings from reasonable and adequately transparent methodological choices, and a strong "convergence of evidence and theoretical and contextual understanding."[25]

In this case, the qualitative exploratory data analysis used here focuses on elucidating the systems of meaning and practice involved in the shift in US public opinion regarding LGBT equality that occurred most strikingly between 2001 and 2015 and that may represent an example of a large-scale deliberative system in practice.

Taking this overall approach, three guiding questions governed the data collection phase of this study as well as the later phases of data analysis. These guiding questions were: (1) Does the available data suggest that the sea change in US public opinion on LGBT equality arose through a deliberative process of public reasoning? If so, (2) Does that process of collective public reasoning appear to have taken the form of a deliberative system as so far theorized? And (3) If a deliberative system appears to have been in operation, what are its properties, including related components, underlying mechanisms, and/or any social meanings that may have fostered or furthered the development of the deliberative system? To explore publicly available materials that might shed light on these three questions, a large and diverse qualitative was collected.

The dataset is comprised of a collection of published materials reflecting occurrences and events related to LGBT equality in the US that are relevant to public engagement on the issue of LGBT civil rights and which took place in the United States between January 1, 1987, and June 26, 2015. While by no means exhaustive, the dataset encompasses a wide and diverse sample of over 8,000 discrete incidents of speech and action, including legal, or other structural developments regarding the public discussion of how historically marginalized LGBT people should be viewed, and incorporated socially and civilly into mainstream American life. The dataset includes examples of public

---

[25] There is an extensive literature on qualitative research methods that spans the social sciences. Followers of the renowned statistician John Tukey, Behrens and Smith (1996) offer a particularly clear and concise account of the contributions and qualities of qualitative data analysis in comparison to quantitative analysis. I rely extensively on their formulation here, see "Data and Data Analysis," in *Handbook of Educational Psychology* (New York: Macmillan Library Reference, 1996), 945–989. All quotations in this series appear on pages 978–979 with the final item appearing on page 985.

speech, news coverage, protest events, public commentary, and related cultural products such as films and television programs as well as materials that reflect public reception and response to those cultural products and newsworthy events.

With the exception of preliminary examples collected during the initial formulation of the research design, the dataset was collected between April 1 and June 26, 2015, with the vast majority gathered during a bulk data collection phase between April 7 and June 15, 2014. In the bulk collection phase, a team of seven volunteer research assistants were asked to engage in a self-directed "scavenger hunt" to locate, via the Internet, any and all items that they individually considered to pertain to public discussion of LGBT issues. Researchers were asked to feel free to use their own discretion and be guided by their own interests and curiosity in selecting materials as well as to take an expansive and inclusive approach to collecting materials that they deemed relevant to public opinion formation on LGBT inclusion and equal civil rights. During the bulk collection phase, a graduate research assistant and I co-supervised the volunteer group and guided the research assistants on technical matters (e.g. database functions, navigation of online databases, various means of using internet search terms, and so on). To avoid biasing the data collection in any particular direction and to foster breadth and diversity in the sample, the seven members of the team were not guided to collect any particular items in the bulk collection phase. Instead, they were left to generally gather materials that came their way following only the general initial description of the project.

To help minimize duplication, maximize diversity and breadth in the materials gathered, and to organize the data to facilitate later analysis, the seven team members were asked to select one or two broad domains of research interest and to focus primarily, but not exclusively, on those areas, storing the materials that they located in a common location in the retrievable database. These general domains were: Sports; Entertainment (mass and niche) including theatrical film, documentary film, TV, music, theater, dance, art, and books (fiction and non-fiction); Community Groups (e.g. Boy Scouts of America); Religion and Faith Traditions; Personalities (celebrities, public figures); Family Life and Friendship; Business and Economics; Public Protest; Legislatures and the Courts; and other extended controversies. Examples of materials in each category were provided as initial guidance but no lists of expected materials were made or issued. To further minimize duplication of entries, if researchers came upon materials of interest that they considered relevant to another domain of activity beyond their primary domain of focus, they were asked to collect it and pass it on to the team member(s) focusing on the relevant area. The researchers were also asked to focus their searches within a given time period between January 1987 (three months before the founding of ACT-UP) and the present date of their research activity sometime between April 7 and June 15, 2014. A general topic area and a specific timeframe thus bounded each researcher's efforts to produce on the whole a longitudinal and topically organized database.

To foster diversity and uniqueness in the search results contributed to the dataset, team members used their own computers and worked in times and places of their own choosing. They were encouraged to use any search engine of their own selection and were instructed in the use of a diverse range of various online databases. Researchers attended a weekly research meeting where technical questions and problems were addressed. To avoid introducing search trends or influencing the search results of others, however, volunteer researchers did not convey in detail what they were locating, nor were they encouraged to circulate among themselves particular items during this bulk collection phase activity. Although the internet was used to collect materials that served as the dataset, the bulk of the materials collected were not originally or exclusively Internet-published sources. Many, if not most, were originally sources from mainstream or niche media outlets including print journalism, television sources, documentary film, and/or published commentary on relevant events or cultural products. The dataset does include, however, some material from Facebook and other social media platforms. All collected materials were stored by topic category as links in an online database using the program Zotero.

To facilitate both security and access, in some cases materials that were downloadable were stored by category as Word documents as backup documentation. In addition, in analyzing all material from the database an extraction was made of those events that were interpreted as being particularly high profile, or potentially significant as turning points. This subset of data totals just over 7 percent of the whole (570 of 8,000). These selected items were separated and placed onto two timelines using the database timeline3D and then also presented in searchable spreadsheets using Excel. One timeline identified key social events across popular culture generally (i.e. across all domains indicated above, such as sports, social groups, religion, and so on). The other timeline focused on legal and/or other structural changes, such as relevant court rulings and shifts in state or federal public policy. These two timelines were also collated into a third in which structural changes were superimposed on the timeline of social milestones. These sequenced extracts from the dataset as a whole were intended to serve in the data analysis phase to offer a representation of whether landmark social events and structural changes arose in tandem or alternatively in sequence, as well as to reveal any "tipping points" in acceleration over time.

After the bulk data collection phase was complete, the data analysis was undertaken in several stages generally consistent with grounded theory analysis as developed by Glaser and Strauss (1967; see also Charmaz 2006). Consistent with their approach, analysis in this case began with a general research problem and a search for hypotheses that may arise from the collected data (rather than hypothesis testing) (Glaser and Strauss 1967, esp. 194–196). The research problem to be addressed here was articulated in the guiding questions, namely again, was a large-scale deliberation taking place at all in this case, and if so how? Exploratory analysis began with an open coding phase – a general application of theoretical sensitivity, looking for any patterns that might suggest concepts or relationships that the data typify.[26] The aim here was to "derive from the data as a whole, a small set of themes or propositions that can be instantiated and confirmed by refer [ence back] to the data" (Behrens and Smith 1997, 981–982; see also Robson 2002, 256). Among the suggestive patterns that emerged was a particularly high incidence in the names of particular individuals in specific domains, such as the almost universal reference to and/or quotation of John Amaechi in the sports-related items in the dataset.

This and two other patterns – social network dynamics and specific patterns in discursive framings – also emerged in this initial open

---

[26] In this work, I retain the two-phase coding technique from open coding to theoretical coding initially proposed by Glaser and Strauss (1967). For further discussion of variations see Barney G. Glaser, *Emergence vs Forcing: Basics of Grounded Theory Analysis* (Mill Valley, CA: Sociology Press, 1992) and David McNabb, *Research Methods for Political Science: Quantitative and Qualitative Methods* (Armonk, NY: M.E. Sharpe, 2004), 384–385.

coding phase. Combined, these patterns suggested to me – as I contend in the chapters to follow – that a deliberative system had emerged along the lines theorized by Mansbridge et al., but that additional empirical underlying mechanisms were also at work in the growth and function of the system. The open coding phase suggested categories of deliberative relationships and themes that were further scrutinized and elaborated in the next phase of data analysis referred to as axial coding. In this later phase, I analyzed the data to determine the specific properties of three core categories of factors contributing to the form of the deliberative system that, I suggest, appeared in the LGBT case. The empirical data collected for this study was also analyzed using event history analysis to trace patterns in events across domains including the common appearance of similar types of catalysts and growth patterns.

In the final phase of exploratory data analysis, I turned attention to providing – and continuing to corroborate through the method of constant comparison – robust and valid descriptions of the overall findings. To do so, I engaged in a round of theoretical sampling defined as "a deliberate search for episodes and incidents that enlarge the variance of properties [under review] and thus put boundary conditions around category definitions and propositional statements" (Behrens and Smith 1997, 982). Here I employed the qualitative research standard of reflexivity in data collection and analysis by adding supplemental data on specific incidents to flesh out event histories that could illustrate particular points, especially points related to (a) the influence of extremism, (b) dense and cohesive social networks, and (c) the persistence of patterns in key events that took place between January and June 26, 2015, after the bulk data collection had been completed.

In this phase, researchers conducted additional searches relevant to targeted events. For the purposes of theoretical sampling, therefore, the period of the case study – though not of the originally collected dataset – was extended to June 26, 2015, the date of the US Supreme Court decision *Obergefell* v. *Hodges*, which declared same-sex marriage to be legal across the nation.[27] The supplemental data taken for the final phase of theoretical sampling is held separately from the original dataset. However, a significant portion of the supplemental data is described in the case study chapters as part of illustrative case event

---

[27] *Obergefell* v. *Hodges*, No. 14–556, slip op. at 23 (U.S. June 26, 2015).

histories. Overall, the findings of this exploratory data analysis are offered in this work through a general theoretical overview provided in Chapter 1 and then elaborated through detailed reference to the data in Chapters 2 through 5.

Additional Relevant Case Study Methods

Most of the applied theoretical analysis in this book is derived from exploratory qualitative data analysis offered in a case study format. In this methodological approach, therefore, case study methods are utilized. For the purposes of statistical inference in scholarly inquiry, case studies are often regarded with some suspicion. Some view case studies as yielding only "one datapoint," and thus too little for generalization. Methodologists who utilize case studies, however, have argued that for the purpose of theorizing the mechanisms at work in complex multifaceted phenomena – *especially toward theory development* – case studies do not operate at the level of statistical inference as, for example, surveys do (Gerring 2007). Rather, they operate at the next higher level of analytic inference, in which each case study provides for *analysis of a class of phenomena*. As such, according to methodologist John Gerring, for the purposes of theory building, theoretical conclusions drawn from a detailed case study constitute a methodologically sound, broad-based inference regarding the phenomenon under study. Moreover, the inferences drawn may be used as the basis to develop theory that has potential applicability to many other examples within the class (Yin 2003, 31–39; Gerring 2007, 61).

Following Gerring and Yin, in this inquiry, the qualitative database collected here has been used as an empirical basis for theory development. Specifically, this case study has been used to develop a theory of the underlying mechanisms at work in the public self-assembly of large-scale deliberative systems. As such, this case study also represents one example of a potentially emerging class of a new phenomenon (i.e. networked deliberative systems). This method is similar to that followed by Manuel Castells in his theoretical consideration of the emergence of a new type of social movement, namely networked social movements (Castells 2012, 2015). Like Castells, I cannot prove through the case study offered here that the mechanisms that I have identified theoretically were active. Nor can I prove beyond a doubt that they account for the observed sea change in American public opinion regarding legal and social equality for LGBT people. Rather, theory is provided here in the spirit of collaboration as an exploratory contribution to further empirical inquiry and debate.

Nevertheless, the LGBT case study offered does illuminate and support the view that, at a bare minimum, times are changing. The theoretical model and framework provided here suggests that the hopes harbored by many that dysfunctional aspects of American democracy (and other democracies as well) can be transformed are not misplaced. Based on the data analysis theorized in this work, I suggest that the means are now available to implement large-scale deliberative democracy. Americans themselves, I further propose, appear to have already built one large-scale deliberative system though which they have made new choices about LGBT equality and made their own public voices heard as a central force in democratic policy-making on this issue. At the time of this writing, other deliberative systems on other issues, such as economic inequality, gender equity, climate change, and racialized violence in the use of force by police, may also be emerging on this model.

Study Scope and Relevance to LGBT Studies

Finally, this study is methodologically interdisciplinary in that it draws upon constructivist theory, social network theory, and knowledge of human cognition produced in numerous disciplines in the social and life sciences. In addition, the centrality here of the LGBT case study makes this manuscript relevant to LGBT Studies, which itself is an interdisciplinary field. Generally, knowledge about LGBT lives is contributed to from various disciplines across the humanities and social sciences including history, literature, art, and political science, as well as, at times, the psychological and life sciences. LGBT Studies as a scholarly field, however, is focused heavily in the humanities, particularly cultural studies, literature, art, history, and queer theory.

There are many ways to tell the story of the evolution of the large-scale recognition of LGBT equality in America. Historians have often told the story of LGBTQI civil rights by narrating tales of resistance, from the early gay and lesbian societies – such as the Mattachine Society and the Daughters of Bilitis – to Stonewall, and by telling illuminating histories such as those of Harvey Milk, the AIDS crisis, and the vivid activism of ACT-UP (Bronski, 2011).[28] Others scholars have drawn the timeline of queer life back to antiquity, tracing same-sex desire and love throughout the ages and around the globe (Rupp 2009). Some writers have focused on the specific lives of LGBT people and their influence or obscurity (Foucault 1990; Middlebrook 1998). Others have told the history of legal changes and continuities over time (Gerstmann 2008; Eskridge 2008). Still others have traced the evolution of how LGBT people have been portrayed in popular culture over decades (Elledge 2010, 2010a, 2010b), and how anti-LGBT discourse has often been linked to partisan and religious subcultures (Burack 2008). Many other narratives also exist, including an alternative account that I offer in Chapter 5 of this book.

Overall, in this work, however, I tell the story of the struggle for equality for LGBT people as part of the story of democracy itself, and as part of how democracy may now be evolving within the epochal shift introduced by the information age. In this story, the effort to gain equality for LGBT people has been pathbreaking not only for LGBT lives, but potentially for all democratic people in that this struggle in particular has prompted, I propose, the first national-scale, deliberative system to be self-assembled by a democratic people. In telling the story of the struggle for LGBT equality this way, however, many important elements of interest to LGBT Studies come within the possible scope of the current project but do not emerge as elements of sustained focus in this book. The potential terrain of the case study conducted here is vast, and a much longer book could be written on the case study alone.

Topics raised by the LGBT case study include, but are not limited to, childhood and family life, bullying, teen suicides, same-sex marriage, military service, state and federal recognition of civil unions and transgender identities, religious perspectives on same-sex relationships, state

---

[28] For simplicity I have followed the current convention and, with a few exceptions, omitted Q and I from the LGBT acronym. These letters otherwise signify queer and intersex respectively. I have also omitted the asterisk from the T* which currently signifies the wide expanse of gender diversity including, gender queer, gender fluid, and other gender variations in identities and practices. Nevertheless, I regard the diverse experiences and needs of gender queer, gender fluid, other gender variant, and intersex people to be highly important both socially and politically. In Chapter 5, I return to these forms of deep diversity to discuss and highlight how these and other expressions of human gender and sexual diversity bear valuable insights for this inquiry.

and federal employment protections for LGBT people, among many others. For the sake of brevity and theoretical clarity, the case study as presented here centers on only a sampling of these elements in order to best demonstrate the underlying conditions of deliberation at work – conditions that made large-scale public deliberation possible. As described in this methodology section, these patterns are theorized from a large sample of public speech and action regarding LGBT civil rights using social constructivism and social network theory as toolkits for analysis.

Consequently, much more could be drawn from the case study materials than is represented or discussed in this book, and most relevant scholarship in LGBT studies goes unaddressed (Currah, Juang, and Minter 2006; Rudacille 2005). There is also limited discussion here of the important fact that much of the public deliberation in the case study period of 1987-2015 focused primarily on gay and lesbian experience – especially same-sex marriage – with less attention given to bisexuality, transgender, and other gender diversity. This pattern in public discussion began to shift significantly in mid-2014 when transgender experience and civil rights claims rapidly gained increased social visibility. In May 2014, *TIME* magazine hailed this shift with a cover story entitled, "The Transgender Tipping Point: America's Next Civil Rights Frontier."[29] Likewise, gender fluidity has also been gaining more mainstream attention.[30] Omissions remain, however, and to date, for example, there has been little public deliberation regarding the equality and needs of intersex people. In short, while the sample used for this case study is extensive and the analysis offered is detailed, both convey only a small subset of what has transpired on this topic that is relevant to LGBT Studies. In the concluding case study chapter, however, the narrative of LGBT civil rights is retold in an

---

[29]　Katy Steinmetz, "The Transgender Tipping Point," *TIME*, published electronically, May 29, 2014, www.time.com/135480/transgender-tipping-point/; see also Buzz Bissinger, "Caitlyn Jenner: The Full Story," *Vanity Fair*, Published electronically, July 2015, www.vanityfair.com/hollywood/2015/06/caitlyn-jenner-bruce-cover-annie-leibovitz.

[30]　For example, see mainstream coverage of Australian model Ruby Rose coming out as gender fluid in a short film entitled "Break Free," Rachel McRady, "Ruby Rose Destroys Gender Roles, Transforms From Female Ideal to Male Ideal in a Short Film 'Break Free,'" *US Weekly*, published electronically, June 17, 2015, www.usmagazine.com/celebrity-news/news/ruby-rose-break-free-film-gender-roles-2015176.

alternative manner that brings aspects of gender and sexual diversity back to the center in the context of democracy's current evolution.

Case Study Overview and Chapter Roadmap

Overall, this book offers a grounded theoretical model for the institutional design and practical formation of a large-scale, publicly self-assembled, deliberative system as it may now emerge in social and political life. I illustrate this model through a central case study of 28 years of US public engagement on LGBT equality. At the heart of the proposed model is a set of underlying empirical mechanisms, three necessary catalysts, and specific practices for overcoming common cognitive obstacles to deliberation that, I suggest, together comprise the necessary components for the practical formation of a large-scale deliberative system. Taken together this practical illustration may show that the US public has itself already created the practices needed to realize deliberative democracy at last. If so, then the story that unfolds in the following chapters may provide a blueprint, including the tools and experiences, by which a democratic public may now construct deliberative systems on any topic of its choosing.

Chapter 1 provides a conceptual overview of the model of deliberative system formation offered in this book. The chapter describes and defines the various underlying elements that foster deliberative system growth. It also highlights the relationships among these various components including the sequential and temporal aspects of these relationships. In Chapter 1, I also discuss the characteristics and dynamics of deliberative systems that distinguish deliberative systems from social movements.

Chapters 2 through 5 together offer an extended case study of public engagement on LGBT equality that illustrates the elements and operation of the model outlined in Chapter 1. The LGBT case study spans a period of 28 years between January 1, 1987, and June 26, 2015. As described above, the collection of materials that forms the basis of this case study includes over eight thousand documents reflecting diverse instances of speech, action, and public reflection in the evolution of public thought and practice related to LGBT equality and civil rights in America. This sampling is comprehensive, and yet it merely scratches the surface of what has transpired. As such, the events and speech acts collected and analyzed in this study do not include the full universe of what took place, but instead represent a significant sampling of diverse events and discourses of many kinds. These materials span numerous domains of social life from sports and entertainment to politics, youth organizations, and religious groups.

This case study investigates a widely recognized shift in public opinion and significant social change regarding the equal treatment and incorporation of LGBT people in the US. In the cultural shift examined in this case study, public opinion polls on LGBT equality indicate that this transformation occurred especially between 2002 and mid-2015. In the fall of 2010 and spring of 2011 in particular, an apparent "tipping point" was reached in which a majority of Americans had shifted their views in favor of marriage equality and the social acceptance of gay and lesbian relationships – a common but imperfect proxy for overall LGBT social acceptance.[31] In addition, from early 2011 the momentum of shifting public opinion correlated with the increasing implementation of measures to secure equal rights for LGBT members of society in local, state, and federal law and public policy. By May 2015, majority public opinion had continued to expand in favor of full LGBT equality, with increasing attention to transgender equality. Also at that time, a new high of 60 percent of Americans polled favored acceptance of same-sex marriage.[32] On June 26 of 2015, in a landmark ruling, the US Supreme Court ruled in favor of constitutional protection of same-sex marriage nationwide.[33]

Based on these and many features of the case study detailed in Chapters 2 through 5, I propose first and foremost, that a successful public deliberation did take place in the US through the vehicle of a deliberative system. The question regarding life in common that was under consideration via the deliberative system was: *Should LGBT people be accepted and integrated into mainstream US society on an equal basis, and if so, how?* As surveyed in chapters to follow, the deliberative system through which this question was addressed arose in

---

[31] For a popular rendering of the concept of a tipping point in social change that is occurring through social networks and social epidemics, see Malcolm Gladwell, *The Tipping Point* (Boston: Little, Brown, 2000).

[32] Katy Steinmetz, "The Transgender Tipping Point"; Justin McCarthy, "Record-High 60% of Americans Support Same-Sex Marriage," *Gallup*, published electronically May 19, 2015, www.gallup.com/poll/183272/record-high-americans-support-sex-marriage.aspx?utm_source=alert&utm_medium=email&utm_content=morelink&utm_campaign=syndication.

[33] *Obergefell* v. *Hodges.*

the United States on the issue of LGBT equality between 1987 and June 2015, and the system remains in operation at the time of this writing. It was through participation in this deliberative system, I suggest, that by 2015 a majority of Americans abandoned anti-gay views in favor of legal equality and full social inclusion, especially for gay and lesbian people.[34] In 2014 and 2015, a shift in deliberative focus was also taking place to consider more fully the equality of transgender and bisexual people as well.[35] Working from this proposal, throughout this remainder of this work, I examine the LGBT case as an example of a potential deliberative system in practice.

Consistent with this, and as predicted by Mansbridge and her colleagues, in this case, public engagement via a deliberative system has operated in and through the established components of social and political systems, including the media, commerce, social organizations, the state, and various segments of the public, as well as the general public as a whole (2012). Likewise the LGBT case study offered in Chapters 2 through 5 provides extensive evidence, both direct and indirect, that, as argued by Robert Goodin (2003), private reflection has played a central role in the public deliberation. Furthermore, as anticipated by Mansbridge et al. the state (defined as any and all governance structures at local, state, and federal levels, including institutions that exercise the military and police powers of the state) also played a significant, but by no means decisive role. The media likewise appears as a pervasive part in this LGBT case study, as does the influence of commercial entities. For example, specific businesses and business leaders within the market economy are seen to serve as nodes of deliberation within the deliberative system. Through advertising and sponsorship, corporations in the LGBT case study are seen to express support or rejection of specific actions relevant to LGBT equality, thereby wielding influence that is sometimes pivotal in shifting the policies of social groups or governmental institutions (Chapter 3).

The LGBT case study offered here also highlights the activities of organizations in civil society including churches, schools, and social groups of many kinds. Nonprofit entities and non-governmental organizations are another component of deliberative systems that are observed in this case study. As anticipated by Mansbridge and her

---

[34] McCarthy, "Record-High 60% of Americans Support Same-Sex Marriage."
[35] Steinmetz, "The Transgender Tipping Point."

colleagues, this dimension includes organizations or individuals that offer expert knowledge on a given area of interest, and groups that focus on fostering social dialogue and social change on issues of public concern.[36]

Social movement actors and advocacy groups are also key deliberative actors in this LGBT case study, just as Mansbridge et al. have generally foreseen (2012). Many of these organizations are single-focused, dedicated to advocacy on LGBT civil rights issues, including such groups as the Gay Lesbian Alliance Against Defamation (GLAAD), LGBTQ Task Force, and Lambda Legal. Such advocacy groups and social movements are regarded as part of deliberative systems in the theory offered by Mansbridge et al. Yet for reasons outlined in Chapter 1, although social movements operate through some of the same underlying mechanisms as deliberative systems, social movements also include processes that diverge significantly from deliberative systems thus distinguishing deliberative systems from social movements.

In addition, various publics represent and comprise diverse social and cultural domains that are also part of deliberative systems.[37] As sociologists have long documented, any given society can be seen as an overarching public (e.g. "the American public") as well as a wide array of diverse publics within the whole that represent various subgroups and their lifeworlds. These publics may include subcultural groups (e.g. sports fans or Boy Scouts), demographic groups, or other publics based on region, profession, partisanship, ethnicity, race, language group, generation, and so on.

Over its four chapters, the case study elaborates how a deliberative system grew in scale from individuals stirring reflection in their own

---

[36] Mansbridge et al. designate reliance on experts, and especially the dominance of technocratic experts in bureaucratic governance, as a problem for deliberative systems that must be resolved (2012, 13–17). While I agree that there are risks, in this empirical research, however, independent knowledge producers are often seen to play an important role in the formation of deliberative systems especially as arbiters of verifiable facts and as necessary contributors to some deliberative catalysts, such as the construction of deliberative packages; for further discussion see especially Chapters 1 and 2.

[37] In this work, I use the term *publics* selectively to acknowledge the diversity within a general public and to refer to cases in which different social domains represent overlapping or divided publics as subgroups within the general public as a whole.

social domains in 1987, to nationwide networks of deliberation and implementation in 2015. Illustrations of key elements of deliberative system formation include examples of actions taken by numerous figures, some socially prominent and others previously unknown. These highlighted actors and their relevant social domains include Ellen DeGeneres (entertainment), Barney Frank (politics), Bishop Gene Robinson (religion), and retired NBA basketball star John Amaechi (professional sports), as well as others in the domains of politics, medicine, and religion and youth groups, including Zach Wahls, an Iowa youth raised by his two mothers, who unexpectedly became a national and international spokesperson on LGBT equality at the age of nineteen. Further, the example of the rapid rise and fall of the Indiana State Religious Freedom Bill in March 2015 illustrates the powerful policy influence and implementation capacity that can be wielded by a fully formed deliberative system.

Finally, the case study offered here focuses on deliberation in the US context. Yet this case study also demonstrates that US public deliberation also interacted with related events and discussions occurring internationally. It reveals that various elements of the US deliberation were observed abroad, and conversely, that public engagement in the US context was also influenced by international events. Moreover, in international relations, legal and social equality for LGBT people became increasingly seen in the period of this case study as a measure of the just and democratic character of a nation, as shown by the United Nations resolution affirming equal human rights for LGBT people worldwide.[38] Although the focus of the case study offered here is on deliberation in the United States, international occurrences suggest that similar deliberations may have been taking place in other societies as well concurrent with the US public deliberation.

The general aim of this case study of US public deliberation on equal civil rights for LGBT people is not to give a full account of what has taken place, but rather to distill from thousands of events that occurred over decades the main social mechanisms at work in the large-scale deliberative system. As illustrated with this case, I contend that a variety of patterns do emerge that reveal the underlying mechanisms at work in the self-assembly of a large-scale deliberative system. These

---

[38] The United Nations Human Rights Council passed this resolution in 2011; see www.ohchr.org/EN/Issues/Discrimination/Pages/LGBT.aspx.

patterns and their significance are discussed thematically in the four case study chapters that follow the theoretical overview in Chapter 1. Specifically, in Chapter 2, I define and provide examples of the three deliberative catalysts that were needed for the deliberative system on LGBT equality to form and grow. In Chapter 3, I offer further illustration of each of these three catalysts and add a focus on the practices and conditions through which deliberative system growth occurred within specific social domains and arguably to a national scale, including also the large-scale capacity to influence public policy. Chapter 4 turns to illustrate how the growth of the deliberative system required overcoming a set of common cognitive obstacles that can stymie new conscious public reflection and engagement on specific topics. Lastly, in Chapter 5, I describe how the growth of the deliberative system and effective deliberation may have been shaped by largely unspoken fears and anxieties that distorted perceptions and hobbled dialogue until these underlying stumbling blocks could be creatively addressed through the deliberative system.

The concluding chapter summarizes the findings of this study and highlights the potential new prospects for realizing deliberative democracy on a national scale. It also addresses the potential for other issue-specific deliberative systems to grow over time and to perhaps merge into one overarching deliberative system. In that possible scenario, deliberative democracy may evolve to take the form of always ongoing collective will formation through commonplace deliberative practice. In its overview, the closing analysis also sheds new light on the related challenge of how humanity might renew the Enlightenment project of pursuing peace and justice through public reason.

1 | Theoretical Overview
Deliberative Systems at Work

Critics have often argued that the ideal of deliberative democracy –
while enchanting in theory – is impossible in practice, particularly on
a large scale.[1] Yet recently, the concept of deliberative systems has
reinvigorated hopes among many scholars that deliberative democracy
may be a meaningful empirical possibility as well as a compelling idea.
This renewed hope has been ignited by a team of theorists, led by Jane
Mansbridge, that has developed a model of deliberative systems related
to, but distinguishable from, a model previously offered by Jürgen
Habermas.[2] Introduced in 2012, their theoretical formulation has
excited significant interest, as well as considerable skepticism and
doubt, regarding the possibility that deliberative democracy could be
realized at last through deliberative systems.[3]

As theorized by Mansbridge et al. (2012), deliberative systems operate through the same diverse array of components through which social
and political life is already formed.[4] These components include the

---

[1] At times, even advocates have conceded that the deliberative ideal may be
impossible to realize even as they have sought the means to do so. See
John Dryzek, "Legitimacy and Economy in Deliberative Democracy," *Political
Theory* 29 (5) (2001): 651–669.

[2] Summation of the theory can be found in Chapter 1 of the book, see
Jane Mansbridge, et al., "A Systemic Approach to Deliberative Democracy,"
in *Deliberative Systems: Deliberative Democracy at the Large Scale*, edited by
John Parkinson and Jane Mansbridge (New York: Cambridge University Press,
2012).

[3] For a survey of response see, David Owen and Graham Smith, "Survey Article:
Deliberation, Democracy, and the Systemic Turn," *Journal of Political
Philosophy* 23 (2) (2015): 213–234.

[4] Jane Mansbridge, et al. 2012, "A Systemic Approach to Deliberative
Democracy." In their work, they also discuss five structural pathologies
including: *overly tight system coupling, system decoupling, institutional
domination, social domination,* and the diversity-related *divisions.* I agree that
these five structural pathologies exist (22–24). In focusing here on underlying
mechanisms, however, I set these overt pathologies aside and focus (beginning in
Chapter 2) on four cognitive obstacles that can, I contend, also disrupt the

apparatuses of the state, the media, and many elements of civil society (e.g. community groups, schools, churches) including prevailing social norms and practices. In their model, deliberative systems are large and broadly encompassing, also featuring considerable redundancy. They propose that while some components may not be democratic in and of themselves, when taken as a totality the system as a whole serves as a vehicle of collective reflection, deliberation, and choice. As they theorize it, such a deliberative systems fulfills three functions of (1) increasing public knowledge, (2) generating mutual respect, and (3) fostering inclusive democratic practice (i.e. epistemic, moral, and democratic functions).

With this theoretical model in hand, however, Mansbridge et al. have indicated that the path to the practical creation of such a deliberative system remains as yet unclear. Consequently, Mansbridge and her colleagues have called on scholars to engage in the development of an empirical "template" by which a deliberative system could be detected and assessed in terms of its fulfillment of the three major functions (2012, 13). Moreover, this practical template or prototype would need to *"evaluate the conditions that support* the various functions of good deliberation" (13, emphasis added). In other words, Jane Mansbridge and her colleagues have identified the next key theoretical step as understanding and modeling the practical mechanisms by which a large-scale deliberative system may come into being.

In this chapter, and in this book as a whole, I undertake this project of providing a working model of the practical emergence of large-scale deliberative systems. In the next sections, I offer a theoretical model of how a deliberative system can develop in practice. This prototype encompasses the diverse components specified by Mansbridge and her colleagues (2012), but it also adds to numerous elements that, I propose, are necessary for practical deliberative system growth and effectiveness. These necessary elements are enumerated and defined in the next section of this chapter and also illustrated through the LGBT case study presented in the next four chapters. These elements of the practical emergence of a deliberative system include: one pervasive and indispensable practice, three common deliberative system catalysts,

underlying mechanisms and conditions necessary for the growth of deliberative systems.

one element of underlying social infrastructure, three facilitating social processes, seven microsteps of public self-assembly, and three conditions that need to be met in order for deliberative systems to unfold on a large scale.

In responding to the call for a theoretical model of the empirical formation of deliberative systems, I approach this project as an exercise in grounded theory development. I seek to bridge a frequent gap between empirical and theoretical research on deliberative practices by developing a theory based on exploratory analysis of an empirical dataset collected expressly for the purpose of this study. If this approach proves effective, it also demonstrates that theoretical work and empirical research may be productively united in mutual engagement in social science, in much the same way that it more frequently is in the physical sciences. In this case, the guiding research question is *both* an empirical and a theoretical question, roughly: What, if any, underlying mechanisms are needed to foster the growth and development of a deliberative system in everyday practice? As described in the introductory chapter, in elaborating the following model, I have turned to empirical examples and case study analysis to make plain the underlying mechanisms at work in the emergence of a large-scale deliberative system.

This chapter is divided in four section. In the first section, I enumerate the major components in the emergence of a large-scale, informal deliberative system that is self-assembled by a given public including the role of individual reflection, three necessary catalysts, and the role of social networks in deliberative system formation. In the second section, I describe the processes of this model of deliberative system growth. These include seven microsteps of public self-assembly, three contingent phases of system growth to a national scale, and processes of policy implementation. In addition, in this section, I identify key cognitive obstacles to public deliberation including fear, implicit bias, and identity threat and describe the significance of issue-specific hidden fears and anxieties. Having highlighted the significance of these potential obstructions, I then identify processes for overcoming or circumventing these cognitive obstacles to public deliberation. In the third section of the chapter, I describe the practical elements that distinguish a large-scale deliberative system from a social movement. While social movements may form part of a deliberative system, they differ in form in important ways. In the final section, I offer five general characteristics of deliberative systems in practice, including theoretical observations on the relationships among these various elements, the timing and sequence of deliberative system growth, and the possible shape of large-scale deliberations over time.

Elements in the Emergence of a Large-Scale Deliberative System

Although a holy grail of research on deliberative democracy has long been the search for a pathway to large, national-scale deliberations, theoretically, a self-assembled deliberative system can emerge on any needed scale, including those of local or organizational cultures. In this model, I propose that deliberative systems are not an object that can be formally planned and constructed, but rather are a social phenomenon that emerges organically within a collective through processes of self-organization. These collectively self-organized systems emerge to meet a specific need for reflection and informed choice on a given topic or a question that is relevant to life in common. Consequently, such deliberative systems are not general, but rather emerge as issue-specific occurrences. In other words, in this grounded model, large-scale deliberative systems are not created by formal design, but instead emerge on a pressing issue unplanned and uniquely shaped through ongoing practices in response to specific needs and problems within the social and political life of a specific collective.[5]

As a phenomenon of social self-organization, I propose here that large-scale deliberative systems also require a number of specific elements that together provide the conditions for a deliberative system to emerge and grow to national scale, or to whatever other scale may be appropriate. As described in the paragraphs that follow and in the case study chapters, taken alone each of these component elements are necessary but not sufficient for system growth. It is through their convergence and operation in concert that large-scale deliberative systems appear to be viable. These necessary elements are: (1) individual-

---

[5] Although it is beyond the scope of this work to address, I have written elsewhere that in the absence of the organic emergence of a large-scale deliberative system a formal deliberative design employed in the UK for national-scale deliberation related to climate change could fulfill some of the same functions. For brief discussion see Edwina Barvosa, "Mapping Public Ambivalence in the Public Engagement with Science: Implications for Democratizing the Governance of Fracking Technologies in the USA," *Journal of Environmental Sciences and Studies*, 5 (4) (2015): 497–507.

level *conscious* reflection, (2) three deliberative catalysts labeled here as deliberative entrepreneurs, deliberative packages, and precipitating events, (3) social networks, which form the underlying social infrastructure for the emergence and expansion of deliberative systems over time, (4) seven microsteps taken in daily life by members of the public toward self-assembly of deliberative networks, (5) three phases of the growth of deliberative systems to large-scale, (6) conditions to be met through the application of communicative techniques used to overcome three cognitive obstacles to deliberation, including finally, (7) efforts to provide materials or insights that can ease or ally the strain of any hidden quandaries – i.e. sets of unspoken fears or anxieties – that may lead members of society to avoid a topic or to consider it only in already comfortable ways. These hidden quandaries may be unique to each topic of deliberation, but they can pose hidden obstacles that can stymie new and fully informed conscious reflection and, in turn, large-scale deliberation growth. In the remainder of this section, I describe these various elements of emerging deliberating systems in turn.

Individual Conscious Reflection: The Foundational Element of a Deliberative System

As described in the Introduction, Robert Goodin has previously suggested that large-scale deliberation could be realized if it could rely on millions of individuals themselves undertaking personal reflection on a topic under widespread consideration. This mechanism would overcome the need to depend on gathering millions of people in direct conversation. Goodin referred to this as "democratic deliberation within" and he regarded it as a necessary aspect of any potential real-world implementation of deliberative democracy (Goodin 2003, 10).[6] The exploratory analysis upon which this proposed theoretical model is based and also illustrated affirms what Robert Goodin has anticipated, namely: in practice, deliberative systems depend heavily, and at some level entirely, on individuals engaging in personal conscious reflection. In that individual consideration, participants are willing to confront

---

[6] The illustrating case study offered in this book both bears out Goodin's theoretical proposal, and sheds more light on exactly how individual reflection can be linked back into the broader collective deliberative process, thereby expanding a deliberative system as a whole. See Goodin, *Reflective Democracy*, (Cambridge: Cambridge University Press, 2003), esp. 7–14.

their own existing views in an informed manner with openness to the possibility that their "deliberation within" may lead them to new conclusions and points of view on a specific question of "how should we live together?" that is under general consideration.

As such, in this proposed model, deliberative systems are made up of millions of acts of personal soul-searching and individual reviews of diverse information and competing ideas. This may include sudden or gradual changes of mind and heart by members of the deliberating public. Personal conscious reflection undertaken by many millions of people is thus the indispensable mechanism and foundational activity of a deliberative system. Yet this action of individual conscious reflection as a vehicle of deliberative systems may itself go unseen and without public witness. As a deliberative system emerges and grows, these acts of personal reflection are likely to occur in solitude and perhaps slowly over time. Sometimes, however, the course of a person's private reflection is made public, as when individuals openly describe the evolution of their thoughts and feelings and name the factors that prompted their reconsideration and, potentially, their arrival at newly developed views and opinions.[7]

Yet more often than not detailed acts of private reflection are seldom seen directly in a deliberative system. Instead evidence that deliberation is taking place on a widespread basis is seen indirectly through its effects, as revealed by speech and action made after deliberation has been undertaken.[8] Indirect observation of the effects of widespread individual deliberation thus can be used to confirm that large-scale reflection and deliberation are taking place. Existing narratives of self-reflection and retellings of the evolution of personal views, for example, can be considered alongside mappings of large-scale changes in opinion

---

[7] One of the most publicized examples of evolution in personal thought has been that of former US President Barack Obama. Although he favored same-sex marriage in a 1996 survey, between October 2004 and May 2012 his views evolved from opposing same-sex marriage to endorsing it. For speeches illustrating the sequential shift, see "Obama's Evolution on Same-Sex Marriage," *The New York Times*, published electronically, May 9, 2012, www.nytimes.com /interactive/2012/05/10/us/politics/20120510-obama.html?_r=0. For additional examples see Chapter 3.

[8] For post-reflection examples and discussion see Chapter 2, including the personal and family narratives conveyed in the documentary film *For the Bible Tells Me So*, in which five families describe their journeys of reflection taken after learning that one of their children is gay or lesbian. Directed by Daniel Karslake. 2007. New York: First Run Features, DVD; running time 98 minutes.

polls and changing social norms and discourses over time. But for the most part, individual reflection, which is the prime and indispensible vehicle of deliberative system formation and operation on this model, will take place in a manner inaccessible to the public eye and thus difficult to measure.

Three Deliberative Catalysts

Given the many obstacles that exist to the formation of deliberative systems, deliberative catalysts are needed to excite the organic formation of such systems. These catalysts serve to excite deliberative activity by providing invitations, enticing opportunities, and easily accessible substantive and verifiable materials that foster and ease entry into deliberative practice. In this model, I propose that the growth and development of deliberative systems takes place to the degree that three specific types of deliberative catalysts – *deliberative entrepreneurs, deliberative packages*, and *precipitating events* – successfully stimulate the flow of deliberative invitations and materials through specific social domains of society and/or through society as a whole. The impetus provided by these three additional components are needed in order for the system to form and expand.

Deliberative entrepreneurs are individuals (or potentially groups) who take it upon themselves to provide invitations and opportunities for others to engage in reflection and deliberation on the topic of common concern. Although their personal views on the topic may be evident, deliberative entrepreneurs do not operate as advocates for a particular outcome (although they may be perceived as doing so at times), but instead operate primarily as proponents of reflection and providers of opportunities for deliberation in which others may decide for themselves. Deliberative entrepreneurs stimulate the formation of deliberative systems by personally circulating welcoming, non-judgmental, invitations and safe opportunities for people of all kinds to undertake new informed deliberation on a given topic.

In general, each deliberative entrepreneur is unique and operates – at least at first – within a single domain of social life, generally the domain in which his or her life and work is centered. These originating social domains may include those of politics, religion, popular culture, education, professional sports, and so on. In addition, however, some deliberative entrepreneurs may identify and operate at the outset in multiple social domains, thus bridging different and sometimes divided social domains in their work as deliberative entrepreneurs. In this, these social "border crossers" may come to operate at the intersection of two or more social domains in ways that can also further facilitate deliberative system growth as described later in this chapter under the heading Processes of System Growth to Scale.

In addition to the work of deliberative entrepreneurs, deliberative packages are cultural products that serve to provide preassembled, verifiable, materials and information for the purposes of deliberative reflection, i.e. high-quality food for thought. For reasons associated with overcoming the obstacle of implicit bias as outlined in this chapter under the subheading Communication Techniques for Overcoming Cognitive Obstacles to Deliberation, deliberative packages as defined in this model must do more than simply take the form of providing deliberation-relevant information. They must present this information in ways that juxtapose competing ideas, views, information, stories, and expressions. Through this pattern of juxtaposition, the package presents materials useful for deliberation in the form of puzzles, paradoxes, and enigmas, or as puzzling and commonly shared problems to be solved. Presenting materials in this fashion induces topic-relevant cognitive load for the audience thereby engaging and activating the capacities for *conscious* reflection, *if* the viewer is willing to undertake the labor of such thought. In addition, this quality of juxtaposing opposites in deliberative packages provides materials for reflection, but also opens up an inviting space for conscious reflection that is safely accepting of all audiences. In this model, this application of even-handed juxtaposition of competing ideas is thus the defining quality of deliberative packages. Yet for reasons discussed in paragraphs to follow, the most effective deliberative packages also utilize no-blame-no-shame framings and other communication techniques that help to overcome other cognitive obstacles to deliberation that are discussed later in this chapter.

When evenhandedly done, the prepackaging of materials for reflection by placing content in productive contrast and tension can assist potential deliberators by providing relevant and trustworthy materials for their use in considering a matter at hand. Members of the public may use such deliberative packages as ready-made opportunities for deliberation, thus concentrating their limited energy on deliberation itself, focusing on the contradictions and issues before them without the need to undertake their own research in advance. Well-crafted deliberative packages can also facilitate individual research by providing a starting point for study. As cultural products, deliberative packages may appear in virtually any format. As illustrated in the LGBT case study presented in Chapters 2 through 5, deliberative packages may take the forms of cultural products that normally circulate in society, including documentary or theatrical films, television or radio programs, songs, fiction, poetry, personal interviews or stories made public through mainstream media or social media such as YouTube, cartoons, satirical skits, historical or other works of nonfiction such as memoirs, public lectures, presentations, or conversations, or recordings of live events that are then circulated in society through various means.

Lastly, precipitating events are unexpected, happenstance, or landmark occurrences that feature and highlight issues under public deliberation. These events thus serve as flashpoints for deliberation by members of the public that can spur reflection among those who are not directly involved in those events. These occurrences, or other precipitating conditions, can trigger flurries of public attention and public discussion providing not only food for thought, but also renewed impetus and energy that can excite new waves of public reflection. In addition, some precipitating events may offer the occasion and/or material for the creation of additional deliberative packages that retell the story of the event in ways that may later circulate in society in new forms, thereby prompting new or renewed deliberation as such event-related deliberative packages circulate. Similarly, unexpected events relevant to a deliberation topic are also opportunities in which deliberative entrepreneurs may step forward to provide new invitations and opportunities to reflection prompted by the precipitating event. In this way, the three deliberative catalysts – while they can be clearly distinguished – are often interrelated and co-occur in practice. Deliberative entrepreneurs, for example, may create or otherwise utilize deliberative packages. Likewise some precipitating events may function also as deliberative packages and so on. Illustrative examples of all three forms of deliberative catalysts are provided in the case study chapters.

Social Networks as Deliberative System Infrastructure

In this model of deliberative system growth, existing social networks serve as the social infrastructure for system development. If and when public deliberation begins to emerge on a specific issue, a deliberative system expands along the pathways of existing social networks. The self-organization of a deliberative system grows as invitations, opportunities, and materials for individual or collective reflection on a matter circulate among people and are increasingly accepted and passed on to others. This circulation and transfer occurs through existing social networks using communication technologies or standard forms of interpersonal communication. This social network basis of deliberative system growth also involves the three deliberative catalysts defined in the preceding paragraphs because these catalysts stimulate the flow of invitations, opportunities, and various materials for deliberation through existing social networks. Therefore, (a) the three deliberative catalysts described in the preceding paragraphs combine with, (b) existing (and potentially growing) social networks, and (c) the processes of individual deliberation to form the necessary underlying infrastructure and mechanisms for the formation and growth of large-scale, and publicly self-organized, deliberative systems.

Processes of System Growth to Scale

With the basic underlying infrastructure and mechanisms now in mind, there are a number of additional processes and conditions that are also necessary to overcome the likely obstacles to deliberative system emergence and growth in specific cases. In other words, the three basic underlying mechanisms and infrastructures of deliberative systems named so far are themselves necessary but not sufficient to produce deliberative system growth to a national scale. This is because, as theorized in this model, deliberative systems can grow to large scale only insofar as deliberative catalysts can excite the flow of deliberative invitations and materials farther and farther throughout existing (or expanding) social networks. This flow of deliberative impetus in turn depends on the extent to which members of the society themselves are willing to further amplify and extend the deliberative process by participating in the creation of a network of deliberators, thereby self-assembling the system. A series of (at least) seven microstep processes are involved in this activity of public self-organization. As these microsteps are optional for everyone, they represent contingent factors in deliberative system growth that may either enhance system growth or alternatively collapse it. These contingent factors and microstep processes are:

1. the extent to which deliberative entrepreneurs or other catalysts inspire members of society to engage in deliberative entrepreneurship themselves in their own way, thereby forming sibling deliberative nodes within the social networks of a society
2. the extent to which deliberative packages are created and flow along through social networks of a domain, including being passed hand-to-hand, thereby providing deliberative opportunities to those in the social network as deliberative packages flow
3. the extent to which members of social networks (individuals, groups, and organizations) accept the invitations to deliberation provided by deliberative entrepreneurs, and use deliberative packages to engage in personal reflection and/or collective discussion and deliberation
4. the extent to which active deliberators pass along in their social networks news that they are reflecting on a matter at hand, and/or the extent to which they convey the reasoning and/or deliberative packages that they are using to do so
5. the extent to which those who are post-reflection or post-deliberation convey their decisions to others in their networks through speech *and action*
6. the extent to which expressions of post-deliberation decisions flow through social networks and serve as information for the reflection of others who are still deliberating, or as implied invitations to reflection for those who are not yet active in personal reflection and/or collective deliberation, and finally,
7. in the case of eventual formation (or confirmation) of a clear consensus public opinion, this microstep is the extent to which post-deliberation members of social networks (individuals, groups, and organizations) act to express the established public opinion and will through social networks in a "siegelike manner"[9] and in ways that can be recognized and applied by policymakers,

---

[9] The language of "siegelike manner" refers to a conceptualization offered by Jürgen Habermas and is discussed at length in Chapter 3 of this work. See "Further Reflections on the Public Sphere," in *Habermas and the Public Sphere*, Craig Calhoun, ed., trans. Thomas Burger, 2nd edition. (Cambridge: MIT Press, 1993), 452.

including issuing strong objections to those policies that contravene the collective will that has emerged. In other words, the seventh microstep is the public's use of its communicative power to shape public policy in accordance with the public will through its deliberative networks.

When undertaken on a large enough scale, these seven microsteps of system self-organization, I propose, may over time excite three stages of deliberative system growth to a large scale. These processes, which arise from the microsteps in the preceding list, are elaborated in the following two sections.

Establishing Feedback Loops that Link Individual and Collective Deliberation

The microsteps listed above, especially steps 4 through 6, represent the creation of feedback loops between private personal reflection and deliberation (i.e. deliberation within) and the potential growth of a larger, all-inclusive, deliberative system of the collective. Alone, people who reflect and deliberate individually may evolve significantly in their own thinking and opinions on any given topic of public concern. But if their opinion and evolving views are not shared and made available to serve as material for the reflection of others, their path of conscious reflection does little or nothing to build and advance the collective project of creating a large-scale deliberation in which all members of a society may have participation and voice. Conversely, if members of a society at large are increasingly engaged in reflection on a given topic, but some individuals persistently turn away and ignore this growing engagement, then a growing deliberative system retains gaps in which members of some social networks are not brought into the deliberative process. In such a case, the deliberative process remains arguably incomplete. Microsteps 1 through 3 are the steps by which all members of a society can be brought into a deliberative process over time and participate themselves not only in the deliberation, but also in amplifying and spreading the deliberation to all parties. The primary obstacle to the success of this process of public self-assembly is likely to be that of disengagement or apathy that is not overcome by the easy availability of welcoming invitations and opportunities to take part with few or no barriers to entry.

Deliberative System Growth to National Scale: Growth in Three Phases

The deliberative catalysts and underlying mechanisms of deliberation sketched above make it theoretically possible to provide individuals and groups with opportunities and ready-made materials for reflection on a matter of public concern. Once these materials exist and circulate, the potential formation of a deliberative system depends on whether individuals accept those invitations to reflection, engage in personal reflection or collective deliberation, and then pass on to others in their own social networks the deliberative packages that they received, and/ or their own deliberative reasoning, and/or any deliberative decisions that they may have reached. When these microsteps are increasingly undertaken then the deliberative system grows. If such system growth takes place and proceeds to a large scale, I propose that this development will generally unfold in three stages of network growth.[10]

Person-Centered Deliberative Networks: The first and earliest of these three growth stages is the formation of person-centered deliberative networks. As illustrated in Chapter 2, in the early stages of a deliberative system, practical system growth is most likely to begin with the efforts of deliberative entrepreneurs to initiate public engagement within some particular social arena in which they are already a member. These fledgling deliberative networks can emerge in any social domain. These domains may include electoral politics, a local unit of a religious denomination, an industry, such as the entertainment industry, professional sports, and so on. Deliberative system growth often thus begins with the activity of a particular person who fosters a network that extends from themselves to those in their own social networks, and then potentially to other social networks in their social domain (and possibly beyond). In so doing, they create what social network scientists call a *person-centered network*. The success of this early stage depends on the contingent factors enumerated as the seven microsteps of public self-assembly. In addition, many different separate person-centered deliberations may be beginning and taking place in different domains.

---

[10] These terms for levels of social networks – person-centered networks, bounded networks, and open networks – are drawn from social network theory, see Kadushin, *Understanding Social Networks: Theories, Concepts, and Findings* (New York: Oxford University Press, 2012), 17.

Domain-Specific Bounded Deliberative Networks: Over time, a second phase of deliberative system growth may emerge in which person-centered deliberative networks may expand and merge with others throughout a specific social domain, until they come to saturate that social domain. This process of deliberative system growth may take place in different social domains either simultaneously or at different times. Each social domain will likely circulate deliberate packages suited to its own specificity, such as faith-related packages circulating in communities of faith, sports-related deliberative packages circulating among sports fans, and so on. In order for domain saturation to take place, deliberative networks would need to have grown and flourished in such a way that over time virtually everyone in the given domain has had an opportunity to reflect on the matter at hand and has formed their own informed and consciously considered opinion on the matter or is in the process of doing so.

In this second stage of potential deliberative system growth, variations in the density of social networks in a given social domain can significantly shape how, if at all, domain saturation comes about. Dense and cohesive social networks characterize some social domains. This category includes close-knit groups such as some religious denominations or professional or social groups. In these cohesive domains, deliberative materials may have trouble gaining a toehold in order to flow unless they originate from *within* those cohesive social networks. But once the flow of these deliberative materials begins, it is more likely to flow quickly and to saturation due to the density of the social networks that prevail in a cohesively networked social domain. Conversely, in those social domains that are very loosely knit with many points of disconnection, there is a greater potential for the flow of deliberative materials to drop off though large gaps and broken ties that characterize such social domains. Examples are provided in Chapter 3 of the LGBT case study, to illustrate the special challenges and opportunities of deliberative system growth in highly cohesive social domains. These examples focus on controversies involving the Boy Scouts of America (BSA) and the National Basketball Association (NBA).

Open, Unbounded, Deliberative Networks: Finally, deliberative systems that have emerged and grown to saturation in specific social domains may then grow to what social network scientists call an *open network*. At this stage, the deliberative system potentially grows in an unbounded manner spreading throughout a society by linking or merging domain-specific deliberative networks, or otherwise coming to span across different social domains, thereby creating a large and diverse deliberative system. It is in this contingent phase of its growth that a deliberative system can reach a national scale. For example, in this phase of system growth, deliberation on an issue in the domains of education, religion, or sports may come to intersect with related deliberations in other domains such as commerce or popular entertainment, resulting in mutually influencing effects among different domains as the deliberative system continues to spread to other areas of the society. As with domain bounded deliberative networks, the key institutional goal is to reach deliberative saturation in which virtually everyone in the society has a meaningful opportunity to reflect on the matter under consideration and has forged, and at some level publicly expressed, their own informed and consciously considered opinion on the issue at hand. Through these three stages of growth, a deliberative system can form and serve as the vehicle for large-scale deliberation and as the vehicle for deliberative democracy. In turn, in this model, deliberative democracy itself is considered to be a process of the formation of a society's collective will.[11]

Implementation: Wielding Public Communicative Power Through a Large-Scale Deliberative System

In this model, in addition to providing the tools for the formation of collective will, in practice a national-scale deliberative system also provides the means to express and powerfully assert the collective will in order to shape law and public policy. Among the criticisms of the ideal of deliberative democracy is that informal talk appears incapable of wielding any form of power to implement the public will in the form of policymaking. In speaking to this issue of implementation, Jürgen Habermas has indicated that public discourses themselves "do not govern" directly (Habermas 1992, 452). He pointed out, however, that mobilized public opinion (i.e. public discourses that express the collective will) do "generate a communicative power that cannot take the place of administration but can only influence it" by withholding

---

[11] For an early thought experiment on collective will formation, see Jürgen Habermas, "Towards a Communication-Concept of Rational Collective-Will Formation: A Thought Experiment," *Ratio Juris* 2 (2) (1989a): 144–154.

legitimacy. He has stated also that this communicative power does not displace bureaucracies and their "inner logic" but rather influences the inner logics of governance "'in a siegelike manner'" by denying the legitimacy needed to validly create policy in the name of the members of the society (452). Thus in this template of large-scale deliberative system growth, the system operates not only as the vehicle for collective will formation, but also, once that will is formed, the system remains in place as the vehicle for further reflection and for the siege-like expression of public will as it has been generated.

Here the siege-like expression of collective public opinion (once formed) is represented by microstep seven. Step seven involves the extent to which members of society use the deliberative system as a self-organized structure to monitor implementation progress and to issue dissent and resistance in a siege-like manner if and when the public will is disregarded in policymaking. Skeptics may insist that such expression is powerless. Yet, seasoned legislators contend that even in a deeply dysfunctional democracy, public opinion has great power when it is effectively conveyed. As former US Representative Barney Frank (discussed in Chapter 2 as a deliberative entrepreneur) has stated: "As influential as money has become [in American democracy], it can be countered by the effective mobilization of public opinion ... the claim [and belief] that big money is politically invincible is especially self-defeating" (Frank 2015, 194). Often, however, seeing is the best path to believing. Chapter 3 of the following case study on LGBT equality offers illustrative examples of the implementation power of public opinion as wielded through a deliberative system.

Conditions Necessary for System Growth: Overcoming Cognitive Obstacles Through Communication Techniques

At least three common cognitive obstacles can block the practice of deliberation as both individual reflection and at the collective level of deliberative system formation. These cognitive obstacles are: (1) implicit bias, (2) the activation of fear, including post-traumatic fear, and (3) the activation of identity-related threats to a treasured sense of self. These three obstacles can be distilled to two overarching hurdles to deliberative practice: inattention and fear activation. These stumbling blocks are distinguishable but interrelated. They are also rooted in the physiology of the human body and cannot be wished away. Rather, as material obstacles they can only be minimized and overcome.

Circumventing the Cognitive Obstacles of Fear and Defense System Activation

The activation of fear in any of the forms just listed will obstruct deliberation because the experience of fear generally activates in the human body a specific physiological system – an emergency defense system – that overrides the slower cognitive system that is the necessary mechanism of conscious reflection (LeDoux 1996). This is because emergencies that truly threaten physical safety require immediate self-protective reaction. The human body has evolved over time to have a psychophysiological system of automatized rapid-response that takes effect and overrides the slower cognitive centers of the brain, which are too slow for the task of immediate self-protection.[12] Neuroscientist Joseph LeDoux describes this aspect of human embodiment stating: "Although we can become conscious of the operation of the defense system, especially when it leads to behavioral expressions, the system operates independently of consciousness – it is part of what we call the emotional unconscious" (128). In other words, when it is activated, the defense system overrides conscious cognition as an *involuntary* response. This override persists *even if a person can sense* that they are operating from fear in a given moment. Physically, we cannot return to exercising the capacity for conscious reflection until the emergency defense system activation subsides. Fear is the emotion that is most often associated with the activation of this emergency-defense system in the body.

This basic fact of human psychophysiology presents a significant challenge to the self-organized formation of deliberative systems. For it means that whenever a human being feels threatened or otherwise significantly fearful *they cannot physically access and use the cognitive centers through which conscious reflection is conducted.* I repeat, that this is true even when people can become aware that they are reacting from fear in a given moment. The human self-defense system is thus, in

[12] For a full discussion see Joseph, E. LeDoux, *The Emotional Brain: The Mysterious Underpinnings of Emotional Life* (New York: Simon & Schuster, 1996).

effect, an onboard emergency autopilot system. When this autopilot is activated by fear, human beings can only react to whatever is transpiring through whatever internalized scripts make up their specific repertoire of fear-based reactions, including but not limited to the fight, flight, or freeze responses commonly appearing in reactions to mortal threat and to trauma. The fear-activated emergency response system is valuable, healthy, and vital to survival in a true emergency. However, common social fears can also activate this emergency autopilot even when no true emergency is present.

Herein thus lies the problem that fearful defense system activation presents for deliberative system formation: defensive, fear-based, autopilot reactions are the antithesis of conscious reflection and deliberation. Even the human body wisely keeps them separate. Yet fearful responses to political discourse are common and often understandable in many, if not all, contemporary democracies. Threat and fear framings are commonplace and are often intended to activate fear regarding issues of political and social concern. Against this grain, deliberative system formation requires that conditions be met such that people have the resources and support necessary to approach challenging topics *without* activating levels of fearfulness that will, in turn, trigger their emergency autopilot systems. In other words, deliberative system growth requires creating the conditions in which fearfulness is minimized to secure the *conscious* reflection that deliberation requires.

Circumventing the Cognitive Obstacles of Autopilot and Implicit Bias

In addition to the self-defense autopilot induced by fear, there is another autopilot system within human psychophysiology that is likewise valuable, but which also opens the door for humans to express a potentially large array of implicit biases in everyday life. In the scholarly literature across numerous disciplines this fact of human cognitive function has been extensively studied and is referred to often as "dual processing."[13] As with the self-defense system, dual

---

[13] Dual processing is addressed in a variety of fields of study including behavioral economics (Kahneman, *Thinking, Fast and Slow* (New York: Farrar, Straus, and Giroux, 2011)), social psychology (David L. Hamilton, ed. *Social Cognition: Key Readings* (New York: Psychology Press, 2005) and Roy F. Baumeister, ed., *The Self in Social Psychology* (Philadelphia: Psychology Press, 1999)), and

processing in everyday thought and action involves two different psychophysiological systems. One system (commonly referred to as System 2) is the cognitive system of slow, conscious, considered reflection. System 2 reasoning requires time and consumes energy – it is genuine work. The second system, System 1, like the emergency defense system, is a system of cognitive autopilot. Its operation is fast and far less energy and labor consuming than conscious reflection.

As an autopilot process, System 1 allows us to run as the immediate frame of reference for thought, feeling, and action one of a large number of internalized social scripts – scripts comprised of previously internalized, neurally encoded sets of meanings, values, and practices. When the mind instantaneously perceives a script as associated with and relevant to the content of a present moment, that script is neurally activated as the frame of reference for perception, feeling, and action in that given moment. As contexts shift from moment to moment, different encoded frames of reference become salient as "working memory" in different instants, in shifts that generally occur without our conscious awareness. Countless internalized scripts exist in the minds of each of us, and perhaps thousands of such moment-to-moment shifts from one activated frame of reference to another occur outside of our conscious awareness throughout every day. The benefit of System 1 autopilot processing is to save the energy, time, and labor required by conscious reflection for those activities where attention is needed most by reducing the energy and concentration used to execute more mundane tasks.

Thus, through System 1 autopilot, humans have the capacity to automatize a wide variety of complex tasks in order to perform them *without conscious attention* and the expenditure of significant energy. While Western cultures have commonly held that people are acting consciously and rationally at all times, scientific estimates today suggest that human beings are likely operating on the autopilot of

neuroscience and the brain sciences (LeDoux, *The Synaptic Self*). Accounts of dual processing vary within and among disciplines, and while the general facts are accepted, research and scholarly debate continues. See Jonathan St. B.T. Evans, "Dual-Processing Accounts of Reasoning, Judgment, and Social Cognition," *The Annual Review of Psychology* 59 (2008): 255–278. For a recent summary of ongoing debates regarding dual processing approaches see Jonathan St. B.T. Evans, and Keith E. Stanovich, "Dual-Process Theories of Higher Cognition: Advancing the Debate," *Perspectives on Psychological Science* 8 (3) (2013): 223–241.

cognitive System 1 up to 80 to 90 percent of the time.[14] While the human autopilot system is necessary to health and well-being, it also brings the attendant risk of unconscious bias. These implicit biases are many and vary in form and content (Kahneman 2011; Banaji and Greenwald 2013). They also arise from the presence within the mind of biased socially constructed scripts that have been inherited and internalized from previous generations – including inherited fears. Biased scripts are then potentially activated and acted upon as frames of reference in specific contexts, typically without conscious awareness and often without the content of these inherited scripts having been consciously considered in advance.

The unconscious (or more accurately subconscious) perceptions, reactions, and actions unfolding under autopilot – which are conventionally regarded as "thought" – are not in fact conscious reflection at all, but instead lack full and attentive reflection and active choice. Moreover such autopilot operations are potentially the majority of the cognitive processing that takes place for most people most of the time every day.[15] This preponderance of unthinking "thinking" is an integral and beneficial part of the human condition. Nevertheless this aspect of human embodiment also presents a significant challenge to deliberation both as individual reflection and as deliberative system formation.

As with fear and the activation of the emergency defense system, the problem that System 1 autopilot presents for deliberative practice is twofold. First, System 1 autopilot risks the introduction of attendant biases, such as cognitive blind spots, self-confirmation bias among

---

[14] For further discussion see Mahzarin Banaji and Anthony Greenwald, *Blind Spot: Hidden Biases of Good People* (New York: Delacorte Press, 2013), 61.

[15] Those who reject these facts as irrelevant to social and political life often do so based on the view that these concepts appear to relieve actors of responsibility for harmful actions that are driven by socially inherited bias. I have suggested elsewhere, however, that theoretically speaking, autopilot cognition might be considered an unconscious associative responses that is "pre-authorized" through the volitional withholding of conscious attention from a task. In other words, what people do on autopilot is not itself an act of conscious choice or agency, but arguably a person *has* exercised agency when making the choice to withhold conscious thought in a given activity or instant, thereby incurring responsibility. For further discussion of the conditions of conscious agency in the self as it is comprised of a multiplicity of socially inherited and internalized scripts see, Edwina Barvosa, *Wealth of Selves* (College Station: Texas A & M University Press, 2008), Chapter 3.

others that may be part of activated autopilot scripts (Kahneman 2011; Banaji and Greenwald 2013). Second, autopilot reactions are the antithesis of conscious reflection and deliberation. Yet thinking without *consciously* thinking is ubiquitous. Worse yet, because thoughtfulness is generally socially prized, people are often loath to believe that they are quite often, and through no fault of their own, *not* engaged in truly conscious thought. Overall therefore, deliberative system formation requires that the conditions be met in which members of society have the resources and support – e.g. time, energy, and high-quality information – needed to engage in the *conscious* reflection necessary for genuine deliberation to ensue. Furthermore, because conscious reflection is effortful work, it is an act of will that must be chosen. No one can force another to do this work. Consequently deliberative system growth also requires creating the conditions for people to choose to engage in the effort of *conscious* reflection that large-scale democratic deliberation requires.

Communication Techniques for Circumventing Cognitive Obstacles to Deliberation

There are various ways to overcome the three cognitive obstacles to deliberation identified so far. In this proposed model, I stress the use of specific communication techniques as mechanisms for creating the cognitive conditions necessary for individual deliberation and for overall deliberative system growth. Specifically, experimental research in cognitive science suggests that people can shift from autopilot to conscious reflection when they come under cognitive load, *and* willingly choose to undertake that load (Kahneman 2011, 39–49). A shift to engagement in conscious reflection (System 2) helps to circumvent the obstacles of autopilot-related implicit bias, because effortful thought allows for the careful review of potentially invalid conclusions drawn as part of automatized reactions (System 1) (44–49). Facilitating a shift from System 1 autopilot to System 2 conscious thought could be accomplished by offering deliberators materials that provide relevant cognitive load in enticing ways that invite the undertaking of that load. In this model, I therefore incorporate the communication technique of creating deliberation materials that foster cognitive load as a key element of generating the conditions of conscious reflection. Communication techniques for this task include presenting ideas in the form of puzzles, paradoxes, or simply as juxtaposed competing ideas. Deliberative materials presented in this way offer a cognitive challenge that invite people to consciously apply their critical capacities. *If* people take up this challenge, then the conditions for conscious reflection are met. In this model, therefore, the defining characteristic of deliberative packages is the quality of juxtaposing competing ideas, thereby providing the conditions for deliberation-relevant cognitive labor. In turn, this can help to minimize the risks of implicit bias associated with unconscious cognitive processing while also prompting new, informed, and independent thought.

Specifically, regarding the obstacle of fear activation and self-defense system–related autopilot and reactivity, here too communication techniques employed in deliberative catalysts are included in this model as methods that can help to minimize the risks of triggering fear. In particular, for example, two of the deliberative catalysts – deliberative entrepreneurs and deliberative packages – serve not only to facilitate the flow of informed opportunities for deliberation through existing social networks (as described previously), but also help to meet the necessary condition of minimizing fear by creating open and non-judgmental framings of issues and circulating open invitations for all to participate in deliberation. In contrast to social movements that generally employ us-versus-them framings (as further discussed later in this chapter), deliberative systems work to shift public discussion from polarizing and divisive framings of issues, to open invitations that welcome all to take part in reflection on a matter of common concern. These open invitations present opportunities for reflection that: (a) are safe and accepting of people as they are, (b) avoid levying judgments of blame or shame, (c) are evenhandedly informed drawing expressions from all concerned parties on a matter, and (d) refrain from privileging in advance particular choices or outcomes of the deliberation, instead affirming that an open choice is secured to all without judgment. Aspects (b) and (d) – blame-free, open opportunities to reflect and choose according to one's conscience – serve to foster a sense of safety in deliberation and thus help to overcome the activation of common social fears and identity threats.

Beyond these communication techniques, in this proposed model, I also suggest that common qualities of social networks can also help to meet the conditions for conscious deliberation and to minimize the activation of hobbling fears. In other words, in addition to being the infrastructure by which deliberative systems grow, social networks also have other qualities that can help a society to overcome the cognitive obstacles to large-scale deliberation. In particular, social networks link people who see themselves as having something in common, and in general, social networks are made up of people who are significantly socially similar.[16] This quality of social networks (called homophily) is especially important because people are often *not* willing to hear divergent views from people who they perceive as different from themselves, but they are more willing to listen to alternative points of view from members of their own social groups (Friedkin 1998, 71). In other words, people are much more likely to listen to differing viewpoints from people who they see as like themselves. The tendency toward homogeneity in social networks can thus help to reduce barriers to hearing (and in turn consciously considering) discrepant views, because the circulation of deliberative materials that occurs via social networks allows competing ideas to be delivered to listeners by people who the recipients see as socially similar to themselves. This mechanism of delivery can thus contribute to greater receptivity to challenging ideas. Moreover, as deliberative systems grow in scale, the self-organized quality of deliberative systems may link different deliberations taking place in various social domains, thus allowing many diverse people to engage in reflection in their own familiar networks, while also taking part in a larger common deliberation in a manner that both admits of and bridges social distance.

The observation that people are generally more prepared and willing to hear views that are contrary to their own from someone they perceive to be like themselves also flags the opposing effect. In that contrast, listeners will tend to dismiss *the same message* if it comes to them from someone they consider to be socially different from themselves, as opposed to someone they see as similar (Friedkin 1998, 71). As such, the perceived social similarity of deliberative entrepreneurs can help open the way to clearing cognitive blind spots caused by implicit bias. Therefore, in practice, deliberative systems on difficult topics are more

---

[16] Social network scientists use the term "homophily" to describe the tendency to homogeneity of social networks. It is possible that homogeneity in social networks can hinder the gathering of diverse people in common cause. For discussion of the possible effects of homophily in undermining solidarity formation in conventional social movements, see Kadushin, *Understanding Social Networks*, 22.

likely to grow and to meet the conditions of conscious reflection on competing ideas, *if* relevant messages are introduced by deliberative entrepreneurs within a wide variety of social networks, especially networks where the idea is unlikely to already be present.

Consequently, deliberative entrepreneurs, who are at the center of, or otherwise contributing to, various social networks, can help to achieve the conditions needed to overcome cognitive obstacles to deliberation in a number of ways, in part by leveraging the sense of social similarity that tends to prevail in most social networks. These communication techniques include providing deliberative invitations and materials that (a) place listeners under cognitive load through their content and narrative messages, (b) activate a sense of social similarity that fosters feelings of safety and ease in familiarity, (c) affirm listener identities, and/or highlight a basis for common identification, (d) ease potential or apparent fears by reframing or reconstructing social narratives that excite fear, and (e) reframe troubling social contradictions and/or propose alternatives to obstructive belief systems in ways that resolve present tensions that may be blocking consideration or reconsideration of a matter at hand. All of these practices serve to help overcome the three common cognitive obstacles to individual reflection identified here and to thus facilitate the growth of deliberative systems. These techniques are illustrated with examples throughout the LGBT case study, especially in Chapters 3 through 5.

Issue-Specific Cognitive Obstacles: The Challenge of Hidden Quandaries

In addition to attending to the cognitive obstacles of fear, identity threat, and autopilot, I also stress the further possibility that other cognitive obstacles may take the form of hidden quandaries defined as sets of unspoken fears and anxieties that are held by large segments of a democratic public. Research increasingly shows that people are not always fully forthcoming, and may be less than fully honest with themselves or others about the things that worry them the most. This pattern of self-stabilizing self-deception is particularly likely when hidden sources of fear or anxiety excite feelings of shame, self-blame, apathy, guilt, suppressed anger, or other painful emotions that feel stigmatizing to admit to, perhaps even to oneself (Barvosa 2008, 119–139). This form of hidden quandary, when widely held among a public, can become a significant hidden obstacle to the formation and success of a deliberative system, especially if the hidden worries also excite fear, identity threat, or issue avoidance.

As illustrated in Chapter 5, in this proposed model I suggest that many if not most issues that are candidates for large-scale public deliberations have some associated hidden quandaries – i.e. sets of largely unspoken fears or anxieties at work that are keeping people from reflecting on the topic or even admitting that there is a problem at all. For example, in the US context, evidence suggests that the vast majority of all US families have some form of significant financial vulnerability and are unprepared for even modest financial shocks, much less for retirement (Rhee and Boivie 2015).[17] Yet many members of US society continue to say that they are financially stable and optimistic and that significant economic inequality, and its related vulnerabilities, is not a troubling issue for them. It is possible to imagine that deep fears and forms of social stigma could be discouraging people from admitting, perhaps even to themselves, the severity of the effects of economic inequality in their lives. By extension, such hidden fear could block many people from stepping forward from this self-generated shadow to begin to deliberate on the matter of economic inequality as a collective.

In Chapter 5, I illustrate the influence of hidden quandaries in an example drawn from the LGBT case study. While the specifics of this hidden quandary are unique to the LGBT case study, this form of obscured obstacle may also obstruct the formation of deliberative systems on other topics. Thus, in addition to the fear-mitigating and autopilot-reducing communication techniques listed in preceding sections, these hidden quandaries may sometimes require deliberative entrepreneurs to read between the lines of angry or pained public discourse on a hot-button issue and to empathetically sense what might be going on beneath the surface of what is being said on a given topic in the public domain in order to address that hidden anxiety.

This is not to say, however, that the hidden fears and anxieties that can stymie the formation of a deliberative system must be fully understood or visible before they may begin to shift or make way for

---

[17] Pew Charitable Trust, "Report: The Precarious State of Family Balance Sheets," January 29, 2015, www.pewtrusts.org/en/research-and-analysis/reports/2015/01/the-precarious-state-of-family-balance-sheets.

conscious reflection. As the illustrative example in Chapter 5 suggests, meaningful deliberation can still potentially emerge even if unspoken fears or anxieties remain unspoken, or even as these are eased or otherwise overcome. As shown in Chapter 5, remedy and reflection may still arise, but these may be slowed or feature strange paradoxes that mark the hidden influences. Overall, the indispensible operative mechanism of a deliberative system growth is not complete self-awareness and fearless public honesty (although these would be beneficial), but rather the willingness to engage in individual reflection, and to take part in the seven microsteps of public self-assembly that cause one's own individual reflection to feed back into the collective deliberation. Thus, even when the hidden fears or worries that may be generating shame or guilt are never publicly acknowledged, open invitations and opportunities for deliberative reflection may still serve as effective mechanisms for deliberative system growth. Through these invitations and opportunities to deliberate, people can, if they choose, confront, reconsider, and potentially let go of unexamined beliefs they have inherited about an issue in favor of newly considered judgments and choices or newly collectively or individually endorsed principles and actions regarding an issue that is under widespread consideration.

Durable Cognitive Obstacles: The Special Case of Individual and Collective Trauma

Trauma is a specific kind of fear activation. As with other forms of fear activation, it is a cognitive obstacle that, I propose, can stymie the growth of public deliberation even when other favorable conditions are present. Activation of post-traumatic fear can be seen as a form of emergency defense system reactivity that arises from the residual pain and wounding of trauma (Van Der Kolk 1996; Scaer 2005, 2014). In recent decades, the study of trauma has taken a somatic turn, focusing on the physical embodiment of trauma encoding in the mind and body. Special focus is often given to trauma-induced expressions of fight, flight, or freeze – the trio of responses common to post-trauma reactivity, which can appear socially as paralysis, shrill or angry resistance, or avoidance (Scaer 2005, 2014). In the context of public deliberation, like other forms of fear activation, the activation of post-traumatic fear physically precludes the use of slow conscious thought (System 2) in the moment of post-traumatic reactivity. The potential for trauma-related fear activation is distinct, however, in that it is often highly durable over time and less likely to evolve or fade away with changing social conditions. Like the soldier with post-traumatic stress disorder (PTSD) who suffers long after the war has ended, post-traumatic fear and reactivity can endure and shape human experience long after relevant social conditions have changed (Scaer 2014). Moreover, post-traumatic fear activation is particularly painful or intense as it typically takes the form of an emotional and physiological state of high arousal that involves the reactivities of fight, flight, or freeze, and which feels to the afflicted person as if the original trauma-tizing event is occurring again in real time.[18] Yet post-traumatic fear activation can occur in the absence of any actual immediate threat. The subconscious recall of an associated memory is enough to trigger the fight, flight, or freeze response of the emergency defense system, thereby override the forms of slow conscious reasoning upon which deliberation depends (Van Der Kolk 1996; Scaer 2005, 2014). Trauma can be experienced by groups and collectives, as well as individuals. There is also some experimental evidence that collective trauma can be transferred to subsequent generations through intergenerational social engagement in families and social groups.[19] Thus collective traumas can affect large segments of a society or even entire societies over time, leaving them more reactive and potentially triggered by commonplace events that might not otherwise have provoked cognition-stopping fear.[20]

Such post-traumatic fear activation is a special obstacle to deliberative system formation because, as with other kinds of fear activation, this intense form of fear must subside in order for those who are

---

[18]   The reactions of fight and flight are often noted in common understandings, but the third reaction of freeze is also significant, see Van Der Kolk et al., *Traumatic Stress: The Effects of Overwhelming Experience on Mind, Body, and Society* (New York: The Guilford Press, 1996).

[19]   In this model, I focus on firsthand experiences of trauma and social inheritances for later generations. But the study of epigenetic influence in trauma indicates that multigenerational transfer of trauma may have a genetic pathway as well. For experimental evidence of the transfer of post-traumatic stress *and reactivity patterns* across four generations of organism, see Brian Dias and Kerry Ressler, "Parental Olfactory Experience Influences Behavior and Neural Structure in Subsequent Generations," *Nature Neuroscience*, 17 (1) (2014): 89–96.

[20]   For examples of the large-scale social impact of collective trauma, see Kai Erikson, *A New Species of Trouble: Explorations in Disaster, Trauma, and Community* (New York: W.W. Norton & Co., 1994).

afflicted to resume conscious reflection. Unlike other fears, however, recovery or avoidance of post-traumatic fear activation may be more difficult to achieve or sustain over time. Consequently, deliberative packages, and deliberative entrepreneurs in general, should seek out and adopt measures to avoid triggering commonly existing traumas. But this may not always be successful, and the shrill and reactive quality of trauma activation may not always be recognized. Moreover, its presence in public discourse may take various forms including explosive anger that, when read only at face value, are potentially divisive or polarizing (Smelser 2004).[21] Given the disruptive potential of individual and collective trauma, it is worthwhile to explore the effects that widespread traumas may have for the emergence of a deliberative system on topics likely to invoke associated trauma. Further inquiry into this cognitive obstacle to public deliberation is, however, beyond the scope of this study. I have not further illustrated this aspect of the model in the LGBT case study in Chapters 2 through 5.

Distinctions Between Deliberative Systems and Networked Social Movements

There are important distinctions to be drawn between social movements and deliberative systems. To distinguish deliberative systems from social movements – which can be part of deliberative systems – it is useful to first define social movements as they have currently evolved and to compare and contrast the two forms. Today large-scale social networks and new communication technologies are common aspects of contemporary social movements. In his recent work *Networks of Outrage and Hope*, sociologist Manuel Castells offers numerous case studies and hypotheses regarding what he refers to as *networked social movements* (Castells 2012). Highlighting recent democracy-related social movements, such as those of the Arab Spring, and other democratization movements around the globe, Castells proposes that what has appeared is a new breed of social movement. This new form of social movement is possible in the information age due to the rise of technology-assisted social engagement and

---

[21] For discussion of this in the context of public reactivity to Mexican immigration and related US cultural diversity, particularly in Arizona, see Edwina Barvosa, "Inner Contradiction to Immigration Quagmire: A Response to Rogers Smith," *Perspectives on Politics* 9 (3) (2011): 559–562.

social platforms that foster the simple and fast mobilization of social networks and the self-organization of people who share common social or political concerns.

Based on his case studies, Castells hypothesizes that networked social movements operate through the formation of a movement community. These movement communities generate and perpetuate themselves through a constructed sense of togetherness. This togetherness, in turn, allows people to overcome their fear of speaking out and to engage in collective action despite the threat of punishment and state coercion. Importantly, the boundary of the social movement community is generally defined by casting an "us-versus-them" divide (Castells 2012, 10). To join such a movement community is often to embrace being among an "us" who is opposing "them." To assert its claims and concerns, such a networked social movement community often deploys its membership to occupy urban spaces as a symbolic form of insurgency. This occupation symbolizes defiance of the oppressive norms of the state, of a specific bureaucracy, and/or other aspects of the prevailing status quo.

Castells argues that by delivering a movement community into the symbolic occupied space, a networked social movement opens a space for its own deliberations in which the movement community itself reflects upon its own needs and priorities (e.g. Occupy Wall Street encampments) (Castells 2012). This movement community deliberative space is ultimately political in character, yet it is predicated on the sharp divide drawn between members of the movement and those who persist in the conventional norms and practices that the movement community rejects. Castells also finds that these social movements are often ignited and animated by "a few individuals, sometimes only the one hero accompanied by an undifferentiated crowd" (Castells 2015, 10). In this sense, the networked social movements analyzed by Castells still tend to be activated by charismatic leadership with all of the attendant advantages and disadvantages of such leadership for movement longevity.

Deliberative systems as theorized in this proposed model and networked social movements as theorized by Castells, share a common reliance on social network formations and new communication technologies for self-organization and growth. But the similarities end there. A key distinguishing factor of deliberative systems as modeled here is that deliberative systems abandon and avoid the use of us-versus-them community building and the external insurgency methods common to networked social movements. As Castells notes, these us-versus-them boundary-setting tactics are often employed in social movements to good effect. Specifically, us-versus-them discourses are especially useful when deployed for social movement formation, for community building, and for group mobilization (Castells 2012). Taking a deliberately schismatic approach can help to gather and energize people in a self-identified collective and embolden movement members to confront and overcome limitations such as fear, apathy, paralysis, isolation, or other emotional obstacles to collective action and voice. This can include engaging in productive forms of anger that, in turn, can help people to develop the momentum and courage needed to engage in common cause. In short, as movement members feel a sense of belonging separate from others who they feel constitute a threatening opposing force, this sense of belonging to a community that is resisting a siege can help people to gather and sustain the strength to engage in activism and dissent.

However, while us-versus-them discourses can be helpful in building community and courage within a social movement, schismatic discourses can also alienate third-party onlookers who are outside of the movement. Observing members of the public can be put off or angered by intense movement rhetoric. Some may simply cease to listen. Other onlookers may feel fear that they themselves are being shamed or blamed by the strong accusations of abuse, subordination, or other wrongdoing. Thus the common us-versus-them approach of networked social movements can be socially divisive, but can also trigger the three cognitive obstacles to individual and collective deliberation, including: implicit bias (including related inattentiveness), fears (including post-traumatic fear), and identity threats. When triggered, these obstacles can obstruct consideration of the issues that social movements are attempting to raise before the general public.

In contrast, as modeled here networked deliberative systems proceed by avoiding us-versus-them framings of all kinds, because the absence of schismatic language helps to foster deliberative system growth. As illustrated with examples throughout the next four case study chapters, deliberative system growth requires generating and circulating open and inclusive invitations to consider a given problem. Thus issues to be addressed via a deliberative system are not framed in us-versus-them terms, but rather as a commonly shared problem – including problems of group conflict or violence – that are best considered and addressed by all. Shame and blame that could trigger fear or inattention are avoided.[22] Avoided too is any pressure on members of the public to ultimately decide on the issue in any particular way. What is encouraged instead is reflection on a specific matter of common concern by all members of the society.

In this deliberative mode, the need to build a movement-based community falls away in favor of the assumption that a society or a social domain is already an interconnected whole that forms one community of common mutual concern in which all are a part. This common membership exists even as members also stand in diverse social locations and relationships to each other, and may hold divergent opinions on specific topics. In this account of deliberative system growth, social networks within larger social domains serve as the principal vehicles by which invitations to reflection flow from one person to the next along with evenhanded information to support such deliberation. Dispensing with divisive framings, two of the deliberative catalysts – deliberative entrepreneurs and deliberative packages – serve to bring public discourse up to an elevated level in which everyone is invited to take part in a public deliberation equally from whatever happen to be their own current viewpoints or social locations.

At first the difference between a deliberative system and a social movement may be difficult to detect. This is in part because social movements are much more familiar to us, and because the LGBT deliberative system (I propose) emerged alongside of, and in interaction with, a social movement that fits the description offered by Castells. While these social phenomena are distinct, deliberative systems and social movements both have a valuable social and political role to play and may often operate in symbiosis. Insurgent social movements, for example, may provide a deliberative system with important resources, including insightful stories, narrative contrast, and resistance to existing conventional norms and practices. Such contrasts offer the productive tensions and contradictions needed as food for conscious reflection in the deliberative system.

---

[22] While some scholars have argued that shame is a necessary component of social change, I disagree for reasons stated in this chapter. It may be, however, that shame is motivating for some social movement efforts, but is counterproductive to the task of developing voluntary, thoughtful, and widespread public deliberation; see Jennifer Jacquet, *Is Shame Necessary?: New Uses for an Old Tool* (New York: Pantheon, 2015).

General Characteristics and Relationship of Elements in Deliberative Systems

In addition to the various elements needed for deliberative systems to emerge and grow, in this proposed model I suggest that, in practice, large-scale deliberative systems also have several general characteristics as follows.

Issue Specificity: In the model of deliberative system formation offered here, deliberative systems are likely to develop as issue-specific systems. While some, if not most, issues of concern in a society intersect with others, a deliberative system is, I propose, unlikely to address all of a society's issues at once at least at this point in time. Instead the exploratory data analysis conducted for this study suggests that deliberative processes are animated by pressing needs and engagement on a specific topic, and are thus not likely to emerge as a single generalized system without a specific focus of attention. Therefore, public deliberation through a growing deliberative system may get underway on some subjects but not on others. The reasons for this may vary. In some cases, lack of deliberative catalysts may prevent system emergence. A lack of public participation in the seven microsteps of self-organization of the system could also prevent system growth. In other cases, the cognitive obstacles to public deliberation discussed in Chapters 4 and 5 could stymie the growth of public deliberation on particular issues even as it proceeds apace on others. Other factors may also cause differences in uptake of topics including variations in public willingness to grapple with a given matter. Moreover, as discussed in Chapter 3, at some stages of deliberative system growth, specific deliberations may take place only within a particular social domain, addressing how the specific issue relates uniquely to that domain. For all of these reasons and others to follow, a deliberative system is likely to be issue specific. In the concluding chapter, however, I suggest some scenarios in which multiple deliberative systems might merge and how large-scale public deliberations might proliferate, stabilize, and morph into one ongoing and overarching system over time.

Framing Effects: Framing effects play a significant role in the emergence and growth of deliberative systems as modeled here. Open and inclusive framings that avoid divisive rhetoric or shame-and-blame discourses are a defining characteristic of deliberative system formation. Among other influences, framing effects impact how well or how poorly the cognitive obstacles to deliberation may be overcome. In the case study developed in Chapters 2 through 5, changes in the framing of key issues had an important impact on how the issues were perceived and addressed by those who engaged in deliberation on the matter over time. For instance, reframing of the issue of "same-sex marriage" to "marriage equality" activated a different emphasis and frame of reference with which to consider this specific factor. This reframing linked the specific issue of same-sex marriage to a larger set of social concerns to do with social and political equality. Thus framing effects can crosscut the single-issue quality of deliberative systems and can, in some cases, draw attention to the interconnection of social and political concerns.[23] Such framing processes have been widely discussed in the social science literature for decades (Benford and Snow 2000) including the literature on implicit bias in behavioral economics (Kahneman 2011, 49–58). In short, deliberative system growth – like social movements and other elements of social change – is a phenomenon in which framing effects play a major role.

Reason Giving & Deliberative Practices Take Many Forms: Much of deliberative theory privileges the giving of reasons as central to public deliberation, and it prioritizes high standards of rationality in reason giving. In this model, however, and in the empirical case study presented in Chapters 2 through 5, reason giving is not the only form of speech that animates a large-scale deliberation as it takes place over time and across all domains of a society. Reason giving is certainly important, but many forms of dialogue, appeal, critique, and particularly storytelling can initiate or provide further impetus for deliberation, reconsideration, and ultimately collective will formation and/or transformation. Thus the template suggested here is wide open as to mode and tone of expression: art, chitchat, prayer, and even silence may be helpful components of a broad deliberative system in a given instance. Although patterns may emerge, it is possible that each deliberative system will vary from the next in its primary forms of animating content. In addition, as other deliberative theorists including Jürgen Habermas have stressed, reason giving is not restricted only to linear

---

[23] My thanks go to Robert Goodin for urging me to highlight several key aspects of this element.

logic. It may also usefully include emotional responses and aesthetic judgments. Moreover, as Habermas has stated in writings on post-secular political life, spirituality-related reasoning for judgment may be also given as valid and valuable reasons, if and when they are offered in ecumenical or non-sectarian forms that are understandable to those who do not share a similar spiritual or metaphysical worldview.[24]

Furthermore, Mansbridge et al. theorize that one of the functions of a deliberative system is inclusivity. This inclusivity extends not only to the inclusion of a diversity of people as participants, but also to a diversity of forms of deliberative engagement. The LGBT case study provided in later chapters shows that a nearly infinite variety of things might prompt engagement with diverse viewpoints on an issue under deliberation. Many contributions, from high art to popular culture expressions, can cause us to reconsider our views and to come face-to-face with contradictions around and within ourselves that can forward personal and collective thinking on a pivotal topic. In this sense, deliberative democracy practiced through a deliberative system may be defined as *including anything and everything that a people do to form and implement their collective will on issues related to how they shall live in common.* As such, a deliberative system can be highly inclusive in its forms of communication as well as in its modes of participation.

Microsteps in Deliberative System Growth are Nonlinear but Synergistic: The model outlined in the preceding paragraphs and illustrated throughout the case study on LGBT equality features a set of seven contingent and interrelated small steps and activities through which a deliberative system is publicly self-assembled, and may grow or potentially stall. These seven microsteps are distinct from, but also

---

[24] Jürgen Habermas has argued the modernity's development is not necessarily defined by increasing secularism and that secular worldviews should be open to the insights offered by citizens who are informed by spirituality and/or various faith traditions. Such traditions can at times productively introduce useful and relevant issues and ideas that may be missing or deemphasized in secular discourses and worldviews, such as an emphasis on the value of expressing love and compassion for loved ones and enemies alike. As such, faith and reason may be interrelated intellectual formations. This recent evaluation refines the Enlightenment project's original flight from religious unreason by recognizing secular spirituality and/or religious faiths (which are often distinguished) as potential sources of valid reasoning. See Jürgen Habermas et al., *An Awareness of What is Missing: Faith and Reason in a Post-Secular Age*, Translated by Ciaran Cronin (Cambridge: Polity Press 2010).

necessary to, the general phases of system growth and to other processes that are part of the model. These seven small but critical micro-steps include accepting invitations to reflection, inspiring others to engage in reflection, and circulating publicly the results of one's own personal reconsideration among others. Not every participant must necessarily complete each step, nor must the steps be accomplished in a linear sequence for the deliberative system to grow. Instead, various steps of the process may be happening simultaneously with many people taking different steps at any given time. In addition, some participants could be seen circling back to undertake steps again on other aspects of a given topic.

While the emergence of deliberative system growth does not require everyone to be on the same step, deliberative system formation does depend on the overall flow of activity that takes place in the system over time. Overall, the material considered in this study shows peaks and valleys in visible activity in which specific catalysts trigger flurries of public engagement punctuated by periods of apparent relative calm. Moreover, as previously described, the growth and activity of the deliberative system depends in part on increasing the flow of deliberative material and activity through social networks. In those networks, the ebb and flow of activity is also synergistic – meaning that the more people take part, the more the flow of deliberative activity increases, and in turn, the more that people take part. Conversely, as the flow of deliberative invitations and materials tapers off, activity in the system ebbs.

The overarching point is that while the elements involved in deliberative system formation are closely interrelated, the timeframe and the sequence in which elements unfold for any particular participant or for any particular deliberation is not predetermined. There are many different contributing factors in deliberative system emergence – including a number of elements that are considered in this model to be necessary but not sufficient for deliberative system growth. Yet conceivably there is no absolutely necessary *sequence* of events that is required for a deliberative system to thrive. It is possible to imagine that a flurry of public conversation and shifting opinion could appear on a topic even before evenhanded deliberative packages appear and circulate. It is conceivable too that a number of large-scale, person-centered, deliberative networks could expand rapidly and lead directly to the formation of a large open deliberative network and a nationwide deliberation, which then back fills into specific social domains that have yet to be saturated on the issue (examples can be seen in Chapter 3).

In short, there is no necessary order of events that must unfold for a deliberative system to form. Instead, the relationships among the various elements of deliberative systems lend themselves to synergies in which the combined effects of various elements of system growth exceed that of any one factor. Those synergies, when they emerge, are likely to be driving forces. Likewise in terms of the timing of deliberative system growth, while deliberative catalysts clearly make a difference in the unfolding of events in the exploratory data analysis in this study, there is nothing in this model or the case study to suggest that it is possible to predict the timing of deliberative system growth. As with many other aspects of life, it is not possible to push the river. If hundreds of millions of people are to deliberate on an issue of common concern, then they will do so only when they are ready, willing, and able. People arrive at the task of reflection on difficult topics in many ways – through happenstance, through changing life conditions, through the influence of friends or family, or by being swept up in the zeitgeist of an era. Thus it is difficult to predict if, when, and in exactly what manner a deliberative system on a given topic will emerge. Logically, it is therefore also unwise to expect it to occur on any particular timeframe.

Nevertheless, many if not all of the elements that are part of this model of networked deliberative system formation are already common in social and political life in the United States. Given the commonplace character, and the easily generated quality of many of the ingredients of deliberative system growth, it is reasonable to expect that members of the US public are likely to pick up the available tools that it has already arguably used to deliberate on LGBT equality to address other issues of primary concern to the public. There is already some appearance of these processes emerging on issues of policing and racial hierarchies, economic inequality, and gender inequity. If people can begin to see networked deliberative practices emerge, it may becomes easier to also see, appreciate, and embrace the potential power of public deliberation and the growing capacity of democracies to become centered on public discussion and engagement, rather than primarily on the electoral practices, which are regarded by so many as having become increasingly less representative of the whole.

No Necessary Outcomes But Potential for Justice Over Time:
Deliberative democracy – including large-scale deliberative systems –

is looked upon philosophically by many in the West as the next evolutionary step in democracy. Moreover, it is regarded as a means of
effectively restoring the Enlightenment project of making conscious
reasoning a positive mainstay of political thought, choice, and action.
Considered as a part of the Enlightenment project in this way, deliberative democracy is meant to respect and enhance the free will of
individuals and the collective. Consequently, there is no guarantee
that a public deliberation would always render an entirely just decision
or course of action as the collective will.[25] However, there is documented evidence that over time, humanity as a whole has become less violent,
less intolerant, less hateful, and less willing to harm or take advantage of
fellow human beings in its choices and actions (Pinker 2011).[26] Dr. Martin
Luther King, Jr. famously quoted Theodore Parker saying, "The arc of the

---

[25] Likewise, civility in public discourse, which can aid public deliberation, may
also ebb and flow, although potentially with unpredictable effects. In 2017, for
example, public discourse in the US on immigration had become increasingly
divisive as a function of the rhetoric of the newly elected US President both
during his candidacy and his first year in office. Some commentators have noted
that even school children are experiencing an increase in hateful anti-immigrant
speech over the previous year, see Nicholas Kristof, "Donald Trump is Making
America Meaner," *The New York Times*, published electronically August 13,
2016, www.nytimes.com/2016/08/14/opinion/sunday/donald-trump-is-mak
ing-america-meaner.html. Yet the ultimate effects of such a shift in discourse on
public engagement can be surprising. In this case, concern over negative political
discourse has brought many new people into political engagement who had been
previously disengaged, resulting in increased calls for new constructive dialogue
among people with differing points of view. Since the 2016 presidential election,
for example, over 4500 women have reportedly undertaken their first run for
elected office, see Mahita Gajanan, "More than 4500 Women Have Signed Up
to Run for Office Since the Election," *Time*, published
electronically December 8, 2016, http://www.time.com/4594114/she-should-r
un-women-election/?xid=newsletter-brief. Moreover, as discussed in Chapter 3,
extremism in public discourse may have the unintended consequence of
prompting new reflection across the political spectrum, potentially ultimately
leading to new expressions of peace and justice from unanticipated quarters, see
Katie Leslie, "George W. Bush Condemns Bullying, Bigotry, Nativism in the Age
of Trump," *Dallas Daily News*, published electronically October 19, 2017, w
ww.dallasnews.com/news/politics/2017/10/19/george-w-bush-blasts-bullying-
bigotry-age-trump
[26] Further evidence may be seen in declining rates of violent crime, see
Ashley Southall, "Crime in New York City Plunges to a Level Not Seen Since
the 1950s," *The New York Times*, published electronically, December 27,
2017, www.nytimes.com/2017/12/27/nyregion/new-york-city-crime-2017.ht
ml?emc=edit_th_20171228&nl=todaysheadlines&nlid=22926683&mtrre
f=undefined

moral universe is long, but it bends toward justice."[27] If this insight and the evidence of humanity's drift toward greater peace and justice carry wisdom, then it is reasonable to hope that deliberative democracy can and will produce fair-minded outcomes most of the time and will ultimately generate a more just society over time. With this in mind, I now turn to illustrate the model of deliberative system growth outlined in this chapter throughout the next four chapters using empirical examples drawn from the case study of US public engagement on LGBT equality.

[27] February 8, 1958. "The Gospel Messenger, Out of the Long Night" by Martin Luther King, Jr., Start Page 3, Quote Page 14, Column 1, Official Organ of the Church of the Brethren, Published weekly by the General Brotherhood Board, Elgin, Illinois. Quote attributed first to Theodore Parker, *Ten Sermons of Religion* (Boston: Crosby, Nichols, and Company, 1853).

2 | Three Catalysts of a Deliberative System

The following case study examines a broad sampling of speech and events in the US public engagement on LGBT equality between January 1, 1987, and June 26, 2015. Taken as a whole, I suggest that this case study illustrates a number of processes, necessary elements and conditions, and patterns of growth and development that repeatedly appear in this example of large-scale public reflection. As noted in the Introduction, I have proposed two additional ideas illustrated with this case study. First, that US public engagement on LGBT equality in this period is an example of the emergence and function of a national-scale deliberative system.[1] Second, that patterns, processes, and apparent conditions of this practical deliberation reveal the underlying mechanisms at work in making deliberative systems emerge and grow, factors not addressed by Mansbridge et al. (2012) in their focus on the role of deliberative systems in fostering informed, fair, and inclusive democratization.

In this and the next three case study chapters, I elaborate these ideas by presenting this case study as an example of the discernible patterns at work in the emergence and functioning of a deliberative system. Throughout this case study, I link these observations with the range of concepts and relationships offered in the theoretical model of deliberative system growth outlined in Chapter 1. At some point, each

---

[1] I propose too that this deliberative system remains in effect at the time of this writing, in late 2017. Through it, some members of US society are still considering concerns related to the equal treatment and incorporation of LGBT people, especially transgender equality and rights. Through the system, the US public continues to assert pressure on policymakers to implement the new public consensus affirming measures for LGBT equality that has already emerged and proposals that contravene the public will have diminished. Alan Blinder, *New York Times*, "Wary, Weary or Both, Southern Lawmakers Tone Down the Culture Wars," published electronically, January 22, 2018, www.nytimes.com /2018/01/22/us/transgender-bathroom-bill-religious-freedom.html?emc=e dit_th_180123&nl=todaysheadlines&nlid=22926683. Implementation is further addressed in Chapter 3.

concept, process, and relationship is illustrated with examples drawn from the case study material. Although I present these concepts as general observations on the data collected for this study, and as components of a template for witnessing and assessing deliberative systems, I reemphasize here as a caveat that this analysis is an exercise in exploratory data analysis. The model presented in this work thus constitutes a working hypothesis that methodologically can be created and illustrated, but not yet confirmed, with the materials presented here. Confirmation would require further study and other collected data (Stebbins 2001, 25). Moreover, while theoretical concepts and hypotheses that emerge from exploratory data analysis are often likely candidates for subsequent validation, new evidence and research would likely further develop these initial insights, bring additional dimensions to light, and add clarity, nuance, and useful amendment.

This chapter is divided into five sections, beginning with an initial overview describing the three main catalysts of deliberative systems as they appeared in the LGBT equality case. The second section narrates the early stages of the nascent deliberative system with an emphasis on the presence and role of deliberative entrepreneurs in the perhaps unlikely settings of organized religion and the US Congress. The third section illustrates deliberative entrepreneurship operating at the center of a large social network. In the fourth section, I describe how deliberative entrepreneurs both shared commonalities and also operated uniquely in the LGBT case. These variations are a function of each person's individual qualities and histories, but they are also a function of the specificities of the social domains in which they operated. In the final section of the chapter, I describe briefly examples of the remaining two catalysts: deliberative packages and precipitating events.

Disproportionate time is thus spent in this chapter illustrating the concept of deliberative entrepreneurs. This imbalance is retained in this chapter for three reasons. First, the overall balance of attention is restored in Chapter 3, where numerous examples of deliberative packages and precipitating events are used to illustrate the role of social networks in deliberative system growth and the emergence of *networked* deliberative systems.

Second, the presence of deliberative entrepreneurs has the potential to be seen as the least likely or least plausible concept by some readers. This is because as readers, we necessarily come to this new phenomenon only with our existing frames of reference. For the most part, our understanding of shifting public opinion and social change employs a social movement framework in which advocacy, resistance, argument, dispute, and insurgency are prevailing forms. Simply put, we do not yet expect to see people foster huge social change by simply asking other people to think for themselves and then helping them to do so by offering materials that aid reflection. Yet this appears to be exactly what has happened in the LGBT case. As this observation may be the most counterintuitive, I spend extra time in this chapter providing evidence that this dynamic was at work in public reflection on LGBT equality.

Third, for reasons just stated, media reports of the activities of the deliberative entrepreneurs described in this case study almost invariably describe the actors in existing social movement terms, such as "advocates" or "activists" and sometimes even as single-issue ideologues who are determined to realize a given social outcome through their persistent social support. I contend, however, that close examination of their words and deeds shows that this conventional portrayal as advocates tends to misrepresent the more nuanced and deliberative role that each had undertaken. In most of these cases, these deliberative entrepreneurs explicitly rejected the role of advocate for a particular social outcome in favor of broadly supporting others in reflecting on their inherited views. In this they urged others to *forge their own consciously reconsidered views* whatever those considered views might ultimately become. In order to move against the grain of dominant media descriptions of these social actors, therefore, I spend extra time illustrating the words and actions that reveal particular figures to be engaged in the work that I am labeling here deliberative entrepreneurship. I then turn to elaborate the other two deliberative catalysts of deliberative packages and precipitating events at the end of this chapter and more thoroughly throughout Chapters 3 and 4.

Overview: Three Catalysts of the LGBT Deliberative System

Among the most striking patterns that appeared in this exploratory study of US public engagement on LGBT issues is the visible appearance and widespread influence of a relatively modest number of people who actively sought to foster public reflection. Given the intellectual and emotional labor involved in self-reflection, it makes sense that for a large-scale public deliberation to emerge across an entire society, a number of catalysts are needed to spark deliberation and to sustain it over time through periodic jump-starts. At least three different, and also interrelated, catalysts gave impetus to the US public deliberation on LGBT equality in the period studied.

As described in Chapter 1, the first catalyst is that of *deliberative entrepreneurs*. This catalyst is defined as topically informed groups or individuals who serve to spark deliberation by visibly and repeatedly issuing public invitations to conscious and informed reflection on a matter that is potentially coming under public consideration. In the LGBT case, some of the individuals who performed this function were already on the public stage and poised to serve in this role. Others were swept to the center of public engagement and controversy in unforeseen ways that they would not perhaps have chosen. In the materials analyzed for this case study, deliberative entrepreneurs emerged in many, if not most, of the major social domains sampled.

The contributions of nine deliberative entrepreneurs are featured at length in this and the next three chapters of this case study. Together these nine figures operate in at least five major social domains; some also operated beyond a single social domain to straddle two or three social spheres, and some catalyzed deliberation at a national level. The public figures highlighted here as having served as deliberative catalysts include: Ellen DeGeneres (entertainment); Episcopal Bishop Gene Robinson (religion); Episcopal Bishop John Shelby Spong (religion); Parnesse Seele (religion and public health/medicine); Barney Frank (politics); John Amaechi (sports); Rick Welts (sports); Zacharia Wahls (politics and community groups); and Daniel Karslake (entertainment and religion). The bulk of this chapter is dedicated to illustrating the concept of deliberative entrepreneurs through numerous examples, including a cluster of instances that occurred in the very early years of system formation.

In addition to these deliberative entrepreneurs, public deliberation on LGBT equality appears to have been also catalyzed by two other elements. These are referred to throughout this work as *deliberative packages* and *precipitating events*. As briefly sketched in the overview chapter, the concept of deliberative packages refers to cultural products that juxtapose competing ideas about the topic under deliberation and includes an implicit or explicit invitation to the audience to use this contrast among ideas to think for themselves about the issue at hand. In the LGBT case, deliberative packages took many forms including documentary films, poetry, flash mobs and other street performances, op-ed pieces, talk show segments, among many others. A variety of examples are offered in Chapter 3, and an illustration featuring a documentary film is discussed in the fourth section of this chapter.

Finally, countless precipitating events also occurred in the LGBT case that spurred public reflection on the question of how LGBT people should be treated in US society. A precipitating event is defined here as any occurrence related to the topic of deliberation that excites new reflection and reconsideration among members of the society. In the LGBT case, precipitating events included the coming out of public figures as gay, lesbian, bisexual, or transgender, the killing or assault of an LGBT person, teen suicides related to the bullying of queer youth, and the election or appointment of a gay, lesbian, bisexual, or transgender person to high office. Such precipitating events also included legal rulings or legislative actions favoring or disfavoring the extension of equal rights and statuses to LGBT people, the exclusion of LGBT people from community groups, workplaces, churches, or families, and public protests in favor of or opposition to the specific recognition of LGBT people by businesses or other organizations. An illustrative example drawn from the case study is provided in the fourth section of this chapter, and a number of illustrative examples appear in the next two chapters as well.

Early Deliberative Entrepreneurs in a Nascent Deliberative System on LGBT Equality

In the late 1980s, social movement efforts arose to draw attention to the urgent public health crisis involving the growing and deadly epidemic of Acquired Immune Deficiency Syndrome (AIDS), which was significantly effecting gay men. The AIDS crisis generated a pressing need for public funding and support for those afflicted (Shilts 1987). While this movement emerged in a time of prevalent anti-gay sentiment, elements of what can be seen as a nascent deliberative system also quietly grew. As discussed in Chapter 1, one of the distinguishing features of deliberative systems, in contrast to most social movement organizing, is that deliberation does not depend on the formation of a community based on an us-versus-them group boundary, as most social movement efforts do. Instead, deliberative systems operate to create opportunities for public reasoning by forming open space for all to reflect on received understanding. At times, this appears as suggestions for reflection that are rooted in already accepted moral and political principles. This anchoring of deliberative space in accepted moral norms serves to highlight familiar ideas and invite people into the deliberative process who might not otherwise see themselves as part of a social movement.

An early example of this dynamic can be seen – perhaps not surprisingly given its ideal democratic function – in the US House of Representatives. This example involves Barney Frank, who I define here as serving as a deliberative entrepreneur. In 1987, Barney Frank was in his sixth year as the Representative from the 4th District of Massachusetts. He was also in the process of coming out publicly as gay. As the work of The Coalition to Unleash Power (ACT UP) and other AIDS-related activism reached new heights, the battle in Congress over AIDS research funding also reached a new peak.[2] In the AIDS funding context, Frank observed that on some legislative topics, including AIDS, some "elected officials would take risks to do what was morally right" (Frank 2015, 114). Reflecting this fact among Congressional representatives, some Democrats and Republicans regarded the AIDS epidemic as a danger not only for gay men but to all, and they therefore felt "a moral duty to vote in ways that would be described – or caricatured – by their opponents as 'pro-gay'" (Frank 2015, 114). The logic of this legislative outlook was one of protecting and serving the common good.

In articulating this particular legislative logic within the House of Representatives, reasoning about public health was directed toward everyone in the domain of the House from within that domain itself. In this process, everyone was invited to reflect and to act upon their own conscience and convictions. Furthermore, all were invited to reflect upon the potential contradiction between their convictions and their actions regarding what was fair and just in light of principles that were already held in common in their immediate domain. Frank himself led this effort in the House of Representatives and served as the focal point and leader for deliberation. He offered reasons for others to take risks for what is "simple common sense" (115). In time, and through this approach, Frank was joined and aided by many others, including some unlikely supporters such as conservative Republican

---

[2] For a digital archive of the work of ACT UP see www.actupny.org/.

Senator Orrin Hatch (R-UT). These new supporters indicated that while opposition existed, they acted as they did on their own emerging convictions.[3] Although Frank at times spoke in terms of pro-gay and anti-gay forces, his perspective in this case reflected what I am calling deliberative entrepreneurship: namely the issuing of open invitations to people from all walks of life and perspectives to reconsider their views regarding a key matter at hand (Frank 2015, 97).

This is not to say that open invitations to reflection and deliberation did away with conflict in this case. The social and political climate of the time was hostile on the matter of the AIDS epidemic. Consequently, some members of Congress who were unwilling to support AIDS research funding actively resisted the congressmen and congresswomen who became willing to support it. This resistance arose in the form of legislative amendments crafted to prevent AIDS research funding recipients from describing gay and lesbian sexual orientation in positive or benign terms. In 1987, these amendments were called "No Promo Homo" riders, although ultimately these were creatively circumvented by a bipartisan coalition – including Senator Orrin Hatch – through the addition of further amendments that eliminated the legal effect of the obstructive riders (Frank 2015, 114–115). Yet despite these efforts, Barney Frank stated that in the larger context of angry activists, a pointedly inattentive president, and the bombastically hateful speech of some politicians, "unfortunately, AIDS advocates did not always recognize how important it was that *majorities* of both the House and Senate had stood up for a bias-free response to the [AIDS] crisis" (Frank 2015, 115, emphasis added). In this episode of legislative action, congressional majorities promoted, in Frank's words, "successful efforts to combat bias" against gay and lesbian people through discussion, reason, and effective will (115).

Frank's analysis flagged an important difference in the components of a deliberative system in contrast to the networked social movements identified and theorized by Manuel Castells (2012). In Barney Frank's assessment, this example public reason and deliberation in the context of the US House of Representatives did not operate through the establishment of a community forged through an us-versus-them

[3] According to Frank, it was conservative Senator Orrin Hatch who conceived the legislative amendments needed to overcome the anti-gay riders. See Barney Frank, *Frank: A Life in Politics from the Great Society to Same-Sex Marriage* (New York: Farrar, Straus and Giroux, 2015), 115.

boundary as social movements commonly do. Instead, it operated to open deliberation to all. It made room for deliberation and personal reflection, thus creating space for shifting views to emerge. It provided also supportive pathways for taking action on the basis of conscientiously held views through votes and other legislative activities. It could be argued, of course, that this form of open invitation for all to deliberate is paradigmatic of any legislative body and is to be emulated in any democratic society at large. This is true. Ideally a democratic body would always, by its very definition and mission, function as just described (Bessette 1994). But in the 1980s, and arguably even more so today, Congress can be seen to be often torn by intense us-versus-them partisanship in which engagement across such divides is anathema to many members.[4] In this sense, Frank's attention to reasoned dialogue and common engagement across segments of the congressional domain expresses a deliberative tradition that is implied but not always observed in legislative contexts.

In any case, evidence of a nascent pattern of public deliberation on LGBT equality is not restricted to Congress in the late 1980s. The materials collected and reviewed here for the years 1987 to 1989 are marked by other examples of individuals creating opportunities and materials for public reflection on LGBT civil rights and the AIDS crisis. Some of these deliberative spaces were created in the perhaps most unexpected domain of established religion. In the domain of religion, at least two people initiated domain-specific deliberation regarding LGBT equality and AIDS in the late 1980s. The first was the Episcopal Bishop of Newark, New Jersey, Bishop John Shelby Spong. In January of 1987, Bishop Spong referenced a report generated by local members of the church and other clergy to urge the Episcopal Church to "deal with reality" by acknowledging and blessing "nonmarital relationships including those between homosexuals."[5] Spong cited his experience in the civil rights movements as the root source of his concern with the extension of equal rights to marginalized people in general. In this, he supported pathways to deliberation within his church and suggested that the poor treatment of gays by the Christian

---

[4] Pew Research Center, June, 2014, "Political Polarization in the American Public," www.people-press.org/2014/06/12/political-polarization-in-the-american-public/.
[5] Ari Goldman, "Newark Bishop Seeking to Bless Unwed Couples: Asks Episcopal Support for Homosexuals, Too," *The New York Times*, January 30, 1987, B3.

Church was itself immoral. He remarked that while he shared with his fellow clergy a desire to uphold the values of "the traditional family," he did not want these "upheld to the detriment of other people."[6] In response, Bishop Spong received widespread criticism and blame for initiating this debate in his ecclesiastical domain.

Nonetheless, Bishop Spong persisted in raising the issue in the Episcopal Church, and proceeded to welcome gay and lesbian people in the Episcopal Diocese of Newark. In 1989, he ordained the first openly gay male minister.[7] He initiated gay- and lesbian-friendly ministries and began the blessing of gay and lesbian relationships.[8] Subject to a firestorm of criticism, Bishop Spong nevertheless continued to foster public debate by drawing attention to contradictions between the moral convictions of the church and its actions with regard to gays and lesbians. As described in a later section regarding Episcopal Bishop Gene Robinson, debate on this issue continued to spread in the US Episcopal Church and within the wider Anglican Communion after the 1980s. Over time, the result of this engagement has been an increasingly visible acceptance and inclusion of LGBT people as members and as clergy in the Episcopal Church.[9]

Secondly, in Harlem, New York, immunologist Pernessa Seele worked among AIDS patients and developed one of the first AIDS education programs in the city. While growing up near Charleston, South Carolina, Seele had seen civic action taking place through local churches. Yet in Harlem she was "shocked and disappointed" to observe AIDS patients dying alone, shunned by congregations in the city. Seele's response was to approach fifty leaders of churches, mosques, and synagogues of Ethiopian Jewish to join one another in education and prayer regarding the AIDS crisis.[10] Drawing together people of various faiths for the specific purpose of prayer and new reflection, Seele created an ecumenical space for the faith community to

---

6   Ibid.
7   Mireya Navaro, "Openly Gay Priest Ordained in Jersey," *The New York Times*, Late Edition (East Coast), December 17, 1989, sec. A.
8   Associated Press, "Jersey Episcopalians Offer A Blessing to Homosexuals," *The New York Times*, Late Edition (East Coast), January 31, 1988, sec. A.
9   For example, in its national website, the US Episcopal Church describes its collective identity as defined in part by the active inclusion of LGBT members.
10 Gretchen Gavett, "Timeline: 30 Years in Black America," *Frontline*, July 10, 2012, www.pbs.org/wgbh/frontline/article/timeline-30-years-of-aids-in-black-america/.

learn new ideas and to contemplate anew on their understanding of the AIDS crisis and the place of gay people in their churches.

At the event, many experienced a shift in their view of AIDS and the legitimate needs of AIDS sufferers. For those who experienced this shift, the next logical step was presented to them: to reconcile their new perception with their deeds by considering the possibility of offering spiritual and practical support to AIDS patients and their families. Seele's 1989 event was the first Harlem Week of Prayer for the Healing of AIDS. The event later expanded beyond Harlem to become the Black Church Week of Prayer and then later into the National Week of Prayer for the Healing of AIDS, which now "involves tens of thousands of churches in the US and worldwide."[11] Seele is an example of an early deliberative entrepreneur on the issue of LGBT equality. Today she continues to foster interfaith engagement with AIDS education and prevention through her organization The Balm of Gilead.

Concurrent with Seele's efforts, other faith denominations were also reflecting on the equal inclusion of gay and lesbian people and taking action through new choices. In 1990, for example, the 101st Annual Conference of American Rabbis (Reform Judaism) opted to formally accept gay men and lesbians as rabbis.[12]

Deliberative Entrepreneurs at the Center of Deliberative Social Networks

It is tempting to interpret the change in US public opinion as a result of a social movement, extended cultural conflict, and/or legal destiny. But the exploratory data analysis offered here suggests that while these factors were certainly present and influential, they are only part of the story. The work of Barney Frank, Bishop Spong, and Dr. Seele in the late 1980s began to create a significant pattern that continues to appear throughout the 28 years of LGBT-related US public engagement considered in this study. As previously stressed, this sample of events and public speech shows the activity of a significant number of deliberative entrepreneurs who visibly and actively generated opportunities for groups and individuals to reflect upon, debate, and deliberate on the

---

[11] Ibid.

[12] Ari Goldman, "Reform Judaism Votes to Accept Active Homosexuals in Rabbinate," *The New York Times*, June 26, 1990, page A1.

question of whether LGBT people should be incorporated into American life on an equal footing, and if so how this should be done. Some of these deliberative entrepreneurs were famous and familiar to the public; others were not. Some were affluent and already influential in various ways, others were of modest means and are known today primarily for their contributions on this issue. Some set out to foster public discussion on LGBT equality. Still others found themselves unexpectedly at the center of a maelstrom of intense public engagement and discussion.

As described in the third section of this chapter, the deliberative entrepreneurs discussed in this case study are diverse and unique individuals. Each one has made, and in some cases continues to make, their own specific and distinctive contributions to US public engagement on LGBT issues. As people they are noteworthy, sometimes peerless, in their own areas of particular endeavor. By coincidence – or perhaps as a formative factor that made each one willing to serve society as they have – nearly all of the deliberative entrepreneurs discussed here have experienced a history of significant adversity of some kind. In some cases, this included poverty, dangerously ill health in themselves or a parent, dislocation, physical or emotional abuse, or some combination of these or other challenges. For some, these hardships arose from being gay or lesbian in an unaccepting society. In other cases, straight individuals had familial or other close ties to LGBT people, and/or strong commitments to social justice, that animated their efforts to foster public engagement on LGBT issues.

To provide specific illustrations of these personal correlates of deliberative entrepreneurship, I describe in the next three sections of this chapter something of the life trajectory of three deliberative entrepreneurs and how their public efforts regarding LGBT equality began. I also describe how the specific words and deeds of their efforts reveal the characteristics of deliberative entrepreneurship. The examples include those of Ellen DeGeneres (entertainment), Bishop Gene Robinson (religion), and NBA basketball player John Amaechi (professional sports). All of these examples (and others) are further discussed in Chapter 3, where their contributions are drawn upon again to elaborate how the efforts of deliberative entrepreneurs can, when certain obstacles are overcome, foster the growth of deliberative social networks within specific social domains, thereby spurring the emergence of large-scale deliberative systems.

Ellen DeGeneres: A Deliberative Exemplar

Ellen DeGeneres is one of the best-known and most widely loved comedic entertainers in America. She is also a television and music producer and has one of the largest social media followings of any public figure. A 2015 Harris poll found DeGeneres to be America's favorite TV celebrity annually for three consecutive years, from 2012 through 2014.[13] Importantly, DeGeneres's appeal also crossed ideological boundaries, as she tied with Bill O'Reilly as the favorite TV personality among Republicans in the poll.[14] Her viewership and social media platform are also among the largest in the entertainment industry. DeGeneres's daytime talk show, *The Ellen DeGeneres Show*, averaged 3.5 million viewers daily in 2013, its tenth year on the air. In that year, her show's viewership was continuing to increase, an unusual pattern in a show so long-running. A social media powerhouse, in 2013 DeGeneres had 17 million followers, and program clips posted on her YouTube channel had been viewed 1.7 billion times.[15] Since that time her social media following has grown to over 29 million followers on Facebook and 22.4 million subscribers to her YouTube channel, which has been viewed over 10.9 billion times.

Ellen DeGeneres rose to prominence from modest means and difficult circumstances. Born in 1958 outside of New Orleans, Louisiana, she was raised by a single mother. She moved often as a child and adolescent, almost annually, and was at one stage abused by her stepfather, a fact that she concealed from her mother for a time in order to spare her mother grief.[16] Comedy emerged as a central component in DeGeneres's life when she discovered that comedy was a means by which she could help to ease the suffering of others. She first discovered the soothing effects of comedy during an extended period of illness experienced by her mother, during which time her mother

---

[13] Allyssa Birth, "Ellen DeGeneres is America's Favorite TV Personality for the Third Year Running," *The Harris Poll*, January 13, 2015, www.prnewswire .com/news-releases/ellen-degeneres-is-americas-favorite-tv-personality-for-the-third-year-running-300019650.html.

[14] Meg James, "For Ellen DeGeneres: Things Are Going Along Nicely," *The Los Angeles Times*, published electronically, April 5, 2013, beta.latimes.com/enter tainment/envelope/cotown/la-et-ct-for-ellen-degeneres-things-are-going-along-nicely-20130405-dto-htmlstory.html.

[15] Ibid.

[16] Lisa Iannucci, *Ellen DeGeneres: A Biography* (Westport: Greenwood Press, 2009), 87.

frequently felt sad and hopeless. DeGeneres noticed that her mother's only joy at that time came from Ellen's ability to make her laugh.[17] This capacity to foster laughter during adversity, and especially in the context of pain, has become a hallmark of DeGeneres's career.

DeGeneres's rise to her current fame is intertwined with, and potentially mirrors, changing US public opinion on LGBT equality. She is often referred to as "the face of LGBT America" and a recent Pew Research Center Survey found her to be by far the most recognized and visible gay or lesbian person in the United States.[18] By the 1980s, DeGeneres was an established comedian. She won the title of "Funniest Person in America" in 1982, and in her broadcast television debut she became one of the first woman comedians ever to be summoned by Johnny Carson to sit in the guest chair after delivering their stand-up routine in their first appearance on the *Tonight Show*.[19] In the late 1990s, DeGeneres had her own successful sitcom. In April 1997, ten years after Barney Frank came out as gay in the realm of politics, Ellen came out as gay in the famous "puppy episode" of her program. DeGeneres's coming out was a popular culture landmark. Many in the LGBT community celebrated DeGeneres's action. For it she was also featured on the cover of *Time* magazine and her show won an Emmy for writing.[20]

But the backlash against DeGeneres, however, was also intense. Upon coming out as gay, DeGeneres experienced death threats and widespread professional and public vilification and rejection.[21] Oprah Winfrey was also caught up in the backlash for having played the role of Ellen's therapist in the puppy episode in order to help DeGeneres in

---

[17]   Ibid, 5.

[18]   Drew DeSilver, "Ellen DeGeneres Is the Most Visible Gay or Lesbian Public Figure in America," *PEW Research Center-FactTank News in the Numbers,* published electronically, June 14, 2013, www.pewresearch.org/fact-tank/2013/06/14/ellen-DeGeneres-is-the-most-visible-gay-or-lesbian-public-figure-in-america/.

[19]   "Ellen DeGeneres – Funniest Person in America," *Biography*, 01:41 [n.d.], https://www.biography.com/video/ellen-degeneres-funniest-person-in-america-20724803639; "Ellen DeGeneres (Sexual Abuse, Coming Out, Oscars)," *YouTube*, 09:37, Barbara Walters interviews Ellen, host of 79th Annual Academy Awards (2007), posted on September 30, 2010, www.youtube.com/watch?v=U-3S7jVBBG4.

[20]   "Ellen DeGeneres-Public Backlash," *Biography*, 01:41 [n.d.], www.biography.com/video/ellen-degeneres-public-backlash-20724291907.

[21]   Ibid.

her task. In the aftermath, Winfrey too became the target of death threats and racialized public vitriol.[22] Sponsors such as JCPenney ended their advertising on DeGeneres's show, which was canceled the following year in 1998 without DeGeneres being personally notified of the cancellation.[23] For three years thereafter, DeGeneres left entertainment. She entered a time of reflection and despair. She did not, however, regret her decision to come out as a lesbian. Today she still describes her coming out as an act that freed her to be herself.[24] Yet the vitriol and scale of her public rejection was far greater than she expected or understood. As DeGeneres has described it, "I felt like I was the exact same person, so I didn't understand how that bit of information on a sitcom caused such a big reaction. I had become the punch line. I had become the target of people's jokes, and it really hurt. I didn't want anyone else to feel that way."[25] DeGeneres had resolved to leave show business. At the urging of a friend and mentor, however, DeGeneres returned to entertainment to try again. She took any entertainment work that she could get and she began to write new comedic material as she lived her life as openly gay.

In the fall of 2001, Ellen again rose to national attention in the unenviable but important role as the host of the annual Emmy Awards. The show was originally scheduled to air shortly after the 9/11 terrorist attacks and it was twice postponed. Organizers wanted neither to celebrate too soon, nor cancel the program in a concession to terrorism.[26] When the awards show was finally held, DeGeneres handled the somber event with impressive grace and skill. She introduced a gentle, mirthful humor that brought relief, but that did not

---

[22] Lacey Rose, "Oprah Winfrey: I Was Called the N-Word after Ellen Came Out," *The Hollywood Reporter*, published electronically, August 22, 2012, www .hollywoodreporter.com/news/oprah-winfrey-ellen-DeGeneres-n-word-coming -out-gay-364529.

[23] "Ellen DeGeneres-Public Backlash."

[24] "Ellen DeGeneres: Meditation Helps Me Shut Down & Feel Good," *MindBodyGreen*, published electronically, October 10, 2011, www .mindbodygreen.com/0-3280/Ellen-DeGeneres-Meditation-Helps-Me-Shut-Down-Feel-Good.html.

[25] James, "For Ellen DeGeneres: Things Are Going Along Nicely," 2013, 7.

[26] Bruce Zabel, "TV Academy CEO Remembers 9/11 – and the Emmys That Almost Weren't," *The Wrap*, published electronically, September 2, 2011, www .thewrap.com/tv-academy-ceo-remembers-911-and-emmys-almost-werent-306 09/.

eliminate or dismiss the collective pain of the nation. At one point in her opening monologue, DeGeneres described her own participation as fortunate in being the most likely to infuriate the nation's attackers. Here she was onstage, she quipped, "a gay woman in a tuxedo surrounded by Jews." After the perfect comedic pause, she added, "Well, I like to do my part."[27]

In this and other humor that evening, DeGeneres's sexual identity was neither erased nor made an issue of division (even as this monologue joke effectively drew a parallel between anti-gay intolerance and anti-Semitism). Instead, openly gay DeGeneres – in her totality – was simply woven into the fabric of the collective. As the host, she deftly attended to both the grief and hope of the passing moment. In so doing, she demonstrated a relatively rare skill of helping others to feel safe and at ease even as they remained attentive to the facts of troubled times. This skill has served DeGeneres and her audiences well ever since. In the next chapter, I argue that her deployment of this skill has also played a role in how DeGeneres has fostered public deliberation on LGBT equality.

On September 8, 2003, after a short-lived sitcom, DeGeneres found her current place as the host of her own daytime talk show. By the end of the year, DeGeneres's new program was nominated for numerous Emmys. Over the intervening years, the show has won more than thirty daytime Emmy awards. It is one of the most successful shows on television and is under contract to continue until 2020.[28] In her daily work, DeGeneres is fully an entertainer who describes herself as "not political."[29] By this I take DeGeneres to mean that she is not confrontational, nor likely to offer an affront regarding LGBT equality or other

---

[27] Lisa de Morases, "Look Back: Ellen DeGeneres Tactfully Opens Post-Sept. 11 Emmys," *Deadline*, published electronically, August 2, 2013, www.deadline .com/2013/08/ellen-DeGeneres-2001-emmys-opening-555866/.

[28] Along the way Ellen has hosted the Academy Awards twice, been the face of major advertising campaigns for Cover Girl and JCPenney, and was named by Secretary of State Hillary Clinton as a Special Envoy on Global AIDS Awareness, see Office of the Spokesperson, "Secretary Clinton Names Ellen DeGeneres as Special Envoy for Global Aids Awareness," US Department of the State, November 2011, https://2009-2017.state.gov/r/pa/prs/ps/2011/11/176773.htm.

[29] Larry Goben, "Ellen DeGeneres on 15-Year-Old Boy, Larry King, Killed for Being Gay," *YouTube*, 02:38, posted on May 8, 2008, www.youtube.com/watch?v=PeM9w3L4H6I; Judy Wieder, "Ellen Again," *The Advocate*, September 25, 2001, 50–63.

issues. In other words, she is not an activist.[30] Toward that end, DeGeneres's talk show has an upbeat format: she dances with her audience, amuses them with her comedic monologue, banters with her DJ, interviews three guests, and offers additional comedy through skits and pranks. DeGeneres's studio audience is made up largely of women, of whom a significant number are straight, white, and middle-aged. These audiences adore Ellen DeGeneres and she warmly welcomes and adores them in return.

Significantly for the purposes of deliberative entrepreneurship, in her stage performance DeGeneres's humor is high-spirited but not mean-spirited. She makes fun of the oddities of human behavior not to ridicule people, but like all jesters, to mirror back to her listeners their unreflective silliness. The effect is to gently reveal to the audience our human foibles both great and small. As noted previously, as a teenager, DeGeneres observed that her humor could lift her mother's mood from sadness. Since then she has recognized that her work also has the power to help people change their own perspectives.[31] In so doing, the comedian intends her work to be positive and to avoid the kind of painful criticism heaped upon her at the time of her own coming out. In conducting her interviews, therefore, DeGeneres indicates that her aim is that no one is ever made to feel uncomfortable and that the conversation goes in a "good, positive, upbeat direction" (DeGeneres 2011, 111). In this, DeGeneres welcomes people to express their best self and their best work. She therefore avoids hurtful gossip and tabloid fodder (however much there may be in circulation), and she is intentionally kind and compassionate. Hilary Estey McLoughlin, president of the company that produces *The Ellen DeGeneres Show*, opines that this generosity of spirit is at the heart of DeGeneres's increasing success: "Ellen is an antidote for the times. She focuses on being kind in a bully culture."[32] As elaborated in Chapters 3 and 4, these practices of positive social engagement can play a catalyzing role in public deliberation as communicative acts that help to overcome the cognitive obstacles to individual reflection.

---

[30] DeGeneres admits to having some "baggage" regarding the appearance of being political. It was suggested that the cancellation of her program in 1998 came as a result of her being, or being perceived, as too political, meaning too much of an advocate or activist, see Wieder, "Ellen Again."

[31] "Ellen DeGeneres (Sexual Abuse, Coming Out, Oscars)," 5:23–5:50.

[32] James, "For Ellen DeGeneres: Things Are Going Along Nicely."

In terms of public deliberation, in her work DeGeneres has also intentionally provided opportunities for members of her audience to reflect upon LGBT experience, as well as on other issues of justice and equality. DeGeneres has done this in at least two ways. First, DeGeneres herself is a walking opportunity to reflect on the question of LGBT equality and social acceptance. Since her return to show business in 2000, DeGeneres's visibility as a comedian and talk show host who is openly gay has offered people the opportunity to consider and debate the merits of valuing equally LGBT people. As audience members enjoy and respect Ellen's work, acceptance of her as an individual entertainer is in tension with simultaneously regarding LGBT people in general with fear, and/or with endorsing conditions in which LGBT people overall suffer exclusion, or other forms of subordination.[33]

The impact of DeGeneres as a visible and well-liked LGBT person appears in opinion polls. In a recent Pew Center public opinion survey, Ellen DeGeneres was found to be by far the most recognizable and most commonly identified gay or lesbian person in America. Thirty-two percent identified DeGeneres as the LGBT public figure who comes to mind first, which is 25 points higher than the next most recognized name, Jason Collins, the NBA's first openly gay basketball player at 7 percent. In the poll, two-thirds of LGBT Americans noted that having well-known people out as LGBT "helps a lot" in the process of making American society more accepting of the LGBT community.[34]

Second, in her work as a talk show host, DeGeneres periodically presents her audiences with real life stories that place expressions of intolerance toward LGBT people in contrast with expressions of love and acceptance. These narratives provide material for audience members to reflect for themselves using the story as a deliberative package. For example, on October 10, 2012, DeGeneres included a guest in her program named Ryan Andresen, who had been involved in Boy Scouts of America (BSA) since the age of 6.[35] Having experienced significant bullying in his life as a gay youth, Andresen chose to create a tolerance

---

[33] The role and importance of tension and contrast in such personal reflection is discussed at length in Chapters 1 and 4.

[34] DeSilver, "Ellen DeGeneres Is the Most Visible Gay or Lesbian Public Figure in America," 2.

[35] TheEllenShow, "A Boy Scout Without a Badge," *YouTube*, 4:52, posted on October 10, 2012, www.youtube.com/watch?v=IGrz6TJk3dA.

wall at his middle school for his scouting public service project. After completing the required twenty-one scouting badges, however, Andresen was denied his Eagle Scout pin because he is gay. While his troop leader had long known of Ryan Andresen's sexual orientation, his presence officially violated the organization's ban on gay youth as members.

News of the BSA's refusal to award the Eagle Scout pin to Andresen drew nationwide attention when Andresen's mother began a petition drive at Change.org. This petition also emerged in the context of a larger controversy over the BSA's ban on gay scouts and leaders – a controversy discussed further in the next chapter. Soon, the Change.org petition gathered 400,000 signatures in support of Andresen being awarded the Eagle Scout pin. In addition, 150 standing Eagle Scouts pledged to donate their Eagle Scout pins to Andresen, including fifty Eagle Scouts from his own troop. Another Eagle Scout, Matthew Kimball, led the pin transfer effort. Kimball, also gay, had received his Eagle Scout status while closeted. Kimball offered his pin as a symbol of his support and respect for Ryan Andresen for being honest and visible in the world as a gay youth.

This story represents a precipitating event in the context of the larger controversy over the BSA's ban on gay scouts and leaders, and public discussion of LGBT equality. Retelling this story also creates a useful deliberative package that places in contrast the BSA's tradition of excluding gay youth, on one hand, with alternative expressions of supportive acceptance by others, including many scouts, on the other. In presenting the story, DeGeneres declared her intention to open space for critical reflection, not to persuade people to adopt a particular perspective, but to give them materials to think for themselves. Near the end of the segment, DeGeneres stated: "You know, I share stories like this because I want people, I think people, you can make your own decision, but just hear all the facts, and keep an open mind, and then you can maybe feel the same way."[36] DeGeneres thus stressed that her intention in the interview was to give her viewers the opportunity to reflect independently on the story and to reach their own decisions based on the available facts in the context of the broader societal debate. In DeGeneres's approach, if audience members reflected and retained their original opinions following conscious reflection, then so be it.

---

[36] Ibid.

DeGeneres also articulated her emphasis on the need for people to think for themselves on other occasions. In an interview for PBS and AOL on making society better, for example, DeGeneres stated:

I hope more people would question their lives and look at it and go "Am I doing that because everybody else before me and my whole family thinks this way and feels this way? Or am I doing it because I really, you know, am following what is really right for me?" I think, we look at society and we look at every ad that's out there and everything that tells us how we are supposed to look and how we are supposed to live and how we're supposed to be, instead of saying: "Is that really how I feel? Is that really what I want to do? Is that really how I want to live?" If more people did that it would be lovely to celebrate our individuality and celebrate our uniqueness.[37]

In this instance, DeGeneres offers an everywoman's account of a scientific, philosophical, and scholarly point. That is, human beings inherit and internalize a range of socially constructed messages and meanings by which they then often unreflectively live their lives. These inherited internalized scripts also often operate as our unconscious biases (Banaji and Greenwald 2013; Kahneman 2011; Barvosa 2008). Yet, these inherited and internalized scripts may or may not support a genuinely positive life for individuals or for groups. As Robert Goodin has likewise stressed, democracy can be improved through an emphasis on individual reflection on matters of common life (Goodin 2003). Thus overall, democracy – which is lived as both collective and individual life – is best served when people consciously examine their social inheritances and choose for themselves what, if any, of that material they wish to keep as guiding elements. In so doing, people can more actively craft their lives through their own conscious choices.[38]

In her work as an entertainer, DeGeneres has consequently created opportunities for people to engage in such self-reflection on inherited ideas regarding LGBT equality, as well as other issues of public concern. The deliberative opportunities that she has generated regarding

---

[37] Makers: the Largest Video Collection of Women's Stories, "Ellen DeGeneres: A Better Society," *PBS AOL*, [n.d.], www.makers.com/moments/better-society.

[38] For an example and related discussion of a method of selfcraft that includes recognizing, assessing, and consciously diminishing selected social inheritances, see Edwina Barvosa, *Wealth of Selves: Multiple Identities, Mestiza Consciousness, and the Subject of Politics* (College Station: Texas A&M Press, 2008), Chapter 6.

LGBT equality include her segment on the murder of 15-year-old gay teen Larry King in 2009; her interview with Candace McMillen, a Mississippi high school senior who spoke out when she was denied entry with her girlfriend to her high school prom in 2010; her interview with 19-year-old Zach Wahls, who addressed the Iowa House Judiciary Committee on marriage equality in 2011 (discussed further in Chapters 3 and 4); and her interview with 14-year-old gay youth Graeme Taylor regarding his public address on behalf of an embattled teacher in 2014.[39]

These and other segments brought forward the voices and experiences of everyday people, often highlighting the noteworthy and sometimes heroic efforts of those doing their part to improve the world. Interspersed with these stories relevant to LGBT equality were also segments in which DeGeneres created space for hearing narratives of other kinds, such as the story of a heroic teen who saved a child from a burning home.[40] She likewise brought attention to thought-provoking stories related to aggression and hate of other kinds, including a segment on the documentary *Bully*, which interviewed a family whose son with Asperger's syndrome committed suicide after being bullied extensively.[41]

Finally, DeGeneres actively defended her statement that she is not an advocate and was not operating politically.[42] Using humor, she at time objected to efforts to portray her as an activist with pro-gay advocacy intentions. In early 2015, for example, conservative Pastor Larry Tomczak published an essay in which he rehearsed an often-made claim that accuses the entertainment industry – specifically naming DeGeneres – as having a "gay

---

[39] Goben, "Ellen DeGeneres on 15-Year-Old Boy, Larry King, Killed for Being Gay,"; TheEllenShow, "Constance McMillen Talks About Her Fight for Equality," *YouTube*, 07:20, posted on October 11, 2010, www.youtube.com /watch?v=B9bZcOsdWt8; TheEllenShow, "Zach Wahls Talks About His Inspiring Speech," *YouTube*, 06:34, posted on February 17, 2011, www .youtube.com/watch?v=gu8RkskFi78; ellenxportia's channel, "An Extremely Inspiring 14-Year-Old Graeme Taylor (2010-11-22)," *YouTube*, 03:48, posted on November 22, 2010, www.youtube.com/watch?v=zRQ07ZpzPGA.

[40] TheEllenShow, "A 14-Year-Old Hero," *YouTube*, 04:38, posted on October 2, 2012, www.youtube.com/watch?v=2PRbqW7eRGg.

[41] TheEllenShow, "Watch the Entire 'Bully' Chat Here," *YouTube*, 15:38, posted on March 23, 2012, www.youtube.com/watch?v=H6RDpOGqeCg.

[42] Goben, "Ellen DeGeneres on 15-Year-Old Boy, Larry King, Killed for Being Gay"; Wieder, "Ellen Again."

agenda."[43] DeGeneres responded to the message with playful but pointed humor. Her reply was widely covered in the mass media, both in the United States and abroad.[44] She closed by stating: "Larry, the only way that I'm trying to influence people is [to encourage them] to be more kind and compassionate with one another. That is the message that I'm sending out. I don't have an agenda. I'm not here to brainwash anyone." DeGeneres then proceeds to a sight gag that gently satirizes the pastor's claim of her supposed brainwashing efforts by unveiling a hypnotist's wheel and a sales pitch to segue humorously to the next segment of the show.[45]

The Uniqueness of Deliberative Entrepreneurs: Bishop V. Gene Robinson and John Amaechi

Ellen DeGeneres is considered here to represent an ideal type of deliberative entrepreneur. The work of other deliberative entrepreneurs analyzed in this case study also exhibits similar patterns, albeit in its own tailored ways. Each worked uniquely to create open space for deliberation, welcoming those who are willing to reflect on new ideas without prompting feelings of judgment or shame for their current perspectives. At the same time, from their various social locations, not all of the deliberative entrepreneurs highlighted here felt the need to draw as bright a line as DeGeneres did between creating deliberative opportunities and other work exhibiting their personal views that might be plausibly read as partisan advocacy or activism.[46] For these

[43] Larry Tomczak, "Are You Aware of the Avalanche of Gay Programming Assaulting Your Home?" *Christian Post*, Accessed June 19, 2015, www .christianpost.com/news/are-you-aware-of-the-avalanche-of-gay-programming -assaulting-your-home-132277/.

[44] Chris Pleasance, "'Larry, it sounds like you are watching a lot of gay TV': Ellen DeGeneres shuts down homophobic pastor after he accuses her of 'promoting homosexual agenda,'" *Daily Mail*, published electronically, January 15, 2015, www.dailymail.co.uk/news/article-2911294/Larry-sounds-like-watching-lot-gay-TV-Ellen-DeGeneres-shuts-homophobic-pastor-accuses-promoting-homosexual-agenda.html.

[45] Paula Reis, "Ellen's Real Agenda," *YouTube*, 02:38, posted on January 16, 2015, www.youtube.com/watch?v=cgKN7MjNrtQ.

[46] TheEllenShow, "Memorable Moment: Ellen's Wedding Monologue!" *YouTube*, 04:18, posted on June 20, 2012, www.youtube.com/watch? v=NeUm3vHYOtw.

other entrepreneurs, the boundaries between deliberative entrepreneurship and political advocacy may be more porous even as their deliberative emphasis remains abundantly clear.

This blend can be seen, for example, in the work of the Episcopal Bishop V. Gene Robinson. Now retired, Bishop Robinson was the first openly gay and partnered Episcopal bishop in the US and in the worldwide Anglican Communion of which the US Episcopal Church is a part.[47] In 2003, after thirty years of service as a priest, Robinson was elected to become the Bishop of New Hampshire, which ignited a firestorm of controversy that fostered extensive debate in his social domain. Like DeGeneres, Robinson too came from a childhood of adversity. Born in rural Kentucky in 1947, at birth he was so ill and his cranium so misshapen that Robinson was not expected to live.[48] But live he did. He grew up in poverty raised by his loving parents, Charles and Imogene Robinson, who were both sharecroppers and a couple of devout Christian faith. Robinson too embraced Christian faith early while also becoming aware that he himself was gay. As a young man, Robinson attempted to abandon his sexual orientation. He married and with his wife Isabella became the father of two daughters. He eventually accepted the inevitability of his sexual orientation, however, and he and his wife amicably divorced. Robinson then came out as gay to his family and to members of his church. He later entered into a new life partnership with Mark Andrew and began a new peaceful phase of his career. In this next eighteen years, he lived in service as a clergyman, as a loving father to his daughters, and as the assistant to the bishop of New Hampshire. In his election as the new bishop in 2003, however, Robinson was swept unexpectedly into the public spotlight as a focal

[47] Lynne Tuohy, "Gene Robinson: First Gay Anglican Bishop Reflects on Tenure in New Hampshire," *The San Diego Union Tribune*, published electronically, December 30, 2012, www.sandiegouniontribune.com/sdut-first-gay-anglican-bishop-reflects-on-tenure-in-nh-2012dec30-story.html.

[48] Expected to die at birth, Robinson was named Vicky Gene Robinson, with both female and male names, to facilitate family recognition and his immediate burial. His injury was so extreme that the family doctor who attended Robinson's birth, seeing Robinson's severely misshapen head, molded it by hand into a greater semblance of roundness to spare Robinson's mother further grief. Haunted by this act of compassion, the doctor only revealed this action to Robinson many years later. Hill Center DC, "Bishop Gene Robinson: Straight Talk About Gay Marriage," posted on September 26, 2013, www.youtube.com /watch?v=jIUs4ITbJXo, 1:58–5:58.

point of growing debate within the Episcopal Church on the inclusion of LGBT people.[49]

While Robinson is often described as an advocate for LGBT civil rights, he is, I contend, better described as a deliberative entrepreneur.[50] Like DeGeneres, Robinson's mere presence in his chosen profession as an openly gay and partnered bishop created controversy. That controversy, in turn, fostered opportunities for others of religious faith to reflect on the equal inclusion of LGBT people in churches of various denominations.[51] It also fostered reflection on issues of sexuality, patriarchy, and the power of churches to advance justice or injustice. On close examination, however, Robinson's contributions persistently invoke the admonition to think for oneself. Rather than accept any particular moral prescription, Robinson urges his audience to reflect upon the contradictory influences that shape faith traditions even in their common focus on human dignity and compassion.

Robinson's urging to self-reflection appears clearly in the area of sexuality. For example, responding to the common admonition to sexual abstinence "just say no" in his book entitled *In the Eye of the Storm*, Robinson urges readers to see the oversimplification in the "just say no" edict and to attend to the greater complexities that human sexuality invokes. Given that many people regard religious leaders as always opposing robust sexual self-expression, Robinson's comments to the contrary – comments that highlight the centrality and beauty of sexuality within human identity – bear quoting at length.

Just say no to which part of sexuality? Say no to hugging, to holding hands, to touching, to kissing, to massage? Say no to fondling? Say no to unbuttoning a blouse or a shirt? Say no to fondling the breast or the chest? Say no to rubbing the legs, to unbuttoning the pants or the shirt? The real question isn't whether or not to be sexual; we are sexual every minute of our lives. The real question is what limits do we need to choose for our sexual activity, and by

[49] Gene Robinson, *In the Eye of the Storm: Swept to the Center by God* (New York: Seabury, 2008).

[50] Macky Alston, *Love Free or Die*, 82 min. New York: Kino Lorber Inc., 2012; HillCenterDC, "Bishop Gene Robinson: Straight Talk About Gay Marriage," *YouTube*, 58:55, posted on September 26, 2013, www.youtube.com/watch?v=jlUs4ITbJXo.

[51] Daniel Karslake, *For the Bible Tells Me So*. 98 min. New York: First Run Features, 2007.

what criteria? We may need to say no to the most intimate expressions of sexual intimacy. But for the health of our bodies, and the health of our souls, we must not say no to sexuality – this marvelous means of communion that enlivens and blesses our daily existence. (2008, 30–31)

In these and other passages, Robinson urges people to think critically and to reconsider the issues of sexuality and the body raised in the controversy over the place of LGBT people in the domains of spirituality and religious faith. To aid public reflection in his books, sermons, and public lectures, Robinson offered information placed in tension (what I refer to as deliberative packages) thus providing contrasting ideas that audiences need to reflect independently on received wisdom.[52]

In another example, Robinson points out the contradictory messages of the Christian Bible on sexuality and same-sex desire. As a result of these tensions, the Bible is both "less clear and less helpful about sex than people are often led to believe," creating gaps that call for careful reflection (31). Robinson describes, for instance, that the early Hebrews regarded human sexuality as never simply a matter of procreation alone. Instead for them, sexuality was at the heart of human identity itself and a gift of grace from God. He notes that this connection is echoed in language as the verb for genital sex is likewise the root for the Hebrew verbs "to know" and "to create" – facts that associate the exercise of sexuality to human capacities for conscious awareness, creativity, and imaginative innovation. Robinson quotes passages from the Song of Solomon in the Old Testament and finds in those words an overt celebration of the beauty and pleasures of the body and the joy of human sexual love (32).

In tension with this, Robinson notes that the New Testament features a greater dismissal and rejection of the body, thereby expressing a mind–body dualism that pushes off the physical expressions of sexual desire. He also notes related contradictions between the dismissal of carnal love and the actions of Jesus, who in the biblical stories continually engages with the physicality of humanity, as expressed in illness, sex, and death, *and* who scandalously befriended women, interacting with them respectfully, and including them as vital in and to his ministry (Robinson 2008, 32–33). In elaborating these tensions as

---

[52] Robinson also does this in his more recent book, *God Believes in Love: Straight Talk About Gay Marriage* (New York: Knopf, 2012).

demanding reflection instead of reaction, Robinson draws his reader's attention to the scholarship that describes biblical text not as literal prescription, but as culturally specific and time-bound expression. He points out that time- and space-specific values do not necessarily bind later cultures and eras. Robinson thus urges readers to reflect on scripture because the contemporary relevance of any biblical passage or sacred text must be determined in each generation and is not inevitable over time. Illustrating this process of moral evolution, Robinson further points out that the Christian Bible is full of stories in which women are treated in ways that are viewed as unacceptable to readers today. These include the taking of multiple wives and concubines, the treatment of women as salable property, and the labeling of a man's adultery with another person's wife as a property crime. On this logic, the biblical prescriptions that supposedly condemn same-sex desire and sexuality in general are by no means as clear or as determining for contemporary life as has been often assumed.

With these facts presented, Robinson does not urge a particular prescription. Instead, he consistently encourages people to cease reacting and instead to carefully reflect. He entreats his readers: "When we talk about the standards of biblical sexuality, let's think carefully about exactly what we mean" (2008, 32–33). Despite his emphasis on fostering reflection on LGBT issues, Robinson, contrary to the perceptions of many, did not limit his activities as a clergyman to LGBT issues. His work as bishop of New Hampshire involved the full range of ministries usual to his post, such as attention to the poor, the sick, and those in need – including a special focus on women in prison.[53] Also, like DeGeneres, Robinson took an open and embracing view of those who rejected him and who disagreed with his views.[54] Inspired by the book *Embracing the Exile* – which recounts the experiences of John E. Fortunato who was vilified as a gay Episcopalian – Robinson adopted a generous outlook toward all those who would despise, scorn, ridicule, or destroy him and his work saying simply that he: "love[s] them anyway" (2008, 13).

[53] Tammy Trahan, "Endowment Fund for the NH Woman's Prison," *YouTube*, 08:12, posted on August 22, 2012, www.youtube.com/watch?v=zJ0edCKUlzU#t=17.

[54] Goben, "Ellen DeGeneres on 15-Year-Old Boy, Larry King, Killed for Being Gay."

In his time as bishop, Robinson nevertheless served as a focal point for an ongoing debate within the Episcopal Church – one that arguably had its origins with Bishop Spong in 1987. Like DeGeneres, Robinson's election to bishop saw him endure death threats, calls for his removal, and an intense backlash from many around the world who objected to the consecration of a gay bishop. Robinson, as well as his partner Mark Andrew, his children, and his former wife, wore bulletproof vests to Robinson's consecration as bishop.[55] Some blamed Robinson, who was *elected* to his role as bishop, for willfully bringing controversy and the threat of schism to the church. Robinson was also pointedly excluded from the decennial Lambeth Conference in 2008, a gathering of the leadership of worldwide Anglican Communion. This was a painful slight from the Archbishop of Canterbury (then Rowan Williams) who called for the American Episcopal Church not to consecrate same-sex unions or recognize gay and partnered clergy.[56] Some Episcopalians left the church, and some churches left the Episcopal denomination in a much-debated schism.[57]

Yet as the controversy raged, Robinson, like DeGeneres, proceeded with graceful good humor, warmth, kindness, and peacefulness.[58] Robinson persistently and with skill and energy presented the tensions at hand to members of the Church in diverse venues and contexts, giving innumerable addresses and sermons, and publishing his writings. In each activity, he created opportunities for greater reflection on the part of others. His manner and presence also fostered changing views. He witnessed a shift in outlook in many individuals who were at first apprehensive to meet him, but who soon relaxed and become accepting as he won them over by his warmth.[59] Many faithfully

---

[55] "Robinson under FBI Protection after Death Threats." *Advocate*, published electronically October 28, 2003, www.advocate.com/news/2003/10/28/robinson-under-fbi-protection-after-death-threats-10294.

[56] Stephen Bates et al., "Preaching to the Converted," *The Guardian*, Published electronically July 14, 2008, www.theguardian.com/world/2008/jul/15/anglicanism.gayrights.

[57] Riazat Butt, "Gene Robinson Goes but Rift Remains: Strain Proves Too Much for Gay Bishop," *The Guardian*, published electronically November 7, 2010, www.theguardian.com/world/2010/nov/07/gene-robinson-anglican-us-episcopal.

[58] Evidence of Robinson's warm and inviting style can be seen in the documentary of his time as bishop, *Love Free or Die*.

[59] *Love Free or Die*; see also the interview for the Endowment Fund for the NH Woman's Prison, www.youtube.com/watch?v=zJ0edCKUlzU.

supported Robinson and other gay and lesbian clergy throughout the controversy. Many more reflected on what the challenge meant for the community as a whole.[60]

In 2009, this ongoing reflection found a culmination in the Episcopal General Convention at which representatives of the US Episcopal Church would formally deliberate and decide by ballot whether it would choose to consecrate gay bishops and to bless same-sex wedding ceremonies in states where same-sex marriage was then legal.[61] At the conference, Robinson did not know what the deliberations would produce. The conference employed formal democratic procedures of floor debate, small group discussion, and breakout sessions for group reflection. During the proceedings, many LGBT church members told their stories, as did many who were deeply torn on the matter.[62] As the collective deliberations unfolded, the issues were debated in impassioned and reflective ways as assembled representatives sought to discern the right path forward. Finally, the assembled bishops voted. As the votes were cast and tallies read, the assembled clergy passed both measures by significant margins voting in favor by two-thirds. As described by Robinson, the announcement of this historic vote was punctuated by an extended silence during which the monumental character of this inclusive choice resounded throughout the assembly.[63] The significance of this decision has extended far beyond the US Episcopal Church. After the rejection voiced by Rowan Williams, the subsequent Archbishop of Canterbury sponsored an initiative against the bullying of LGBT people and urged a change in the tone of worldwide Anglican communications to be more accepting of people of all sexualities and genders.[64] Today, in his retirement, Gene Robinson continues his work in public engagement, dedicating his time to fostering civility in political speech and public discourse.

---

[60] Rev. Susan Russell, "And Here's to You, Bishop Robinson," *The Huffington Post*, published electronically November 13, 2012, www.huffingtonpost.com/rev-susan-russell/and-heres-to-you-bishop-robinson_b_2119963.html.

[61] Laurie Goodstein, "Episcopal Vote Reopens a Door To Gay Bishops," *The New York Times*, July 14, 2009, A11.

[62] For documentary footage of deliberations at the 2009 General Assembly see *Love Free or Die*, at 49:00–1:14:00.

[63] Ibid, 1:10:00–1:14:00.   [64] Russell, "Here's to You, Bishop Robinson."

Domain-Specific Deliberative Entrepreneurship: John Amaechi and the Domain(s) of Professional Sports

The example of Bishop Robinson suggests two further points about deliberative entrepreneurs. The first is that the specifics of the activity of each entrepreneur is unique and grows from his or her own expertise in their chosen fields. Second, the work and immediate impact of a deliberative entrepreneur is generally focused in their particular domain where they are actively engaged. For example, in the social domain of American professional sports, as late as 2013 no active professional player was out as gay in any of the four major sports leagues. In that year, NBA player Jason Collins became the first openly gay player.[65] Public statements and the experiences of past participants indicate that the levels of anti-gay intolerance in American professional sports had been high.[66] This climate of intolerance and bullying had also extended beyond US professional sports to prevail in youth and collegiate sports around the world.[67]

In the domain of US professional sports, and particularly in professional basketball, deliberative entrepreneurship also can be seen in the influence of retired NBA player and psychologist John Amaechi. Amaechi has actively and consciously served to foster discussion of LGBT inclusion in professional sports in America. In the materials compiled for this exploratory study, Amaechi stands out as being referred to, interviewed, or otherwise quoted in nearly every piece of material collected on LGBT issues related to professional sports between 2007 and mid-2014.[68] Unlike some other deliberative entrepreneurs, Amaechi consciously intended at the outset of his activity to

---

[65] Howard Beck and John Branch, "With the Words 'I'm Gay,' an NBA Center Breaks a Barrier," *The New York Times*, published electronically April, 29, 2013, mwr.nytimes.com/2013/04/30/sports/basketball/nba-center-jason-collins-comes-out-as-gay.html.

[66] PEW Center Research, "A Survey of LGBT Americans: Attitudes, Experiences and Values in Changing Times," In LGBT in Changing Times, PEW Research Center (Washington DC: PEW Center Research, 2013), 38; Erik Denison, and Alistair Kitchen, *Out on the Fields: The First International Study On Homophobia in Sport* (Sydney: Bingham Cup Sydney 2014, 2015).

[67] See *Out on the Fields*.

[68] From a social network theory perspective, this high rate of incidence of Amaechi's name in the sample indicates that Amaechi has a high degree of social network centrality in his domain. The significance of this for the growth of public deliberation on LGBT equality in sports is discussed in Chapter 4.

assist in the task of fostering public debate and consideration on LGBT equality. Born in Boston – the son of a Nigerian father and English mother – Amaechi was raised near Manchester in the United Kingdom. His mother single-handedly raised Amaechi and his siblings while she also worked as a physician. As a child, Amaechi sometimes joined his mother as she made homecare visits to families who had loved ones facing death. He witnessed her uncanny ability to alleviate the suffering of others and to ease their minds into a peaceful collaboration with her directives for patient care. Watching her work, the young Amaechi imagined his mother as a kind of healing Jedi.[69] Inspired, Amaechi vowed to learn to help others as his mother had, but in his own fashion. While still a youth himself, he also promised himself that he would someday work to help youth. This vow was animated in part from his own sense of childhood discomfort. As an adolescent Amaechi was pudgy, bookish, and 6' 8" in height, which together made him feel like a "pathetic freak." Amaechi became drawn to basketball after a stranger in the street told him he could be great. As he began the against-all-odds climb to the NBA, basketball became for Amaechi a way to succeed and to overcome his feeling of being socially misfit. In time, his growing awareness of his hidden sexual identity as a gay man, however, added to Amaechi's sense of alienation. In his memoir, *Man in the Middle*, Amaechi noted that he felt "sexuality was nothing less than a form of torment, a booming tinnitus and blinding light all around as I tried to study and play and do good works" (2007, 110). This unease was unabated even as Amaechi became a much-lauded college basketball player in the US. After playing college basketball at Vanderbilt and Penn State, Amaechi later played in the NBA for five seasons before retiring in 2003.

Amaechi was out as gay to his teammates during his time in the NBA. He then came out to the wider public in 2007, making him the first NBA player to do so. He recounted the experience of being a closeted NBA player in his memoir (2007). Like Robinson and DeGeneres, upon entering the public stage as a gay man, Amaechi received death threats and shunning from the public as well as from some members of the sports community. In a compelling interview, he described how his

---

[69] DiversityInc, "John Amaechi: Hate Speech Goes Way Beyond the N- and F-Words," *YouTube*, 31:24, posted on November 15, 2011, www.youtube.com /watch?v=rLteJkaoGnU.

public announcement occurred between the time of a departure from and arrival to a particular airport. On the outbound journey, Amaechi was stopped by fans in an airport bar and showered with praise and interest. Upon his return, however, he was met with disregard and aversion. One mother pulled her child away from him in the airport. Once again, Amaechi was experiencing what it meant to feel like an outcast. Some active NBA players also immediately denigrated Amaechi, although others actively expressed their support.[70]

In the face of this backlash, however, Amaechi remained committed to generating public engagement on LGBT issues in the domain of sports. Moreover, as time went on, he engaged more heavily in fostering public discussion. Amaechi himself was inspired to prompt public conversation by others who had taken professional risks to be out as gay, particularly actor Sir Ian McKellen who appeared as the Grand Marshal of the LGBT pride parade in Manchester, England. Seeing McKellen take such a public stand, Amaechi said:

Even [in] my cynical heart I felt a flutter a little bit. I thought that there was a man who was standing up for me, and it was a moment when I decided I had to move out of my comfort zone. Having retired in England, I['d] really got comfortable there. I decided it was time to come back to America and see if we could start a new debate.[71]

As described in further detail in Chapter 4, in the years following, Amaechi made good on his commitment to foster public discussion on LGBT equality in American professional sports. Informed in part by his new career as a psychologist, Amaechi emphasized in his deliberative activities the value of using language in positive and inclusive ways that can help people to feel safe, valuable, and able to proceed with greater feelings of hopefulness.

In his efforts to foster public discussion, Amaechi rejected the view that only a select few could wield "the amazing power of mindfully used words" to foster well-being and hope in others. Often citing the

---

[70] Amaechi's description of being publicly shunned after coming out literally stunned his interviewers in a segment of *Highly Questionable* on ESPN, "John Amaechi on Not Coming Out While Playing in the NBA," *YouTube*, 02: 41–04:07, posted on November 17, 2011, accessed June 23, 2014, www .youtube.com/watch?v=NlW8aa_ZKMw, accessed June 23, 2014.

    Human Rights Campaign, "John Amaechi," *YouTube*, 01:14, posted on September 20, 2007, www.youtube.com/watch?v=pknJt10nBlo.

[71] Ibid.

example of his mother's work, Amaechi has urged everyone to learn the necessary skills to thoughtfully attend to people in each moment. To prevent any misperception that deliberative entrepreneurship is an activity only for exceptional people, it is worthwhile to quote Amaechi's words to the contrary at length.

My mother used words in a way that it felt like they gently fell onto your brain and stayed there forever. These are skills that we can all have. In a world where people use discourteous language and hateful speech, this [form of attentive, kind and mindful speech with each other] is the antidote. And this is something that we can do every day. It's amazing to me the power of this in the scheme of things. The way that you can help saddened people feel hopeful; the way that you can help people who have been victims find that strength of their own. And the way that in organizations—especially in times of crisis, especially at times when the world seems chaotic and unstable—. . . you can use words to make people feel that they belong and that they are safe and that they are capable of coping.[72]

Here Amaechi notes that the skills of positive and mindful communication with others is a key activity in making social life better for everyone in ways still needed today.

In this analysis of the catalyzing influence of deliberative entrepreneurship, I suggest that this type of positive communication also served Amaechi in playing a key role in fostering public deliberation on LGBT equality in the domain of professional basketball (Amaechi 2007, 48). In Chapters 4 and 5, I draw upon Amaechi's contributions to further illustrate how speech promoting a sense of safety in others was a necessary ingredient in overcoming the three major cognitive obstacles to deliberation in the LGBT case and, in turn, aiding deliberative system formation.

If the contributions of deliberative entrepreneurs like Amaechi, Robinson, DeGeneres, Frank, Spong, Seele, and others have been key catalysts in the development of broader public engagement and reflection on LGBT equality, then the question remains as to the mechanisms by which their active invitations to deliberation aided the formation of a large-scale deliberative system. In the next chapter, I address this question by illustrating a number of concepts and relationships that

---

[72] DiversityInc, "John Amaechi: Hate Speech Goes Way Beyond the N- and F-Words."

appear as patterns in the case study examples used in this analysis. On the whole, social network dynamics played a vital underlying role in how deliberation emerged and grew in specific social domains, and then spread across domains to eventually crisscross the nation as a whole. In the next section, however, I first describe the two other deliberative catalysts, deliberative packages and precipitating events.

Deliberative Packages and Precipitating Events

As described by Mansbridge et al. (2012) deliberative systems are vehicles for the collective consideration of the question: *"How shall we live together regarding this specific matter?"* As briefly sketched in the overview chapter, the concept of deliberative packages refers to cultural products of all kinds that invite the audience – implicitly or explicitly – to reflect anew on an issue of common concern. Deliberative packages are thus catalysts for deliberative system formation, including individual reflection as part of collective consideration. Deliberative packages are further defined in this proposed model as cultural products that juxtapose competing ideas and information about a topic of deliberation thereby providing useful verifiable materials that a person may use to think for themselves about an issue. This juxtaposition of opposing ideas relevant to a deliberation topic is a defining characteristic of a deliberative package. For as described in Chapter 1, the work of contemplating the contrast between competing ideas provides the means for relevant cognitive load for the deliberator. This, in turn, creates the conditions for minimizing the influence of unconscious inherited bias by shifting from cognitive autopilot (System 1) to conscious effortful thought and reflection (System 2) as is necessary for independent deliberation.

Presenting ideas in the form of puzzles, contrasts, or conundrums can provide issue-relevant cognitive load as part of the effort to prompt and support conscious reflection. In other words, undertaking cognitive load is necessary for people to engage in *conscious* reflection lest they instead unconsciously default to the automatized application of previously internalized social scripts as frames of reference in a given topic. As discussed in further detail in Chapter 4, such simple script activation, in contrast, brings up the likelihood that the immediate perceptions and thoughts of a person are not new independent thought, but rather merely the triggering of already internalized views, including

any related implicit bias that they may have subconsciously internalized on the topic. This core component of deliberative packages thus
serves the vital purpose of providing ready-made content as an inviting
vehicle that people can use, if they choose, to step out of cognitive
autopilot into conscious reflection and thought.

In addition to the core element of juxtaposing competing ideas and
thereby presenting a kind of thought puzzle or conundrum that
prompts conscious thought, the most effective deliberative products
also have other qualities. First, the most helpful deliberative packages
frame issues creatively and avoid couching topics in us-versus-them
terms, thereby declining to shame or blame listeners for currently
holding any particular viewpoint. Such open framings welcome all
comers to (re)consider the issues at hand without prejudgment, asser-
tions of guilt, shame or blame, or other judgmental elements that might
suggest personal criticism or rejection. As further illustrated in
Chapter 4, these additional qualities help to minimize the activation
of common fears and identity threats that can, in turn, trigger the
unconscious activation of fear-based, self-defensive scripts that exist
in the psychophysiology of the viewer. Refraining from judgment of the
audience, in turn, enhances the capacity of a deliberative package to
engage listeners and inspire new conscious reflection (see Chapters 1
and 4 for further discussion). Second, deliberative packages also aid
deliberation when they provide listeners with space to experience
a sense of social similarity with the creators of or voices heard in
a given deliberative package. As discussed in detail in Chapter 3, people
are more likely to be open to divergent ideas when those ideas are
articulated by people with whom they feel a sense of social commonality. By fostering such a sense of social similarity and identification
with speakers, well-crafted deliberative packages make it easier for
listeners to encounter and consider unfamiliar ideas or perspectives
that clash with their own existing viewpoints.

Beyond the core requirement of juxtaposing competing ideas on
a deliberation topic, deliberative packages may be created in virtually
any format. They might be long or short, fiction or nonfiction, tell
a story or sing a song. Deliberative packages may include poetry,
television programs, storytelling in any form, films (theatrical or documentary), radio programs, personal interviews publicized in print or
other formats, YouTube clips, novels, plays, skits, cartoons, memoirs,
historical works, public lectures, presentations, and recorded audio or

imagery of live-action events that are then circulated in society via social media. Deliberative products may be created with the active intention of providing food for thought for public reflection, or they might do so inadvertently.

The LGBT case study included countless deliberative products that circulated as ready-made content for reflection in the deliberative system. An example of a deliberative package can be seen in the documentary film written and directed by Daniel Karslake entitled *For the Bible Tells Me So* (2007). As discussed more extensively in Chapter 3, the documentary was consciously designed by Karslake to foster informed and mutually respectful conversation and new reflection on the commonplace idea that Christianity and the Christian Bible condemns LGBT people and requires contemporary Christians to do so as well. At ninety-eight minutes running time, the documentary is a cohesive whole that is also made up of shorter segments on different facets of the issue of LGBT equality. The documentary is an ideal illustration of a deliberative package that presents the repeated juxtaposition of relevant competing ideas. It also displays the evolution in thought on LGBT acceptance of five sets of Christian parents, each with a gay or lesbian child. Alongside the stories of each family, Karslake provides verifiable relevant information about the issue of religious perspectives on gay and lesbian life. In omitting any voiceover, the filmmakers create open space for the audience to review and decide for themselves on the diverse and contradictory materials shown. While the filmmaker's leanings may be inferred, they are not expressed. Instead, throughout the work the film's creators offer no judgment on any of the views expressed and never suggest to the viewers what opinion they themselves should ultimately embrace.

Overall, the film contrasts the stories of five different families of Christian faith who learn that one of the family's children is gay or lesbian. These narratives put faces and life stories to the issue of LGBT equality and provide information upon which viewers can consider the stakes in US society's collective struggle to better understand and decide how to incorporate sexual and gender diversity. These familial stories place side-by-side competing ideas and experiences and also reveal the evolution of thought that occurred among the Christian families depicted in the film. Observing these narratives gives viewers the opportunity to reflect on different paths and to consider how they themselves might decide in similar situations, as well as to consider the larger question of LGBT equality.

In addition to these stories, the documentary contrasts competing ideas and information throughout the film in various sub-topical segments interspersed with the unfolding tale of each family. For example, the film includes a segment on biblical literalism. The segment begins with Mr. and Mrs. Poteat – the parents in one of the five families – describing how they subscribe to and teach the view that the Bible decries homosexuality as "an abomination" and how this conviction has informed their view of their daughter's coming out to them as a lesbian. With this opening, the segment then segues to six person-on-the-street interviews with people who are asked: "What do you think the Bible says about homosexuality?"[73] The answers vary strikingly. One offers the view that homosexuality is absolutely forbidden, while another states that homosexuality is a sin, while a third states that Jesus does not address the issue in the New Testament, and a fourth observes the Bible regards is as "unnatural." A fifth person indicates that she "know[s]" that the Bible says homosexuality is wrong, and that she takes it on faith that the Bible is the word of God because that is what she was taught, although she does not analyze the Bible deeply herself. Lastly a sixth person indicates that while he has read "snippets" of the Bible and he believes what "right wingers" say about what the Bible says about same-sex desire, he concludes by saying, "But in terms of what I know, and what I've read? I haven't actually read it."[74] The documentarians then place this array of six diverse views in contrast with the views of a number of religious scholars and clergy whose lifework involves Biblical interpretation.

These scholars and clergy hail from different denominations, races, nationalities, and genders and they include Reverend Dr. Peter Gomes (Harvard Divinity School), Reform Rabbi Brian Zachary Mayer, Archbishop Desmond Tutu (Anglican, archbishop emeritus Cape Town, South Africa), Reverend Susan Sparks (American Baptist Church), Reverend Steve Kindle (Clergy United), Reverend Dr. Lawrence Keene (Disciples of Christ), and Reverend Irene Monroe (public theologian). Each contributor provides different insights that call into question the conventional reading of the Bible as condemning same-sex desire as an

---

[73] The term homosexuality is used here reflecting the language commonly used in the film and in the time period that it surveys. Over the 28-year timeframe of this case study the socially preferred terms shifted as cultural norms and the ongoing public debate also evolved.

[74] Karslake, *For the Bible Tells Me So*, 18:46–20:00.

abomination. Reverend Gomes, for example, indicates that: "There are [only] about six or seven verses in all of Scripture that speak even remotely to what we might call homosexual activity or homosexual conduct."[75] Moreover, Reverend Kindle stresses that to take the Bible literally ignores some important illuminating factors. Among these elements, for example, Rabbi Mayer notes that there are many things that are innocuous and unobjectionable today that are referred to as abominations in the Bible, including the comingling of crops and the wearing of linen and wool together. Likewise others point out the abominations of eating shrimp or rabbit are not commonly regarded as problematic today. In this they stress that singling out this language regarding homosexuality is a selective reading.

In addition, the meaning of the word abomination itself shifts significantly if it is read in an historically grounded and contextualized manner. Reverend Keene indicates that in the context in which the Bible was written, the term "abomination" referred to a violation against established ritual; it was not used to refer to something as being "innately immoral." He points out, for example, that it was not innately immoral to eat pork, yet it was understood as an abomination because it trespassed against the religious rituals of the day. Reverend Sparks likewise indicates that in the historical era in which the Bible was written, cultural and religious norms prized procreation as a means for Jewish culture to survive and thrive. In that context, procreation was emphasized and prioritized as life and death matter. This emphasis on procreation is also echoed in what Mrs. Poteat describes about her own understanding of biblical teaching and her resulting opposition to gay and lesbian sexual identities.

Finally, in other presentations of competing ideas, the segment ends with two further contrasts in which the logical extension of taking the Bible literally plays out. The first is fictional; the second is non-fiction. The first and fictional contrast involves a clip from the television program *The West Wing,* in which the US president, played by Martin Sheen, subversively asks the advice of a hardline religious opponent of LGBT equality. Sheen repeats and (for illustration) affirms to her the claim that she makes that homosexuality is an abomination. The activist replies that she herself is not the author of this view, but rather that the Bible prescribes it at Leviticus 18:22. Sheen responds

---

[75] Ibid, 18:12–24:30.

affirmatively granting her statement. He then says, based on this model of interpreting scripture, that he would like to sell his daughter into slavery as sanctioned in Exodus 21:7, and Sheen asks the activist what she thinks a fair price would be for his daughter. Sheen follows this question by also noting that his Chief of Staff insists on working on the Sabbath, a violation for which Exodus 35:2 instructs that "he should be put to death." Sheen asks the activists whether he himself is morally obligated by the Bible to kill his Chief of Staff, or whether it is acceptable to call the police to do so.

The contrasts presented fictionally in this clip from *The West Wing* are mirrored in the next scene, which features an interview with Reverend. Dr. Mel White, who favors LGBT acceptance ecumenically across all churches. White describes having given many interviews on live radio programs, during which he has often been asked in hostile terms about the common interpretation of the Bible as condemning homosexuality as an abomination. White describes, for example, being asked on a Seattle radio program whether he knows the scripture at Chapter 20 of Leviticus, which is often read as stating that a sexual encounter between two men is an abomination punishable by death. In the Seattle instance, Dr. White asked the caller: "Who should do the killing, us church people?" The caller responded: "No that's the civil authority's job ... God said it first and it's our job to obey."[76] The segment closes without comment with the image of a religious painting in which an elderly man is depicted with a halo reading a Bible. Here the violence invoked by some who oppose LGBT equality is left to speak for itself alongside expressions of love, compassion, and acceptance in a manner that lets viewers decide for themselves.

This practice of presenting differing views, facts, and ideas in a thought-inviting tension also appears throughout the film in other segments. These include a short animated sequence called "Is It a Choice?" in which common stereotypes are juxtaposed with scientific information and narratives from gay and lesbian perspectives.[77] Another segment includes the self-narration of Mrs. Poteat as she recounts the evolution of her own thought. She describes how watching a talk show featuring a conventionally masculine gay male couple speaking of their love for each other awakened in her an awareness that one of her own obstacles to accepting her daughter's lesbian

[76] Ibid.   [77] Ibid, 39:09–43:47.

identity was that she was thinking of the issue through exaggerated and derogatory stereotypes of gay men and lesbians. Mrs. Poteat also came to see that she was focusing on imaging same-sex desire and sexual practice rather than reflecting on the deep love that can exist between gay and lesbian couples, just as it can for heterosexual couples.[78]

Repeatedly throughout the film, expressions of violence invoked by some who oppose LGBT equality are presented without comment from the filmmakers. For example, expressions of violence occur in the story of the family of Bishop V. Gene Robinson of New Hampshire (who is also discussed earlier in this chapter as a deliberative entrepreneur). Robinson's election and consecration as the first openly gay and part-nered bishop in the Episcopal Church became a precipitating event that itself catalyzed intense deliberation on LGBT equality within the US Episcopal Church and throughout the worldwide Anglican Communion. The documentary shows side-by-side both angry outcry and jubilation that the event of Robinson's election as Bishop excited. While the film does not judge, it also does not flinch from showing the violence at times involved in the cultural struggle over LGBT equality. It shows viewers without comment, for example, handwritten death threats and attacks written to Robinson by total strangers, alongside the joyful congratulations of congregants who had long known Robinson and his work in the Diocese of New Hampshire. In this deliberative package, this technique of setting opposites side-by-side accomplishes the task of evenhandedly presenting information that potential deliberators need in order to reflect on the issues at hand. The film is an honest effort to invite this reflection and to help people to think for themselves on a controversial topic. In order to catalyze public deliberation in this way, deliberative packages like *For the Bible Tells Me So* preassemble and present in one easily accessible package materials that can foster meaningful, informed, and conscious reflection on the topic of common concern for those who are willing to undertake the task.

The third deliberative catalyst seen in the LGBT deliberation case is that of precipitating events. Precipitating events are defined as events that occur relevant to the deliberation topic that excite further delib-eration and reflection among members of the public. In the LGBT case, precipitating events included the coming out of public figures as gay,

[78] Ibid, 46:21–48:40.

lesbian, bisexual, or transgender, the killing or assault of an LGBT person, teen suicides related to bullying of queer youth, the election or appointment of a gay, lesbian, bisexual, or transgender person to high office. Precipitating events also included legal rulings or legislative actions favoring or opposing the extension of identical legal rights and statuses to LGBT people, the exclusion of LGBT people from community groups, workplaces, churches, families, and public protests in favor or opposition to specific recognition of LGBT people by businesses or other organizations.

In some cases, tipping points in the evolution of public opinion regarding the social equality of LGBT people, including affirmation of same-sex marriage, were significant shifts that occurred not long after precipitating events. For instance, as noted previously, the shift in public opinion in favor of same-sex marriage emerged as a majority opinion several months after a series of widely covered teen suicides among bullied LGBT youth. These tragic events spawned many responses, including a social media campaign called "It Gets Better," begun by Dan Savage and his partner Terry Miller in which thousands of people, including public figures, organizations, businesses, and government agencies, created YouTube videos affirming the message that life as an LGBT person gets easier after adolescence (Savage and Miller 2012).[79] The campaign was picked up and emulated around the globe. It also sparked debate and critique within and outside of LGBT communities by those who considered the message to be misleading, stating that things do not necessarily get better in adulthood.

The example of LGBT teen suicides suggests two points. First, happenstance events can be important triggers for public reflection. It is not possible to determine with certainty whether public awareness and reflection on teen suicides in the late summer and fall of 2010 fostered the shift in public opinion that occurred in spring of 2011. What is clear is that the suicides, as unexpected events, fostered a rise in public notice and media coverage, as well public expressions – and perhaps related private conversation – that likely heightened the level of deliberation that was taking place.

Second, this example illustrates the interrelationship of the three deliberative catalysts. It demonstrates that precipitating events and deliberative packages, as well as the activities of deliberative

---

[79] For the campaign see itgetsbetter.org/about/.

entrepreneurs, often intersect and frequently converge in time and place. For example, deliberative entrepreneurs issued invitations for new public deliberation in the context of media coverage of numerous teen suicides. In turn, these contributions of deliberative entrepreneurs often became deliberative packages that could be circulated and used to reflect on the issues at hand in the context of the tragic precipitating events. In the information age and networked societies, such deliberative packages are often circulated through social networks as well as via the media. These deliberative packages are forwarded by email, reposted in blogs and tweets, and sometimes go viral such that millions may see them both from afar in the moment and also at later times. As these cycles of the circulation of catalysts are repeated in and over time, the contributions of deliberative entrepreneurs and deliberative packages flow throughout society, sometimes with renewed impetus created by precipitating events. As these three catalysts spread invitations to deliberation over time the potential arises for nearly everyone in the society to be faced with deliberative opportunities on the topic at hand. As such, these three deliberative catalysts, along with the underlying mechanism of social network dynamics and individual deliberation, together formed the material elements of the deliberative system on LGBT equality.

3 | Social Networks in Deliberative System Growth and Implementation Power

Centers of concentrated communication that arise spontaneously out of microdomains of everyday practice can develop into autonomous public spheres and consolidate as self-supporting, higher-level intersubjectivites, [human interactions] only to the degree that the lifeworld potential for self-organization and for the self-organized use of the means of communication are utilized. *Forms of self-organization strengthen the collective capacity for action.*[1]

—*Jürgen Habermas*

Discourses do not govern. They generate a communicative power that cannot take the place of administration but can only influence it. This influence is limited to the procurement and withdrawal of legitimation. Communicative power cannot supply a substitute for the systematic inner logic of public bureaucracies. Rather it achieves an impact on the logic "in a siegelike manner."[2]

—*Jürgen Habermas*

In the previous chapter, I suggested that the sea change in US public opinion on LGBT equality emerged through the workings of a large-scale deliberative system that was self-assembled by members of US society. This deliberative system integrated all of the many components outlined by Jane Mansbridge and her collaborators (2012) but also required three additional catalysts as underlying mechanisms. I have identified these catalysts as deliberative entrepreneurs, deliberative packages, and precipitating events. All three of these are further illustrated in this chapter through continued discussion of deliberative

---

[1] Jürgen Habermas, "The Normative Content of Modernity," in *The Philosophical Discourse of Modernity: Twelve Lectures*, Trans. Frederick G. Lawrence (Cambridge: MIT Press, 1990), 364, emphasis added.

[2] Jürgen Habermas, "Further Reflections on the Public Sphere," in *Habermas and the Public Sphere*, Craig Calhoun, ed., trans. Thomas Burger, 2nd edition. (Cambridge: MIT Press, 1993), 452.

system growth in the LGBT case. While I theorize that these three catalysts were vital to system growth, I illustrate in this chapter that they were *necessary but not sufficient* underlying mechanisms for the formation of a large-scale deliberative system.

Instead, the growth and development of a deliberative system took place in the LGBT case only to the extent that these three catalysts could effectively stimulate the flow of deliberative invitations and materials through existing social networks. When those invitations to collective deliberation and/or personal reflection were accepted and passed on in existing social networks, then deliberative system growth occurred along those networks. Thus social networks – both existing and newly emerging – formed the vital social infrastructure for the formation of a deliberative system. In other words, considered generally, deliberative systems are *networked* deliberative systems that emerge organically as human interest and engagement grows and spreads throughout existing social networks and/or foster new social network development. The presence of existing social networks as the social infrastructure of deliberative systems allows those systems to accommodate and incorporate social diversity. By linking different social networks engaged in deliberation in their own domains, large-scale deliberative systems can bring millions of diverse people into linkage within the overall system through ties that vary in degree and strength but that altogether contribute to the overall cohesion of the system.[3]

In form therefore, this model of deliberative systems parallels the finding of Manuel Castells regarding social movements – namely that in the information age, social movements have become *networked* social movements (Castells 2012). Yet deliberative systems are also distinct from social movements in ways that are described in Chapter 1, and also discussed with regard to the distinctive contributions of deliberative entrepreneurs in Chapter 2. This chapter is dedicated to elaborating how social networks facilitate deliberative system growth to a national scale. In addition, this chapter describes how a national-scale deliberative system can be a powerful mechanism by which public

---

[3] For an alternative discussion of networks in deliberative systems with a focus on bureaucratic and governing networks, see John S. Dryzek and Simon Niemeyer, *Foundations and Frontiers of Deliberative Governance* (Oxford: Oxford University Press, 2010), esp. 126–130; John Dryzek states, "Networks are a kind of adaptation to complexity," 129.

opinion can decisively influence public policy and other organizational policymaking. The core insights of this chapter are captured briefly in its two epigraphs by Jürgen Habermas. First, the public self-assembly of a deliberative system is a form of self-organization that can be part of daily life and common to everyday practices including those of our most immediate relationships. Second, while the deliberation itself is not governing, the power of large-scale communication influences the prevailing logic of governing systems in a "siegelike manner." This process is illustrated in this chapter. As the illustration reveals, the implementation power of a deliberative system also relies on the social infrastructure of large-scale social networks.

This chapter is divided into four parts, each part draws examples from the LGBT case study to illustrate how social networks serve as the vehicle of the public self-assembly of deliberative systems. In the first section, I outline the manner in which deliberative entrepreneurs, deliberative packages, and precipitating events operate to stimulate the formation of a deliberative system through the social structure of social networks. Specifically, I provide empirical examples of the underlying role of social networks in deliberative system formation in the LGBT case study related to V. Gene Robinson (religion), Ellen DeGeneres (entertainment), and John Amaechi (professional sports). I also include examples that introduce three additional deliberative entrepreneurs, Daniel Karslake (entertainment and religion), Rick Welts (professional sports), and Zacharia Wahls – a young Iowan who at age 19 serendipitously emerged as a national and international deliberative entrepreneur on LGBT equality. Although examples of deliberative entrepreneurship continue to appear throughout this chapter, the first section primarily highlights the pivotal role of deliberative packages and precipitating events. These two elements supply the material flow of deliberative opportunities through social networks, which in turn provides the practical impetus for deliberative system growth.

In the second part of the chapter, I build on earlier analysis of the development of deliberative networks to large scale. The section elaborates on the shift from deliberative saturation within a given social domain (e.g. the entertainment industry, the Episcopal Church) to system crossover into other social domains (e.g. other business sectors, governmental bureaucratic systems, and the domain of professional basketball). In this LGBT case study, as deliberation spread from one social domain to the next, the deliberative system as a whole grew larger and more encompassing.

The third section focuses on the special case of highly *cohesive* social domains, i.e. spheres that are densely networked such as close-knit communities or enclaves. In closed and close-knit domains it is more difficult for deliberation catalysts to gain access to these spheres from outside of those domains. In such cases, the flow of deliberative networks from other domains can be stymied by the relatively sequestered and tight-knit quality of cohesive social networks. Although such high cohesion may forestall the entry of deliberative materials flow from outside of a domain, however, if deliberation can begin within these tightly knit social domains, then the flow of deliberative materials may be faster and more pervasive than in less dense social systems. Two examples of dense, highly cohesive, social network domains are used here to illustrate these particular network dynamics. These examples are those of the Boy Scouts of America (BSA) and the National Basketball Association (NBA). The delayed emergence of public deliberation on LGBT issues in these two domains serves to illustrate the potential for the growth of deliberative systems into areas previously not open to considering the issue at hand.

In the final part, I illustrate that if a deliberative system expands far enough by spanning more and more social domains, a deliberative system may reach a national scale, achieving saturation across all of the social domains of the society. At such a point, the deliberative system forms an open social network that is all-encompassing. At this scale, a deliberative system may also become a vehicle by which public opinion can be expressed powerfully on a large scale and with swiftness in what Habermas called "a siegelike manner." As illustrated in this section, this capability gives public voice, opinion, and will weighty influence in policymaking.

Public Self-Assembly of a Deliberative System: The Role of Social Networks

The evidence analyzed in this study suggests that social networks are the underlying social mechanism by which deliberative systems are self-assembled by the public. To understand the relationship of social networks as the sinew of deliberative systems, it is necessary to survey, at least briefly, the main characteristics of social networks in relation to social domains and the flow of information and social activity. Social network science and social theorists emphasize that all social domains are comprised of social networks.[4] As readers likely know, social networks are known to be composed of the ties and connections – weak or strong – that exist between and among individuals and groups (Granovetter 1973). Social networks are thus ubiquitous in our lives, ranging from the ties among a group of friends or a family, to the social networks that link members of larger social groups, including entire societies and potentially members of a society's far-flung diaspora. For example, the well-known social domains of sports, popular culture, religion, politics, and youth culture in any society are all made up of an array of social networks, from simple pairs and trios of individuals – dyads and triads – to large and complex networks of interconnected people (Kadushin 2012). Some constitutive social networks are dense, cohesive, and significantly encompassing. Other social networks contain significant gaps, or structural "holes," in which some members and/or sectors of a domain are only weakly linked – or not linked at all – to other members of the domain.

In the current historical period, referred to often as the information age, social formations are significantly shaped by: (a) new information technologies that have heightened the rapidity and ease with which information may flow through social networks both locally and globally, and (b) the establishment of commercial and social productivity based on or largely dependent upon the flow of information through social and technological networks (Castells 1996, 32).[5] As noted in the Introduction, the historical development and technologies of the information age are not themselves sufficient to produce large-scale deliberative systems. Nevertheless, the ease and simplicity of accessing local and global social networks that mark the information age appears to be

---

[4] In this chapter I introduce and define concepts from social network theory as needed. For further detail see Charles Kadushin, *Understanding Social Networks: Theories, Concepts, and Findings* (New York: Oxford University Press, 2012).

[5] In his three-volume grounded theoretical treatment of the information age, social theorist Manuel Castells describes the networked society as a deepening pattern in the larger transformation from the industrial age to the current period in which the primary mode of production has shifted from industrial output to a technology-assisted, information-based, mode of development; see especially Manuel Castells, *The Rise of the Network Society* (Malden: Blackwell Publishers, 1996), 16–17.

among the necessary underlying conditions of the emergence, successful growth, and evolution of deliberative systems.

As such, the social networks that permeate society also constitute a key component of deliberative systems. Since the 1970s, new information technologies have ushered in an age in which the networking of society and commerce has become faster, easier, and more pervasive than at any time in world history. Consequently, today's social networks vary in density and size ranging from small email-linked friendship groups to the global financial system. Social networks can be informal, but they can also incorporate elements of formal institutions as components, including the state, the media, and commercial enterprises, knowledge-producing agents and institutions such as universities and think tanks, and other groups as well as formal and informal collectives and organizations of all kinds.

The materials analyzed here for this LGBT case study suggest that in the US public discussion of LGBT equality, the three catalysts outlined in Chapter 2 stimulated the flow and circulation of invitations and materials for deliberation through social networks, thereby forming a key underlying mechanism by which the deliberative system was self-assembled by the general public. These relationships and processes are described in the remainder of this section with reference to various examples.

Deliberative Entrepreneurs as Social Network Nodes

Within their primary social domain of activity, deliberative entrepreneurs stand in a social network as what social network scholars call a "network node." Social network scientists define such person-nodes (also called "ego-nodes") as a social network that originates with an individual rather than with a group or other organization (Kashudin 2012, 17). In the simplest terms, all social networks are made up of nodes and their relationships, which are referred to as "ties." If two person-nodes are linked in a network, this means that they are connected by some relationship (i.e. a tie). Those ties may flow in one direction or the other, be reciprocal, or occur via a third node.

In the formation of a deliberative system, deliberative entrepreneurs place invitations to deliberation and deliberative materials (i.e. deliberative packages) into an existing social network. Those invitations and deliberative packages may then enter into the flow of information already moving through the network. As illustrated in this LGBT case study, the degree to which a deliberative entrepreneur (or any deliberative catalyst) is successful in fostering public deliberation on a given question depends on at least seven contingent factors, each of which is also a microstep process in the larger activity of the public self-assembly of a large-scale deliberative system. These factors are:

1. the extent to which deliberative entrepreneurs or other catalysts inspire members of society to engage in deliberative entrepreneurship themselves in their own way, thereby forming sibling deliberative nodes within the social networks of a society
2. the extent to which deliberative packages are created and flow along through the social networks of a domain, including being passed hand-to-hand, thereby providing deliberative opportunities to those in the social network as deliberative packages flow
3. the extent to which members of social networks (individuals, groups, and organizations) accept the invitations to deliberate provided by deliberative entrepreneurs, and use deliberative packages to engage in personal reflection and/or collective discussion and deliberation
4. the extent to which active deliberators pass along in their social networks news that they are reflecting on a matter at hand, and/or the extent to which they convey the reasoning and/or deliberative packages that they are using to do so
5. the extent to which those who are post-reflection or post-deliberation convey their decisions to others in their networks through speech *and action*
6. the extent to which expressions of post-deliberation decisions flow through social networks and serve as information for the reflection of others who are still deliberating, or as implied invitations to reflection for those who are not yet active in personal reflection and/or collective deliberation, and finally,
7. in the case of the eventual formation (or confirmation) of a clear consensus public opinion, this microstep is the extent to which post-deliberation members of a social network (individuals, groups, and organizations) act to express the established public opinion and will through social networks in a "a siegelike manner"[6] and in ways that

---

[6] Habermas, "Further Reflections on the Public Sphere," 452.

can be recognized and applied by policymakers, including issuing strong objections to those policies that contravene the collective will that has emerged. In other words, the seventh microstep is the public's use of its communicative power to shape public policy in accordance with the public will through its deliberative networks.

An illustrative example of these processes at work in the LGBT case can be seen in the example of Bishop Gene Robinson, who partly inspired and aided another deliberative entrepreneur, filmmaker Daniel Karslake. In 1997 Daniel Karslake was a director and producer at the PBS program *In The Life,* which was then the only televised news magazine dedicated to exploring LGBT experiences in America. Karslake noticed with concern that few, if any, segments of *In the Life* addressed the issue of religion. However, he was aware that many Christian denominations were engaged in internal dialogue and conflict over how to incorporate LGBT people. Karslake approached his executive producer, who reluctantly approved Karslake to produce a biography segment on an openly gay, Harvard-based, theologian, Reverend Irene Monroe, highlighting her work as a street theologian in Boston, Massachusetts.

The day after the segment aired, a young gay man in Iowa wrote an email to Karslake. It read as follows:

Last week I bought the gun. Yesterday I wrote the note. Last night I happened to see your show on PBS, and just knowing that someday, somewhere, I might be able to go back into a church with my head held high, I dropped the gun in the river. My mom never has to know. [7]

This email communication changed Karslake. In his words, it "changed everything I thought and felt about this issue," and "after getting that email, I decided that really everything I was about was going to be trying to get the word out about the fact that God didn't necessarily hate gay and lesbian, bisexual, and transgender people. That perhaps, maybe, God loved them for who God made them to be."[8] Karslake became committed to becoming what I am calling a deliberative entrepreneur. The emergence of numerous deliberative entrepreneurs is the

---

[7] Daniel Karslake, "New Interview with Bishop Gene Robinson and Director Dan Karslake," *For the Bible Tells Me So.* 98 min. New York: First Run Features, 2007, 01:20–02:12.

[8] Ibid.

first microstep process in the public self-assembly and growth of a large-scale deliberative system.

In Karslake's case, even emerging as a self-selected deliberative entrepreneur depended on social networks. In 2003, Karslake connected with Robin Voss, a married mother and grandmother living in Orange County, California, where conservative social and political views are common. Voss had been conflicted about how to understand the contradiction between her religious beliefs – which contained a rejection of LGBT people – and her positive experience of having gay friends. She attended a workshop at a local Presbyterian church entitled "What Does the Bible Really Say about Homosexuality?" Expecting a "fire and brimstone" damnation of LGBT people, Voss instead received an opportunity to reflect again on received wisdom. She walked away feeling healed by her experience in the workshop and, like Karslake, committed to getting the word out that there were other ways to reflect on the question of LGBT equality and inclusion from a religious perspective. Once connected, Karslake and Voss set out to make a documentary that would ultimately be entitled *For the Bible Tells Me So*. Almost immediately after Karslake and Voss reached their decision to make a documentary, Gene Robinson was elected as the next bishop of New Hampshire – emerging as the first openly gay and partnered bishop in the worldwide Anglican Communion. This precipitating event generated a firestorm of worldwide media coverage and a backlash erupted around Robinson including death threats. Through Robinson's heavy layers of security, including FBI protection, Karslake somehow connected with Robinson, who agreed to take a featured part in the documentary film.

Karslake's documentary includes portraits of the lives of five sets of Christian parents, each of whom respond in different ways to learning that they have a gay or lesbian son or daughter. These five families include the Robinsons (Gene, Charles, and Imogene); former US Representative and presidential candidate Dick Gephardt, his wife Jane, and daughter Chrissy; Mary Lou Wallner, whose daughter Anna committed suicide after having been rejected as a lesbian by her mother; Phil and Randi Reitan and their son Jake; and David and Brenda Poteat and their daughter Tonia. The stories are varied and compelling. Each conveys a different journey of reflection on the part of the parents as people of faith, each confronting the tension between their love for their child and the religious teaching that they had long embraced.

Interwoven with the stories of these five families are commentaries and diverse scholarly information provided by noted theologians, including historical knowledge generated by scholars of antiquity. As noted in Chapter 2, these contributors include Archbishop Desmond Tutu, Reverend Peter Gomes, Reverend Irene Monroe, Rabbi Brian Zachary Mayer, and others. All offer scholarly reasons why the scriptural texts are not rightly interpreted as condemning gay and lesbian people.[9] Taken as a whole, this documentary film becomes what I call a deliberative package. It carefully places into tension competing ideas on gay and lesbian inclusion – i.e. stating prevailing views in contrast to alternative perspectives – with the express aim of fostering conscious reflection and informed conversation on a matter of public disagreement. As Karslake describes his effort:

The main reason I wanted to make this film—the main reason the whole team wanted to make this film—was to elevate the conversation about religion and homosexuality to a higher level. We've done enough screaming at each other. We've done enough accusing each other of hatred and bigotry. It's time to start to understand that there might be a way that we can live together and be together in faith—maybe not by always agreeing—but by sharing this idea that really what it all comes down to is love.[10]

The emergence of new deliberative entrepreneurs like Karslake and Voss is an example of the first microstep in deliberative system growth at work. This process is visible here as Robinson, the unknown Iowa youth, and others who engaged with Voss in fostering reflection in her community of faith all inspired Karslake and Voss to work as deliberative entrepreneurs. In relation to those who inspired him to take action, Karslake, in turn, became a sibling person-node in a deliberative social network by actively providing deliberative packages and opportunities to reflect for others in the domain(s) of faith communities.

Karslake's documentary thus also exhibits the second and third microstep processes of deliberative system growth, specifically the creation and flow of deliberative packages through social networks, and the resulting creation of deliberative opportunities for others via existing social networks. In addition, Bishop Robinson also describes microstep four in the eagerness of audience members to pass along the DVD of *For the Bible Tells Me So* to family members:

---

[9] Karslake, *For the Bible Tells Me So*.   [10] Ibid, 09:33–10:06.

When I have appeared with Dan at various screenings of the film, almost the first question out of anyone's mouth is, "When can we get a copy?" Probably the most common experience I've had in talking to people just after they've seen the film is: "I've got to send this to my parents. I've got to send this to my brother, my sister, my cousin. . ."[11]

Bishop Robinson's experience suggests that the deliberative package of *For the Bible Tells Me So* was likely passed hand-to-hand through immediate social networks, often beginning with family units. Karslake also emphasizes how the open and non-accusatory framing of the film is designed to foster this kind of person-to-person sharing of the movie in family and other social networks:

Now that the DVD is out I am convinced that a great number of people who maybe do not share an affirmation of gay and lesbian people—primarily based on scripture—might come to see this film because a son or a daughter or a husband or a grandmother or a cousin has put the movie in front of them and has said: "You know what, *this is not a hating film, this is not a separating film. Would you, just for me, take a look at this movie? And maybe we can talk.*"[12]

If such an invitation is issued and accepted, then a part of a deliberative system has been built. Any personal reflection that the film then excites constitutes the individual democratic reflection described and emphasized by Robert Goodin in *Reflective Democracy* (2003). The follow-up talk among two or more people then constitutes further deliberative practice. In these microsteps, people can reflect on the narratives, concepts, and tensions raised in the film. In turn, the ideas of the film can be related to lived experience and to potential new attitudes and choices.

This scenario offers an example of the self-assembly of a deliberative system at work within families or among friends using a film as a deliberative package. In the case of *For the Bible Tells Me So*, however, although the film is well regarded and has won numerous awards, it is not possible from the materials that I collected for this case study to quantify how often this deliberative network growth took place using

---

[11] Ibid, 08:30–08:45.
[12] Karslake, *For the Bible Tells Me So*, 09:04–09:33, emphasis added.
The importance of deliberative packages that do not employ shame and blame discourse is addressed again in Chapter 4 and Chapter 5 as a key element on overcoming cognitive obstacles to deliberation on sensitive topics.

the film, or how often invitations to deliberate using it were accepted or passed along to others.

Zach Wahls, Viral Videos, and the Visible Flow of Deliberative Catalysts

In other cases, however, the flow of deliberative packages through social networks is more clearly visible. A useful example can be seen in the unplanned influence of Zach Wahls and the deliberative person-centered network that formed around him. Zach Wahls emerged into the ongoing deliberation about equal rights for LGBT people on January 31, 2011. At age 19, Wahls – the son of lesbian parents in Iowa, a college student, and an Eagle Scout – addressed the Iowa House Judiciary Committee speaking in opposition to a proposed constitutional amendment that would ban same-sex marriage in the state. The amendment had arisen in response to the Iowa Supreme Court ruling that overturned the state's ban on same-sex marriage.

In his address to the House Judiciary Committee, Wahls offered a personal statement in which he stressed a variety of points.[13] Overall, Wahls proposed that his positive experience and healthy development as the straight child of lesbian parents debunked the myth that same-sex couples were unable to provide a child with the loving and supportive parenting needed for children to thrive. Now a college student majoring in engineering and a small business owner, Wahls challenged the legislators to rethink their views on same-sex marriage based on Wahls's positive example. Moreover, he submitted for consideration his experience that the hardships of growing up in a same-sex parent household came not from what his two mothers offered, but instead from the refusal of others in American society – including other families, schools, hospitals, and the government – to recognize LGBT families as "real families" (Wahls 2012, 7–9).

[13] Wahls's address is often read as advocacy. Wahls certainly described himself as an advocate and in his interview with Ellen DeGeneres, both treated his testimony as social movement activism. Nevertheless for reasons offered in the second part of this chapter, in my analysis I interpret the structure of Wahls' address and its inclusive form as consistent with contributions that I have been describing as deliberative entrepreneurship. The full text of Wahls's address also appears in Zach Wahls and Bruce Littlefield, *My Two Moms: Lessons of Love, Strength, and What Makes a Family* (New York: Gotham Books, 2012), 7–9.

It is possible that nothing would have come from Wahls's address. Every day in America excellent and impassioned addresses are made at hearings large and small that have little or no larger influence. But in a time of video-equipped smartphones and in what Manuel Castells calls our "networked age," Wahls's address was captured on video and circulated via social media.[14] Without his knowledge, the Iowa House Democrats posted the video of his address to YouTube on February 1 (Wahls 2012, xiv). Wahls' comments quickly went viral. By Friday, four days later, it had been viewed one million times.[15] The video and the viral online response received coverage by many major media outlets and the Wahls family gave a live television interview from their home. The following week, Wahls appeared with Ellen DeGeneres on her daytime talk show. By that time, the video had tallied 1.5 million views.[16] The video of Wahls's testimony went viral a second time in late 2011, becoming the most watched political YouTube video of the year with 18 million views, surpassing videos by President Obama and Texas Governor Rick Perry.[17] In 2012, Wahls published a memoir, *My Two Moms*, telling the story of his family and offering, in his words, "an exploration of the values my moms taught me, values driven home by my journey to [becoming an] Eagle Scout" (Wahls 2012). By September of 2012 – nineteen months after his initial address – Wahls was designated to speak on marriage equality at the Democratic National Convention.[18]

---

[14] Iowa House Democrats, "Zach Wahls Speaks About Family," *YouTube*, February 1, 2011, www.youtube.com/watch?v=FSQQK2Vuf9Q. The hearing was also covered by the mass media, for details see Wahls, *My Two Moms*, 6.

[15] For a scholarly analysis of this phenomenon, see Bill Wasik, *And Then There's This: How Stories Live and Die in Viral Culture* (New York: Viking, 2009).

[16] TheEllenShow, "Zach Wahls Talks about his Inspiring Speech," *YouTube*, posted on February 17, 2011, www.youtube.com/watch?v=gu8RkskFi78.

[17] Iowa House Democrats, "Zach Wahls Speaks About Family," *YouTube*, February 1, 2011, www.youtube.com/watch?v=FSQQK2Vuf9Q; "Zach Wahls, Iowa Student, Pro-Gay Marriage Speech Goes Viral," *The Huffington Post*, published electronically December 1, 2011, www.huffingtonpost.com/20 11/12/01/zach-wahls-iowa-student-marriage-equality_n_1123020.html.

[18] Ryan Grim, "Zach Wahls Speech Backs President Who Backs Gay Marriage," *The Huffington Post*, published electronically September 9, 2012, www .huffingtonpost.com/2012/09/06/zach-wahls-speech-_n_1862752.html; National Journal Staff, "Zach Wahls' Speech: Full Text from the Democratic National Convention." *National Journal*, published electronically September 6, 2012, www.nationaljournal.com/s/101428/zach-wahls-speech-full-text-from-democratic-national-convention?mref=search-result.

The Wahls example demonstrates the self-assembly of deliberative systems through at least five of the seven microsteps of deliberative system formation previously outlined in this chapter. It is especially illustrative of the second, third, and fourth microstep processes, which are more difficult to assess in the Karslake example. First, Wahls's address, together with the public response to it and its media coverage, demonstrate process two, centered on the creation of deliberative packages (e.g. here the original address) and their flow through existing social networks. In this case, that flow initially took place through a rapid viral response via YouTube and coverage by diverse media outlets.[19] Wahls' initial intention was only to speak to an assembled legislative audience and for his views to be considered in the immediate legislative action. In this, Wahls certainly wanted his voice to be heard. But he, like DeGeneres and Robinson (Chapter 2), had no idea what would be the larger ramifications of his actions.

In addition, the Wahls example also demonstrates microsteps three and four. In these the flow of deliberative packages is fostered by various entities (e.g. individuals, groups, and organizations) operating as nodes in different social networks that accept and participate in invitations to deliberate, and/or pass along news of their own reflections through their social networks with the intention of fostering further reflection in others. An example of this can be seen in the network link created between Wahls and Ellen DeGeneres through his interview on her talk show. As described in Chapter 2, DeGeneres consciously engaged in activity as a deliberative entrepreneur in part by bringing forward stories that provided material for her viewers to think about the issue of social and legal equality for LGBT people.[20] DeGeneres not only featured Wahls, but also asked him to present how others had used his public testimony as a means of personal reflection and deliberation. The following is their exchange:

---

[19] For Wahls's narrative of the construction of his address and the full text see *My Two Moms*, 2–9.

[20] DeGeneres saw the coverage of Wahls and invited him to tell his story, saying to him on her show, "Well I saw it immediately and I wanted to have you on as soon as I even saw you. So I am happy to have you here." She later adds: "And also that's why I think it's important the more that people see. I mean we have always had this struggle throughout history in any kind of fight for equality. There's been a fight for equality in many different areas. We are still having this fight today, which is outrageous to me, but the more we put a face to it and people can see that you are a straight man raised by two women and such an amazing guy." TheEllenShow, "Zach Wahls Talks about his Inspiring Speech."

DEGENERES: And have you been contacted by anyone, you know, that maybe you changed their minds?

WAHLS: Yeah, well I got a Facebook message from a guy who was shipping off to Afghanistan in two weeks. He was raised in the Deep South, [and was] in his words raised anti-gay. And he said that after seeing my testimony he felt that his mind had really been changed. He had been really anxious about the repeal of don't ask, don't tell and I changed his mind on that too. That just really blew me away. I didn't change the mind of the legislators, they still voted to pass the bill, which was really disappointing. To have this kind of impact on a state, national, and even international level has been really such a blessing. And to be able to come on here, to your show and share my story and my family . . .[21]

The exchange between DeGeneres and Wahls shows several of the public self-assembly processes at once. First, the exchange demonstrates microsteps two and four, in which the deliberative materials are flowing through social networks from their origin, but are also passed along by others to their own social networks – in this case, the 3.1 million average daytime viewers of *The Ellen DeGeneres Show*. This flow is not restricted to the immediate viewers, for the interview was then reposted to YouTube for further amplification through online reposting and additional viewing. Moreover, the DeGeneres–Wahls interview was itself later nominated for a media award by the advocacy and media watchdog organization the Gay and Lesbian Alliance Against Defamation (GLAAD), which further disseminated and amplified the message of the original deliberative package.[22]

In addition, this and other portions of the interview also show microsteps three, four, five, and six in operation. Wahls described being contacted by many people in response to his testimony, all of which then represent new network ties (microsteps three and four). He states: "You know I have gotten a lot of Facebook messages and emails

---

[21] It should be stressed that in the analysis offered here, Wahls himself did not change anyone's mind. Instead only the young Southern man himself could have changed his own mind. A more accurate description is that Wahls provided resources and an occasion with which the young Southern soldier, and others, could consciously reflect on their received, inherited views and potentially reach new – or at least more consciously rendered – views on the matter at hand.

[22] GLAAD, "GLAAD Media Awards," www.glaad.org/mediaawards/nominees/2012/zach-wahls-ellen-degeneres-show.

from people who think I am inspirational, but I'm really a testament to my parents."[23] Among those replies is that of the soldier from the American South, who conveys that he accepted the opportunity presented by Wahls' testimony to reflect upon and ultimately change his socially inherited views (microstep three). In addition – as a recently active deliberator and now post-deliberation person – the soldier's statement of his own conclusion then contributes to collective deliberation by putting his feedback back into the deliberative network via Wahls, thereby creating a feedback loop (microstep five). In this, the soldier's revised views and reasoning flow through social networks (microstep six). In addition, the soldier expresses his anticipated sense of how his new outlook will change his perspective *and his actions* during his upcoming military deployment (exhibiting microstep five). In turn, as Wahls narrates the soldier's example, he increases the flow – and thus the potential influence – of the soldier's reflection to the over 3 million viewers of DeGeneres's television show (i.e. her existing social network). Wahls thus reissues the soldier's reply as a new deliberative package (microstep two) that may or may not be accepted by others as an opportunity for further reflection (microstep three).

These first six microstep processes of the public self-assembly of a deliberative system can also be seen outside of the domain of popular entertainment in other domains, and at smaller, yet still influential, scales. For example, for Wahls's testimony to gain 18 million views by the time of his appearance at the Democratic National Convention in 2012, news of the testimony was likely passed hand-to-hand, friend-to-friend, and colleague-to-colleague via simple digital means and social media.[24] In many, if not most cases, news of the Wahls testimony was shared by people who were personally unknown to Wahls, but who themselves passed on the video to express their wish of fostering discussion on LGBT equality in their own social networks. For example, within the legal domain, Wahls's address was reposted in the blog *Children and the Law* published by the Southwest Juvenile Defender Center. The blogger used a quote from Wahls as the title: "I was Raised by a Gay Couple and I'm Doing Pretty Well." Its author, Ashley Pierce, concluded, "The young man is an incredibly talented speaker and even if you disagree with his overall point, I think it is a valuable video to

---

[23] TheEllenShow, "Zach Wahls Talks about his Inspiring Speech."
[24] Wasik, *And Then There's This*, 2009.

watch."[25] Here Pierce serves as a deliberative entrepreneur encouraging others of any viewpoint to view Wahls' performance.

Still other examples stem from Wahls' numerous public appearances, some of which were covered by media outlets. In a networked society, each public appearance at which Wahls presented his message becomes an opportunity for the greater flow of his deliberative materials within a specific social domain – and hence, the further growth of a deliberative system in that domain and as a whole. Like a pebble dropped into a pond, the ripple effects of each of Wahls's interventions cannot be fully traced. Yet evidence of his interpersonal influence emerges in unlikely places, suggesting that deliberative social networks can permeate society in diverse and complex ways. One example can be seen in a report in the *Huffington Post* on Wahls's address to the Democratic National Convention.

In the comments section, one commentator praises Wahls, whom he had met when Wahls performed a book reading on a cruise ship. The unlikely personal contact with Wahls on a vacation made a significant impact on the respondent, who was commenting to publicly express – and thus potentially amplify across this network of readers – his supportive sentiments.[26] How many additional people became open to Wahls's deliberative message through the favorable words of this one enthusiastic man? Did his endorsement have influence in the *Huffington Post* venue, or perhaps more so when he voiced his view in other contexts? In a complex and fast-growing deliberative network, it may be impossible to quantify the scope of such influence, but its presence is evident.

Finally, even microstep one – the inspiring of new deliberative entrepreneurs – can be seen in the Wahls example. Wahls himself had been inspired to speak before the Iowa House Judiciary Committee and contribute to ongoing societal debate by others who had already contributed in their own ways. In particular, he notes having been inspired to speak out by the website *It Gets Better*, which provided videos of encouragement for LGBT youth in distress in the sorrowful wake of a series of LGBT teen suicides in late 2010. In addition, Wahls was

---

[25] Ashley Pierce, "I Was Raised by a Gay Couple and I'm Doing Pretty Well," *Children and the Law Blog: A Publication of the Southwest Juvenile Defender Center* (n.d.), childrenandthelawblog.com/raised-gay-couple-im-pretty-well/.

[26] Grim, "Zach Wahls Speech Backs President Who Backs Gay Marriage," *The Huffington Post* (2012).

dismayed at the success of the vote to remove from office in November 2010 the three Iowa Supreme Court Justices who had ruled in favor of marriage equality. Wahls felt regret for not having campaigned on their behalf and sadness at the loss of young lives due to intolerance toward LGBT youth. His response was to take the next available opportunity to do his part to forward the ongoing conversation.

Deliberative System Growth – Expansion into New Social Domains and the Influence of Social Network Cohesion

In this model of deliberative system growth, I suggest that as public deliberation advances the size and scope of a deliberative system and whether it expands to a nationwide scale depends on at least three other contingent developments. These developments are:

1. the spread of a deliberation to new social domains previously relatively untouched by that deliberation
2. domain saturation in which entire social domains are saturated by the growing deliberative system such that nearly all, or a strong majority, of those in a domain are at least familiar with the issues being discussed, and
3. crossover influences occur among different social domains, such that deliberations in one domain influence those of other domains

Overall, at the macro level of system growth, these three contingent factors contribute to the expansion of deliberative system growth through domain saturation, expansion to new domains, and domain crossover. Of these three contingent developments, crossover influence among domains may especially help to grow the deliberative system to a national level as deliberative network segments begin to crisscross and overlap among multiple social domains.

Consequently, as discussed in the paragraphs to follow, a primary factor shaping the flow of deliberative catalysts into new domains and new crossover influence is the degree of *group network cohesion* that characterizes social domains at the frontier of a growing system. In addition, as illustrated in the LGBT case, social movement organizations and commercial enterprises can also play important roles in the formation of cross-domain deliberative networks and influence. Growth to larger scales also shows the media and social media as key conduits for the flow of deliberative packages and the visibility of precipitating events and deliberative entrepreneurs. In turn, robust social network flow facilitates the first six – and potentially ultimately all seven – microsteps of deliberative system assembly and function. In the next section, I offer a set of examples to illustrate the influence of group/network cohesion as a contributing factor that has a mixed influence on the growth of deliberative systems to a large scale.

Deliberating Homophobic Slurs in the NBA

The LGBT case illustrates how deliberative system growth could emerge in social domains with little or no previous deliberative activity on LGBT equality. In general, this growth occurred as deliberative catalysts and social pressure for reconsideration were carried into new social spheres from ongoing deliberations in other domains. An example of new system development can be seen in American professional sports, and most especially the National Basketball Association (NBA) beginning in the spring of 2011.[27] Up to that time, personal statements indicate that the climate in the NBA had

---

[27] I focus here on the NBA. However, anti-gay cultures have also prevailed in other domains of professional sports including the National Football League (NFL) and Major League Baseball (MLB), extending at times beyond teams to fans as well. In 2011 not a single active player was out as gay in the NFL, NBA, or in MLB. Thus case examples could be drawn from other sports to demonstrate processes of deliberative system growth. Arguably, of these the NBA has had the most extensive development of a deliberative system. However, an illustrative example can be seen in baseball in the formation of a small self-assembled network responding to homophobic taunting by NY Yankees fans. This scrutiny and response involved GLAAD, the NY Yankees, and Sean Chapin, who created and posted a video overlaying footage of the taunting with statistics about LGBT teen deaths and suicide. I would identify Chapin as a deliberative entrepreneur based on his stated aim of creating a video intended to foster reflection. In Chapin's words: "The video's purpose is to call attention to the anti-gay bullying and harassment and offer peaceful and positive solutions towards making our world a better place. This video does not support treating anyone with violence, and I do not support violence of any kind. I believe that everyone should be treated equally with dignity, respect, and full equal civil human rights." For details see: Aaron McQuade, "New York Yankees to Take Action Against Homophobic Fans." *GLAAD*, published electronically October 14, 2010, www.glaad.org/2010/10/14/new-york-yankees-to-take-action-against-homophobic-fans.; SeanChapin1, "Homophobia Literally Kills: Yankees Game," *YouTube*, Video, 01:39, posted on October 12, 2010, www.youtube.com/watch?v=Gpq4RKYd4wQ.

not been open and accepting of gay men and that coming out as gay has been perceived as an immanent detriment to one's career in sports either as a player or as a manager.[28] As a result, in 2011 no active professional basketball players (or a player in any of the four major sports) were out as gay. Only in 2013 did an active NBA player, Jason Collins, come out. Prior to this, a few NBA players had come out as gay but only after their retirement.

The most visible of these former players was John Amaechi, who came out as gay in 2007. Amaechi is discussed in Chapter 2 as an active and intentional deliberative entrepreneur on LGBT equality in the US. As indicated there, when Amaechi came out publicly, while some were supportive, many fans also shunned him and some NBA players, including Tim Hardaway, openly criticized him. Hardaway announced to the media after Amaechi's disclosure: "You know, I hate gay people... it shouldn't be in the world or in the United States."[29] Overall, while some of Amaechi's former teammates remained supportive, others were not and Amaechi experienced the kind of public censure that many out LGBT people had experienced.

In 2011, Amaechi was joined in coming out by Rick Welts, then president and CEO of the Phoenix Suns. Welts began to engage actively in fostering public discussion of LGBT equality in the NBA and he saw his coming out as not only a personal choice but as a decision that could help others to reflect and to feel more at home within the NBA.[30]

---

[28] See John Amaechi and Chris Bull, *Man in the Middle* (New York: ESPN Books, 2007); see also PEW Research Center, "A Survey of LGBT Americans: Attitudes, Experiences and Values in Changing Times," In *LGBT in Changing Times*, PEW Research Center. (Washington DC: PEW Center Research, 2013), 38; and Erik Denison and Alistair Kitchen, *Out on the Fields: The First International Study on Homophobia in Sport* (Sydney: Bingham Cup Sydney 2014, 2015).

[29] Hardaway later apologized. Yet his comment continued to circulate as emblematic of a systemic problem in the domain of men's professional sports, see Lateef Mungin, "Expert: Use Gay Slurs Controversy to Tackle Homophobia in Sports," *CNN*, published electronically May 27, 2011, edition.cnn.com/20 11/SPORT/05/26/gay.slur/. For a description by John Amaechi of being publicly shunned after coming out, a narrative that literally stunned his interviewer, see Highly Questionable on ESPN, "John Amaechi on Not Coming out While Playing in the NBA," *YouTube*, Video, 02:41–04:07, Posted on November 17, 2011, accessed June 25, 2014, www.youtube.com/watch?v=NlW8aa_ZKMw.

[30] Dan Barry, "A Sports Executive Leaves the Safety of His Shadow Life," *The New York Times*, published electronically May 15, 2011, www.nytimes .com/2011/05/16/sports/basketball/nba-executive-says-he-is-gay.html?_r=0.

At the time of his coming out, Welts described the NBA saying: "This is one of the last industries where the subject is off limits ... Nobody's comfortable in engaging in conversation."[31] This inhospitable culture of silence began to shift in April 2011, when a cluster of events occurred that catalyzed a sudden surge in attention to the issues in the domain of the NBA. A cluster of events precipitating this surge in attention occurred between April 11 and May 15 of 2011.

These specific precipitating events unfolded in rapid sequence. On Monday, April 11, Rick Welts had dinner with his long-time friend and colleague, NBA Commissioner David Stern. Welts came out to Stern and discussed his intention to soon publicly come out as gay. Welts had worked in professional basketball for decades and was (and remains) prominent and widely respected in the field. In coming out, Welts would become the first openly gay person in NBA management. Welts was apprehensive and uncertain what the fallout of his announcement would be for his career. Stern, who had long believed Welts was gay but had never felt able to raise the issue, assured Welts of his support.

By coincidence the following day the NBA began filming a public service announcement (PSA) against the use of homophobic slurs that starred two Phoenix Suns players, Grant Hill and Jared Dudley.[32] Further, as fate would have it, on the same night as filming began, NBA player Kobe Bryant used a homophobic slur on the court during a televised game.[33] The slur was caught on video by a fan with twitter handle @Jose3030 and posted to Twitter where it immediately went viral. On April 13, NBA Commissioner Stern fined Bryant $100,000 for the verbal offense. The incident deepened Welts's resolve to come out. Welts did so in a feature article in the

---

[31] Ibid.

[32] "NBA – Think Before You Speak," *YouTube*, Video, posted on April 13, 2012, www.youtube.com/watch?v=T31cOFkZFig.

[33] The NBA commission issued the fine and it is unclear what influence the Welts-Stern dinner may have had in the official response to Bryant's use of the anti-slur on the court soon thereafter. The LGBT advocacy group GLAAD claimed to have some influence on the commissioner's decision. Seth Adam, "Breaking: Lakers' Kobe Bryant Fined $100k after GLAAD Speaks Out," *GLAAD*, published electronically April 13, 2011, www .glaad.org/2011/04/13/breaking-lakers-kobe-bryant-fined-100k-after-glaad-speaks-out/.

New York Times on May 15 and his announcement generated extensive news coverage.[34]

These happenstances – a combination of spontaneous and pre-planned events – unfolded in ways that fostered heightened public awareness and reflection on LGBT issues in professional sports, especially basketball, in different ways. Welts announcement, as a precipitating event, came as a surprise to many fans and NBA participants. But his social status as a well-liked and highly respected man in the NBA community prompted continued respect on the part of many and a new awareness for others. Moreover, Welts, who gave many in-depth interviews after coming out in the *New York Times,* began to actively foster deliberation in his many public appearances. Like other deliberative entrepreneurs, his words were relentlessly evenhanded. He avoided the blaming and condemnation of anyone, and he urged new reflection on the chilling atmosphere of don't ask, don't tell that had prevailed in the NBA.

While the domain of the NBA had not yet been touched by the national conversation on LGBT equality, the influence of deliberative activity in other domains likely shaped the public reception of Welts, which varied dramatically from the public coming out experience of John Amaechi only four years before. Coincidentally, the experience of both men – the journey from the closet to the light of public expression – was mediated by air travel. Amaechi traveled outbound in glory and affirmation, but returned to the cold air of rejection. Rick Welts held his breath during a transcontinental flight awaiting the public response to his announcement of his sexual orientation. Asked by an interviewer from *TIME* magazine a few hours after landing, Welts described this arduous last moment of uncertainty:

SEAN GREGORY: It's been a few hours now, but what has the reaction been to the public announcement?

Rick Welts: Overwhelming. One of the ironies of it is I was actually on a flight from the West Coast to New York when the story posted

---

[34] Barry, "A Sports Executive Leaves the Safety of His Shadow Life,"; "Suns Prez Rick Welts Reveals He's Gay," *ESPN,* published electronically May 15, 2011, www.espn.com/nba/news/story?id=6553603; "NBA Executive Rick Welts on Coming Out," *YouTube,* Video, 6:11, posted on May 18, 2001, www.youtube .com/watch?v=EkEN22yYGvE; "NBA Exec Rick Welts Announces He's Gay," *TIME,* Video, 7:41, [n.d.], content.time.com/time/video/player/0,32068,9474 76098001_2072000,00.html.

online. I knew that was going to be the case, somewhere 40,000 feet up in the air with no wireless, out of touch with the world. Somehow my life was changing forever down on the ground somewhere. So when the wheels touched down at JFK, I took a deep breath and reached for the Blackberry and turned it on. It exploded with e-mails from the time I touched down to the time I got to the gate. I think I was able to get through a dozen or more and probably had a few tears along the way just from people who already reached out with their encouragement.

Welts described the timing of his public disclosure as a "culmination of a long personal journey" in which he overcame the fear that had been driving his secrecy. In his words, "the fear that drove that was that if that aspect of my life became public, it would limit my ability to follow what was really my passion ... I was concerned that that disclosure could limit what I would be able do with my career."[35] The positive public and professional response helped to further put his personal fears to rest.[36]

Yet Welts also emphasized and demonstrated in his subsequent actions that his motivation was to help others and to foster communication that would help the sport. For reasons further explored and theorized in Chapter 4, Welts's coming out, as an NBA insider, and the positive response to his doing so also made it possible for others to potentially present themselves as LGBT more freely as well. New social connections emerged from Welts' disclosure and existing network ties also carried new information about the LGBT presence in the sport, thereby providing other opportunities for new reflection (system assembly microsteps two and six). For example, as Welts once described in an interview: "Today, actually in your green room, I was just reading an e-mail *from somebody who is an Executive in sports who I don't know* who just said, 'Thank you. This is going to make a difference in my life.' And that's really I guess the motivation. Not I guess, it was the motivation for choosing such a public route to do this."[37] Thus, these events

---

[35] "NBA Exec Rick Welts Announces He's Gay," *TIME*, Video, 7:41, [n.d.], content.time.com/time/video/player/0,32068,947476098001_2072000,00.html.

[36] "NBA Executive Rick Welts on Coming Out," www.youtube.com/watch?v=E kEN22yYGvE. "*Interviewer:* And just so it's clear, the response within the NBA has been what? *Rick Welts:* Just spectacular. You know, I've heard from several of the NBA owners in the last 48 hours, so many of my coworkers."

[37] Ibid.

were not simply a happy ending for Welts, but the beginning of a new phase of his influence on a new conversation in the NBA.

From the moment of his disclosure, Welts worked as (what I call in this model) a deliberative entrepreneur. His contributions were relentlessly kind, evenhanded, and he frequently issued open invitations for informed reflection on the matter at hand, often providing his own story as material and as an occasion for people to engage in conscious deliberation on how the NBA should address LGBT equality. When faced with opportunities to be critical if not outright cynical toward the NBA's approach, Welts consistently opted instead to positively stress the productive potential for all to learn. In response to one interviewer he stated:

INTERVIEWER: Now look, I know the NBA has been putting together PSA's, public service announcements within array of players and all that. Now that's wonderful, but it seems to me the only thing that would really solve this is others following your example. Isn't that right? When it becomes part and parcel of daily life; a PSA on TV just doesn't do it.

RICK WELTS: Well, you know, *I think we're going to learn from this*, about what happens. I don't know what my future is. I don't know where my career is going to go. I don't know what opportunities I will have. I think that's part of the big problem with players. There is no example out there. No one's ever done it. Nobody really knows what's going to happen. I think, based on the incredible outpouring that's come to me because of this, I think it will be encouraging for others to do the same.[38]

In this exchange, Welts does not back away from or downplay the gravity of the state of de facto don't ask, don't tell in the NBA. But nor does he engage in shaming or blaming discourse. Instead he positions himself with the collective as a whole saying that "we" will learn from this. He then stresses a positive note about the prospects and the potential that through such learning the future could be better for all. Here Welts provides food for thought on a serious and detrimental collective problem, but does so in a positive way such that no one who may have contributed to or ignored the problem feels accused, criticized, blamed, or shamed. All are instead encouraged to learn and

---

[38] Ibid, emphasis added.

engage in the collective growth. The difference in framing may be subtle (or not), but as discussed in greater detail in both Chapter 4 and Chapter 5, this approach to fostering deliberation is key to overcoming a number of obstacles to the emergence and growth of large-scale deliberative systems.

Welts takes a similar evenhanded and relentlessly kind approach to the incident involving star player Kobe Bryant's televised use of the anti-gay slur on the basketball court. He speaks of the event in relationship to his own willingness to come out as follows.

Well, the irony of the timing is, it was the day before that I had been sitting in David Stern, the commissioner's, office to kind of discuss this with him. *And then the next night, Kobe went off. You know, I think it reinforced it probably was the time [to come out] because I think that'll probably be remembered also as a teaching moment. And I think he's apologized for it. I think he regrets doing it very much but it was a conversation starter for sure and it led to another step in the dialogue.*[39]

With these words Welts does not issue a condemnation of any kind to Bryant or the many who sought to excuse his conduct. Rather Welts hastens to foreground the better part of Kobe Bryant's response (his apology) and to emphasize the episode for its deliberative value as a "teaching moment" that ultimately served as "a conversation starter for sure" and "another step in the dialogue." In taking his generous approach, Welts persists in describing the problem but also opens space for forgiveness, dialogue, and ultimately for social transformation depending on how that public dialogue unfolds. In this, Welts demonstrates the catalyzing role of deliberative entrepreneurs to promote safe, informed spaces for reflection as described in Chapter 2.

Welts's observation that the Kobe Bryant incident and his response to the NBA fine would spark significant public engagement on the matter was accurate. The public conversation about Bryant's use of the word and the resulting $100,000 fine was extensive. Expressed views ran the gamut from strong critique of Bryant and praise for the NBA fine as a response,[40] to dismissal of the slur as an acceptable part

---

[39] Ibid, emphasis added.
[40] "Kobe Bryant Fined $100,000 for Gay Slur," *ESPN*, published electronically April 15, 2011, sports.espn.go.com/nba/news/story?id=6344596.

of a high-intensity game.[41] As a moment of deliberative system growth, NBA fans on couches and at computers across the country now had numerous deliberative packages at hand with which to rethink practices long prevalent but not commonly discussed or, until then, scrutinized. Some responses, such as that of NBC's John Krolic were particularly evenhanded, at once praising Bryant and the sport while offering reasons why the tolerance for homophobic language could harm fans and youth across the country with effects that are out of sync with the values and intent of the sport and the role model status of a player like Bryant.[42]

This and other interventions opened space for fans to reflect on various questions. Why was the use of homophobic slurs frequent on the court and in locker rooms? Did it matter? What impact did the practice have within the domain of basketball and beyond? In these events and the conversations and reflections that they generated, NBA fans were urged to consider the effect on LGBT people of the common use of the slur far beyond the moment of the game. Some fans defended homophobic slurs as meaningless artifacts of the heat of the moment.[43] Other fans drew upon concerns raised in other domains, especially teen suicides and the problem of bullying, and made it relevant to the NBA and to Bryant, asking Bryant and NBA leadership to consider taking positive action. One fan, Lyn Greenberg, wrote to the *LA Times*:

Given the number of kids who look up to Kobe Bryant, the loose use of this slur among kids, the rate of harassment of gay teenagers, and the number of them who commit suicide every year, the best outcome here would be for Kobe to turn a negative into a positive: He could make a public service commercial for the Trevor Project, the "It Gets Better" Project, or one of

---

[41] "Anti-Gay Slurs Become Popular Fine Material in NBA," *Baltimore Sports Report*, published electronically May 23, 2011, baltimoresportsreport.com/anti-gay-slurs-becoming-popular-fine-material-in-nba-15773.html.

[42] Krolik writes: "This is a beautiful game, and people of all races, religions, and sexual orientations should feel comfortable playing it, watching it, and enjoying it. When the most respected player in the league by players, coaches, and media members alike gets caught uncorking a gay slur and nobody has a problem with it, it can give the impression that the NBA doesn't care about creating a welcoming environment for all of its fans." John Krolik, "Kobe Bryant May Have Used a Gay Slur," *NBCSports*, published electronically April 13, 2011, probasketballtalk.nbcsports.com/2011/04/13/kobe-bryant-used-a-gay-slur/.

[43] "Anti-Gay Slurs Become Popular Fine Material in NBA," *Baltimore Sports Report*.

the gay-straight alliances, urging teenagers to drop use of that word and sensitize them to the impact on their classmates.[44]

In this example, deliberation within the domain of the NBA was fueled by issues already extensively reviewed in the domain of popular culture as a result of the precipitating events (teen suicides) and the deliberative package makers named by Greenberg.

As the conversation on the Bryant slur and fine unfolded, the deliberative entrepreneurship of Amaechi also played a major facilitating role. As these events were scrutinized and discussed in the sports media and mainstream media outlets, Amaechi was sought for comment innumerable times. In the controversy over Bryant's slur and fine, in particular, Amaechi was quoted widely. Of Bryant's initial slur Amaechi stated on April 14, "I'm surprised that people are surprised." He indicated that it was "common language" when he played, and that in the absence of visible efforts by the NBA, "there's no reason for it to somehow get better."[45] Here Amaechi highlighted the tension between what people want to believe about the NBA and what actually exists, thereby providing deliberative material.

Bryant's initial response was to defensively downplay the event, including a half-hearted apology expressed with his initial intention to appeal the fine. Amaechi's comments evolved to highlight tensions in Bryant's response relevant to public deliberations originating in domains beyond, but also ultimately related to, the NBA. Amaechi remained evenhanded, and stated in a *New York Times* commentary essay, "Kobe Bryant isn't some great, bigoted monster, as some have implied."[46] But Amaechi went on to address Bryant directly, relating stories that illustrated the harm that Bryant's words had done.

---

[44] "Letters: Kobe Bryant Creates a Stir with a Slur," *The Los Angeles Times*, published electronically April 16, 2011, articles.latimes.com/2011/apr/16/spor ts/la-sp-letters-20110416.

[45] Cindy Boren, "Gay Former NBA Player Surprised by Surprised Reaction to Kobe Bryant Slur," *The Washington Post*, published electronically April 14, 2011, www.washingtonpost.com/blogs/early-lead/post/gay-former-nba-player-surprised-by-surprised-reaction-to-kobe-bryant-slur/2011/04/14/AF19utdD_bl og.html.

[46] John Amaechi, "A Gay Former N.B.A. Player Responds to Kobe Bryant," *The New York Times*, published electronically April 15, 2011, offthedribble .blogs.nytimes.com/2011/04/15/a-gay-former-player-responds-to-kobe-bryant/; the even-handedness of Amaechi's response as well as its passion are reissued in other coverage, see "Kobe Bryant Sorry; Lakers Make Plan," *ESPN*, published electronically April 15, 2011, www.espn.com.au/nba/news/story?id=6361970.

In particular, Amaechi highlighted the example of a Los Angeles gay youth who had contacted him about Bryant's outburst asking for Amaechi's help. Amaechi wrote regarding this youth: "You are his idol. He is playing up, on the varsity team, he has your posters all over his room . . . but this week he feels less safe and less positive about himself as he stares adoringly into your face as you said the word that haunts him in school every single day."[47] Here – and as discussed further in Chapter 4 – Amaechi responds to the request and the pain of a young person to prompt reflection on the part of an all-star player and celebrity, as well as all of those following the story. This relay of expression of concern, appeal, and response to the pain of anti-gay speech is an example of the flow of deliberative materials through existing (and growing) social network (microstep processes two, four, and six).[48]

In advancing this flow of expression as food for public deliberation, Amaechi further asked Bryant to stop fighting the fine and "use that money and your influence to set a new tone" by indicating that homophobic slurs are never acceptable. Amaechi also praised Bryant as a brilliant player and a person "powerful enough to make an important change in the way we look at real equality in sports and in general," and finally Amaechi also expressed hope that it was not too much to ask for "the occasional good deed" worthy of Bryant's status as a sports superhero.[49] Here, like Welts, Amaechi pulls back from the rhetoric of shame and blame to issue an evenhanded explanation of the negative impact of anti-gay slurs in ways that nevertheless also emphasized the value and dignity of those who, as a result of following constructed and widely accepted social norms, have unwittingly inflicted pain and indignity on others. As discussed further in Chapter 4, this approach is particularly important for circumventing the major cognitive obstacles to public deliberation. For as patterns in this case study illustrate, by affirming the valuable and heroic qualities of Bryant, Amaechi creates a space in which Bryant can feel no fear of rejection, and thus no need to be defensive. Freed from the fear of rejection, he can get on with the key business of thinking anew about his (most likely heretofore unreflective) habits and actions.

---

[47] Amaechi, "A Gay Former N.B.A. Player Responds to Kobe Bryant."
[48] DiversityInc, "John Amaechi: Hate Speech Goes Way Beyond the N- and F-Words," YouTube, Video, 31:24, Posted on November 15, 2011, www .youtube.com/watch?v=rLteJkaoGnU.
[49] Ibid.

As the controversy and the discussion that it fostered unfolded, Bryant's views clearly evolved. After his early defensiveness, his public comments shifted first to accepting responsibility, stating: "The comment that I made, even though it wasn't meant in the way it was perceived to be, is nonetheless wrong, so it's important to own that." By Friday of that week, however, Bryant's language indicated a new understanding of the impact of his example, and the broader conversation about LGBT experience. On a talk show that day, Bryant stated: "It was just stupid and ignorant . . . In this situation, *seeing how many people were affected, it helps you understand* the weight that comes from that word. *That's why it's very important for me to communicate how sorry I am* to [have] use[d] the word [emphasis added]."[50] On that same Friday, the Lakers announced a new collaboration with the Gay and Lesbian Alliance Against Defamation (GLAAD) to co-develop positive initiatives described by a Lakers spokesperson as "ways to help educate ourselves and our fans, and to help keep language like this out of our game."[51] In less than a week's time, the league leadership and key figures in the NBA had become linked – via a social movement organization – into the broader US public deliberation on LGBT equality.

When Welts came out on May 15, his announcement excited new discussion about the climate for gay men in the NBA in the context of the broader national conversation. In an interview at ESPN, Welts was asked why the world of sports had lagged behind in addressing LGBT issues. Welts had no answer but confirmed that the problem "still exists" in the field and described it as "totally out of step, probably with where our society is today."[52] Welts also indicated that Bryant's use of a slur had deepened his resolve to come out and that his aim in doing so very publicly was to assist public reflection. As indicated previously, Welts gave numerous interviews emphasizing the potential for positive dialogue; he stated in one instance: "There really could be an opportunity here to further the dialogue on this subject and perhaps even help some people that might be struggling with the same issue."[53] Moreover, in discussing how Bryant's use of a homophobic slur related to the timing of his own coming out, Welts contributed to sustained attention on the issue of anti-gay slurs, thereby provided ongoing opportunities for public reflection.

[50] "Kobe Bryant Sorry; Lakers Make Plan."   [51] Ibid.
[52] "NBA Executive Rick Welts on Coming Out."
[53] "NBA Exec Rick Welts Announces He's Gay."

In the following weeks, Welts achieved his aim of fostering dialogue on LGBT issues within the NBA.[54] Following his coming out, Welts joined Amaechi in being frequently asked to comment on relevant events, and opportunities soon appeared. On May 23, for example, Joakim Noah used a homophobic slur toward a belligerent fan during the Eastern Conference game watched by nearly 11 million viewers – reportedly the second most watched game in cable television history.[55] Noah was immediately fined $50,000. Unlike Bryant, Noah was immediately apologetic, stating: "What I said wasn't right. I don't want to disrespect anybody. That's not what I'm about. I just got caught up . . . and I'm going to face the consequences as a man."[56] When asked for comment, Welts expressed his disappointment in witnessing an anti-gay slur as "the thought that comes to mind when you're most frustrated." But Welts also praised the league for its efforts to clarify acceptable speech, saying: "For that I'm grateful and I think it's progress and I think it's a teachable moment."[57] Welts's evenhanded comments placed contrasting elements in tension and contradiction, fostering cognitive load and thus the opportunity to more conscious reflection.

Ironically, Noah's anti-gay language arose during the same game in which the NBA aired the public service announcement featuring Grant Hill and Jared Dudley. The PSA had been produced in collaboration with the social movement organization Gay, Lesbian and Straight Education Network (GLSEN) as part of their *Think Before You Speak* education campaign. In the segment Hill states: "Using gay to

---

[54] Welts's contributions continue to date. Living openly gay, Welts continues to provide insight to fans and support of the leagues efforts to create inclusivity. NBC Bay Area, "Rick Welts on Being Gay in the NBA," *NBC*, Video, 04:24, Posted on March 22, 2013, www.nbcbayarea.com/news/sports/The-Interview-Rick-Welts-199248831.html. After coming out, Welts resigned from the Suns to accommodate his partnership, prompting false concerns he had been pushed out. Welts is now affiliated with the Golden State Warriors. Matt Brooks, "Phoenix Suns' CEO Rick Welts–First Openly Gay Top Sports Executive – Resigns," *The Washington Post*, published electronically September 9, 2011, www.washingtonpost.com/blogs/early-lead/post/phoenix-suns-ceo-rick-welts–first-openly-gay-top-sports-executive–resigns/2011/09/09/gIQApTIYFK_blog .html?utm_term=.ca1a3481cdd6

[55] Jonathan Abramsmay, "Noah Fined $50,000 for Antigay Slur," *The New York Times*, published electronically May 23, 2011, www.nytimes.com/2011/05/24/ sports/basketball/bulls-noah-apologizes-for-using-antigay-slur.html?_r=0.

[56] Ibid.   [57] Ibid.

mean dumb or stupid – not cool." Dudley contributes: "It is offensive to gay people."[58] For attentive viewers, the combination of these two opposing events in one game offered an unplanned deliberative package in which fans could reflect on the tension between prevailing practices of anti-gay speech and competing messages that such speech creates a hostile environment with potentially dire effects. At that time, extensive media coverage of recent teen suicides had highlighted the terrible consequences of intolerance expressed in spoken words. As Amaechi had written in the *New York Times* with regard to Bryant: "Right now in America young people are being killed and killing themselves simply because of the words and behaviors they are subjected to for being perceived as lesbian or gay, or frankly just different."[59] In their comments, both Welts and Amaechi kept the contradictions in view while offering affirmation that the problem could be solved.

It is impossible to say from the evidence at hand how many sports fan took these opportunities to reflect. Yet by late May of 2011, some sports commentators were echoing Welts and Amaechi by calling for these and other anti-gay slurs in sports to be used as events for transforming the climate in all the professional sports.[60] Moreover, by the time that Jason Collins came out in 2013, the public response to Collins in open forums such as the *New York Times* was overwhelmingly positive and supportive.[61] The difference between this later public response and the response to Amaechi's announcement in 2007 is striking. I contend that the key difference is that Collins came out at a time when the tipping point in the major shift in public opinion had passed. The discourse around teen suicides and the sense that youth like

---

[58] Mungin, "Expert: Use Gay Slurs Controversy to Tackle Homophobia in Sports"; the campaign would continue with another *Think Before You Speak* PSA appearing the following year during the Super Bowl, see "'Think Before You Speak,' Anti-Gay Bullying Campaign Produced by GLSEN, to Air at Super Bowl (Video)," *HUFFPOST GAY VOICES*, published electronically February 1, 2012, www.huffingtonpost.com/2012/02/01/think-before-you-speak-anti-bullying-super-bowl_n_1247349.html.

[59] "Kobe Bryant Sorry; Lakers Make Plan."

[60] Mungin, "Expert: Use Gay Slurs Controversy to Tackle Homophobia in Sports."

[61] Howard Beck and John Branch, "With the Words 'I'm Gay,' an N.B.A. Center Breaks a Barrier," *The New York Times*, published electronically April 29, 2013, www.nytimes.com/2013/04/30/sports/basketball/nba-center-jason-collins-comes-out-as-gay.html#story-continues-8.

Wahls were thriving in the homes of same-sex couples had provided material upon which a US majority had as of May 2011 taken up new perspectives. This, in turn, spread to other domains where deliberation had not yet taken place.

Overall, these elements of this case study illustrate that in the public self-assembly of a large-scale, nationwide, deliberative system, the growth of the system occurs as saturation in a given social domain and then potentially extends to other social domains. In this process of crossover, the deliberative system can grow to span multiple social domains. As it increasingly does so, it may also grow, theoretically at least, to a national level. As discussed at the end of this chapter, the results of deliberation-related transformation can be enduring. To date, for example, the NBA has retained its zero tolerance policy on homophobic slurs.[62]

Social Network Cohesion and the Expansion of Deliberative Systems into Resistant Domains: The Example of the Boy Scouts of America

As a deliberative system grows and spreads across social domains, the social cohesion of social networks within a domain can play a significant role. However, the influence of social cohesion is not uniform and social cohesion can either foster or alternatively undercut deliberative network growth depending on related circumstances. In social network theory, high levels of cohesion in social networks take the form of "a network of heterogeneous interpersonal ties" (Friedkin 1998, 69). Social cohesion appears as (1) "inclinations to remain within the group, and (2) members' capacities for social control and collective action." As such, group cohesion can be based on relatively weak ties of "acquaintance and collegiality" such that not everyone in the group needs to be connected. A cohesive group thus may have a large proportion of weak ties in which members of the group are perhaps two or more steps removed (Friedkin1998, 69). In cohesive groups, leaders of the group both become more central to the social

---

[62] Mitch Lawrence, "Amar'e Stoudemire Fined $50,000 by NBA for Using Gay Slur in Twitter Exchange with NY Knicks Fan," *New York Daily News*, published electronically June 26, 2012, www.nydailynews.com/sports/basket ball/knicks/amar-stoudemire-fined-50-000-nba-gay-slur-twitter-exchange-ny-knicks-fan-article-1.1102702.

network of the group (in having more ties) and tend to "embody more of the norms of the group than the followers" (Kadushin 2012, 54).[63] As a result, in a highly cohesive network, when the influence of leaders reinforces and sustains existing norms, values, and practices, change becomes more difficult. Conversely, in a highly cohesive network, when the influence of leaders tends toward transformation, it can foster rapid change due to the close-knit qualities of cohesive networks.

The implication of these qualities of social networks for deliberative system growth is that if large-scale deliberative systems are moving toward decisions that would create social change in practice or policy that is unwelcome to the leaders of cohesive groups, then those groups may be more impervious to deliberation and/or to the resulting change. Alternatively, if the leaders (who are central nodes) of a cohesive group endorse the evolution in thought that is being produced by large-scale public deliberation, it is more likely to spread quickly throughout the network(s) that make up that cohesive group.[64] As such, the quality of group cohesion can have crosscutting effects for the potential for large-scale public deliberation to permeate highly cohesive social groups.

An example of both can be seen in the case of the Boy Scouts of America (BSA), which long resisted the inclusion of LGBT participants as members and as leaders. More recently, however, the BSA has also exhibited both a rapid shift in policy toward including gay and

---

[63] In general social networks tend toward homogeneity. The process by which this occurs is still debated, however, see Charles Kadushin, *Understanding Social Networks: Theories, Concepts, and Findings* (New York: Oxford University Press, 2012), 54.

[64] The contrast between the BSA and the NBA is an example of this impact of leadership. For example, NBA commissioner David Stern's leadership on the equal inclusion of gay men in the sport exhibited strong endorsement for extending respect to gay members of the profession and larger society. His efforts led a demonstrable and comparatively quick turnaround in the domain as illustrated by variations in responses to gay men coming out between 2011 and 2013. At the time of Rick Welts's coming out in 2011, the *New York Times* reported of Stern: "Asked weeks later about the persistent perception of the NBA and other men's team sports as homophobic, Mr. Stern removed his glasses, rubbed his eyes and said, "I think we're going to get there." Barry, "A Sports Executive Leaves the Safety of His Shadow Life." By the time Jason Collins came out in 2013, however, Stern commented with good reason that, "the overwhelming positive reaction does not surprise me ... Our players are knowledgeable and sophisticated on this issue ... I would have expected them to be supportive, and they are." Beck and Branch, "With the Words 'I'm Gay,' an N.B.A. Center Breaks a Barrier."

transgender scouts and a protracted deliberation regarding adult LGBT participants. The Boy Scouts of America has a long history of trailing behind the curve of American social change. The BSA is the largest private youth organization in the country. It is an iconic group in the American cultural landscape and it touches the lives of millions. In its first hundred years (1910–2010) there numbered over 52 million Boy Scouts, including two million as Eagle Scouts. Scouting activities build bonds and the organization often inspires deep loyalty. As such, it qualifies as a "primary group" in which face-to-face interactions become self-defining and involves "the sort of sympathy and mutual identification for which 'we' is the natural expression" (Cooley 1909, 23). Developing this sense of collective is consistent with BSA's express mission, which "is to prepare young people to make ethical and moral choices over their lifetimes by instilling in them the values of the Scout Oath and Scout Law." In the Scout Law, "a Scout is trustworthy, loyal, helpful, friendly, courteous, kind, obedient, cheerful, thrifty, brave, clean, and reverent."[65]

Although it is a private organization, the Boy Scouts of America has enjoyed a privileged relationship to the state, including special access to public lands and resources. Moreover, US presidents have served as the Honorary President of the BSA since 1911, and numerous acts of Congress have affirmed and sustained the privileged status of the BSA in times of controversy.[66] Controversy has arisen especially around the BSA's exclusionary practices based on race, ethnicity, gender, religion, and sexual orientation. Exclusions have impacted scout membership, paid leadership, and adult volunteers, both men and women. As wider societal norms of inclusion have changed, the BSA has been relatively slow to transform. In the case of racial inclusion, for example, the BSA did not remove its racial exclusions until 1974.

Historically, the BSA has resisted changing its practices and persisted in excluding LGBT youth and leaders against considerable public and

---

[65] Boy Scouts of America, "100 Years in Review, 1910-2010," *Boy Scouts of America*, ner-area2.org/wp-content/uploads/2014/10/210-031_WB.pdf.

[66] The US Congress itself granted charter to the BSA in 1916 under Charter 36 of the US Code, thus designating it an organization of national and patriotic importance. The charter confers an honorific status designed to provide official honor and prestige to group activities. Other Congressional support includes the 2002 Boy Scouts of America Equal Access Act, which requires local schools to provide spaces for scouting activities. See www2.ed.gov/about/offices/list/ocr/boyscouts.html.

legal pressure to do so. The organization has been sued numerous times for its various practices of exclusionary membership and hiring.[67] In response, the BSA has often claimed First Amendment protections for the right of free association, arguing that as a private organization, it has immunity from anti-discrimination law. The US Supreme Court upheld BSA immunity – to great skepticism among some legal scholars – in 2000 in *Boy Scouts of America v. Dale*.[68] By that time, well-known individuals, religious organizations, and corporate sponsors had also pressured the BSA to include LGBT participants to no avail.[69]

After long resistance to admitting LGBT members, however, the BSA itself partially changed course between May of 2012 and May 2013. This shift appears strongly related to the larger public deliberation on LGBT equality and civil rights. As in other contexts, deliberative entrepreneurs played a role. On May 30, 2012, Eagle Scout Zach Wahls – who is previously discussed in this chapter (and again in Chapter 4) as a deliberative entrepreneur – approached the Annual National Meeting of the Boy Scouts of America. Wahls presented the BSA with a petition signed by 275,000 people asking the BSA to drop its ban on gay scouts and leaders.[70] The petition drive had been organized via the website Change.org by 32-year-old Jennifer Tyrell, who had been serving as den mother for the Cub Scout Troop to which her 7-year-old son Cruz belonged. Tyrell had been dismissed from her role as a den mother the month before, however, when it became known that she is a lesbian.

Zach Wahls was already well known to members of the media due to his influential 2011 address on marriage equality to the Iowa House Judiciary Committee. Dressed in his Eagle Scout uniform, Wahls spoke informally to BSA leaders and also gave a press conference outside of the BSA meeting. Many major media outlets attended the press

---

[67] See for example, *Curran* v. *Mount Diablo Council of the Boy Scouts*, (1998), *Randal v. Orange County Council, Boy Scouts of America* (1998), *Yeaw v. Boy Scouts of America*, (1997).

[68] *Boy Scouts of America v. Dale*, (2000).

[69] "Spielberg Resigns from Boy Scouts Board," *Hollywood.com*, published electronically n.d., www.hollywood.com/general/spielberg-resigns-from-boy-scouts-board-57167345/; Rabbi Dan Polish, and Judge David Davidson, "Commission on Social Action to URJ Congregations: Boy Scouts of America," *Religious Action Center of Reform Judaism*, published electronically January 5, 2001, rac.org/commission-social-action-urj-congregations-boy-scouts-america.

[70] Christina Ng, "Eagle Scout Challenges Boy Scouts' Anti- Gay Policy with Petition," *ABCNews*, published electronically May 30, 2012, abcnews.go.com /US/eagle-scout-challenges-boy-scouts-anti-gay-policy/story?id=16459135.

conference. *Good Morning America* covered the story under the heading "Eagle Scout Challenges Boy Scouts' Anti-Gay Policy with
Petition" and named a list of celebrities who had signed the petition
including Ellen DeGeneres, Julianne Moore, Ricky Martin, and others.
ABC News interviewed Jennifer Tyrrell regarding her experience of
dismissal, about which she said, "I actually felt devastated. I was heart-
broken. I cried a lot. I still feel sad about it a lot. It's 2012 and nobody
deserved to be treated like that." She described that to her the saddest
element was her son missing out on taking part in Cub Scouts. She
shared that her young son did not fully understand what was taking
place, stating, "He just loves everybody and doesn't understand how
others couldn't."[71] The touching story of Tyrell and her son Cruz now
circulated nationwide through the media. As such, Tyrell's story,
including the related petition, served as a deliberative package for
people within US society, and a catalyst for the microstep processes
of the public self-assembly of deliberative systems. In addition, shortly
after the press conference, Intel, a sponsor of the BSA, announced that
it would cease its financial support for the organization because of its
policy on LGBT participants. Intel did so, in part, because it too had
received a petition asking it to withhold its funding from BSA.[72]

External pressure had long been ineffective at altering the policy of
the highly cohesive BSA. Thus the relevant question for deliberative
system formation in this case is: What eventually triggered new deliberation growth within this close-knit group? Theoretically, once such
deliberation began it could grow significantly in part because of the
cohesion of the group. Network scientists find that in cohesive groups,
information flows quickly. Sociologist and network specialist Noah
Friedkin finds in his research that members of "cohesive groups are
more likely to be aware of each other's views on an emergent issue than
are actors who are not members of the group" (Friedkin 1998, 70).
In cohesive groups, group attention to discrepant viewpoints generally
takes the form of increased levels of communication, particularly in
face-to-face communication. Consequently in this case, news of the

---

[71] Ibid.
[72] Rich Ferraro, "Intel Will Not Fund Boy Scouts of America until Ban on Gay
Scouts and Scout Leaders Ends," *GLAAD*, published
electronically September 21, 2012, accessed on August 11, 2014, www.glaad
.org/blog/intel-will-not-fund-boy-scouts-america-until-ban-gay-scouts-and-
scout-leaders-ends.

petition brought against the exclusion policy by Wahls, an Eagle Scout, would have traveled quickly, not only through the media, but also through the informal networks of the Boy Scouts.

Arguably therefore, the most important element to prompt new deliberation within a cohesive group in the BSA case was that someone who had undeniable and valued status as a group member delivered a challenge to BSA policy from within the group itself. In this case, the catalysts for deliberation came via a member of the Boy Scout's most honored group, from an Eagle Scout, who respectfully presented a request to the national assembly following its established protocols. Wahls himself unquestionably embodied the values of BSA, yet he also favored inclusivity. So much is scouting a part of Wahls' identity, that his book *My Two Moms* is structured with each chapter titled and themed with a value instilled in him by his mothers and his experience as a Boy Scout, beginning with "be prepared" (Wahls 2012).

To what extent did the request brought forward by Wahls foster a new round of internal deliberation on the question of how, if at all, LGBT people should be included in the BSA? It appears that deliberation did emerge in both formal and informal ways. Formally, the issue was immediately discussed at the 2012 annual meeting where it was decided that opinions would be solicited within the BSA for the next year of the BSA Annual National Meeting. Between the national meetings in May 2012 and 2013, the BSA formally fielded surveys and requests for feedback to be incorporated into closed-door discussions among BSA leaders at their regularly scheduled administrative gatherings.[73] The BSA's organizational structure includes both national and regional councils, within which local councils and troops are established by charter. Troop charters also require the sponsorship of a local organization, typically a church or civic group. There is evidence that a range of formal deliberations took place at these multiple levels to review the policy, which had been in place for over 30 years. The ultimate decision to accept gay youth as members was arrived at by a vote of the adults assembled to represent their regional councils at the 2013 Annual National Meeting. In these various ways,

[73] Josh Israel, "Internal Survey Shows Many Boy Scouts and Parents Believe Discriminatory Policy Harms Organization," *ThinkProgress*, published electronically, March 22, 2013, thinkprogress.org/lgbt/2013/03/22/1764441/boy-scouts-97-percent/.

the decision was formally democratized through the established deci-sion-making mechanisms of the BSA.

In addition, however, segments of the scouting community also orchestrated informal deliberations, particularly the group Scouts for Equality and the Inclusive Scouting Network. In 2012, Zach Wahls established the Scouts for Equality (SFE) after the BSA affirmed its policy of excluding gay scouts and leaders in what was effectively a don't ask, don't tell policy. SFE was (and remains today) a scouting alumni group that includes over 8,000 Eagle Scouts. As an advocacy organization, SFE was dedicated to fostering inclusive policies at BSA while also exhibiting BSA values and supporting the organization of BSA as a whole.[74] The SFE Board of Directors and staff were comprised of a highly accomplished group of volunteers headed by Zach Wahls as executive director. Among the group's achievements was its successful drive to obtain two million signatures on petitions urging the BSA to end its discriminatory practices.

Although it was a grassroots advocacy group, Scouts for Equality consciously adopted practices of speech and action that accepted all perspectives, while also supporting the BSA as an organization and the broader BSA community. As SFE described itself at the time of the controversy: "Consistent with the BSA's policy, Scouts for Equality believes that showing respect towards the beliefs of others is consistent with the Scout Oath and Law. *We expect all of our members to show reverence and respect for all religious beliefs and philosophical posi-tions* (emphasis added)." Scouts for Equality thus functioned as a deliberative entrepreneur in its intent and its practice in three specific ways.

First, the explicit aim of the group was to foster discussion that might eventually lead to people changing their minds and, in turn, changing BSA policies. As they state: "Scouts for Equality is leading a respectful, honest dialogue with current and former Scouts and Scout Leaders about ending the Boy Scouts of America's discriminatory policy against

---

[74] The Group's mission statement is: "Scouts for Equality is a Boy Scouts of America alumni association dedicated to ending the BSA's ban on gay members and leaders. As Scouts, we believe discrimination goes against the values our movement teaches us and has no place in Scouting's future. The creed and principles of the Scout Oath and Law will drive our mission as we work to save a great cultural icon: the Boy Scouts of America," accessed August 1, 2014, www.scoutsforequality.org/.

gay Scouters."[75] This dialogue was fostered informally, and included shedding light on stories of how the exclusionary policies of BSA affected the lives of youth and families such as Terrell and her son Cruz, and also Ryan Andresen, whose experience of being denied his Eagle Scout pin because he is gay had gained national attention (see Chapter 2). These stories put a face and a name to the negative impact and lived experience of BSA policies, policies that still seemed principled to some scout leaders.

Second, the group recognized that by simply being present and participating as scouts who believe in inclusive practices, their visibility alone could change hearts and minds. SFE stated: "By embodying the values of the Scout Oath and Law, we believe we can restore the social relevancy of one of this country's great cultural institutions: the Boy Scouts of America. "[76] In engaging in scouting activities while endorsing inclusive principles, these scouts demonstrated for others the potential for uniting tradition, faith, service, and equality for all. This component of visible expression also took the form of a creating a new scout badge developed by the network for inclusive scouting. By wearing the badge, members of SFE could indicate to all that they were scouts who favored inclusive practices, as well as discretely identifying oneself as a safe contact person for an LGBT participant who was struggling under what was effectively BSA's don't ask, don't tell policy.[77] In addition to exhibiting deliberative entrepreneurship, all of these activities involved the contributing microsteps of the public self-assembly of a deliberative system.

Third, the SFE actively created opportunities for deliberation on the part of members, and provided outlets for new reflections to be

---

[75] www.scoutsforequality.org.
[76] Neal Broverman, "Watch: Zach Wahls Debates Father of Scout Opposed to Ending Gay Ban," *Advocate*, published electronically February 4, 2013, www.advocate.com/youth/2013/02/04/watch-zach-wahls-debates-father-scout-opposed-ending-gay-ban; Ryan Houlihan, "Zach Wahls Appears on CNN to Debate against Boy Scouts Anti-Gay Policies," *GLAAD*, published electronically April 22, 2013, www.glaad.org/blog/zach-wahls-appears-cnn-debate-against-boy-scouts-anti-gay-policies.
[77] The square knot badge was originally created in connection with the Inclusive Scouting Network led by Mark Noel, an Eagle Scout and troop leader who had been ousted when it became known that he is gay. In 2014, the Inclusive Scouting Network merged with Scouts for Equality, and Noel served as a member of the Board of Directors, accessed on August 1, 2013, www.scoutsforequality.org/inclusivescouting.net and https://our-team/.

expressed and heard throughout the scouting community and beyond. For example, on May 10, 2013, Scouts for Equality held a national day of action to mobilize scouts and their leaders nationwide to support a shift in policy. Events were held across the country and a rally was held in Bethesda, Maryland, across from the National Capital Area Council headquarters.[78] Eagle Scouts, present and former den leaders, and Council Chairs attended. GLAAD reported on the event quoting from a long string of participants offering their reasons for rejecting the ban. Most pointed out the ban as discriminatory and contrary to the principles of scouting regarding acceptance and respect for others. Former den mother and committee chair Jody Benjamin pointed to the contradiction in which the ban on gay scouts placed leaders: "The Scouts are asking me to be a liar or to do a really hurtful thing to a child. I can't do it, and so I think it's wrong."[79] In turn, the organization Think Progress, as well as GLAAD, circulated these statements through their own media units. Wahls also engaged in public debates, including a debate on CNN with Edward Whelan, who alleged in a *New York Post* Op-Ed piece that gay Boy Scout leaders would molest scouts. Another CNN-sponsored debate featured Wahls debating John Stemberger, who strongly supported the ban on gay scouts.[80]

In this manner Wahls functioned as a deliberative entrepreneur within the domain of the BSA/SFE catalyzing new deliberation with the close-knit organization. This example illustrates the theoretical model in which the circulation of personal reasoning and perspectives from *within* a highly cohesive group is the most promising way to foster significant reflection and reconsideration in such a group, as exhibited among BSA members and leaders. This pattern likely arises because, as described previously, in highly cohesive groups, group attention to discrepant viewpoints generally takes the form of increased levels of communication, particularly in face-to-face communication. Furthermore, in general, cohesive groups are already characterized by patterns of compromise and reciprocity. As Noah Friedkin states: "Frequent communication [within cohesive groups] tends to embed

---

[78] Ryan Houlihan, "Video: Scouts for Equality Rallies to Include All Boy Scouts," *GLAAD*, published electronically May 13, 2013, www.glaad.org/blog/video-scouts-equality-rallies-include-all-boy-scouts.

[79] Ibid.

[80] Houlihan, "Zach Wahls Appears on CNN to Debate against Boy Scouts Anti-Gay Policies."

opinions in a supporting fabric of arguments and information and also allows adjusting these supports as circumstances change" (Friedkin 1998, 70). Thus, heightened communication, interpersonal influence – and by extension invitations and opportunities to consciously reflect on issues of LGBT inclusion – rippled throughout this cohesive group.

Likewise, as Friedkin states, because cohesive group members are commonly "embedded in a field of interpersonal tensions and conflicts [this status] encourages reciprocity and compromise" (Friedkin 1998, 70). Thus, emergent discrepant opinions within the group can become highly salient and more likely to be addressed. In addition, some network theorists propose that because cohesive networks can be self-referential, and therefore often tend to conserve their existing norms and practices, the potential for social change (here via deliberative practice) may *require* polarization, in which two poles of thought develop within the group. In such cases of polarization, if the group is to survive as a collective, those members in the moderate middle must choose and lead down a middle pathway in order to preserve the group at all. If the bonds of the group are strong enough and avenues for effective resolution emerge, then the group may shift in its norms and practices and cohere. If not, then polarization may lead to a final fragmentation of the group (Kadushin 2012, 47–50).[81]

The level of individual reflection and deliberation elicited by these and other BSA events cannot be quantified with the data collected for this case study. What is clear, however, is that at the time of the 2013 annual meeting of the Boy Scouts of America, the three highest-ranking BSA leaders took the opportunity in a closed meeting to urge board members and delegates to consider admitting gay members as a compromise move on the only common ground that had emerged: namely, that kids are better off participating in scouting. Chief executive Wayne Brock is reported to have said, "This is not about what's legal, but what's compassionate, caring, and kind." The vote of the

---

[81] In this case, the Boy Scouts of America appears to be remaining largely intact. John Stemberger, however, who opposed the inclusion of gay scouts and leaders, has formed an alternative scouting group for boys called Trail Life. Trail Life USA describes itself as a "Christian Outdoor adventure program that emphasizes and teaches biblical moral values and requires all adult members to agree with, sign, and abide by the Trail Life USA Trinitarian Statement of Faith and the Statement of Values," www.traillifeusa.com/.

delegates approved the inclusion of gay scouts by 61 percent.[82] In this decision, however, the BSA left in place its ban on LGBT scout leaders. Thus deliberation and activism regarding the ban on LGBT scout leaders continued thereafter.

In the incorporation of the BSA into the growing nationwide deliberative system on LGBT civil rights, it took one year for the BSA to voluntarily rescind its longstanding, and long-defended, ban on gay youth after the Wahls petition. This rapid shift occurred after many previous years of fighting to retain the ban in the courts. The BSA deliberation, including sometimes-heated debate, appears to have had its own organizationally based discourses and its own internal catalysts. Arguably, the large-scale national deliberative system may not have so much entered the domain of the BSA, as instead helped the deliberative entrepreneurs within the BSA itself to foster deliberation within the cohesive group. The overarching deliberative system facilitated this by helping to produce a high degree of national visibility for the stories of hardship arising from BSA membership policies. Through the larger deliberative system, the personal impact of the BSA's ban on gay scouts could be seen and heard in ways that were less possible without the flow of stories throughout large-scale networks.[83]

Moreover as public opinion in the broader society moved in favor of LGBT equality, corporations and other entities began to express these new norms in ways that financially impacted the BSA. Increasingly, corporations rescinded funding to the BSA in compliance with their own nondiscrimination policies. Those discontinuing former sponsorships included Disney, Intel, Caterpillar, UPS, Merck, local governmental agencies, and many chapters of the United Way. Among these, numerous organizations and other philanthropists opted instead to

---

[82] Erik Eckholm, "Boy Scouts End Longtime Ban on Openly Gay Youth," *The New York Times,* published electronically May 23, 2013, www.nytimes .com/2013/05/24/us/boy-scouts-to-admit-openly-gay-youths-as-members.html ?_r=0.

[83] The growth of new technology that makes it possible to witness various forms of injustice is not new. Much has been written on the effect of television coverage of war zones on the public perception and opinion. The difference here is that social media and public-centered sites such as *Change.org* make it possible for incidents that would not have been considered noteworthy enough for media coverage to gain public attention through the actions of citizens themselves in their being able to access broad social networks with relative ease through social media.

sponsor Scouts For Equality thus creating additional impetus for the BSA leadership to reflect anew on the consequences of its action.[84] In these actions, communication flowed through financial means, but these financial shifts and the nondiscriminatory logic behind them were also reported in and circulated widely via the mass media, and within the cohesive BSA as well.

In 2013, under the new inclusive policy Eagle Scout Pascal Tessier became the first openly gay Boy Scout at sixteen years of age. Under the BSA policy excluding LGBT adults from participating as scout leaders, however, when Tessier would come of age at eighteen, he would be again banned from participation as a gay adult. In the spring of 2015, however, when Tessier became eighteen years of age and officially ineligible to continue in scouting under BSA policy, a New York council defied the formal BSA policy and hired Tessier as a camp counselor.[85] Moreover, in a call to further reflection and change, on May 21, 2015, then current BSA President and former US Secretary of Defense Robert M. Gates urged the BSA to end its ban on LGBT leaders stating, "We must deal with the world as it is," he said, "not as we might wish it to be."[86] Former Secretary Gates stated that he expected to see movement on the issue by October 15, 2015. Ahead of schedule, the BSA removed its blanket ban on LGBT adult participation on July 27, 2015. In addition, in January of 2017, the BSA announced that it would also include transgender boy scouts by accepting new boy scouts on the basis of the gender identity listed by the applicant, rather than what appears on the applicant's birth certificate.[87]

---

[84] Sponsors include Lockheed Martin, Caterpillar, Intel, UPS, Merck, and the Bill and Melinda Gates Foundation, see www.scoutsforequality.org/donate/.

[85] Malak Monir, "Boy Scouts in New York Hire Openly Gay Camp Leader," *USAToday*, published electronically April 3, 2015, http://www.usatoday.com/story/news/nation-now/2015/04/03/boy-scouts-first-openly-gay-camp-leader/25266357/.

[86] Erik Eckholm, "Boy Scouts' President Calls for End to Ban on Gay Leaders," *The New York Times*, published electronically May 21, 2015, https://www.nytimes.com/2015/05/22/us/boy-scouts-president-calls-for-end-to-ban-on-gay-leaders.html?mtrref=query.nytimes.com&gwh=D82B67CA9249E97B2CCE9987B715ED6B&gwt=pay.

[87] Niraj Chokshi, "Boy Scouts, Reversing Century-Old Stance, Will Allow Transgender Boys," The New York Times, published electronically Jan 30, 2017, www.nytimes.com/2017/01/30/us/boy-scouts-reversing-century-old-stance-will-allow-transgender-boys.html.

Meanwhile, Zach Wahls has continued to develop his work and his social network(s) as a businessman, social entrepreneur, public speaker, and author. His public appearances have reverberated through blogs and other communication media.[88] He has been increasingly regarded as a resource for youth development and for the betterment of women as well. In late 2014, Wahls became the first man ever to deliver the keynote address in the twenty-year history of the Iowa Women's Foundation Annual Luncheon. The executive director Dawn Oliver Wiand stated: "I cannot think of a better and more fitting speaker. Zach knows first-hand how it feels to be viewed as 'different' and, through his mothers, he has seen the difficulties that still exist for Iowa's women. Zach's success in advocacy is something that we can all learn from."[89] Through these opportunities Wahls continues to play a role in the unique and highly cohesive domain of the BSA as it continues to adjust to the new social norms that have arisen through US public reflection on LGBT equality.

In the next section, I offer more evidence that large-scale deliberative systems are not only effective vehicles of collective will formation, but that they are also effective tools for wielding public influence and for implementing the public will in law and public policy.

The Implementation Power of Deliberative Systems: Witnessing the Policymaking Weight of the Public Will

So far the case study provided here illustrates an arc from the early stirrings of public deliberation to the formation of a mature, networked, national-scale, deliberative system. In the largest-scale of the LGBT deliberative system, virtually everyone has been invited to reflect on the subject of LGBT equality at some point as the issue first saturates specific social domains and then, over time, all of society. Public deliberation may or may not result in changed opinions. But in the

---

[88] Alisha Carter, "Zach Wahls Tells His Story to Spread Same Sex Marriage Awareness at the Intersect Conference Presented by Elon University," *Blog Writing for the Public Good*, published electronically February 24, 2013, www.alishadcarter.wordpress.com/2013/02/24/zach-wahls-tells-his-story-to-spread-same-sex-marriage-awareness-at-the-intersect-conference-presented-by-elon-university/.

[89] Iowa Women's Foundation, "Zach Wahls to Speak at the Iowa Women's Foundation Luncheon," *IWF*, published electronically June 9, 2014, www.iawf.org/zach-wahls-to-speak-at-the-iowa-womens-foundation-luncheon/.

case of LGBT equality in the US, the significant evolution of US public opinion is clearly visible in public opinion polls. Polls conducted between 2010 and 2012 mark the emergence of new majorities favoring laws, policies, and social norms that put into practice a new embrace of LGBT equality, especially on the social acceptability of same-sex relationships, and support for marriage equality.[90] In 2010, Gallup polls showed that for the first time, a majority (52 percent) of Americans considered gay and lesbian relationships to be "morally acceptable."[91] By 2012, that number had risen to 56 percent and Gallup declared this majority acceptance to be "the new normal."[92] In the time period of this case study (1987–June 2015), that majority continued to expand, according to Gallup reaching a new high of 60 percent in May 2015 (and later 63 percent in May 2017).[93] As rates of social acceptance of gay and lesbian relationships rose rapidly, public opinion favoring marriage equality also rose. A CNN poll found over 50 percent approval for same-sex marriage in the fall of 2010. Several months later Gallup also reported an over 50 percent approval rating in May of 2011.[94] A new small majority in favor of

[90] It is possible that this evolution in public opinion follows the same pattern of shifting practices in the adoption of new technologies. For statement of this frequently observed pattern, see Everett Rogers, *Diffusion of Innovations* (New York: Free Press, 2003).

[91] Lydia Saad, "Americans' Acceptance of Gay Relations Crosses 50% Threshold," *Gallup*, published electronically May 25, 2010, www.gallup.com /poll/135764/Americans-Acceptance-Gay-Relations-Crosses-Threshold.aspx. The bulk of the shift was attributed by Gallup to "a big jump in acceptance among moderates. ...[attended also by] a 16-point jump in acceptance among Catholics, nearly three times the increase seen among Protestants." At that time a majority of liberals were noted to have been accepting since 2006, while acceptance among conservatives remained low.

[92] Lydia Saad, "U.S. Acceptance of Gay/Lesbian Relations is the New Normal," *Gallup*, published electronically, May 14, 2012, www.gallup.com/poll/154634/ Acceptance-Gay-Lesbian-Relations-New-Normal.aspx.

[93] Justin McCarthy, "Record-High 60% of Americans Support Same-Sex Marriage," *Gallup*, published electronically, May 19, 2015, www.gallup.com /poll/183272/record-high-americans-support-sex-marriage.aspx?utm_source= Gay%20marriage&utm_medium=search&utm_campaign=tiles, and 2017 Gallup poll findings with summary of poll data over time, see "Gay and Lesbian Rights," *Gallup*, published electronically, news.gallup.com/poll/1651/gay-lesbian-rights.aspx

[94] McCarthy, Justin. "Same-Sex Marriage Support Reaches New High at 55%." Gallup (2014), published electronically May 21, 2014. www.gallup.com/poll/ 169640/sex-marriage-support-reaches-new-high.aspx.; Nate Silver, "CNN Poll Is First to Show Majority Support for Gay Marriage." *Five Thirty Eight Politics*,

marriage equality had thus emerged and has since grown to 64 percent in 2017.[95]

As a new US public consensus emerged in favor of gay and lesbian equality, the survey results revealing this new public will also indicated that the most significant predictor of changing views on LGBT equality was whether respondents personally knew an LGBT person (Pew Research Center 2013a, 8–17). At first, this may not appear to be a matter of deliberative influence. Yet to see the deliberative element, recall from this chapter's previous description of deliberative entrepreneurship by Robin Voss and Daniel Karslake, that for Voss it was the contradiction between the traditional norms and teaching of her religious group identity and the experience of her personal identification and relationships with specific LGBT individuals that prompted her to new reflection. Thus the tension between the norms of her religious identity and the joyful experiences of her relationships and connection to specific and unique LGBT people created for Voss the initial contrasts and cognitive load needed for her to take steps to rethink their inherited anti-gay perspectives. In other words, in Voss's case, and apparently that of millions of others, personal deliberation was prompted by – and deliberative material provided within – the experience of having competing relationships (including related identifications) that contained contradictory meanings, values, and practices regarding LGBT equality. Experiencing this kind of identity contradiction as a deliberative package is perhaps among the most motivating drivers for new individual deliberation because a personal desire to effectively negotiate, integrate, and retain existing group and individual relationships that are in tension and conflict can be especially strong (Barvosa 2008, 212–228).[96] I propose that as more and more people came out as

published electronically August 11, 2010, fivethirtyeight.com/features/cnn-poll-is-first-to-show-majority/.
[95] "Gay and Lesbian Rights," *Gallup*.
[96] This discussion employs a common typology of three types of identities. These types are group or *social identities, personal identities*, which are the unique identities we have with specific individuals, and one's own *self-identity*, which refers to a person's identity in relationship to oneself. All three of these forms of identity are commonly conceived in much of social psychology as identity schemes, such that identities are comprised of sets of internalized identity-related meanings, values, and practices, contents that can potentially shift and transform over time, thereby altering the material referents for any particular identity. For further discussion of these concepts in relation to how social conflict can shape the self and identity contradictions, and how identity-related

LGBT as part of personal growth and/or as part of social movement engagement, more and more non-LGBT people who had existing relationships with those out LGBT individuals gained proximate, personal, and high-stakes opportunities to reflect again on received social norms and dictates that rejected LGBT equality. Under these conditions, Voss – and perhaps many others – sought out new knowledge and resources to help her engage in new reflection as part of this very personal deliberative opportunity. For these reasons, in the LGBT deliberation the personal truly was the political. This is so because the question of public will under consideration focused exactly on love and friendship in how members of US society would choose to relate to their own LGBT friends, neighbors, and fellow Americans. Those who happened to know LGBT people simply had opportunities for this deliberation to come directly to their doorstep.

As the public consensus favoring LGBT equality reached new heights, numerous legal transformations also arose in this time period that mirrored shifting public views. These included the US Supreme Court's overturning the of the Defense of Marriage Act (DOMA) and the US Supreme Court's ruling affirming the legality of same-sex marriage on June 26, 2015, an event that marks the closing date for this case study. In addition, after 2012 the focus on gay and lesbian equality visibly shifted and broadened to increasingly highlight other LGBT issues. Increased attention to equal rights for transgender persons, for example, became much more widely expressed in public engagement as media coverage and discussion of transgender experience and rights rose rapidly in 2014 and 2015.[97] Overall, if, as I have proposed, US public engagement on LGBT equality represents an example of a large-scale, self-assembling, deliberative system as the vehicle for deliberative democracy, then the majority favoring LGBT equality may still continue to grow over time, especially as

self-transformation can advance social change as it did in the case of Robin Voss, see Barvosa, *Wealth of Selves* (2008) esp. 131–139, 141–174, 176–179, and 221–229.

[97] Katy Steinmetz, "The Transgender Tipping Point," *TIME*, published electronically, May 29, 2014, www.time.com/135480/transgender-tipping-point/; for other milestone coverage Buzz Bissinger, "Caitlyn Jenner: The Full Story," *Vanity Fair*, published electronically, July 2015, www.vanityfair.com/hollywood/2015/06/caitlyn-jenner-bruce-cover-annie-leibovitz; and a series of opinion pieces and curated stories "Transgender Today," a project of the *New York Times*, www.nytimes.com/2015/05/04/opinion/the-quest-for-transgender-equality.html.

implementation of these new values and norms continues to unfold. In 2014 and 2015, many people who had once posed the staunchest opposition to LGBT equality had already changed their minds or were considering how to adjust and reconcile their views with the new US majority view.[98] Some new deliberative entrepreneurs, such as evangelical youth leader Matthew Vines, began facilitating new reflection among the most resistant segments of the American population.[99] Thus even after a new majority view had been reached in 2011, meaningful support for LGBT equality continued to emerge from new and often unexpected quarters. As discussed below, this pattern of expansion also continued in 2017, even in the context of the distinct shift in tone and intention of the new US President elected in 2016.[100]

While a significant shift in US public opinion on LGBT equality has undoubtedly occurred, the question for many critics of deliberative democracy has been how, if it all, could deliberative democracy – *if* it could be formed – proceed to implement the will of the people in law and public policy? Public deliberation is, after all, just talk that is at best the production of ideas and discourse. In the second epigraph to this chapter, however, Jürgen Habermas speaks to this issue of implementation power. As discussed also in Chapter 1, Habermas acknowledges that deliberative discourses themselves "do not govern" (Habermas 1992, 452). Instead, they "generate a communicative power that cannot take the place of administration but can only influence it" by withholding legitimacy. In other words, the communicative power of deliberative democracy cannot displace bureaucracies and their "inner logic," instead communicative power influences the logics of governance "'in a siegelike manner'" by denying the legitimacy necessary to validly govern (452).

---

[98] Jim Hinch, "Evangelicals Are Changing Their Minds on Gay Marriage: And the Bible Isn't Getting in Their Way," *Politico Magazine*, published electronically, July 7, 2014, www.politico.com/magazine/story/2014/07/evangelicals-gay-marriage-108608. But also, Michael Paulson, "With Same-Sex Decision, Evangelical Churches Address New Reality," *The New York Times*, published electronically, June 28, 2015, https://www.nytimes.com/2015/06/29/us/with-same-sex-decision-evangelical-churches-address-new-reality.html

[99] Religion & Ethics NewsWeekly, "Matthew Vines on God and the Gay Christian," *YouTube*, Video, 05:45, Posted on November 7, 2014, www.youtube.com/watch?v=IGWc2ZbjxZY.

[100] Matt Apuzzo, "Aiding Transgender Case, Sessions Defies His Image on Civil Rights," *The New York Times*, published electronically, Oct 15, 2017, www.nytimes.com/2017/10/15/us/politics/jeff-sessions-transgender.html.

Habermas's argument that the governing impact of public deliberation through communication that is "siegelike" has proven prophetic in the LGBT case, although often no large-scale public siege was necessary for implementation to occur. As the new public will became clear, many religious denominations, for example, changed their policies and discourses to equally incorporate LGBT members.[101] Likewise, major government bureaucracies followed suit. By 2015, for example, the US Navy had issued new standard protocols to equally incorporate transgender service members, revising its policies from employment benefits to gender-neutral dress uniforms, and the US Air Force had eliminated transgender identification as grounds for discharge.[102] Thus even in bureaucracies recognized as slow to transform such as the military and/or those containing high-level leadership resistant to change, there was early evidence that movement toward implementation of the public will on LGBT equality – especially new measures toward transgender equality, had begun to steadily unfold.[103]

An example of this can be seen with regard to transgender equality in military service, where incremental implementation has proceeded despite the fact that in July 2017 the new US President Donald Trump initiated efforts to reinstate the former ban on the open military service of transgender military personnel. In the wake of the surprise presidential edict, however, numerous events and responses arose to suggest that a formal policy affirming the full rights of transgender

---

[101] David Masci and Michael Lipka, "Where Christian Churches, other Religions Stand on Gay Marriage," *Pew Research Center*, published electronically, July 2, 2015, www.pewresearch.org/fact-tank/2015/07/02/where-christian-churches-stand-on-gay-marriage/. For an example of mainstream media coverage of these shifts, see William N. Eskridge Jr., "It's Not Gay Marriage vs. the Church Anymore," *The New York Times*, published electronically April 25, 2015, www.nytimes.com/2015/04/26/opinion/sunday/its-not-gay-marriage-vs-the-church-anymore.html?mtrref=www.google.com&gwh=D6D0BC43A6E60DFF0917E01C22D84803&gwt=pay&assetType=opinion.

[102] Ed Pilkington, "US Air Force: Being Transgender is No Longer Grounds for Discharge," *The Guardian*, published electronically June 5, 2015, www.theguardian.com/us-news/2015/jun/05/us-air-force-transgender-no-discharge.

[103] Dan Lamothe, "Pentagon Celebrates LGBT Pride While Changes to Its Transgender Policy are Stalled," *The Washington Post*, published electronically June 8, 2016, www.washingtonpost.com/news/checkpoint/wp/2016/06/08/pentagon-celebrates-lgbt-pride-while-changes-to-its-transgender-policy-are-stalled/?utm_term=.4373844e2185.

military members to serve and enlistment openly in the military was on track to be implemented and to some degree was already unofficially in effect. Among these responses, the Defense Secretary Jim Mattis used his discretionary authority to freeze the President's ban pending further study and review.[104] As multiple lawsuits were filed on equal protection grounds, two federal court rulings also blocked the Trump ban, and ordered that transgender applicants be allowed to enlist openly in the military beginning January 1, 2018.[105] In the interim, new relevant studies gained significant press coverage widely circulating evidence that the medical costs attendant to military service of transgender personnel is tiny in the overall military budget, thereby contradicting the fiscal concerns animating the President's ban.[106] Moreover, dozens of high-ranking military personnel, some active and many retired, publicly expressed the view that the transgender ban should be reversed and that it poses a risk to unit cohesion and, in turn, to military readiness.[107] Moreover, in a window of opportunity afforded by federal court rulings blocking the President's intended ban, the Pentagon authorized payment of its first gender confirmation surgery for

---

[104] Dan Lamothe, "Transgender Ban Frozen as Mattis Moves Forward with New Review Options," *The Washington Post*, published electronically, August 29, 2017, www.washingtonpost.com/news/checkpoint/wp/2017/08/29/pentagon-chief-mattis-freezes-trumps-ban-on-transgender-troops-calls-for-more-study/?utm_term=.3810097d1a59.

[105] Dan Phillips, "Second Judge Blocks Trump's Transgender Ban in the Military," *The New York Times*, published electronically, November 21, 2017, www.nytimes.com/2017/11/21/us/transgender-ban-military.html?mtrref=www.google.com&gwh=F371BE81F8D2D6F7F0E0C0D28881D886&gwt=pay; Tim Stella, "Transgender People Can Enlist in Military on Jan 1, Judge Says," *NBC News*, published electronically November 27, 2017, www.nbcnews.com/feature/nbc-out/transgender-people-can-enlist-military-january-1-judge-says-n824381

[106] John Tozzi and Rebecca Greenfield, "Here's How Many Trans People Serve in the U.S. Military," *Bloomberg*, published electronically, July 26, 2017, www.bloomberg.com/news/articles/2017-07-26/here-s-how-many-trans-people-serve-in-the-u-s-military.

[107] Sam Levin, "Top Military Officials Call on Trump to Reverse Transgender Ban," *The Guardian*, published electronically August 1, 2017, www.theguardian.com/us-news/2017/aug/01/donald-trump-transgender-ban-us-military; Ron Nixon, "Coast Guard Still Supports Transgender Troops, Commandant Says," *The New York Times*, published electronically August 1, 2017, www.nytimes.com/2017/08/01/us/politics/coast-guard-commandant-general-zukunft-transgender-troops.html?mtrref=www.google.com&gwh=9DE9EB6B664064FD415856B800F46867&gwt=pay

a transgender service member; the medical procedure took place on November 14, 2017.[108] After her surgery, the service member, Air Force Staff Sargent Ashlee Bruce, indicated that throughout the months of uncertainty, military officers were categorically supportive, consistently reassuring her that everything would work out well in time. She stated, "Everyone in the leadership said it would be O.K; they never wavered."[109] Near the end of December 2017, the Trump administration chose to no longer seek to block the enlistment of openly transgender personnel in the US military, and open enlistment began on January 1, 2018.[110] This example of incremental movement toward the equal incorporation of transgender personnel into the US military reveals that while hills and valleys may arise, the implementation of the new public will on LGBT equality can occur even in slow changing bureaucratic domains such as the military, and even against the intentions of the US Commander in Chief. Nevertheless, in a new development on March 23, 2018 (as this book went to press), the administration announced a proposed policy that would effectively ban transgender personnel, yet with latitude for exceptions. The policy is subject to public comment before enactment. Thus its legitimacy could still be publicly rejected in the "siegelike manner" that has checked other policy efforts.

In other cases when government institutions have defied the public by refusing to implement the public will on LGBT equality, they have sometimes suffered a "siegelike" onslaught of public outcry that delegitimized their acts. This outcry has occurred in the form of an outpouring of public resistance that wields the kind of legitimacy-withholding communicative power identified by Habermas. In the case study explored here, the most striking example is the intense public

---

[108] Courtney Kube, "Pentagon to Pay for Surgery for Transgender Soldier," *NBC NEWS*, published electronically, November 14, 2017, www.nbcnews.com/ne ws/us-news/pentagon-oks-surgery-transgender-soldier-military-hospital -n820721.

[109] Helene Cooper, "Transgender People Will Be Allowed to Enlist in the Military as the Court Case Advances," *The New York Times*, published electronically December 11, 2017, www.nytimes.com/2017/12/11/us/politics/ transgender-military-pentagon.html.

[110] Tom Porter, "Trump Administration Abandons Bid to Bar Transgender Recruits from U.S. Military," *Newsweek*, published electronically December 30, 2017, www.newsweek.com/trump-administration-abandons-bid-bar-transgender-recruits-us-military-766242.

pressure placed on the State of Indiana in 2015 when the Indiana state legislature disregarded majority US public opinion on the equal treatment of LGBT people. This example, I propose, demonstrates how a fully functioning national-scale, networked, deliberative system does have, as Habermas anticipated, the power to change the logic of legislative outcomes or other forms of governance. In short, the State of Indiana sought and ultimately failed under intense public pressure to institute new laws that would have reinstated the right to discriminate against LGBT people in commerce. The incident itself was brief, with a reversal coming in a mere seven days.

On March 26, 2015, then Indiana Governor Mike Pence (subsequently elected as US Vice President to President Donald Trump) signed into law a religious freedom bill that allowed businesses to refuse to serve LGBT people on the grounds of religious observance. The law was met with immediate and widespread public opposition objecting to the law as discriminatory toward LGBT people. This massive communicative response to the Indiana religious freedom law featured widespread public dissent, including a practical backlash of expressive boycotts and canceled events by businesses, government entities, entertainers, and others. The list of participants expressing resistance represents an extensive array of commentators, including many public figures, from many walks of life in the United States. Many people, organizations, and institutions called for long-term boycotts and other forms of extended censure. Most immediately influential was the cancellation of upcoming events and travel plans and/or instituted bans on future travel to or events in Indiana by numerous groups and institutions. A publicly reported list of participants in this uncoordinated response was published in *The Washington Post* including as follows.[111]

Many sports figures and organizations, both professional and collegiate responded to the Indiana law, including in some cases the canceling of upcoming travel or events in Indiana. In professional sports such outcries came from the National Association for Stock

[111] Hunter Schwarz, "Your Guide to All the People and Businesses Protesting Indiana's 'Religious Freedom' Law," *The Washington Post*, published electronically March 31, 2015, www.washingtonpost.com/news/the-fix/wp/2 015/03/30/here-are-all-the-people-and-businesses-protesting-indianas-religious-freedom-law/?utm_term=.8efb72e55576. In the following summary: *Indicates the cancellation of immediate or future business travel plans to Indiana. **Indicates those that instituted a public or organizational travel ban to Indiana.

Car Racing (NASCAR), the NBA, the Indiana Pacers basketball team, and basketball players Jason Collins and Kareem Abdul-Jabbar. In collegiate athletics respondents included the National Collegiate Athletic Association (NCAA), Kevin Ollie,* the University of Connecticut Men's Basketball Coach, and Pat Haden,* then the Athletic Director at the University of Southern California.

A significant number of businesses and professional organizations across a number of sectors also engaged in the public dissent. Among these were forty signatories to a joint letter signed by company chairs, founders, and CEOs of a wide range of companies including many technology companies. These businesses included, "Affirm, Zynga, Yelp, SalesForce, Square, Twitter, Lyft, AirBNB, Azon JuriMed Group LLC, Ebay, YCombinator, Zillow Group, Mixbit, Homejoy, Evernote, IfOnly, NextDoor, NextLesson, Quip, Formation 8, Elance-odesk, Path, BackOps, North Technologies, jawbone, Cisco Systems, about.me, Sidecar, Sequoia Capital, PayPal, Glassdoor, Emerson Collective, Alphalight, Penny Mac, and Sherpa Ventures."[112] Among social media enterprises, Square, Twitter, Yelp, and Yahoo also voiced their opposition. In the service and retail industries, those who articulated resistance included Angie's List, Gen Con, the Gap and Levi Strauss & Co., Salesforce,** Accenture, Eli Lilly, Subaru, and Marriot. Business and labor organizations also took part including, the American Federation of State, Country, and Municipal Employees (AFSCME) Women's Conference,* the Association of Flight Attendants, and the Indiana Chamber of Commerce.

In addition, numerous entertainers, celebrities, and political figures also spoke out publicly against the Indiana law, including Ellen DeGeneres, Cher, George Takei, Larry King, Miley Cyrus, MC Hammer, Stephen King, the musical group Wilco,* Hillary Clinton, New York City Mayor Bill De Blasio, California Lieutenant Governor Gavin Newsome, and many others.

Finally, a significant number of governmental agencies and educational institutions also took steps in the form of travel bans or public statements. These included the State of Connecticut, Washington State, and the District of Columbia. The municipalities of Indianapolis, New York City, Oakland, San Francisco, Portland, OR; Rochester, NY, and Seattle, WA, as well as a number of colleges and universities

---

[112] Ibid.

that also instituted travel bans or made public statements of objection. Religious organizations did not respond in large numbers but some did so, including the Disciples of Christ.

Although negative public opinion about the law was widespread, this rapid outpouring of negative public response over a seven-day period appears to have clustered into the social domains of sports, popular culture entertainment, business, politics, and the state. Significantly, these are also many of the same social domains in which deliberative networks had already formed as highlighted in this case study. Hence, these social domains were already heavily networked on the issue, and through those networks responses (some collaborative) were amassed quickly and decisively. As a result of this avalanche of public resistance, then Indiana Governor Pence was forced to reverse his previous claim that the law would stand. Pence had declared unequivocally after signing the bill that he would not endorse alteration of the law. Yet in the face of such strong public expressions of objection, the law was revised after only seven days.[113]

In this example, I suggest that public communicative power was amassed and wielded through a large-scale deliberative system. In this proposed model of practical deliberative system formation, the public achieved power to change legislative policy because the majority could express its recognized public opinion and will through the deliberative system in a "siegelike manner" thereby conferring or withholding legitimacy on policymaking. In this case, through an onslaught of expressed public disapproval, including various boycotts, the public withdrew the presumption of democratic legitimacy calling for a change in the governing logic of the statute. Under the pressure of this revocation of legitimacy, lawmakers felt compelled to promptly rewrite the statute to address public outcry. In this controversy, the political reputations of the state and then Governor Mike Pence suffered a severe blow, news of which also flowed widely.[114] Moreover, the flurry of events also appears to have prompted new public reflection

---

[113]   Monica Davey and Laurie Goodstein, "Religion Laws Quickly Fall Into Retreat in Indiana and Arkansas," *The New York Times*, published electronically, April 2, 2015, www.nytimes.com/2015/04/03/us/rights-laws-quickly-fall-into-retreat.html?action=click&contentCollection=U.S. &module=RelatedCoverage&region=EndOfArticle&pgtype=article.

[114]   Amanda Terkel, "Indiana Hires PR Firm To Rebuild Image After 'Religious Freedom' Fiasco," *The Huffington Post*, April 13, 2015, www.huffingtonpost .com/2015/04/13/indiana-pr-firm_n_7056268.html.

on "religious freedom" laws in general. A growing percentage of Americans polled reported disfavoring them after the incident, while their popularity had been rising beforehand.[115] Moreover, efforts to instate such laws have been unsuccessful and by 2018 efforts to do so have waned as lawmakers recognize that efforts to institute these law in opposition to the public will are untenable.[116]

A striking contrast exists between Barney Frank's experience of widespread opposition to funding AIDS research in Congress in 1987 (discussed in Chapter 2), and the Indiana example of widespread public resistance to anti-LGBT legislation in 2015. These two episodes provide illustrative bookends to the emergence and growth of public deliberation and the evolution of US public opinion on LGBT equality over a 28-year period. I have suggested in this exploratory study that a self-assembling, networked deliberative system has formed and functioned to facilitate public reflection both as a collective activity *and* as inner reflection on the part of countless individuals. As Noah Friedkin articulates in the epigraph to the next chapter, this kind of social metamorphosis can be viewed as a human drama that is produced by a clash of diverse viewpoints. In the crucible of that clash, different worldviews are either reconciled into new opinions that create a new social equilibrium, or those diverse opinions become "fixed in irreconcilable opposition" (Friedkin 1998, 163). In the case of LGBT equality, a new social equilibrium emerged in the US that strongly favored equality for LGBT people. In this resolution, I propose that the US public used a self-assembled deliberative system to democratically answer the question: *How should LGBT people be treated in American society?* In answering this question, what had been an outlying perspective in 1987 became the status quo majority opinion in 2015.

In the next chapter, I further explore this case study illustrating the theoretical model of deliberative system formation, and the position that a large-scale deliberative system has emerged in the US and grown

[115] Aaron Blake, "Religious Freedom Laws Suffer Another Blow – in Public Opinion," *The Washington Post*, published electronically, April 24, 2015, www.washingtonpost.com/news/the-fix/wp/2015/04/24/the-upshot-of-indiana-opposition-to-religious-freedom-laws-rises/?utm_term=.19bd54dcf27d.

[116] Alan Blinder, "Weary, Wary, or Both, Southern Lawmakers Tone Down the Culture Wars," *The New York Times*, published electronically, January 22, 2018, www.nytimes.com/2018/01/22/us/transgender-bathroom-bill-religious-freedom.html.

to a national scale on the issue of LGBT equality. I focus next on three common cognitive obstacles to the development and growth of large-scale public deliberation, especially deliberative systems on painful or thorny topics about which some people may feel emotions such as fear, pain, or guilt when faced with relevant facts. Among other things, I explore how the fluidity and flexibility by which identities and social norms can be formed *and transformed* over time offer key pathways by which some of these cognitive obstacles to public deliberation can be overcome.

4 | Overcoming Cognitive Obstacles: Implicit Bias, Identity Threats, and Fear

> Social differentiation sets the stage for a drama ... Each such drama presents a story concerned with the events that have reduced, maintained, or even increased differences of opinion between certain individuals and their social positions, but the basic process entailed in this stream of events is also timeless and ubiquitous—the repetitive balancing of Self and Other in the formation and maintenance of an opinion.[1]
>
> —Noah Friedkin

The previous two case study chapters illustrate that there are many contingent factors in the emergence and growth of a large-scale deliberative system. In this chapter, I further demonstrate that beyond the three deliberative catalysts and the social networks that carry those catalysts, the formation of a deliberative system also depends on the circulation of materials that can help people to overcome or circumvent common cognitive obstacles to effective, informed, and unbiased judgment, particularly under conditions of uncertainty. The once dominant model of human beings as always thoughtfully rational has been long disproven and modified by scholarly research. Across numerous disciplines in the second half of the twentieth century, scholars have developed detailed knowledge of the fact that rather than consistently issuing evenhanded and informed rational judgments, humans of all intellectual skills routinely employ heuristic frames of reference, various mental models, and other cognitive shortcuts that commonly produce biases in judgment (Kahneman, Slovic, and Tversky 1982; Bargh and Chartrand 1999). These biases in judgment generally occur outside of conscious awareness. Thus, they are often difficult to detect, frequently durable, potentially widely held, and in many cases potentially socially damaging (Banaji and Greenwald 2013; Kahneman

---

[1] Noah E. Friedkin, *A Structural Theory of Social Influence* (Cambridge: Cambridge University Press, 1998), 163.

2011, 50–70). Consequently, to be effective – and perhaps even to form – deliberative systems must include elements that can help members of a society to overcome the cognitive obstacles that can disrupt effective and unbiased judgment for both individuals and collectives.

In this chapter, I elaborate on this aspect of deliberative systems by identifying three major cognitive obstacles to deliberative system growth to a national scale. For each obstacle, I also introduce observations from the case study materials regarding a series of practices and mechanisms that have demonstratively contributed to circumventing or otherwise overcoming these cognitive obstacles in the LGBT case. Each example from the LGBT case included here illustrates and supports the proposition that prevailing over these perennial cognitive obstacles is, theoretically at least, another necessary but not sufficient factor in the emergence and growth of a deliberative system. In other words, together with (a) deliberative catalysts (Chapter 2) and (b) existing social networks (Chapter 3), practices that help people to overcome cognitive obstacles to deliberation also serve as an underlying mechanism at work in the practical empirical formation of large-scale public deliberation.

Before entering into this discussion, however, it is important to observe at the outset that bias mitigation discussed in this chapter is distinct but not isolated from the other mechanisms of deliberative system formation. There is significant interconnection between the form of deliberative entrepreneurship and well-designed deliberative packages and the task of overcoming implicit bias and other cognitive obstacles. Both theoretically and empirically, the most effective deliberative catalysts have significant impact in fostering public deliberation exactly because they contain elements that create safe spaces for conscious reflection and do so in ways that avoid the conditions that generally foster implicit bias and other disrupters of judgment. The linkage between this element of deliberative systems and the techniques discussed in Chapter 2, for example, can be seen in the case of Zach Wahls as he burst onto the public stage in 2011. Recall that Zach Wahls' initial address to the Iowa Judiciary Committee had an extraordinary impact, both in the magnitude of its reach and in the extent and significance of its influence. Within days, millions of people had watched the address. Ultimately, at least 19 million people observed the three-minute speech as it was relayed through social media and amplified also by the mainstream media. Wahls' words – offered in a speech he did not intend to share beyond the room of people that he addressed – catapulted an unknown nineteen-year-old to major political visibility as an invited speaker at the Democratic National Committee Convention only eighteen months later. Among the most impressive elements of the Wahls phenomenon was the changes of mind and heart reported by people from subcultures that have traditionally discounted or rejected LGBT people. Recall from Chapter 3 that when asked by Ellen DeGeneres if Wahls had been contacted by anyone whose mind had been changed by his words, he stated:

Yeah, well I got a Facebook message from a guy who was shipping off to Afghanistan in two weeks. He was raised in the Deep South, [and was] in his words raised "anti-gay." And he said that after seeing my testimony he felt that his mind had really been changed. He had been really anxious about the repeal of don't ask, don't tell and I changed his mind on that too. That just really blew me away.[2]

The impact of Wahls' address, and other striking changes in hearts and minds discussed throughout this case study, suggests that woven into Wahls' speech, there were qualities that helped listeners to hear new information and to face, and potentially overcome, implicit bias and other cognitive obstacles to reflection – communication characteristics that made this particular catalyst powerfully influential.

This chapter explores elements and qualities of communication practice that can help deliberators to sidestep cognitive obstacles to deliberation. The chapter is divided into five sections. In the first section, I briefly introduce the dimensions of the self that constitute the basis for the three cognitive obstacles to deliberation discussed in this case study. In the second section, I sketch the first obstacle of implicit (or unconscious) bias and describe how this obstacle was circumvented by both Wahls as a person and by the specific content of his address at the Judiciary hearing. In the third part, I sketch the second cognitive obstacle of fear and the third obstacle of identity-related threat. In the LGBT case, these two obstacles were commonly intertwined, so in this

---

[2] As stressed in Chapter 3, however, Wahls did not literally change anyone's mind. It was the young man who changed his own mind. Instead Wahls provided materials and an occasion in which others could reflect anew on their socially inherited (and often unexamined) views and to potentially reach new outlooks on the matter at hand, or perhaps arrive at the same view but in a consciously derived manner.

section I describe the practices apparently used to overcome these obstacles in combination. In the fourth section, I turn to the influence of extremism and its often unintended role in providing perspectives that can help members of society with deeply held but unexamined beliefs to gain a reflective distance on those beliefs by encountering them in fanatical forms. This encounter can trigger conscious critical reflection on these entrenched ideas and their potential bias. Throughout all four sections, examples from the case study further illustrate the role of social networks in shaping the emergence and flow of deliberative practice. Finally, in section five, the chapter ends with examples that illustrate how stories of visible changes of heart on an issue that circulate within social networks can also spark additional reflection among others and foster shifting public opinion through the deliberative system.

Formations of the Self and Three Cognitive Obstacles to Public Deliberation

The human self is not uniform. Instead, because human beings are most often shaped by many different social influences, each person has many different aspects to the self. Likewise, human subjectivity – defined here as embodied consciousness – is not usually comprised of one identity but rather of a multiplicity of identities. Within a person's overall sense of self, therefore, people today often identify variously, including identifying with various social roles as parents, as children, as co-workers, as friends, and so on. They may also identify with regions, towns, specific ethnic groups or other subcultures, and also with specific ideas and beliefs. The meanings of these ideas and beliefs are often interwoven into the cluster of meanings that make up specific identities themselves (frequently known in social psychology as identity schemes) (Barvosa 2008, 59–60). At times, the different aspects of the self that each person inherits from social influence may be in conflict with each other. These socially derived inner conflicts (when unresolved) can foster within each person inner turmoil, tension, and disjunctures between different internalized systems of beliefs and practice. For these reasons, people in modern times are frequently seen to function as "walking contradictions," who at times express divergent points of view and perspective that depart from what they openly avow about themselves (159–174). This quality is not theorized here as a personal fault, but rather as an attribute gained honestly through the complexity of social life as it shapes each individual and the social collectives to which people belong and feel connection.

Managing this inner array of divergent, sometimes conflicting, pieces of the self is, however, not always easy. Doing so can also involve blind spots toward aspects of the self that have shaped us outside of our adult awareness, often rooted in experiences in early life or through casual contact or exposure to circulating social norms and beliefs. Contrary to the view (now discredited) that the empirical self is *automatically* fully self-knowing and self-consistent, scholars in diverse fields have confirmed commonplace experience that it can be difficult to fully know and understand oneself at times. In light of this opaque quality of the self it is not always easy for human beings to manage and live through their inner complexity with full self-awareness and consistency toward their own avowed principles. To explore fully the political consequence of the inner diversity of each self is beyond the scope of this study.[3] What matters here is that one result of the socially inherited inner complexity of each person is the existence of three cognitive obstacles to critical reflection and deliberation in everyday circumstances. These three cognitive obstacles, which are related to the social formation of the self, can impede the emergence of deliberative thought in any one person or group. In turn, these obstacles can stop or slow the growth of deliberative systems. In turn, overcoming these cognitive obstacles in practice is a pivotal factor in the practical formation of deliberative systems.

Therefore understanding and taking into account the multiplicity of specific formations within the self becomes an important part in whether or not potential deliberators *can even hear* the diverse opinions and view expressed by others, much less meaningfully and evenhandedly reflect on what others offer. Thus, as described in the introduction, philosopher Jürgen Habermas was clearly justified in shifting focus from subject-centered reason to communication and discourse ethics to address the enduring problems of human violence and unreason, and his vision has been fruitful. Yet within this case study, the philosophical discussion comes back full circle to considerations of self and subjectivity in that deliberative democracy in the form of deliberative systems

---

[3] For extended discussion see Edwina Barvosa, *Wealth of Selves: Multiple Identities, Mestiza Consciousness, and the Subject of Politics* (College Station: Texas A&M University Press 2008) esp. Chapters 3, 5, 6 and conclusion 208–221.

appears to still require detailed attention to the non-unitary qualities of the self that Habermas's predecessors, Horkheimer and Adorno, had urged as the next most important element to consider in understanding the failure of the Enlightenment project of human reason to realize peace. Ultimately, if a deliberative system can be seen as an exercise in collective will formation, as I propose in this work, then by extension the condition and state of the reasoning and willing self becomes a matter of key consideration in the practical emergence of deliberative practice, including the need for attention to any inner fragmentation, fears, or identity-related inner conflicts that can disrupt reasoning and will.

In the following two subsections of this chapter, I offer a brief sketch of each cognitive obstacle and illustrate how circumventions of them appeared in the examples of US public discussion of LGBT equality explored in this study. It is beyond the scope of this chapter, however, to describe the complex brain science that explains how these three cognitive obstacles arise.[4] Instead, I briefly describe these obstacles, their effects, and potential remedies as exhibited by the story of Zach Wahls' Judiciary hearing address, and the public response to it. This illustrative example sheds further light on how Wahls' message would have had such great appeal and impact – not as a fluke of chance, but because of its capacity to help resolve inner tensions of the self that were likely operating as underlying sources of cognitive obstacles to deliberation.

Sources of Inattention and Implicit Bias: The Automatized Replay of Internalized Social Scripts

One of the most important recent scientific discoveries recognized as having enormous – but as yet not fully mapped – importance for political science is the study of implicit bias, also known as

---

[4] For general audience surveys of the relevant brain science see Joseph E. LeDoux, *Synaptic Self: How Our Brains Become Who We Are* (New York: Viking, 2002); Norman Doidge, *The Brain That Changes Itself: Stories of Personal Triumph from the Frontiers of Brain Science* (New York: Penguin Books, 2007); see also John A. Bargh and Tanya L. Chartrand, "The Unbearable Automaticity of Being," *American Psychologist* 54 (7) (1999): 462–479. For a short summary of operation of identity threat and unconscious bias in the context of policing see Edwina Barvosa, "Unconscious Bias in the Suppression Policing of Black and Latino Men and Boys: Neuroscience, Borderlands Theory, and the Policymaking Quest for Just Policing," *Politics, Groups, and Identities* 2 (2) (2014): 260–283.

unconscious bias.[5] Unconscious bias can influence all human
thoughts and actions and may infest what are assumed to be conscious choices with the influence of unexamined (and often unde-
tected) bias. The details of this are complex, but the highlights can be
stated briefly. In short, neurologically, human minds are primarily
shaped by many social imprints placed in them through means often
beyond our control and frequently outside of our awareness.[6]
The human mind and body are also interconnected into an integrated
body-mind that is equipped with a variety of complex embodied
systems and subsystems of thought, emotion, action, and reaction.
Among those systems is a dual-processing system of thought and
action.[7] In this dual-processing system, one subsystem is that of
conscious, carefully considered, slow, and reflective reasoning and
thought. This is commonly referred to in the scholarly literature on
dual processing as System 2 and it is characterized by cognitive work
that is time and energy intensive. The other subsystem, System 1, is
a system of cognitive autopilot. This system is fast and far less energy

[5] See for example, Tali Mendelberg, *The Race Card: Campaign Strategy, Implicit
Messages, and the Norm of Equality* (Princeton: Princeton University Press,
2001).

[6] LeDoux, *The Synaptic Self*; See also Daniel Kahneman, *Thinking, Fast and Slow*
(New York: Strauss and Giroux, 2011); Mahzarin R. Banaji and
Anthony Greenwald, *Blind Spot: Hidden Biases of Good People* (New York:
Delacorte Press, 2013); and Max H. Bazerman and Ann Tenbrunsel, *Blind Spots:
Why We Fail To Do What's Right and What To Do About It* (Princeton:
Princeton University Press, 2011). For a detailed discussion of these
understandings of the self and identities in relation to social constructivism and
blind spots to hierarchical racial formations see also Kathleen D. Cole, "Thinking
Through Race: Social Construction, Social Cognition, and the Unconscious
Maintenance of Racial Hierarchy," Ph.D. Diss., Political Science (University of
California, Santa Barbara, 2013).

[7] The dual processing is addressed in a variety of fields of study including
behavioral economics (Kahneman, *Thinking, Fast and Slow*), social psychology
(David L. Hamilton, ed. *Social Cognition: Key Readings* (New York: Psychology
Press, 2005)) and Roy F. Baumeister, ed., *The Self in Social Psychology*
(Philadelphia: Psychology Press, 1999)), and neuroscience and the brain sciences
(Le Doux, *The Synaptic Self*). Accounts of dual processing vary within and
among disciplines and while the general facts are accepted, research and scholarly
debate continues, see Jonathan St. B.T. Evans, "Dual-Processing Accounts of
Reasoning, Judgment, and Social Cognition," *The Annual Review of Psychology*
59 (2008): 255–278. For a recent summary of ongoing debates regarding dual-
processing approaches see: Jonathan, St. B.T. Evans, and Keith E. Stanovich,
"Dual-Process Theories of Higher Cognition: Advancing the Debate,"
Perspectives on Psychological Science 8 (3) (2013): 223–241.

and labor consuming. Through System 1 we have the capacity to automatize a wide variety of complex tasks in order to perform them without conscious attention and thus with less energy and time. Simply put, System 1 allows us to use as the frame of reference for thought, feeling, and action in a given moment onboard scripts comprised of previously internalized sets of meanings, values, and practices. Like momentarily activating a computer program, the mind instantaneously perceives (through webs of association neurally encoded in the mind) those scripts that are neurally linked as relevant to specific elements of a present context and moment, and then activates those relevant scripts as frames of reference for immediate perception, feeling, and action in that moment (Kahneman 2011, 50–58). Innumerable scripts exist in the mind and perhaps thousands of moment-to-moment shifts among them occur throughout each day. These shifts in frames of reference generally go unnoticed by us even as they take place and shape our perceptions, actions and experiences.

In Western cultural traditions, it was once commonly held that people are consciously thoughtful and rational at all times. But the scientific evidence is now clear, however, that we are not. In fact, while estimates vary, and precise rates are impossible to establish, it is considered most likely that people are operating on their autopilot (System 1) up 80 to 90 percent of the time (Banaji and Greenwald 2013, 61). While the human autopilot system is necessary to health and survival, it also brings forth the attendant problems and risk of unconscious bias. Among our internalized scripts, there will inevitably exist scripts that contain social biases to which we have been exposed. At times, this exposure comes early in life and often without our awareness. Therefore, whatever biased scripts we carry within ourselves we typically inherit these biases through no fault of our own and often without our knowledge. When activated in System 1 autopilot, however, these inherited biased scripts can serve as the source of unconscious bias. These, in turn, can come to be expressed socially as implicitly biased thoughts, feelings, words, and actions.

Democratic deliberation, in contrast, requires *conscious* thought. In light of the existence of System 1 as significant to the human condition therefore, deliberation as public reason itself can be seen in part as a practice of overcoming unconscious activation – i.e. leaving autopilot – to *consciously* reflect, evaluate, reason, and feel about matters of common concern, and thereby to reach conscious and deliberate choices of individual and collective will. As such, deliberative systems must create the conditions under which participants switch from their autopilot into the practice of conscious thought in order to newly reflect on matters at hand. The most direct way to induce entry into System 2's state of conscious thought is to place oneself under a relevant cognitive load by applying focus to a challenging problem, puzzle, or other task that requires concentrated effort. The undertaking of an effortful cognitive task activates and takes place in the slower and conscious processes of System 2, thus reducing the risk of unconscious bias.

Other remedies for the problem of implicit bias in social domains (e.g. banking and commerce, education, policing, bureaucratic govern-ance) are as yet unknown and many scholars despair of any resolutions (Banaji and Greenwald 2013, 166–167). Yet the data analyzed in this study of public engagement on LGBT equality suggests that overall, in many cases, implicit bias appears to have been not only circumvented in particular moments, but also ultimately transformed in the minds of many through the deliberative processes outlined in this chapter and in Chapter 5. Occurring on a large scale, the overcoming of inherited anti-LGBT bias in turn generated the emergence of a new social consensus in favor of LGBT equality. The public reception of Zach Wahls' address to the Iowa Judiciary Committee offers material by which to theorize and illustrate this process of transforming inherited social bias. The specific practices that helped to overcome implicit bias are described in detail in the next section.

Fostering Attention: Zach Wahls and the Ingredients of Network Popularity

From the perspective of social network science, the rapid rise of Zach Wahls from college student to influential public figure is a story of the increasing network centrality – or popularity – of Wahls. Within any given social network, different nodes in the network will have varying degrees of centrality, defined as the sheer number of connections to other nodes (i.e. mutual connections, one-way ties, or ties via another node) (Kadushin 2012, 31–32). As I argue below, two things likely enabled Wahls' rapid rise in popularity and influence in the growing deliberative system. The first contributing factor was his expression of social similarity with his mainstream audience. The second was the unique way that his testimony opened a safe space of reflection for listeners by at once affirming their identities and easing their potential fears, while also enticing listeners to do the work of reconsidering their existing ideas about LGBT families. Regarding the last of these, Wahls placed commonplace rejecting views alongside and in tension with alternative accepting attitudes that could be adopted about LGBT people. Before exploring these two factors, however, it is helpful to initially review the constitutive aspects of network centrality and how these elements also relate to the work of deliberative entrepreneurs like Wahls.

As noted in Chapter 3, Noah Friedkin is a social network scientist who has studied and theorized the sources of interpersonal influence within small-scale social networks. Friedkin's theory of interpersonal influence may be helpfully applied to theorizing the formation of deliberative systems that are catalyzed by the contributions of deliberative entrepreneurs – both well-known figures and newcomers such as Wahls. Friedkin's structural theory of social influence indicates that the network centrality of an actor has two components: power and activity. Trends toward centrality that are arising from *power* include a person's authority, their degree of expertise, and/or their degree of widespread identification. Centrality arising from *activity* involves levels of "gregariousness, expansiveness, or intensity of purpose" or what might be called the attractions of charisma or verve (Friedkin 1998, 76). Consequently, these qualities shape both a person's prospect for network centrality *and* the likelihood that a person has interpersonal influence within a network. In relation to deliberative systems, I propose that these centrality factors of activity and power also influence the degree to which a deliberative entrepreneur may foster deliberation in others and/or grow the deliberative system by inspiring others to engage in the seven microsteps of deliberative network growth, which are the means by which large-scale deliberative systems are self-assembled by a public (for description see Chapter 1 and Chapter 3).

In terms of his potential for social network centrality (i.e. for becoming a popular person-node in a social network), Wahls showed an immediate aptitude for public engagement. First, Wahls self-selected to address the Iowa House Judiciary Committee, and he then accepted follow-up opportunities to speak and write about his life when others might have declined to engage in either. Although Wahls did not yet have extensive professional experience in the public domain, he possessed important gifts of eloquence, analysis, and social and political courage – what Friedkin calls verve – that Wahls had cultivated as an Eagle Scout and as a student active in his community. Wahls thus arguably would have scored high on Friedkin's centrality factor of activity in ways that made it easy for people to be drawn to him as a messenger. Arguably, Wahls may have also rated moderately on the centrality criteria of power as a result of special expertise arising from his family life. Wahls was not widely known beyond his family and social circle at the time of his testimony, but his ability to effectively deliver first-hand knowledge of what it is to grow up as the child of a lesbian couple conferred on him an insight that amounted to expertise, and therefore the power to provide knowledge that was at the time still relatively scarce.[8]

Overall, with his eloquence and energy, Wahls united an appealing gregariousness and intensity of purpose with uncommon expertise in the experience of growing up with lesbian parents. Applying Friedkin's theory of network centrality and interpersonal influence then, Wahls' strengths in the two constitutive categories of activity and power made him well suited to sparking the astonishingly rapid and extensive rise in his public connectedness (i.e. network centrality) that he was soon to experience. Yet even these key qualities seem inadequate to entirely explain the intense and sustained response of so many members of the American public to his contribution. It seems plausible therefore that other influences may also exist that gave Zach Wahls the capacity to prompt thoughtful *conscious* attention to his message from many members of his rapidly growing audience. Another potentially contributing factor – one also drawn from social network theory – is that social similarity was an important ingredient in Wahls achieving a remarkable level of network centrality and social influence in a short period of time.

Fostering Openness: Wahls, Social Similarity, and Influence Among Others in Social Disagreements

In addition to the attributes of network centrality, the potential for a message such as Wahls' address to effectively serve as material for

---

[8] Wahls indicated that among the youth he knew at that time who were raised by openly gay parents, none were older than 25 years of age. Wahls, *My Two Moms*, xiii.

conscious deliberation can also be informed by Noah Friedkin's theory of interpersonal influence in networks. Friedkin argues that interpersonal influence in matters regarding discrepant views among people depends in significant part on whether or not the person attempting to engage others with a new or discrepant viewpoint is perceived as socially similar to or socially different from the listener. In other words, the degree to which a person voicing sentiments that compete with prevailing norms and practices is attended to by listeners often depends on how much a listener can identify the speaker as socially similar to themselves. Drawing on his experimental findings, Friedkin notes that when members of society who are deemed far removed from the listener bring competing views forward, the message is easily dismissed. This is because the message is seen as having little immediate social relevance to the listener. In contrast, when a person who is perceived as socially similar brings discrepant views or messages forward, there is much greater potential for that new view to be considered as salient by listeners. As Friedkin puts it: "Structural similarity [i.e. closely related social location] can establish salience, which encourages [the first actor/listener] *i* to respond to [the second actor/speaker] *j's* opinion on an issue. However, not only must *i* be aware of *j's* opinion on the issue, *i* must *also* be aware of their structural similarity" (Friedkin 1998, 71).

I suggest that theoretically, perceptions of social similarity likely played a role in the favorable and rapid public uptake of Wahls' address to the Iowa House Judiciary Committee. Dressed in a suit and tie for his testimony, Wahls immediately established his similarity of social location to the Committee members, to the chairman, and, by implication, other possible listeners. Wahls began: "Good evening, Mr. Chairman. My name is Zach Wahls. I'm a sixth-generation Iowan and an engineering student at the University of Iowa. And I was raised by two women."[9] The first of these would have likely resonated as social similarities with the members of the committee – the last, of course, is at the heart of Wahls' difference. As his comments proceeded, Wahls revealed a variety of his other identities, elements that may have expressed social similarity to a wide range of different people. Wahls identified himself as a small businessman, as having scored in the 99th percentile in the ACT, as an Eagle Scout, as a nineteen-year-old, and as having a sister. He indicates

---

[9] Iowa House Democrats, "Zach Wahls Speaks About Family," *YouTube*, February 1, 2011, www.youtube.com/watch?v=FSQQK2Vuf9Q.

that his family life includes church, family dinners, and family vacations. Wahls describes his family life as including the enjoyment of good times and struggles, and he names his family's loving commitment to each other as the foundation of his family life. Wahls also did not identify himself as gay, thereby leaving listeners with the impression that he is likely straight.

In presenting himself in this way, Wahls claimed similarity in social location not only for himself but also for his family. He compared himself and his family to both the committee chairman and to all Iowan families by saying:

I am not really so different from any of your children. My family really isn't so different from yours. After all your sense of family doesn't derive its sense of worth from being told by the state: "You're married. Congratulations." The sense of family comes from the commitment we make to each other. To work through the hard times so we can enjoy the good ones. It comes from the love that binds us. That's what makes a family.[10]

With these words Wahls not only identified himself with the chairman, but also identified his family experience as similar to that of the committee chairman, and by extension, his colleagues in the Iowa Legislature as a whole. Wahls further asserted that the value of LGBT family life – like all families – is intrinsic to the love and care within it and thus cannot be conferred or stripped by the state. With this logic, Wahls shows that his family is similar to loving families everywhere.

In Friedkin's theory of interpersonal influence, if Wahls' effort to identify his similarity to the chairman and his colleagues is successful, then those listeners become at least more open to listening to Wahls' message despite the divergence of that message from their own existing views.[11] While it cannot be confirmed using the case study materials analyzed here, I suggest that social similarity was an important contributing factor in how Wahls' address was not rejected out of hand by his listeners and was ultimately embraced by many.

[10] Ibid.
[11] It is a worthwhile thought experiment to consider what might have occurred if Zach Wahls had appeared instead in casual attire, described himself as born out-of-state, and taken a more accusatory tone. Any or all of these factors could have made Wahls seem as "other" to many listeners, such that the identical message may have been heard as divisive. In this alternative scenario, Wahls's message may not have resonated with so many listeners and been more likely to be dismissed by those holding opposing views.

Fostering Conscious Reflection: Wahls and Cognitive Load Against Bias and Blind Spots

In addition, based on the difference in labor required by conscious thought (System 2) versus automaticity (System 1), I further propose that Wahls succeeded in minimizing the risk of unconscious bias by placing his listeners under significant, yet inviting, cognitive load. The major difference between cognitive autopilot (System 1) in which humans can function with minimal attention on the basis of internalized scripts, compared to conscious thought (System 2) is the expenditure of effort. Experimental studies indicate that one sure way for humans to move from autopilot to conscious reflection is to engage with a puzzle or other activity that requires cognitive effort (Kahneman 2011, 32–46). In other words, undertaking cognitive load is a necessary and effective pathway to conscious thought. In his address, Wahls provided materials for significant and relevant cognitive load in the turns and shape of his message. Wahls was by age nineteen a championship-level debater, and in his address he employed a common debate maneuver of turning around a prevailing argument such that the viewpoint under scrutiny can be seen as having a self-defeating consequence.

For example, Wahls turned around the contention that adding a gay marriage ban to the state constitution would solve the alleged "problem" of LGBT families. In turning this argument, Wahls proposed that the constitutional amendment could not actually devalue or end same-sex couple headed families, but it could have devaluing effects for Iowa. Having already reframed the value of LGBT families as based in love, Wahls made clear that while the legislation at hand would not and could not dismantle his family life, it would instead damage the valuable legal and legislative face of Iowa. He stated, "What you're voting [on] here isn't to change us … it's to change how the law views us; how the law treats us. You are voting for the first time in the history of our state to codify discrimination into our constitution" (Wahls 2012). In this claim, Wahls proposed that a same-sex marriage ban amendment would: (a) legislate discrimination by formally establishing a second-class citizen status, and (b) end the legislative tradition in which Iowa's constitution is the least amended in the nation.

With this statement, Wahls turns the legislative contention on its head *while still maintaining his link of social similarity to the legislators* and reiterating that link with inclusive phrasing such as "our constitution." Likewise, Wahls also turned around the pro-amendment argument by casting it as producing a negative legacy that is greater for legislators than for the LGBT families themselves. In this reversal, Wahls suggested that the proposed amendment would not protect children or families, for they do not need protection, and LGBT families would continue and thrive. Rather the true harm at hand in taking the action under consideration would be that the Judiciary Committee would create a legacy of formal discrimination. Moreover, in doing so, a point of Iowan constitutional pride would be destroyed. In presenting his views in this form of a reversal of common arguments and juxtaposing them with unexpected outcomes and competing views, I would argue that Wahls placed his listeners under significant cognitive load, requiring his audience to think consciously in order to follow his logic. By placing the listener under relevant cognitive load but doing so in an inviting way, Wahls made it more likely that the listener would shift out of autopilot (System 1) into System 2 and thus pay attention and engage in conscious reflection. Such conscious thought, in turn, supports – at least momentarily – the reduction of the risk of implicit bias as listeners engage in new independent thought.

The contributing factor of social similarity combined with providing relevant cognitive load potentially opened the door for widespread public engagement with Wahls' message and fostered significant consideration of it for many. Yet these elements may not have been enough to excite the enthusiastic embrace of so many strangers or to kindle major reconsideration of long-held views by many, including the soldier from the South who had been steeped in anti-gay sentiments since childhood. Were there other factors at work that may have helped produce such eager uptake? I suggest in the next section that two other cognitive obstacles to deliberation were overcome by Wahls' address in a way that may have relieved inner tensions and related distress, thereby prompting personal relief and in turn the enthusiastic embrace of Wahls and his message.

Fears and Identity Threats: Two Additional Cognitive Obstacles to Public Deliberation

The Cognitive Obstacle of Fear involves the physical emergency reactions to common fears. In addition to the dual-processing system, the human body-mind also has an onboard system to process perceived danger (LeDoux 1996, 128–129). Via elements of the brain including the amygdala, "this system detects danger and produces responses that maximize the probability of surviving a dangerous situation in the most beneficial way." These responses include the common reactions of fight, flight, or freeze (LeDoux 1996, 128; LeDoux 2002, 7–10). When this defensive survival system (which is typically emotionally experienced as fear) is activated, humans are literally incapable of slow, conscious thought. When triggered the survival mechanism overrides the system of conscious thought because is too slow for effective emergency response. That override of the conscious thought subsystem (System 2) will continue until fear subsides and the emergency system is no longer active as the operating system for thought, feeling, and action.[12] The fear/defense system responds subconsciously both to immediate physical threats and to socially learned fears. Very importantly therefore, when people are afraid, *they are not physically capable of slow, effortful, conscious reflection* because they literally cannot physically access their capacity for conscious refection, as it has been overridden by the emergency safety reaction system of the body-mind.

To effectively engage the human capacity for conscious thought and reflection, therefore, deliberative products and deliberative entrepreneurs must practice fostering deliberation in ways that ease the relevant fears of potential deliberators. It is important to note that for *social* fears that trigger the momentary suspension of conscious thought, those fears are socially constructed. As discussed at length in Chapter 5 social fears are social formations that are subject to processes of social reconstruction and therefore may be transformed (collectively and individually) at any time or left to persist indefinitely. In short, the source of thought-stopping social fears can be often removed through social means such as changing norms and discourses. In the LGBT case materials analyzed for this study, the basis for articulated social fears tended to be linked also with how people identified themselves. That is, their beliefs about LGBT

---

[12] While it is possible to become consciously aware that we are fearful and operating from fear as a self-observation, *we are not physiologically capable* of overriding the activation of the emergency/defense system until our emotion of fear has subsided. As LeDoux states: "Although *we can become conscious of the operation of the defense system*, especially when it leads to behavioral expressions, the system operates independently of consciousness – it is part of what we call the emotional unconscious." Joseph, E. LeDoux, *The Emotional Brain: The Mysterious Underpinnings of Emotional Life* (New York: Simon & Schuster, 1996), 128 emphasis added.

inequality had often become interwoven into their own senses of self and related to their own identities involving sexuality, family, and community.[13] I propose therefore that Wahls' response was especially effective because it addressed both social fears and identity–related concerns and threats at once. Before turning to the remedies to be seen in the Wahls example, however, it is helpful to first sketch identity threat as a third and independent cognitive obstacle to public deliberation.

Identity threat as deliberative obstacle is defined as the fearful defense of a treasured sense of self. When a person's identities and sense of self are threatened, the resulting fear can – as with fear in general – temporarily make the reasoning centers of the brain inactive in favor of the emergency response center and its encoded scripts of self-defense. Thus, identity-related threats can obstruct public deliberation by literally and physically disabling the capacity for conscious thought and reasoning that deliberation requires. Some issues of public concern invoke a variety of issues and ideas that can be seen as threats to a person's sense of self. If these issues cannot be articulated in identity protective ways, then the mere mention of them can be enough to activate a fear response and make conscious reasoning impossible to access until the fear subsides. In this sense, identity-related threats and fears can be a major stumbling block to the formation of deliberative systems because they can disrupt conscious thought on a given issue. This may occur even if the sense of identity threat is felt subconsciously rather than consciously, and even if there is truly no substantive threat.

The possibility of identity threat can be direct, or it can take hold through the inner complexity and multiplicity of the self. To understand this, it is helpful to first recall that human subjectivity (i.e. the embodied consciousness) is generally comprised of a multiplicity of identities, as well as a multiplicity of encoded partial identities, beliefs, fears, concepts, and other elements sometimes referred to as schemas.[14] These diverse elements are written in the brain as neural encodings – i.e. physical neural pathways that are laid down in the brain as imprints of

---

[13] I return to this factor in the next chapter through an alternative narrative of the emergence of new public opinion on LGBT equality. For discussion here, however, I group social fear and identity threat as two obstacles interrelated into one in the LGBT case. In the case of other potential deliberative systems, the sources of social fears and identity threats might be more distinct.

[14] For an interdisciplinary theoretical framework of the multiple identities and overall multiplicity of the self, see Barvosa, *Wealth of Selves*, 54–82.

social life. Thus, as stated previously, identities can be seen as collections of related imprints of meanings, values, and practices associated with the specific identity. Together, these diverse encodings comprise an identity scheme – a set of internalized elements with which a person identifies and claims their identities with others in everyday life. The elements that a person uses to claim their identities may shift over time and can be consciously and actively revised (Barth 1969). In many cases, however, given identities defined in some evolving manner persist over time as a key component of the self and of a person's sense of self and self-esteem.

Identity threats take two general forms. Both involve a threat to a treasured sense of self. In the first form, two aspects of the self (e.g. entire identity schemes or other identity-related content, such as ideas or beliefs) contradict each other in a way that threatens a treasured sense of self. When this tension is brought to mind by passing circumstances, the threat to the self is also activated and can thus trigger a fearful, self-protective reaction in some form, such as denial or self-contradiction. For example, in the contemporary US, members of American society typically have internalized *both* (a) a belief system of and commitment to favoring racial equality, and (b) internalized stereotypes and scripts of racial inequality.[15] In the post–civil rights era, however, most Americans identify themselves with a commitment to racial equality. At the same time, members of US society inevitably have been exposed and socialized to messages of racial hierarchy and thus have internalized scripts of racial inequity encoded in their minds as a (typically involuntary) social inheritance.[16] Thus when issues that invoke ideas of race or racial

---

[15] Despite decades of efforts to shift US culture in ways that eliminate discourses of racial inequity, studies show that even small children are well versed in the longstanding accounts of racial bias as early as the age of 5. In 2010, CNN and university researchers repeated the Clark Doll Experiments originally conducted in 1939. The studies showed both Black and white children exhibiting racial bias by ages 5 and 6 based on their social learning. The Doll study was influential in the 1954 decision in *Brown v. Board of Education*. The 2010 repetition of the experiment produced nearly the same results as it had in 1939, with high levels of racial bias appearing across a broad cross-section of children. The results indicate that socialization to racial stereotypes and discourses of racial hierarchy are still very common in the US. See www.cnn.com/2010/US/05/13/doll.study /index.html.

[16] The internalization of scripts of racial bias is as common among people of color as among whites; everyone in the country receives this socialization. For an ongoing study – including access to self-study – of the pervasiveness of socialization to racial bias and other common biases in the US, see www.implicit .harvard.edu/implicit/.

inequality come up in social contexts, including opportunities for deliberation, the issue of race can trigger this inner contradiction between contrary elements within the self that are linked to race. Activation of this inner conflict can, in turn, threaten a treasured sense of self as committed exclusively to racial equity. The social fear of being *perceived* as racist often feels like a threat to one's own positive sense of self. When severe, this fear can in turn activate the embodied emergency response systems, thereby temporarily overriding the capacity to access the systems of conscious thought (i.e. System 2) often resulting in avoidance or blind spots regarding issues of racial inequity (Banaji and Greenwald 2013).

In the second form of identity threat, there is not necessarily an inner contradiction at work. Instead, something passing in a given moment presents a perceived threat to a person's sense of self that is sufficient to activate identity-related fear. These activated fears might include fear of change, fear of being unable to claim existing identities, fear of being excluded from an identity group on the basis of one's actions or views, and so on. In this second form, identity threats are perceived as an external threat to a valued identity or other positive sense of self. These threats, in turn, activate fears and potentially the embodied emergency-response system that overrides the System 2 capacity for conscious reflection until the fear subsides.

In the case of US public engagement on LGBT equality, many LGBT movement claims for equal inclusion appeared to have triggered identity threats associated with existing ideas of the traditional family for many (thus reluctant) observers. In addition, by February 2011, growing public acceptance of LGBT equality may have intensified inner conflict between two contradictory belief systems for many, specifically conflict between: (a) the belief in social equality as a founding principle on one hand, and (b) inherited judgmental views that LGBT lives are wrong and thus unworthy of equality on the other. Many may have attempted to "manage" this inner conflict by attempting to avoid the issue, through defensiveness, or by feeling intense discomfort or other emotions whenever they encountered the issue. The growing success of the LGBT civil rights movement and emerging social trends toward the validation of same-sex marriage – identified by 2011 as marriage equality – would have likely exacerbated these inner tensions for some members of US society. These tensions likely would have been felt on the surface as social fears of change and threats to one's current identities with traditional forms of family and community.

Like other threats – real or simply imagined – identity threats often excite a defensive reaction; although specific responses will vary. As I have suggested elsewhere, however, there are at least four common responses to stimuli that are experienced as identity threats (Barvosa 2008, 109–139). These four reactions are used to relieve the tension of such threats and any related identity contradictions that they involve. These common responses include: (1) the screening out from conscious thought information that appears to pose an identity threat (i.e. mind blindness), (2) knowingly recognizing self-contradictory information but acting only in identity-affirming ways that may also violate ones avowed principles, (3) engaging in self-deception that *un*knowingly validates only self-affirming points of view, and (4) consciously and thoughtfully engaging with self-contradictory ideas and materials presented and intentionally resolving or managing the contradiction itself through active choice and reflection. On the whole, the perception of identity threats often excites self-defensive responses (one of the first three items) that thereafter take the form of cognitive blind spots to challenging information, or as self-identity affirming biases that will appear as either consciously held or implicit bias.[17]

All of these responses to identity threats (either inner contradictions or direct threats) pose a problem and obstacle for deliberative system formation. This is because democratic deliberation requires democratic subjects to *consciously* think and feel about the matters under consideration. Identity threats can undermine deliberation by triggering – consciously or subconsciously – self-defensive reactions that diminish a person's capacity to consciously reflect on new information, and to shift out of autopilot in order to diminish the risk of implicit bias. Such

---

[17] In previous work, I have discussed at length how politically relevant internal contradictions come into being in the self and how our individual responses to them significantly shape our impact in the world. For elaboration see Barvosa, *Wealth of Selves*, esp. 136–139. For a case study of these defenses in daily life at the intersection of sexual, gender, and racial hierarchies and a *successful* effort to overcome blind spots through engagement with historical facts, see also ibid, 175–206. Conversely, for discussion of how such identity-related contradictions can foster blind spots and unconscious biases that, in turn, sustain racial hierarchies in the post–civil rights era, see ibid, esp. 208–227; for related discussion of dissociation leading to mind-blindness shaped by racial conflict, see also Banaji and Greenwald, *Blindspot*, 57–58.

identity threats, however, often arise as perceived contradictions between one's identities and the information or other aspects of life that are being encountered. *To the extent that this contradiction can be resolved, however, identity threat can be eased or removed as an obstacle to deliberation.* For this reason, deliberative packages that affirm the identities of listeners and avoid threatening those identities will open space for deliberative thought and reflection. In contrast, messages that shame, blame, or otherwise unintentionally threaten identities may go unheard by skeptical observers because they activate self-defensive responses that include cognitive blind spots or self-affirming implicit bias regarding the issue at hand. Likewise, deliberative entrepreneurs who welcome and affirm all listeners are more likely to be heard and acknowledged by listeners, even those who have strongly held views that diverge from what is being offered by the entrepreneur in a (potentially) deliberative encounter. The example described above of Wahls' influence on a young soldier raised in the Deep South is a helpful illustration.

Negotiating Fear and Identity Threat: Wahls and the Deliberative Obstacle Course

Wahls' address successfully fostered individual reflection and deliberation because, I suggest, it provided the ingredients by which listeners could *overcome a range of social fears that they may have felt related to LGBT issues.* At the outset, Wahls himself as a speaker, and his message, were likely viewed together as a deliberative package. This deliberative package was not only highly attractive in having the qualities of network centrality (as described in preceding sections); it was also framed in a way that made it safe and welcoming for anyone to approach. Wahls charismatically provided information in an appealing, disarming way intended to help those with discrepant views to feel drawn in enough to the message to reflect upon it.

At least some of the social fears held by many in early 2011 involved fear of an unknown future for traditional marriage in family life if same-sex marriage and LGBT-led families became socially accepted. Some of this type of social fear rested on concerns about the effects on children. In the materials analyzed for this study, by 2011 the impact of same-sex marriage on children was either still largely unknown or perceived as negative in the minds of many. In contrast, Wahls offered impressive living proof that marriage equality would generate great kids. Moreover with his words, Wahls helped to create and deepen a sense social similarity between LGBT-headed families and all other families via the commonality of a commitment to familial love.

Thus by describing his social similarity in this way, Wahls not only helped to reframe prevailing discourses (further elaborated below) but also likely operated to allay fears of difference and change, which may have been exciting perceptions of identity threat among those who identified with traditional family. As Wahls stated:

My point is that our family really isn't so different from any other Iowa family. When I'm home, we go to church together. We eat dinner. We go on vacations. But, you know we have our hard times too; we get into fights ... my mom Terry was diagnosed with multiple sclerosis ... But you know we're Iowans, we don't expect anyone to solve our problems for us ... We just hope for equal and fair treatment from our government. (Wahls 2012, 7)

After humbly listing his impressive achievements, Wahls stated: "If I was your son, Mr. Chairman, I believe I'd make you very proud" (Wahls and Littlefield 2012, 7). With these words, Wahls at once affirmed the identities of the listener(s) and allayed possible fears of change or of losses potentially arising from embracing LGBT equality. In so doing, Wahls made it possible for listeners from any form of family to identify with his own family. This approach at once not only stabilized the concept of traditional family, but also opened space within that definition of traditional family for LGBT families to be included rather than excluded from the fold.

In addition, Wahls' address also offered ways for listeners to *overcome the potential obstacle of identity threats as threats to a treasured sense of self*. Wahls' address did this in several ways. First, it opened options for listeners to identify with him not as someone threatening to their own self-understanding, but as simply another person from a traditional family (one narrated by Wahls as a church-going, family-dinner loving, and vacation-sharing nuclear family). In laying this groundwork for common identification with his audience, Wahls as a messenger operated to (a) prevent activation of identity threats in the first place, and (b) offer resolutions to underlying identity threats that were likely the basis of fearful identity-based responses to LGBT equality. In so doing, Wahls also avoided framings that judged or blamed others and instead emphasized commonality between himself as a child of same-sex parents and his listeners.

In addition, Wahls also offered a turnaround in his argument that held opposing views in tension (creating relevant cognitive load) and also resolved the commonly perceived conflict between supporting LGBT equality and embracing known forms of family life. In the alternative analysis offered by Wahls based on his own life, marriage equality was not about the end of traditional family life, but instead about the continuity of middle America – raising good kids, going to church, having family dinners, and tackling the daily challenges of family life. Explicit in this logical turn was an inclusive shift in who might embrace LGBT equality: i.e. *all those who favor marriage equality may also favor family life with familiar outcomes and comfortable reasons for familial pride.* This analytical turn presented new options for thinking about the issues and new avenues for peaceful inner resolution for those who were conflicted about the matter, especially those conflicted on identity-related grounds. The possibility of reconciling support for marriage equality with belief in traditional family offered by Wahls opened new space for reconsideration without a sense of needing to abandon or fear for one's cherished senses of self or values.[18] Most importantly, it also opened space for people – *if they chose through their own reflection* – to peacefully let go of inherited and often unexamined biases about the inequality of LGBT people, bias often expressed as opposition to same-sex marriage. In these specifics of his testimony, therefore, Wahls provided materials to overcome the potential obstacles of fear and identity threat. In so doing, Wahls' address also provided a sample pathway by which people could resolve some painful inner conflicts for themselves. I suggest that is it likely for this reason that Zach Wahls' three-minute address was taken up so eagerly by millions, passed through social networks so widely, and embraced and considered with such enthusiasm.

The three cognitive obstacles and potential remedies illustrated in this chapter are summarized in Table 4.1.

---

[18] As previously noted, in other parts of his address Wahls also listed the range of his multiple identities (business owner, student, Eagle Scout, person of faith), thus offering a wide range of identities to which a many different people could identify in some way or another with him. Wahls and Littlefield, *My Two Moms*, 7–9.

Table 4.1 *Cognitive Obstacles and Potential Remedies*

Cognitive Obstacles (among the public as potential deliberators)	Message Presenter Attribute/Practices	Message Content Attributes/Practices
Inattention	*Activate social similarity (positive use of similarity bias – see network centrality)*	Feels safe and interesting
Implicit Bias	*Activate social similarity* *Foster sense of warmth and safety; minimize activating fears*	Feels safe and interesting; Involves relevant cognitive load
Fear	*Minimize fear activation*	Eases apparent fears; Reframes troubling social contradictions (and/or)
	Activating a sense of social similarity can help to ease immediate fear of otherness or expected judgment	Reconstructs obstructive belief systems
Identity Threat	*Affirms listener identities, and/or highlights basis for common identification (activates in-group)*	Reframes troubling social contradictions (and/or) Reconstructs obstructive belief systems

Remaking Norms in Community & Family: Examples of Cognitive Obstacles Overcome

Zach Wahls' address to the Iowa Judiciary Committee in February of 2011 is one of many examples in this case study in which people express the important idea that the boundaries of existing social categories, especially of the traditional family, could be simply expanded to accommodate LGBT lives. In fact, these kinds of social reconstructions commonly appeared in public expressions as early as at least 2004. In this development, there are many examples of the public circulation

terms of here's a father who embraces his daughter no matter what, even straight people would come up to my dad and say, "you know, I think it's wonderful about your daughter, and the relationship that you have." I think people were really inspired by it.

JANE GEPHARDT: So many people came up to us [saying], "you know my son is gay and I am just so happy that you came out and you said it." Or someone else will say, my sister, my cousin; the stories just come flying out of people. *They come up and they cry in front of you, it's the most amazing experience that we've had with this.*[20]

The Gephardt family's narration of how many lives were touched by their reflective choices illuminates how social networks play an important role in supporting the extension of public engagement, including individual reflection. It also points to the level of distress and tension experienced by many people and how observing others take a new path eased their anxieties and fears about adopting a new outlook themselves. In this way, the underlying structure of deliberative system growth via social networks also fostered the overcoming of cognitive obstacles to conscious reflection.

The Influence of Extremism in Deliberation: Mirrors for Conscious Self-Reflection?

The preceding section highlights a variety of positive ways that specific deliberative practices and framings can help a deliberative system to grow by providing opportunities and resources for overcoming cognitive obstacles to deliberation in both individual and collective reflection. However, Mansbridge and her colleagues theorize that in deliberative systems not all moments need be democratic in order to ultimately forward the process of deliberative democracy when a deliberative system is considered as a whole (2012). Similarly, the LGBT case materials explored for this study, also show that social engagement on a topic need not be evenhanded or kind in order to further critical reflection and public engagement on the topic of LGBT equality. A number of examples can be seen in the context of anti-gay extremism that was sometimes received critically by other

[20] Daniel Karslake, *For the Bible Tells Me So*, 98 min. New York: First Run Features, 2007, emphasis added.

conservatives. Progressives too sometimes practiced extreme and uncivil engagement as noted in examples below.

In general, extremism can have a variety of effects on a culture. It is beyond the scope of this study to fully explore the influence of extremism on the public deliberation on LGBT equality, particularly fundamentalist-influenced extremism.[21] What is clear from this case study, however, is that the expression of extremist positions can, at times, foster new reflection and expressions in unintended ways. At times extremism can inadvertently foster more moderate positions and/or embolden a strong pushback, sometimes from unexpected sources. Examples of this pushback can be seen, for example, in controversies involving two organizations designated as hate groups by the Southern Poverty Law Center: Westboro Baptist Church[22] and One Million Moms.[23] It is impossible to quantify from the materials analyzed here how widely these examples fostered critical reflection or whether they changed minds within polarized camps. But both cases excited critical pushback from conservatives and/or conservative media outlets that were not commonly engaged in debunking anti-LGBT rhetoric.

The first example can be seen in the case of the Westboro Baptist Church (WBC), which is unaffiliated with any established church and is designated as a family-based cult and hate group. The Southern Poverty Law Center states: "Westboro Baptist Church is arguably the most obnoxious and rabid hate group in America."[24] The group is well known for its hateful speech directed toward LGBT people and for its anti-Semitic speech. Among the group's efforts, in 2005 it began to picket the funerals of fallen US soldiers as an opportunity to spread its message suggesting that the death of soldiers is the divine retribution for human sin. In their protests, WBC carried signs with slogans such as "God Hates Fags" and "Thank God for Dead Soldiers."

[21] For a survey of literature on rightist extremism in America see, Kathleen Blee and Kimberly Creasap, "Conservative and Right-Wing Movements," *Annual Review of Sociology* 36 (2010): 269–286.
[22] See www.splcenter.org/fighting-hate/extremist-files/group/westboro-baptist-church.
[23] The parent organization of One Million Moms is the American Family Association. See www.splcenter.org/fighting-hate/extremist-files/group/american-family-association.
[24] SPLC Extremist File at www.splcenter.org/fighting-hate/extremist-files/group/westboro-baptist-church.

Public reaction to this practice has been one of general disgust. But this common outrage has been also expressed in some unlikely quarters. In 2006, for example, a member of the WBC was interviewed on the Fox News channel program *Hannity and Colmes* regarding their picketing of the funeral of National Guard Sergeant Daniel Sepster who had been killed in Iraq. During the show, host Sean Hannity lost his patience and exclaimed:

I'm going to be honest; we've had a lot of nutty people on this show over the years. You are as mean and as sick and as cruel as anybody that I've ever had on this program. And the fact that you use religion to justify your hatred this way is frankly, [pause] it's mind numbing. Do you *really believe that* when you hold up your signs [saying] "thank God for IEDs"?[25]

At the time of this writing, this video of Sean Hannity's appalled outburst has been viewed on YouTube over 5.6 million times.[26]

Other objections to WBC from unexpected quarters have also emerged. Over time, for example, a nationwide band of motorcycle groups joined together to shadow the WBC to military funerals, creating a human shield between mourners and the protestors.[27] The shield effort was not always peaceful in consequence. On some occasions, WBC members have been assaulted for disrupting funeral processions. In one instance, for example, a fight broke out at the funeral of Staff Sergeant Donna Johnson, who was a lesbian. The scuffle was captured on two cell phone cameras and footage from both was posted online and discussed by commentators.[28] It is impossible to verify from evidence of these similar incidents how often these events were used by members of the public for reflection on LGBT equality and to what effect. What is clear, however, is that these examples in the LGBT case

[25] "Pissed Off Fox News Reporter Loses It on Air!!!," *YouTube*, Video, December 2, 2015, www.youtube.com/watch?v=bO7kz_yt4rs, emphasis added.
[26] For a related discussion of how extremist discourse can prompt meaningful deliberation with a focus on Australian populism and conflict in Northern Ireland see John Dryzek, *Foundations & Frontiers of Deliberative Governance* (Oxford: Oxford University Press, 2010), 82–83.
[27] Tiffany Ondracek, "Biker Group vs Westboro Baptist Church," *YouTube*, Video, 12:06, Posted on January 12, 2013, www.youtube.com/watch?v=vnxm6p_Azt8.
[28] See commentary by David Pakman: David Pakman Show, "Video: Soldier Attacking Protester at Funeral," *YouTube*, Video, 03:51, Posted on October 16, 2012, www.youtube.com/watch?v=MBNCS2YM3GY.

suggest that *a mature deliberative system can generate its own checks and balances in the expression of extremism*, including dismissals, by people across the spectrum of opinion on LGBT civil rights.

In addition, it is possible that radical extremism in the form of hate speech can inadvertently provide a deliberative package that gives some somewhat similarly minded but less extreme observers a critical distance on perspectives related to their own outlooks – in this case, conservative anti-LGBT outlooks. Examples of extremism cast into stark relief the hateful impacts of some views when they are taken to their logical extreme. In viewing these more extreme versions of conventional narratives, people potentially came to reflect anew on these discourses and/or to dis-identify with the extreme position and, by extension, their own less extremely articulated variants. This shift may be especially encouraged when even a known conservative commentator like Sean Hannity of Fox News finds the extreme approach offensive and cruel. At a bare minimum, the contribution of extremist groups to networked deliberative systems can vary and have unintended consequences for extremists and their message.

In some instances, extreme or extremely misguided contributions spark significant satire. The humor directed at extremism appears to both raise the visibility of these extreme expressions and to highlight more reflective responses to it. Highly popular programs by satirists Stephen Colbert and Jon Stewart served this function in the case study period.[29] Their lampooning of the use of extreme anti-gay rhetoric used humor to provide a critical distance on events that may, in some cases, have felt too sadly tragic or frightening to comfortably observe and reflect upon without the softening mediation of humor. An example can be seen in Michael Moore's 1999 video "A Protest Against Protests" in which Moore juxtaposed footage of ordinary Americans engaged in extraordinarily hateful speech and violence against LGBT people with voiceovers of common rhetorical statements describing America as: a "land where everyone is equal under the law ... where discrimination on the basis of race, creed, or sex is a thing of the past."[30] Placing these conflicting words and deeds in productive

---

[29] Amber Day, *Satire and Dissent: Interventions in Contemporary Political Debate* (Bloomfield: Indiana University Press, 2011).

[30] rainbowrockmom, "Michael Moore vs Westboro Baptist Church," *YouTube*, Video, 07:33, Posted on January 9, 2008, www.youtube.com/watch? v=Ra_fAYl4Th4.

tension created a deliberative package in which Americans could witness the gap between the collective walk and talk in American life regarding LGBT equality.

At one point in "A Protest Against Protests" Moore proceeded to satirize the Westboro Baptist Church by bringing a volunteer brigade of flamboyant, openly gay men to a series of Westboro Baptist Church protests. The groups arrives in an RV painted pink and labeled the "Sodomobile." Moore then films impromptu exchanges between the volunteer group and the WBC protestors carrying anti-gay signs with hateful messages. In creating this juxtaposition, Moore humorously provides food for thought: for in these unscripted exchanges, even the most deliberately campy, over-the-top, and stereotypically "extreme" expressions of gayness appear in contrast as profoundly more reasonable, fair, and compassionate than any member of Westboro Baptist Church. The video – which I defined as a deliberative package – was publicly screened and has been viewed on YouTube over four million times. It is impossible to verify from the materials collected and analyzed here, however, whether or not viewers used the film as deliberative material. However, there is evidence in the example offered in the next paragraph that other deliberative packages did help people to reflect on inherited and settled views, which suggests that Moore's video may have done so as well.

In some cases there is clear evidence of public engagement with extreme anti-LGBT positions that are not articulated from the social fringe. In 2012, former Texas Governor, and then-presidential candidate, Rick Perry issued a campaign advertisement video entitled "Strong." In the advertisement Perry states: "There's something wrong in this country when gays can serve openly in the military but our kids can't openly celebrate Christmas or pray in school. As president, I'll end Obama's war on religion." [31] Among other things, the statement homogenizes all Christians as opposed to equal civil

---

[31] The full text of the video states: "I'm not ashamed to admit that I'm a Christian, but you don't need to be in the pew every Sunday to know there's something wrong in this country when gays can serve openly in the military but our kids can't openly celebrate Christmas or pray in school. As president, I'll end Obama's war on religion. And I'll fight against liberal attacks on our religious heritage. Faith made America strong. It can make her strong again. I'm Rick Perry and I approve this message." "Rick Perry for President 2012 Ad 'Strong,'" *YouTube*, Video, Posted on December 7, 2011, www.youtube.com/watch?v=kxzONeK1OwQ.

rights for LGBT people and invents a religious war. Once posted on YouTube, the video went viral, exciting general disgust (800,000 dislikes). It also inspired a number of satirical memes that circulated over the Internet.[32] Even conservative teenagers who viewed the video found it offensive.[33] News of the blowback was extensively covered in the mainstream media thereby circulating its influence even more widely, including the news that one of Perry's top aides considered the video "nuts."[34]

Contrary to Perry's intent, numerous Christians were turned off by the ad. Communications scholar Stephen Farnsworth was quoted as saying, "The worst thing to be in American politics is a joke."[35] Some viewed the advertisement and the satirical response to it as having irreparably damaged Perry's campaign. This kind of political gaffe might have been overlooked on other issues. But to the extent that a large deliberative system had self-assembled around LGBT issues, the extreme (and nonsensical) account was taken up into the feedback loops of the social networks of the system. Perry's intention of using social division to his political advantage backfired, and instead underscored the logical fallacies and mean-spiritedness of his anti-gay bias. In turn, his extreme example not only discredited him, but also added new deliberative material to what was already circulating through what I suggest was by now an extensive deliberative system on LGBT equality.

Lastly, in some cases of extremist engagement, the efforts of extremists elicited not only critical distance on extreme views of existing viewpoints but also vehicles for people to express their commitment to alternatives. In 2012, for example, the organization One Million

---

[32]   Funny Or Die, "Rick Perry – Weak," *YouTube*, Video, 01:08, Posted
       on December 22, 2011, www.youtube.com/watch?v=1C5a0w5TPGw; Funny
       Or Die, "Jesus Responds to Rick Perry's 'Strong' Ad," *YouTube*, Video, 01:34,
       Posted on December 23, 2011, www.youtube.com/watch?v=yxyEkrxsWP8.
[33]   TheFineBros, "Teens React to Rick Perry's Strong," *YouTube*, Video, 06:35,
       Posted on December 29, 2011, www.youtube.com/watch?v=B4yMvQGE7MY.
[34]   Sam Stein, "Rick Perry's Anti-Gay Iowa Ad Divides His Top Staff,"
       The Huffington Post, published electronically, December 8, 2011, www
       .huffingtonpost.com/2011/12/08/rick-perry-anti-gay-iowa-ad-divides-top-staff
       _n_1136587.html.
[35]   The Associated Press, "Rick Perry's 'Strong' Religious Message Sparks Strong
       Religious Response," *Haaretz*, published electronically, December 13, 2011,
       www.haaretz.com/world-news/rick-perry-s-strong-religious-message-sparks-
       strong-religious-response-1.401178.

Moms called for a boycott of JCPenney in protest of JCPenney having hired Ellen DeGeneres as a spokesperson. DeGeneres responded to the effort of the One Million Moms on her talk show indicating that although she does not usually address such topics, in this case she said, "my haters are my motivators."[36]

DeGeneres humorously debunked the group, and thanked those who supported her in the controversy, including especially JCPenney, which had held to their decision to welcome her as a spokesperson (ironically, JCPenney was among the sponsors who dropped advertising on DeGeneres's program when she came out as gay in 1997). DeGeneres also displayed and read out responses placed on the One Million Moms website as part of her monologue, stating:

I would like to read just a few comments from the Million Moms Facebook page. This is on their page. Not that there's anyone counting but for a group that calls themselves the One Million Moms, they only have 40,000 members on their page. They're rounding to the nearest million and I get that. Here are some of the comments that people have written on their Facebook page.

The first one is: "Love Ellen and everything she stands for. I'm going to shop there more now!"

Then here's another one: "Guess I have to starts shopping at JC Penney now."

Here's another one: "Way to go JC Penney for not giving in to bullies. Stand your ground."

And then: "I am a Christian and part of a traditional family and I support Ellen and now JC Penney!!"

DeGeneres concluded with a restatement of what she stands for indicating:

I usually don't talk about stuff like this on my show, but I really want to thank everyone who is supporting me. If you don't know me very well, if you're just watching maybe for the first time, or you're just getting to know me, I want to be clear. Here are the values that I stand for. I stand for honesty, equality, kindness, compassion, treating people the way you want to be treated and helping those in need. To me those are traditional values. That's what I stand for.[37]

---

[36] TheEllenShow, "Ellen Addresses Her JCPenney Critics," *YouTube*, Video, 04:36, Posted on February 7, 2012, www.youtube.com/watch?v=_zNKTTtAXCs.

[37] Ibid.

DeGeneres's response itself became a precipitating event. With it, the feedback loops of social media launched and spread new opportunities for reflection, but they also issued invitations for people to take up action as a way to raise their voices against hatred. Among the digital age responses were a Twitter hashtag: "#standupforellen" and a video of a flash mob staged before a JCPenney that circulated widely.[38] Soon One Million Moms abandoned the campaign, which sparked celebration and more circulation of narratives of the incident.[39] One Million Moms launched other campaigns that were heaped with further ridicule, which, in turn, generated yet more negative attention. While ridicule, satire, and extremism on any side of an issue are generally not expressing an intention to foster affirming open dialogue, the examples considered here suggest that, at times, all of these can play an important role in fostering reflection and the circulation of materials needed for public deliberation to unfold.

Visible Changes of Heart: The Deliberative Value of Crossing Social Divides

The exploratory analysis of the longitudinal data for this study reveals that by 2012, some longtime opponents of same-sex marriage had begun to change their own views of what should be socially and legally accepted with regard to same-sex relationships and marriage. Conservatives who changed their minds also appeared increasingly willing to express that change of heart publicly. For example, on June 23, 2012, David Blankenhorn published an opinion piece in the *New York Times* entitled, "How My View on Gay Marriage Changed."[40] Blankenhorn had authored a book called *The Future of Marriage* and given expert witness testimony against gay marriage in the legal challenges to the constitutionality of California's Proposition 8, which had defined marriage as between one man and

---

[38] "#Standupforellen and Thank JCPenney for Making the Right Choice," *GLAAD*, [n.d.], www.glaad.org/standupforellen.

[39] "Ellen Degeneres' JCPenney Partnership Boycott Dropped by One Million Moms," *Huffpost Gay Voices*, published electronically, March 8, 2012, www .huffingtonpost.com/2012/03/08/one-million-moms-drops-ellen-degeneres-jc-penney_n_1332651.html.

[40] David Blankenhorn, "How My View on Gay Marriage Changed," *The New York Times*, published electronically, June 22, 2012, www.nytimes .com/2012/06/23/opinion/how-my-view-on-gay-marriage-changed.html.

one woman. Now in his article, however, Blankenhorn was announcing and explaining his change of view stating, "The time has come for me to accept gay marriage and emphasize the good that it can do." While Blankenhorn declined to recant his previous statements, he regarded them as less important than other benefits of accepting same-sex marriage. In his explanation, he offered three overarching reasons for changing his view of how Americans should live together regarding marriage equality: (1) equal dignity for the love of same-sex couples, and (2) comity in living together peacefully as a society, and (3) respect for emerging public consensus. To the extent that his comments also speak to an understanding of how people might approach democracy itself, they bear quoting at length. According to Blankenhorn:

But there are more things under heaven than these [personal] beliefs. For me, the most important is the equal dignity of homosexual love. I don't believe that opposite-sex and same-sex relationships are the same, but I do believe, with growing numbers of Americans, that the time for denigrating or stigmatizing same-sex relationships is over. Whatever one's definition of marriage, legally recognizing gay and lesbian couples and their children is a victory for basic fairness. Another good thing is comity. Surely we must live together with some degree of mutual acceptance, even if doing so involves some compromise .... especially on this issue, I'm more interested in conciliation than in further fighting. A third good thing is respect for an emerging consensus.[41]

Such a publicly announced sea change by a longtime opponent of same-sex marriage is a striking expression of the forms of conscious reflection and public reasoning that can occur via a deliberative system. Equally striking is that, as the full piece reflects, Blankenhorn has not so much surrendered his belief in the difference in same-sex love and relationships as he has come to see that refusal of their validity is destructive to society as a whole. For him as an active conservative, everyone has a stake in "basic fairness," "mutual acceptance," and "emerging consensus." These are powerful and important claims that have value across the political spectrum. Blankenhorn's change of heart and mind is an example of the operation of the deliberative system at work as theorized in this work, and previously by Jürgen Habermas, and by Mansbridge et al. (2012).

[41] Ibid.

Reversals of view among conservatives who previously had been strongly opposed to equality for LGBT people became increasingly common as US public engagement continued. Theoretically, narratives of these reversals of viewpoint among conservatives would have then flowed through the social networks of fellow conservatives, many of whom were still opposed to LGBT equality. In this development, these revised viewpoints would place competing perspectives into existing conservative social networks. Perhaps for this reason, many such expressions of reversal of opinion among conservatives drew significant attention. One example can be seen in a speech by Washington state legislator Maureen Walsh (R. 16th District, Walla Walla), a Republican who described her soul-searching consideration of gay marriage. In her address on the legislative floor, she described how, as a widow, she could identify with the loss of the comfort of the ties of marriage. She described as a matter of conscience deciding to vote in favor of same-sex marriage to affirm that bond of marriage for all, including her own daughter who had come out as a lesbian. The video of Walsh's address went viral.[42]

There are many other examples. Ted Olson, a well-known conservative attorney successful on landmark cases (including *Bush* v. *Gore*), served to the surprise of many as a strong conservative advocate for gay marriage. He worked, for example, as an attorney in the legal battle to designate California's Proposition 8 as unconstitutional. Olsen wrote that although the voters had affirmed Prop 8, the law "embodies an irrational and discriminatory classification that denies gay men and lesbians the fundamental right to marry enjoyed by all other citizens." Moreover, Olson contended that the voters who approved Prop 8 were *not* necessarily engaged in malice. Rather, quoting Justice Anthony Kennedy, Olson found that bias may arise "from insensitivity caused by simple want of careful, rational reflection or from some instinctive mechanism to guard against people who appear to be different."[43] Here Olson's analysis, as well as the Court's, is consistent with that offered throughout this book, that unconscious bias and identity

---

[42] The Young Turks, "Amazing Gay Marriage Speech Goes Viral (Maureen Walsh)," *YouTube*, Video, 07:14, posted on February 10, 2012, www.youtube .com/watch?v=eH5egFXHJnQ.

[43] Maura Dolan, "Perils of Laws Like Prop 8 Cited by Lawyer," *Los Angeles Times*, published electronically, October 20, 2010, www.search.proquest.com /docview/759120229?accountid=14522.

threats can be significant triggers for the expression of socially inherited prejudice.

The Special Deliberative Contributions of Border Crossers: While Olson's message circulates in society like any other, coming from him as a conservative it was heard differently, and potentially had much more weight and influence in conservative social networks than when the same or similar messages were articulated by others. As discussed in previous sections with reference to the principles of network centrality, this is because within social networks, research shows that people tend to be open to discrepant messages primarily when those who deliver them are seen to be similar to themselves. In contrast, people of any ideological bent tend to remain closed to discrepant messages when those who bring them are perceived as socially far removed from themselves. By crossing the partisan divide in his legal advocacy, Olson brought different perspectives on LGBT equality into conservative social networks in ways that may have meaningfully shaped public engagement on same-sex marriage in those domains.

Consequently, as a well-known conservative attorney working as an advocate on an issue widely regarded as a liberal issue, Olson also served as what I have referred to in other writings (following Chicana philosopher Gloria Anzaldúa) as a border crosser. In this context, a border crosser is someone who operates in some part of his or her life across at least one prevailing social divide (in Olson's case a partisan divide) (Barvosa 2008, 225–228). Commonly for such border crossers, some observers may question and contest their group belonging and identities from both sides of the social divide. For Olson, his position on marriage equality led some conservatives to reject him and to question or refuse his identity claims to being a fellow conservative.[44] But Olson's strong and emotionally committed position, the fair content of his claims, and his willingness to take professional risks for them appear to have caused others in his conservative networks to reflect again on the matter and to consider what inherited biases they themselves might have been laboring

---

[44] For discussion of his emotional commitment as well as rejection by fellow conservatives, see Nina Totenberg, "Ted Olson, Gay Marriage's Unlikely Legal Warrior," *NPR*, Morning Edition, published electronically, December 6, 2010, www.npr.org/2010/12/06/131792296/ted-olson-gay-marriage-s-unlikely-legal-warrior. For attention to the activity of Olsen as a partisan border crosser see also The Young Turks, "Conservative Destroys Fox News on Gay Marriage," *YouTube*, Video, 06:15, Posted on August 9, 2010, www.youtube.com/watch?v=eytGQXWD05M.

under.[45] In this sense, border crossers like Olson have a special role to play in deliberative systems because they introduce into relatively homogeneous social networks insights and views that are uncommon in those social domains because they are socially divided or otherwise far removed from other social networks.

In other cases, visible changes of heart and mind served to debunk circulating narratives that were ultimately determined to be false. For example in the fall of 2011, John Smid, a highly visible gay conversion therapy activist, declared that gay conversion therapy was ineffective, and that while he had been a longtime advocate he was reversing this position.[46] In other cases, visible reversals among political elites potentially served to normalize the acceptance of LGBT equality as well as to prompt more thought among others in their networks, thereby growing the deliberative system. In June of 2012, the marriage of Mary Cheney (daughter of Dick Cheney) and Heather Poe also prompted conservatives to note the significant impact of the visibility of LGBT conservatives. Lawyer and conservative blogger John Hinderaker quoted fellow conservative Jimmy LaSalvia of GOProud as saying: "Mary and Heather have had a tremendous impact on the way America views gay people ... Simply by living their lives openly, honestly, and as authentic conservatives, they have done more to change hearts and minds in this country than any gay advocacy group."[47] In the blog post, Hinderaker declared himself to be "reconsidering [his] stance on gay marriage," and adopting a more "nuanced position."[48] This reconsideration did not extend to partisan divides in general. Presumably in jest, Hinderaker mused that he might come to favor gay marriage "but only for conservatives."[49] At times, conservatives who described themselves as resistant to rethinking the issue themselves, such as Senator

---

[45] For further discussion of this kind of self-reflection and social border crossing as a form of *intrapersonal politics* and as a political action significant in the resolution of large-scale political conflict, see Barvosa, *Wealth of Selves*, 159–206, 221–229.

[46] See GateKeeper50hotmail, "Pray Gay Away Guy Quits & Admits He's Still Gay," *YouTube*, Video, 08:30, Posted on October 18, 2011, www.youtube.com /watch?v=9zRS5ZO72AI.

[47] John Hinderaker, "Rethinking Gay Marriage," *Powerline*, Posted on, June 22, 2012, www.powerlineblog.com/archives/2012/06/rethinking-gay-marriage.php.

[48] Ibid.

[49] Ibid. Hinkderaker continued "At the moment anyway, it strikes me as a principled position." Fellow conservative attorney Ted Olson would have disagreed.

Rand Paul (R-KY), acknowledged that rethinking the issue had become the norm.[50]

Finally, and conversely, those who persisted in extreme, unreasonable, or illogical positions or those who failed to be evenhanded in their advocacy often found their displays of rigidity placed into the public domain for consideration by others. As with the influence of extremism, such displays of rigidity in the face of growing norms of reconsideration may have also prompted reflection by observers. This occurred not only for conservative opponents to LGBT equality, but also for LGBT movement advocates as well. The remainder of the blog post by Hinderaker, for example, featured LGBT activists invited to the White House who had posed before a portrait of Ronald Reagan, flipped the bird at the image of the former US president, and then posted the photos on Facebook.[51] Likewise, the Gay and Lesbian Alliance Against Defamation (GLAAD) was criticized for hypocrisy in granting a GLAAD Media Award to a blogger who was known to frequently engage in partisan defamation of conservatives.[52] Other examples involved conservative advocates – particularly appointed or elected public officials working in the public trust – were captured on video in the public domain making reactive, unreasonable, apparently thoughtless, and clearly biased, commentary opposing equal civil rights for LGBT people.[53]

[50] Could Rand Paul Support Gay Marriage? Rand Paul indicated: "Society's changing, I mean, people change their minds all the time on this issue, and even within the Republican Party, there are people whose child turns out to be gay and they're like, oh well, maybe I want to rethink this issue. So it's been rethought. The President's rethought the issue. So I mean, a lot of people have rethought the issue." Peter Hamby, "Hambycast: Rand Paul's campus challenge," *CNN politics*, published electronically October 3, 2014, www.cnn.com/2014/10/03/politics/rand-paul-hambycast/index.html?utm_source=dlvr.it&utm_medium=twitter. Rand Paul's non-committal shrug was also amplified by social media, Maria Santos, "Rand Paul Shrugs about 'Rethinking' Gay Marriage," Red Alert Politics, published electronically, October 3, 2014, www.redalertpolitics.com/2014/10/03/rand-paul-shrugs-rethinking-gay-marriage/.
[51] Hinderaker, "Rethinking Gay Marriage." Hinderaker reposted the videos within the blog.
[52] Caroline May, "GLAAD Honors Biased Gay Blogger after Applauding $100K Fine for Kobe Bryant," *The Daily Caller*, Published electronically, May 27, 2011, www.dailycaller.com/2011/05/27/glaad-honors-biased-gay-blogger-after-applauding-100k-fine-for-kobe-bryant/.
[53] One example can be seen in this video of Congresswoman Vicky Hartzler (R. 4th District MO) ThinkTank, "Gay Student Confronts Anti-Gay Republican," *YouTube*, Video, 09:00, Posted on July 5, 2011, www.youtube.com/watch?v=SsrN5fXnhYM.

In these various cases, new communication technologies heightened the capacity to provide wide access to public statements that would have otherwise had a narrow and fleeting audience. These contributions to transparency also provided material for greater reflection on all sides of an issue by offering a third-party window on public expression, and thus a new critical vantage point on what, in many cases, appeared to be biased practices and discourses that had been established as societal norms. The degree of civility or incivility with which such forms of transparency are accomplished, however (i.e. how people's expressions are treated), appears to make a difference in whether what is revealed elicits reflection or instead a reactive rejection. Incivility can potentially increase social cleavages and polarization by exciting fear or identity threat as previously discussed in this chapter. In contrast, civility can better foster movement toward new reflection and the formation of a clear collective will.[54] The importance of the treatment that is given to the ideas of potential deliberators is discussed further in Chapter 5. Here, I propose only that when attempts at transparency are read as an attack, they may contribute more to enduring social division than to the democratic practices of basic fairness, mutual acceptance, and respect for emerging consensus rightly described and valued by the former same-sex marriage opponent David Blankenhorn.

---

[54] Lambdalegal, "Sh*T Homophobic People Say," *YouTube*, Video, 01:59, Posted on January 13, 2012, www.youtube.com/watch?v=SVEmHcz-SBs. As this example demonstrates, LGBT advocacy organizations also placed highly partisan material into circulation. This raises a question as to whether the primary audiences for such contributions were already convinced of their views, and by extension whether the democratic value to the deliberative system of these contributions exceeded the risks of increasing polarization through unnecessarily insulting discourse. At the same time, increasing the visibility of anti-LGBT rhetoric created the possibility for accountability and transparency that was especially important in the LGBT case, in which the presence of high levels of anti-gay bias was often denied.

5 | *Hidden Quandaries and Implications for Deliberative Democracy*

The notion that we have limited access to the workings of our minds is difficult to accept, because, naturally, it is alien to our experience, but it is true: you know far less about yourself than you feel you do.[1]

—Daniel Kahneman

The linguistic turn did transform reason and unitary thinking, but it did not drive them out of philosophical discussion.[2]

—Jürgen Habermas

As described thus far, the case study of US public engagement on LGBT equality offered in the previous three chapters has various implications for both theories of deliberative democracy and the institutional design of deliberative systems. As such, it potentially illuminates the current evolutionary stage of democracy. Among the implications of the case study are new vantage points on Jürgen Habermas's theoretical work, as well as new ways of seeing the evolution of democracy in relation to the overarching project of creating peace and social justice through public reason. To further address these matters, in this Chapter, I turn to describing some surprising aspects of the LGBT case study that suggest an alternative narrative of what transpired to shift public opinion over a 28-year period. This alternative narration is then used to illustrate an additional set of barriers to successful deliberation that may appear on some topics. These barriers take the form of unspoken fears and anxieties that present cognitive obstacles to meaningful reflection, and also therefore to deliberative practice (see Chapter 1).

---

[1] Daniel Kahneman, *Thinking, Fast and Slow* (New York: Farrar, Straus, and Giroux), 52.
[2] Jürgen Habermas, "The Unity of Reason in the Diversity of Its Voices," in *Post Metaphysical Thinking: Philosophical Essays*, trans. William Mark Hohengarten (Cambridge: MIT Press, 1992), 139.

Like implicit bias, these undeclared fears and subconscious obstacles – which I refer to here as hidden quandaries of personal fears and apprehensions – may operate outside of the conscious awareness of members of society. Yet these hidden quandaries can nevertheless block or slow the emergence of topic-specific deliberative systems and/or create related social contradictions that reflect these hidden quandaries. As such, deliberative catalysts must address these obstacles in order for the deliberative system to grow and for an ongoing deliberation to move forward effectively. Deliberative catalysts can be designed to help remove or ease obstructive social fears and anxieties and many of the catalysts described in this LGBT case study so far did this kind of fear abatement. Yet the final resolution of hobbling fears is ultimately an individual undertaking. Thus releasing the fears and apprehensions that can block inner reflection and collective deliberation is a task that, theoretically at least, each person would need to engage in personally for themselves but also with potential assistance from the whole.[3] If so, then one implication of this book for the relationship between deliberative democracy and the Enlightenment project of overcoming humanity's least productive beliefs and practices is that a necessary element of peaceful democratization is the task of personal healing and growth in which the fears and anxieties that obstruct the use of public reason are released.

Overall, in this chapter I extend the LGBT case study to consider outlying data points that gesture to an alternative view of what transpired to spark the sea change in US public opinion on LGBT equality. Before and after this counter narrative, I also highlight various implications of a publicly self-organized deliberative system on LGBT equality for democratic theory- especially for a Habermasian revision of the Enlightenment project on one hand, and for empirical deliberative practice on the other. This chapter is divided into three sections. In section one of the chapter, I briefly articulate how the case study on LGBT equality further illuminates the possibility for revising the Enlightenment project through public reason. In section two, I offer an alternative narration of how the US public came to favor LGBT equality based on outlying quantitative data that suggests that public acceptance of legal aspects of LGBT equality dates back to the 1970s. In this alternative narrative sketch, I explore hidden fears and internal

---

[3] I thank Robert Goodin for helpful discussion on this point.

contradictions within the self can stymie public deliberation and the observance of publicly avowed principles. In section three, I draw upon this alternative narrative to identify five general implications for public choice in the practical formation of deliberative systems.

Deliberative Systems in the Enlightenment Project: Habermas Revisited

The LGBT case study presented so far in Chapters 2 through 4 brings attention back to the origins of the idea of deliberative democracy in the work of Jürgen Habermas, and his effort to overcome the failures of the Enlightenment project by reconceiving reason itself. In Habermas's vision, public reason would become communicative reason – a process of reasoning conducted by a people in concert with each other in an attempt to democratically determine ways and means to solve the most pressing problems of common life (1992). Using this refashioned form of public reason, humanity would have in hand the tools needed to restore the promise of the Enlightenment by using reason to generate lasting peace and justice that could override old patterns of violence, intolerance, and discord. Habermas's vision has been embraced by many as a hopeful promise, but disregarded by others as an abstract fantasy. Yet deliberative democracy's friends and critics alike have often wondered how this feat of democratic magic could be rendered in daily practice. How in the face of the seemingly endless inequities of power and voice that plague contemporary democracies could deliberative democracy form?

As illustrated in the case study presented in the three preceding chapters, however, I have proposed that a large-scale, self-assembled, and networked deliberative system has formed in the US on the topic of LGBT equality. Moreover, this deliberative system has functioned as the vehicle for US public deliberation on the general question: *Should LGBT people be accepted and integrated into mainstream US society on an equal basis, and if so, how?* This empirical example of an actual deliberative system suggests that deliberative democracy is not simply an appealing theory that is impossible to realize. Instead, deliberative democracy is now a practical possibility. Without our having fully sensed it yet, the ideal of deliberative democracy has at last taken material form as a deliberative system that is already in operation on the issue of LGBT equality. The formation of this deliberative system has also depended in part on the emergence of new communication tools that have recently become commonplace.

In light of the case study presented so far therefore, I suggest that Jürgen Habermas's vision for deliberative democracy in daily life appears now to be practical on many fronts. As Habermas had stated repeatedly, the practice of deliberative democracy could not be produced, but rather had to arise from society itself as a form of self-organization (Habermas 1990c, 364; 1990b, 315; 1992, 146). The LGBT case study that I have offered shows exactly this pattern. If a deliberative system has existed as I have proposed, then it arose as a form of public self-assembly. The system was built from one network node to the next, hand-to-hand by people urging each other to reflect and choosing to reflect themselves on the often-unexamined belief systems that they had inherited within social life.

As Habermas has also stressed, inequities of power and conditions of social domination and subordination are not overriding obstacles to the formation of communicative reason or deliberative democracy. Instead public deliberation could emerge spontaneously under conditions of subordination such that domination becomes an occasion for the use of public reason (Habermas 1990c, 364; 1990b, 315; 1992, 146). Here too, the LGBT case study presented in this work suggests that this aspect of Habermas's vision is empirically possible. If it has existed, the US deliberative system on LGBT equality arose from domination, specifically the longstanding and pervasive subordination of the gay, lesbian, bisexual, and transgender minority in the US. At the time of this writing, millions of people who are not members of the LGBT minority are now nonetheless consciously committed to realizing and consistently maintaining in law, policy, and social practice the social and legal equality of LGBT people.

These developments, which seemed impossible less than a decade ago, point out the practical possibility that using communicative reason as the tool of deliberative democracy is not only possible, it could (as Habermas envisioned) restore in new form the Enlightenment project of creating peace and justice through reasoning. This revised Enlightenment project proceeds not by cold logic alone, but through reasoning broadly defined to include emotional judgments, aesthetics, creative aspirations, spiritual principles, and also by people reasoning with each other in direct and indirect ways. In Chapters 3 and 4 of this case study, stories involving Ellen DeGeneres, Zach Wahls, Gene

Robinson, David Blankenhorn, Ted Olsen, Dick Gephardt, and many others demonstrate in a practical manner *how* the process of hearing the reasons of others – including the emotions and aesthetic judgments of others – prompted many people to reflectively let go of their socially inherited and often unexamined views and to replace them with new outlooks. In many cases, these new outlooks were fashioned by individuals themselves from ideas and information shared by others in and through the deliberative system on LGBT equality. In this way, as reasoning took place one person at a time, the collective will of the whole emerged from the deliberative processes that were often undertaken individually by participants.

In sum, one overarching implication of the case study offered here is that Habermas's account of communicative reason is more powerful and more practical than previously thought. It is only now, with the emergence of new communication technologies that make new forms of fast communication and self-organization among large publics possible, that the Habermasian vision of deliberative democracy can emerge in practice. If the case study offered here provides new perspective on the practicality of Habermasian deliberative democracy, however, then it also suggests that the views of Habermas's mentors regarding the importance of the multiplicity of the self also holds valuable insight for rebuilding the Enlightenment project on higher ground.

Meeting the Unknown Self in Deliberative Systems: The Potential Influence of Hidden Fears

The extended examples offered in Chapter 4 of the LGBT case study imply that Max Horkheimer and Theodor Adorno – Habermas's mentors and predecessors in the Frankfurt School tradition of Critical Theory – were right to point out that the long-prevailing presumption that the self is unitary (i.e. an internally uniform, self-consistent, self-transparent, subject of reason) was both incorrect and relevant to redeeming the Enlightenment project. The fiction of the unitary self is not only misleading, it has been often at work in the many atrocities *not* averted by the Enlightenment project, including the modern persistence of violence, genocide, hatred, and war. The fact of the multiplicity of the embodied self has been long discussed in Western thought. Yet in many ways it is an uncomfortable fact about the self from which many still often turn away. This inner multiplicity – comprised of a plurality of inner systems of perception and response, as well as clusters of mismatched social imprints, identities, and often obscured but discordant beliefs – make us as human beings, (as noted by Daniel Kahneman in the first epigraph to this chapter), far less knowledgeable about the workings of our own minds that we think.

Yet the inner multiplicity of the self is not a personal failing to shun, but rather a lived social and physical inheritance that is an unavoidable part of the human condition. The multiplicity of every person is a product of (a) the multiple cognitive subsystems of human embodiment, and (b) the countless neurological imprints absorbed by everyone from their socially diverse and contradictory environments both over their lifetime and in each new day of their lives. Psychologist Kenneth Gergen refers to humanity's inherited multiplicity as *multi-being*. As Gergen states, "the ideal of an internally integrated, harmonious, and coherent mind is replaced by a view of the person as fundamentally disorderly and inconsistent."[4] Depending on the socialization a person has received, each person comes to contain an extensive inner diversity that often includes numerous contradictions. As Gergen describes it:

...for anything we hold as reasonable and good, we also harbor its opposite. For every activity we embrace, we are also capable of alien activity. Every good liberal knows very well how to engage in hate talk; every religious fundamentalist knows the attraction of sin; every adult can be a baby; every responsible official has the potential for corruption.[5]

This internal multiplicity and contradiction can be a source of conflict, but also a rich resource and repertoire for action, understanding, and empathy toward oneself and others in life. In short, inner multiplicity of the mind absorbed from social environments is unavoidable and also a source of both risk and opportunity.[6]

---

[4] Thus in contrast to the philosophical myth of an isolated, bounded self whose reason operates outside of social influence, Gergen notes that each person is "socially embedded" and operating in and through our relationships as we "carry the residue of multiple relationships" with us. Kenneth J. Gergen, *Relational Being: Beyond Self and Community* (Oxford: Oxford University Press, 2009), 137. For extended discussion of the multiplicity of the self and its relationship to political life and social change, see also Edwina Barvosa, *Wealth of Selves: Multiple Identities, Mestiza Consciousness, and the Subject of Politics* (College Station: Texas A&M University Press, 2008).

[5] Gergen, *Relational Being*, 138.

[6] For examples of this risk and opportunity with regard to agency in context of fascist violence, see Barvosa, *Wealth of Selves*, 83–108.

These facts about the multiplicity of the self are not esoteric. They are practical matters of human thought, feeling, and action that can foster or obstruct the workings of deliberative systems. As such, they appear in the LGBT case study in important ways that are further elaborated below. On the whole, multiplicity within the self – while valuable in many ways – is related also to the root causes of all of the cognitive obstacles to deliberation discussed in Chapter 4. The inner multiplicity of the self takes many forms including self-fragmenting fears, self-protective and self-dividing blind spots, and common avoidance of seeing and/or embracing difference in others and potentially in oneself.[7] These and other manifestations can block both private reflection and public deliberation as well as the effort to implement one's personal will (or the collective will) by *consistently* living by one's own avowed principles. Collectively, if a democratic society proclaims a principle but is not observing it – failing to walk its talk – then that collective inconsistency will likely have its origins, or at least a companion reflection, in the corresponding internal conflicts of members of that society (Barvosa 2008, 207–221). As Chapter 4 of the LGBT case indicates, resolution of such blockages though a deliberative system also therefore involves, and can foster, the resolution of the same collective obstacle as it occurs within the self. To illustrate this implication with an empirical example, in the next section, I turn to telling an alternative story of the shift in US public opinion on LGBT equality providing a look into underlying quandaries that may have shaped what transpired.

An Alternative Narrative of Shifting US Public Opinion on LGBT Equality

So far in this work, I have told a conventional story about shifting US public opinion on LGBT equality. But there is an alternative narration that is arguably more consistent with all of the available empirical data. This second narration requires giving attention to two outlying data points in American public opinion polls. I highlight and analyze them both here in turn. First, in 2002, 85 percent of Americans polled by Gallup stated that they supported legal equality for "homosexuals"

---

[7] For description of a fourth obstacle of trauma, including both collective and individual trauma, see Chapter 1 of this book.

in the workplace (in the language of the time). Almost as many endorsed protecting gay and lesbian people through laws against hate crime. This means that as early as 2002 the vast majority of Americans already believed in legal equality for LGBT people (or, more accurately, at least for gay men and lesbians). In fact, Gallup polls show majority support for legal equality for gay and lesbian people as far back as 1977 when 56 percent agreed that gay and lesbian people should have equal legal protections at work.[8] Thus "paradoxically" in Gallup's words, Americans long endorsed the *legal* equality of gay and lesbian people but did not accept the *social* expression of same-sex relationships.

Examining this paradox retrospectively in 2002, Gallup reported it by saying "there is still significant ambivalence about the overall acceptability of homosexual relations in American society." Gallup found in a 2002 poll that "substantial numbers of Americans continue to say – as they have for the past quarter century – that homosexual relations should be neither acceptable nor legal." In this, the Americans polled pointedly excluded same-sex marriage and partnership benefits as unacceptable.[9] Meanwhile they nevertheless endorsed by large majorities legal equality of opportunity and protections from hate crime for gay and lesbian people. In other words, over several decades US public approval and disapproval of LGBT equality can be seen as oddly bifurcated in favoring public-oriented rights, while denying domestically oriented rights. Yet as political scientist and constitutional scholar Even Gerstmann has stated, "In truth, there is no such thing as gay rights. There are only legal and constitutional rights that must be applied equally for all people" (Gerstmann 2008, 4). The Gallup polls show that as far back as 1977, majorities of Americans appear to have agreed with Gerstmann's point, at least at some level, that gay and lesbian members of society should have legal equality.

If majorities of Americans already endorsed equal legal protections from discrimination for gays and lesbians in the 1970s, and even more so by 2002, then what did Americans deliberate on regarding LGBT people with such obvious anguish between 2002 and 2015? Did a deliberation actually take place? If so, what was it about? I submit that yes, Americans did truly deliberate on the issue of extending full

---

[8] Frank Newport, "Homosexuality," *Gallup*, published electronically, September 11, 2002, www.gallup.com/poll/9916/homosexuality.aspx.
[9] Ibid.

civil rights to LGBT people, especially between 2002 and 2015. Moreover, many people have reported that the process often felt painful and wrenching.[10] What is not clear, however, is that in this intense and conscious process of public reflection that Americans ultimately made a novel choice that a majority of Americans had not already expressed belief in at the outset over several preceding decades.

The paradoxical Gallup poll data suggests alternatively that through public deliberation the majority of Americans did not decide something new. Rather, the majority of Americans *became consciously willing to consistently act upon the values of equality that they already held,* but which they had not consistently observed with regard to LGBT people due, I propose, to an inner conflict and ambivalence regarding some aspects of the issue. In this sense, public deliberation served as *a vehicle for collective will formation in the form of clarifying the collective will and fostering the letting go of fears or other cognitive obstructions that prevented consistent application of that collective will.* In other words, through a large-scale public deliberation, Americans clearly did construct their preferences and came into their own firm individual and collective will on this matter. More specifically, in the process of public engagement and deliberation, Americans reflected on their own competing beliefs, and in so doing, consciously chose to live as a people according to their societal value of equality. By 2015, the collective will of Americans to live together in equality with regard to sexual and gender diversity was thus no longer a paradoxical glimmer in an opinion poll muddied by ambivalence and competing beliefs. Rather by 2015, the public choice that it was right to live in common on an equal footing had become clear and strong. What then can be understood from the evidence of prior belief in these views?

Resolving Inner Conflict Regarding Common Sexual Experience: Clarifying the Collective Will

If it is plausible that the recent US public deliberation on LGBT equality has been an exercise in *clarifying* the existing collective will of Americans, then this raises a second question. If the societal belief in legal equality already long existed, then why was there a struggle of

---

[10] Daniel Karslake, *For the Bible Tells Me So.* DVD. 98 min. New York: First Run Features, 2007.

competing beliefs in the first place, and why would that anxiety have focused on domesticity and interpersonal relationships, but not on discrimination in employment or in hate crime? I cannot answer this question with certainty. However, a second outlying data point suggests a possible theoretical answer. In 2015, Gallup polls found that Americans estimated the number of gay and lesbian people in America to be 23%. Yet extensive polling also in 2015 (interview n = 58,000, January–April 2015) found that only 3.8% of Americans actually identified as gay, lesbian, bisexual, or transgender.[11] In contrast to this, the public estimate is widely off the mark, identifying more than one in five men as gay. Additionally, this large overestimate by the American public is not new. It has been a stable finding for over a decade, with similar results having appeared in 2011 (mean = 25%) and in 2002 (mean among male respondents = 21%, mean among female respondents = 22%). Gallup has suggested that this finding reflects a lack of familiarity with demographic data among the public.[12] Perhaps that is true.

Another possibility for the overestimate, however, is that the incidence of same-sex attraction, arousal, and related sexual expressions are much more common in the general population than is generally acknowledged. Evidence for this possibility can be found in the studies of human sexuality conducted by Alfred Kinsey in the mid-twentieth century. The studies were based on sexual case histories of over 16,000 people, including both males and females. Kinsey's study revealed that for men and women, same-sex arousal, and some degree of same-sex sexual activity, was fairly common (a finding that has been consistently replicated since Kinsey's original study). Among men, same-sex activity tended to appear at different stages of the life course, and among women, it tended to rise gradually over time.

Likewise, Kinsey found that for unmarried men as a whole, same-sex activity comprised a sexual outlet for 27.3 percent of those studied (Kinsey 1948, 259). Similarly, by age 40, 19 percent of females had engaged in same-sex contact that was "deliberately and consciously…

---

[11] Frank Newport, "Americans Greatly Overestimate Percent Gay, Lesbian in U.S.," *Gallup*, published electronically, May 21, 2015, www.gallup.com/poll/ 183383/americans-greatly-overestimate-percent-gaylesbian.aspx?utm_source= Americans%20Greatly%20Overestimate%20%20Percent%20Gay,% 20Lesbi&utm_medium=search&utm_campaign=tiles.

[12] Ibid.

intended to be sexual" (Kinsey 1953, 453). As Kinsey summarized with regard to males, "a considerable proportion of the population, perhaps the major portion of the male population, has at least some homosexual experience between adolescence and old age" (1948, 610). The percentage among preadolescent boys he gauged to be 60 percent, and he noted the presence of "an additional group of adult males who avoid overt contacts, but who are quite aware of their potentialities for reacting to other males" (610). Kinsey's studies thus found same-sex activity to appear at rates quite similar to the overestimates of LGBT identified people long found by Gallup.

For Kinsey, the fact that same-sex desire and experience appeared so commonly in his study was a matter of scholarly interest, but not one of great surprise. Kinsey noted at length that similar patterns of same-sex activity could be seen throughout the animal kingdom (Kinsey 1953, 449–450). Thus, to the extent that human beings are a species, the appearance of same-sex sexual expression among human beings was to be expected. The data identifying this largely unspoken phenomenon was consistent with what was already generally known about other living creatures. Some scholars of LGBT studies today continue to draw parallels between human sexual and gender diversity and similar expressions of diversity common elsewhere in the animal kingdom (Roughgarden 2009). Nevertheless, the commonality of same-sex activity and gender diversity in nature has not generally rendered such diversity socially acceptable in human societies. As Milton Diamond has stated: "One thing that we have to remember from Darwin to Kinsey, to any great thinker about sexuality, is that variation is the norm. Biology loves variation. Biology loves differences. Society hates it."[13] What may be the consequence of such social hatred toward, or the erasure of, sexual diversity as a nonetheless common aspect of human embodiment and experience?

I propose that lived experience, or at least awareness, of fairly widespread same-sex sexual arousal and activity could be the source of the US public's consistent overestimate of the number of people *who actually identify* as gay, lesbian, bisexual, or transgender. Social hostility toward the sexual diversity associated with physical embodiment, such as those articulated historically by various religious

---

[13] Milton Diamond, quoted from the documentary film *Middle Sexes: Redefining He and She*, www.youtube.com/watch?v=jaPsiGutGPQ, 6:06–6:24.

denominations and other social conservative, could also be another source. In any case, the resulting tension between constructed social discourses condemning same-sex sexual expression and the commonplace awareness of such experiences, could create within the self, and within the collective, a long-term contradiction between what people believe from social influence that they "should" be and what they actually are. Within the American mainstream, this tension would likely have been an underlying tension, going mostly unspoken. But the repressed returns. I propose that this stuffed-down inner contradiction showed up socially as both: (a) social practices and social narratives that prohibited and punished as invalid fairly commonplace same-sex erotic practice, especially as part of ongoing relationships and domesticity, and (b) the paradoxical Gallup poll findings that revealed self-contradictory beliefs endorsing LGBT equality in law, but not in the bedroom.

If this further interpretation is plausible, then the inner contradiction described here was not publicly avowed, yet it nevertheless underlay, and likely also drove, the resistance to acknowledging the larger pervasiveness of same-sex attraction and sexual expression in the US mainstream.[14] The denial of the obvious – particularly the obvious in oneself – is uneasy work however. Ambivalence is a way to accomplish that work (Barvosa 2008, 140–174). Thus the public ambivalence toward public versus private and/or domestic expressions of same-sex sexual activity found by Gallup served – most likely without conscious awareness – as a means to manage internal tensions and contradictions until such time as conscious reflection, choice, and action could be

----

[14] For empirical research on the power of this form of denial including self-deception and the relationship of self-deception to hostility toward gay men, see Henry Adams, Lester Wright, and Bethany Lohr, "Is Homophobia Associated with Homosexual Arousal?" *Journal of Abnormal Psychology* 105: 3 (1996): 440–445. The study illustrates sexual self-deception by recording the denial expressed by homophobic men who demonstrate sexual aroused while watching male same-sex pornography. The strength of their resulting erections was measured by a strain gauge fitted to the phallus, yet almost all respondents denied having any physical arousal. In other words, the intention to deny their own sexual attraction resulted in dissociation from their own bodies and from the observable facts of their anatomical response, *even* when evidence of the facts was literally in their lap. Such a strong aim to obscure same-sex desire even from oneself would most likely arise from the internalization of socially constructed messages that homosexual identity and/or same-sex erotic practice is somehow bad.

taken to resolve these tensions at both the individual and collective levels.[15] This opportunity finally came along in the words of Zach Wahls, whose contributions to public deliberation are discussed at length in Chapter 4. In three minutes before the Iowa House Judiciary Committee, Wahls offered a social reconstruction of traditional family that collapsed the socially constructed opposition between "traditional family" and same-sex unions and domesticity.

In this reconstruction, what had been internally fragmented as socially forbidden, yet also ever-present for many *beyond* the LGBT minority, was now suddenly – and on the good authority of a straight child of a lesbian couple – narrated as completely compatible with traditional family life. Wahls's words brought physical realities that had been laboriously denied and anxiously hidden suddenly *within the bounds* of social acceptance. Why was Wahls's address so stratospherically successful and appealing? I suggest that it was because Wahls' reconstruction could quickly relieve the inner tensions caused by circulating beliefs that denied legitimacy to the otherwise valid sexual reality of lived experience. It is perhaps no wonder that Wahls's message spread virally to great acclaim. In the viral flow of the bootlegged video of Wahls's address, perhaps much of the US public heaved a metaphorical sigh of relief at being unexpectedly unburdened of a heavy false belief and its daily anxieties. Suddenly – although still at an unspoken level – more people could not only endorse same-sex marriage, they could perhaps feel relief that their widowed Aunt Tilly and her inseparable friend Madge were no longer to be worried over, or politely overlooked, as a companionship potentially beyond the pale. Wahls's address was presented online in February of 2011. Four months later in May 2011, Gallup tracked the first US majority public opinion poll in favor of same-sex marriage.[16] A majority of the US public suddenly felt ready to accept marriage equality. Coincidental in its timing or not, in so doing, the US majority affirmed domestic and social equality alongside of the legal equalities that they had long endorsed, but not yet consistently acted to realize.

[15] Ambivalence can also be consciously used to manage contradictory circumstances, for further discussion, see Barvosa, *Wealth of Selves*, 140–172.

[16] Frank Newport, "For First Time, Majority of Americans Favor Legal Gay Marriage," *Gallup*, published electronically, May 20, 2011, news.gallup.com/poll/147662/first-time-majority-americans-favor-legal-gay-marriage.aspx.

Evolving Collective Will and the Changing Self in Deliberative Systems

If this alternative narration is tenable, then I propose that it is also possible to see the American public deliberation on LGBT equality between 2002 and 2015 in a different way than it has been so far narrated. The potential emergence of a deliberative system is not only a development in the evolution of democracy. It is the emergence of an institutional form in which a deliberative system succeeds as an open and informal technique – a process *encompassing anything and everything that people do to facilitate the formation of clear collective will* – a process that also facilitates, and may at times require, the personal growth of the members of the public who take part. In other words, deliberative democracy exercised via deliberative systems can be seen as a process of collective will formation that involves the healing of any internal wounds and/or inner conflicts held by participants that obstruct conscious reflection and will.

In the LGBT case, I propose that this can be seen empirically in a paradoxically bifurcated expression of public opinion on LGBT equality that shifts as Americans undertook the opportunity to resolve – through conscious collective reflection – existing intra-societal conflicts between awareness of biologically shaped (though not determined) patterns of sexual expression, and socially constructed norms and narratives that harshly judge human sexual expression as it truly is. The reflective resolution of this inner conflict cleared the way for the development of a *clear collective will* endorsing the equal treatment of LGBT people consistent with existing democratic values. It was thus potentially through a combination of personal reflection and the resolution of inner blockages to conscious thought that public deliberation produced a new consensus in which the US public is no longer wavering on the issue, as it did between 2002 and 2010, but is instead deciding decisively *to act* upon their new or renewed sense of what is right in keeping with their democratic value of equality. Rendered in 2015 as a conscious choice, this new consensus takes the form of recognition, equal treatment, and accommodation of LGBT needs and experiences both under the law *and* in social norms and practices.

This shift spans religious and non-religious members of the US public alike in ways that also challenge common narratives, and some stereotypes, that surround the sea change in US public opinion on LGBT equality. For instance, there remains a perception that the social marginalization of LGBT people in the US is overwhelmingly attributable to the intolerance of religious Americans alone. While religious extremism and in tolerance certainly exists, and in some cases persists, and has been influential as shown in the LGBT case study here (e.g. Westboro Baptist Church), the perception that people of faith have been in recent times *categorically* (or solely) intolerant of LGBT people is not borne out by available data. Recall from Chapter 2, for example, that it was several religious groups in 1987 that made some of the earliest moves to acknowledge LGBT people in their communities. Likewise, across this case study some of the most influential domain-specific deliberations took place in religious spheres such as in the US Episcopal Church. By 2015, polls show that among the religiously observant in America, the strongest moral judgments against LGBT equality were held by a majority of only one subcategory of those who regarded themselves as religious.

Aggregate Gallup data from 2011–2014, for example, showed that a majority of Americans who attend church around once per month or most weeks but *not* every week considered gay and lesbian relations (in the language of the survey) morally acceptable. Moreover, these polls showed that people who are religious but who attend church seldom or never considered gay and lesbian relations morally acceptable by large majorities.[17] Statistically, the only group of religious Americans among which a majority consider gay and lesbian relations morally unacceptable are those who attend *every* week. Yet even among these weekly attendees, 31 percent held that same-sex relationships are morally acceptable. This stratification renders highly religious, strong opponents of LGBT equality as outliers even among religious members of US society (and a clear

---

[17] As Gallup's Frank Newport put it, "Clearly then the strongest views about the moral acceptability of gay or lesbian relationships are confined to the *most* religious segment of American society." Percentages expressing moral approval are as follows: once per month church attendees 59%, most weeks but not every week 51%, seldom attend 71%, and never attend 81%. Frank Newport, "Religion, Same-Sex Relationships and Politics in Indiana and Arkansas." *Gallup*, published electronically, April 3, 2015, www.gallup.com/opinion/poll ing-matters/182300/religion-sex-relationships-politics-indiana-arkansas.aspx? utm_source=Religion,%20Same-Sex%20Relationships%20%20and%20Polit ics%20in%20&utm_medium=search&utm_campaign=tiles,%20emphasis added.

minority in the population overall).[18] Overall there was a 20-point gap between the strong moral judgments against gay and lesbian relationships of most weekly churchgoers, and the next most often church-attending group.

The point of attending briefly to this data is twofold. First, despite stereotypes to the contrary, within this category of religious Americans – as within nearly all other social categories – there is significant diversity. Resistance to LGBT equality does not characterize all religious people. Moreover, secular society has historically also constructed and circulated discourses, practices, and social norms that were denigrating and hostile to LGBT people.[19] Second, therefore, the source of long-term societal tension and group hostility toward an LGBT minority plausibly has had less to do with religion per se, and more to do with an intense rigidity on the part of many people – religious and non-religious alike – in the face of empirical sexual and gender diversity.[20] This rigidity may have many sources including personal fear and anxiety, socially inherited bias, lack of awareness and familiarity with LGBT lives, and other factors including fears promulgated by religious doctrine or by secular narratives of intolerance that have also circulated widely. Therefore to succeed as a vehicle for large-scale public deliberation on the question of how the US LGBT minority should be incorporated into US society, the deliberative system had to somehow address these hidden quandaries of fear or anxiety toward difference, including possible differences within the self. In so doing, the deliberative system also provided the means for facing inherited biases and blind spots in productive ways.

Has the emergence of this new consensus meant that *all* underlying ambivalences involving sexual and gender diversity are now resolved in mainstream America? Not necessarily. At the close this case study in 2015, there remained evidence that members of the US public might still be conflicted in other way(s) associated with the sources of same-sex orientation, an underlying concern that might also extend to the

---

[18] Ibid.
[19] This point is reiterated by Bishop V. Gene Robinson in his description of how he came to be taught secularly as a child that homosexuality was regarded as wrong and unacceptable. See interview with Daniel Karslake in *For the Bible Tells Me So*, bonus material, 6:50–7:43.
[20] As well as perhaps a socially constructed and learned tendency toward narcissism of the kind: "What does that person's difference say about me?"

sources of gender diversity and transgender identities.[21] Over time, American perspectives have changed as to the source of same-sex sexual orientation by slowly moving toward an explanation rooted in nature. This shift has correlated with increasing acceptance of LGBT equality. The more that LGBT identity has been understood to be a product of nature, and not a social choice, the more Americans have become willing to accept LGBT people on an equal footing. Yet the view that LGBT experience has a social origin also persists, and some, but not all, of this can be explained by partisan or conservative religious commitments to the view that LGBT experiences are always purely a matter of choice.[22]

If there remains some underlying inner tension on the origin question of nature versus nurture, this strain appears inattentive to the more nuanced versions of the "born this way" discourse that have also circulated in US society. Again, Kinsey is a helpful resource. As Kinsey put it with regard to human embodiment:

The inherent physiologic capacity of an animal to respond to any sufficient stimulus seems, then, the basic explanation of the fact that some individuals respond to stimuli originating in other individuals of their own sex—and it appears to indicate that every individual could so respond if the opportunity offered *and one were not [socially] conditioned against making such responses.* (1953, 447 emphasis added)

Thus Kinsey held that the possibility of same-sex arousal, attraction, and sexual expression is simply a possibility associated with human embodiment, and is a natural fact that can be shaped (or distorted) by social factors, but only to a degree.

---

[21] Wavering can be seen in Gallup polls over a recent three-year period. The number of Americans polled reporting belief that sexual orientation is innate fell between 2013 and 2014, but rose again to a new high of over 50 percent in 2015; See Jeffrey M. Jones, "More Americans See Gay, Lesbian Orientation as Birth Factor," *Gallup*, published electronically, May 16, 2013, www.gallup.com/poll/162569/americans-gay-lesbian-orientation-birth.factor .aspx. Justin McCarthy, "Americans' Views on Origins of Homosexuality Remain Split," *Gallup*, published electronically, May 28, 2014, www.gallup .com/poll/170753/americans-views-origins-homosexuality-remain-split.aspx. Jeffrey M. Jones, "Majority in U.S. Now Say Gays and Lesbians Born, Not Made," *Gallup*, published electronically, May 20, 2015, www.gallup.com/poll/ 183332/majority-say-gays-lesbians-born-not-made.aspx.

[22] Newport, "Religion, Same-Sex Relationships and Politics in Indiana and Arkansas."

In this account, the actual experiences of same-sex sexual desire and diverse gender self-expression (both of which are also seen widely in nature) logically vary from one person to the next, as well as in and over time in any given person's life course (Roughgarden 2009). Moreover, sexual and gender diversity vary based on a combination of *both* physical and social factors. Yet the interaction of those two factors would be so deeply intertwined as to make it impossible to know with any certainty the reasons why someone has come to identify as LGBT, while someone else does not, despite also having had same-sex sexual experiences, or engaging in diverse gender expressions. Gallup itself noted this interpretation in 2004, when they quoted Canadian Mitchell Raphael, then Editor-in-Chief of a gay culture magazine called *Fab*. As Gallup quoted Raphael: "Sexuality exists along the spectrum. Some people may be stuck at one point, many shift over time."[23] As such, Raphael further observed that the "environment/nature debates simplify a complicated process – but are effective as a tool of political manipulation for people who seek simple solutions."[24] In this still marginalized view, sexual orientation is a complex mélange of biological and social factors, the interplay of which is virtually impossible to untangle.

This alterative narration of the complexity of sexual identity and expression, however, contradicts prevailing conventional narratives of sexual expression as static, entirely inborn, and determining. Yet this oversimplified "born this way" discourse has opened the way for people to feel safe reconsidering and widely accepting LGBT equality. As such, it has served as a vital narrative that could allay the hidden quandaries of underlying social fear that had heretofore appeared as deep and unexplained contradictions in the minds of the US majority. These contradictions were between, on one hand, deeply held beliefs and principles of equality for LGBT people in public protections, and on the other hand, support for everyday practices subordinating LGBT people in domestic matters. Under the fear dissolving "born this way" discourse, the US deliberation on LGBT equality, especially on same-sex marriage, moved forward more quickly to reconcile long-established principles with practice.

---

[23] Josephine Mazzuca, "Origin of Homosexuality? Britons, Canadians Say 'Nature,'" *Gallup*, published electronically, November 2, 2004, www.gallup.com/poll/13930/origin-homosexuality-britons-canadians-say-nature.aspx.
[24] Ibid.

But the simplified "born this way" discourse – useful at one level – also potentially leaves in place conflicting inner beliefs about the sources and origins of sexual and gender diversity. If so, does this remaining inner conflict undermine further public engagement on equality for the transgender minority? Is it responsible for the relative quiet regarding bisexual expression, intersex identities, or gender fluidity that still prevail at the time of this writing? These questions are impossible to answer from the LGBT case study offered here. What is visible, however, at the levels of theory and institutional design is that it is possible at any time to deploy the ever-present tools and practices of social construction to foster democratization through deliberative systems. These language-mediated tools of social construction are the practical mechanism by which humanity generates the meanings, values, and practices (i.e. discourses, ideologies, and structures) in and through which human beings live at any given time. Constructivism thus matters enormously because it is through the practices of social construction that humanity itself creates and sustains its own circumstances – including its most trying problems – over time. With these same tools humanity can, at any time, construct new meanings, values, and practices in order to shift its circumstances and solve its most pressing problems. Patriarchy, for example, when it is expressed as a limiting and hierarchical gender binary is not a phenomenon that is simply found. It is socially created, and it is daily either recreated or transformed in everyday practice.[25] Men and women alike have socially created and recreated the gender binary over and over, moment by moment, year after year, century after century, and millennia after millennia. Yet there is nothing necessary about this perpetuating outcome. The same constructivist toolkit by which humanity constructs a limiting gender binary is the same toolkit by which humanity could at any time – if it chose to do so – create a more freeing alternative framework of gender. In short, the tools of social transformation are always at hand, and are part of the workings of a deliberative system.

[25] Patriarchy, however, is not universal in form and appears in many variations. For a classic reference to the importance of this for social change of gender relations, and for foundational discussion of iterative change in gender norms, see Judith Butler, *Gender Trouble* (New York: Routledge, 1990).

Five Implications for Deliberative Systems as an Institutional Design

Overall, I propose that there are several implications of regarding deliberative systems as operating, at least in part, through personal healing and growth to resolve hidden quandaries. Unresolved hidden quandaries can stymie effective deliberative system formation by creating roadblocks to reflection comprised of private fears and inner conflicts related to a deliberation topic. These fears may also fragment the self through unproductive personal and social contradictions. With the preceding alternative narrative of the sea change in US public opinion on LGBT equality as a reference point, I propose that there at least five implications for deliberative systems of the influence of hidden personal quandaries. These are: (1) addressing the cognitive obstacles to public deliberation is a necessary part of the conditions needed to foster deliberative systems, (2) practices of social constructivism matter, both as a common cause of, and a remedy for, many cognitive obstacles to deliberation, (3) the curative effects of antidote-like social constructions (such as that offered by Zach Wahls in 2011) may be shaped and constrained by timing and happenstance, such that as previously alluded to, (4) deliberative democracy can be seen as an open-ended exercise in collective will formation, including any and all activities that forward conscious reflection on self and society toward the creation of a common will, and (5) there are no necessary outcomes: all parts of the status quo are human formations, and the transformation of that status quo through deliberative systems is, by extension, a contingent matter of choice and will involving specific decisions. Extensive elaboration of these five implications is beyond the scope of this chapter and would require further study. Each implication is, however, illustrated briefly here in turn with reference to the LGBT case study offered in Chapters 2 through 4.

Circumventing Cognitive Obstacles is Vital to Deliberative System Growth

First, cognitive obstacles to public deliberation are real and difficult to identify and address except by focused attention. Cognitive obstacles – namely fears, implicit bias, and identity threats – are powerful and disruptive. They can prevent either the formation of collective will or, as in this Chapter's alternative narration, disrupt self-consistent obser-vance of that will in law, policy, and social practice. Moreover, because these obstacles are the manifestations of inner anxieties and fragmenta-tions of which people may be unaware or ashamed, their presence may not be superficially obvious to observers or openly declared by those who experience them. In such cases, they exist as hidden quandaries. Fears, for example, may be shunted aside through pride or quiet shame. Other cognitive blocks to personal reflection may persist outside of conscious awareness. Implicit biases, likewise, may lurk in patterns of inattention or as blind spots that are rationalized by extreme skepti-cism. Anxiety arising from identity threats may be cloaked by angry aggression or justified through extreme forms of taking offence. Whatever the details, these cognitive obstacles are related to inner multiplicity of the self – i.e. of different levels of cognitive systems or of divergent socially encoded content – and while such cognitive blocks can prevent deliberation they are often not clearly visible on the sur-face. As a result, practical designs and efforts to foster public delibera-tion must take into account the possibility of unseen obstacles and intervene to diminish their effects. In the LGBT case study, deliberative entrepreneurs such as Ellen DeGeneres, Zach Wahls, Gene Robinson, and others undertook these preventative/facilitating measures by fram-ing deliberation in ways that mitigated the effects of implicit bias, identity threats, existing fears – both visible fears and those undeclared.

Social Construction: Effective Tools for Resolving Cognitive Obstacles to Public Deliberation

Second, and as noted by Jürgen Habermas in the second epigraph to this chapter, the linguistic turn has dramatically changed the way we under-stand human reason, and by extension, public reasoning in deliberative democracy. Constructivism, as a key expression of the linguistic turn, has thus changed how we understand science, the self, identities, inher-ited bias, as well as societal norms and practices, including all social structures. As monumental as this new understanding is, however, it is not well integrated into the scholarly literatures on deliberative democ-racy. As Mark B. Brown has described, "contemporary democratic theorists, nurtured on Thomas Kuhn, may be predisposed toward this moderately constructivist view of science, but they have done little to explore its implications for democracy," (Brown 2009, ix).

In scholarship specifically on deliberative democracy, constructivism is rarely mentioned and sometimes considered to be necessarily at odds with Habermasian thought.[26] Yet the processes of social construction have important implications for democracy, including deliberative democracy formed through large-scale deliberative systems.

Among the most important implications of constructivism is how the social reconstruction of identity formations can contribute to the evolution of public deliberation. An illustration appears in Chapter 4 in how deliberative entrepreneur Zach Wahls successfully invites new reflection among people committed to rejecting LGBT equality. He does this in part by juxtaposing the idea of the "traditional family" defined exclusively in heterosexual terms with a narrative of traditional family as already incorporating same-sex couple headed households. Wahls's alternative reconstruction offered a reconstruction of the concept of a "traditional family" – one based on love, meaningful engagement, and mutual support, rather than on a traditional patriarchal nuclear structure. Wahls's revised social construction thus provided a cognitive solution to an inner conflict experienced by many people between respecting the equality of LGBT people on one hand, and preserving a traditionally valued identity with family on the other. In this example, the practice of social reconstruction resolved this inner contradiction by casting LGBT families within the fold of tradition. Related social fears could then diminish, and in turn, this new ease appears to have facilitated a breakthrough for many Americans in their reflection on the issue of LGBT equality. Without a Wahls-type social reconstruction of the definition of acceptable family, many Americans appear to have felt blocked from reconsidering the issue of LGBT

---

[26] This omission likely has its origins in a philosophical disagreement between Foucault and Habermas in which Foucauldian poststructuralism (one account among many of constructivism) was thought for a time to be entirely incompatible with Habermas's perspectives. In fact, even in his critiques, Habermas acknowledged considerable common ground between them, including perspectives on deep contingency and social formation of self and society made known by the linguistic turn. He stated, "Communicative reason too treats almost everything as contingent, even the condition of the emergence of its own linguistic medium." See "Unity of Reason the Diversity of Its Voices," (1992, 140). The extraordinary contributions of both Foucault and Habermas inform this work. In it, I provide analysis primarily in the terrain on which they found agreement.

equality by their need to preserve their existing identifications with traditional family life.[27]

Conversely, while the practice of social construction can solve the inner conundrums that stymie new reflection and deliberation, it is also past social constructions that likely generated those painful inherited conundrums in the first place. Sometimes those social constructions may have never served a peaceful purpose. In other cases, now-unhelpful social constructions were at one time useful, but have now lost their productive value. Consider for example contemporary feminist discourses regarding gender diversity. The prevailing feminist interpretation is that gender is always and entirely a social construction with no meaningful extra-social correlation to the physical body. This claim has historically served a feminist purpose by debunking the view that women are subordinate to men based on physical differences – also known as biological essentialism. But today declaring this level of irrelevance of embodiment in gender is implausible when considered in light of transgender experience.

The strikingly transformative effects of hormones on the body, the emotions, and the physical capacities of a transgender person in gender transition suggest that many factors that are coded masculine or feminine have embodied correlates that can shift as human embodiment transforms. Nevertheless, feminism is right to insist that hierarchical and patriarchal social constructs of binary gender difference have in fact contributed to cruel forms of gender subordination for millennia. This idea of a gender binary – which constrains both women and men – is not universal, but rather emerged as normative around the globe in modern times through the cross-cultural dispersal of discourse and practices of the gender binary via Western colonialism.[28] The colonial spread of socially constructed ideas of a gender binary often displaced other more nuanced cultural norms that acknowledged gender diversity. Numerous pre-colonial indigenous cultures around the globe, including, for example, many Native American tribes,

---

[27] For an example of discussion of such resistance on grounds of identity with traditional family involving Senator Rand Paul (R-KY), see Maria Santos, "Rand Paul Shrugs about 'Rethinking' Gay Marriage," *Red Alert Politics*, published electronically, October 3, 2014, www.redalertpolitics.com/2014/10/03/rand-paul-shrugs-rethinking-gay-marriage/.

[28] Anthony Thomas, *Middle Sexes: Redefining He and She*, HBO Documentary Films, 2005, 44:00–52:00.

previously had multiple gender categories that acknowledged gender diversity (Roscoe 2000; Nanda 1999). Many Eastern cultures today continue, as they have for millennia, to regard everyone as having both masculine and feminine dimensions to the self. In these traditions, both femininity and masculinity have qualities that are considered assets in life that confer benefits as well as a responsibility to balance masculine and feminine expression in the self as needed to produce harmony (rendered, for example, in ancient Chinese culture, with the interpenetrating concepts of yin and yang).

In keeping with these varied historical accounts of gender complexity and diversity, more contemporary alternative narrations of gender diversity have arisen. Among these alternative narratives of gender are some that draw on scientific accounts of sexual and gender diversity found in the animal kingdom (Roughgarden 2009). For instance, one possible – and scientifically plausible – description of both sexuality and gender diversity is that both are arrayed along a spectrum, as referred to previously in this chapter with regard to sexuality in the quotation from Mitchell Raphael. In such an account, each person's gender expression can be seen as situated along a spectrum from strong blends of both masculine and feminine toward the center of the spectrum, to weak blends with a dominance of masculine or feminine toward the ends of the spectrum in a manner that admits of varied gender expression in everyone from moment-to-moment, in and over time. How any particular person comes to express their gender as they do in any given instant is a product of both nature and nurture, embodiment, social construction, and choice, in which choice is made under conditions shaped by constraint, freedom, and specificity. Like sexual expression defined along a spectrum, the expression of gender on this narrative blends the physical *and* the social in ways that are so complex and intertwined as to be inseparable. On this alternative account, the nature versus nurture question dissolves in favor of recognition of the influence of nature *and* nurture, and choice. This turn makes definitive explanation of gender expression impossible. Moreover even if such explanations were feasible, they would remain irrelevant to the commitment that members of a society may have to implementing practices of gender equality.

It is possible to imagine this or other social constructions of gender as someday supplanting the now prevailing notions of a supposed gender binary. For deliberative democracy, the potential value of this social reconstruction is that *everyone* might be recognized as a unique expression of sexual and gender diversity. By extension, everyone would deserve equal treatment and respect even if and when their particular diversity has no special name or category. This matters because, as Kinsey noted, social prohibitions can operate to refuse the significance of embodiment and, as a result, distort or erase human diversity that would otherwise be expressed in the absence of moralizing judgments about simple facts of human embodiment and diversity. There is nothing necessary or predetermined in whether such alternative narratives come into social ascendancy, just as there was nothing necessary about Zach Wahls facilitating the expansion of the definition of traditional family to include same-sex marriage. What is clear, however, is that practices of social construction are ubiquitous and operate as both a cause and remedy for the cognitive obstacles to public deliberation within deliberative systems. As such, deliberative systems – and scholars of deliberative democracy – need to take social constructivism seriously in order to witness all of the working parts of the deliberative systems that may emerge through public self-organization.

Timing and Happenstance: Uncontrollable but Key Factors in Collective Will Formation

Third, if the construction of alternative social narratives can ease the inner contradictions of competing belief systems within the self (and society), then timing and happenstance beyond anyone's control nevertheless also shape how and at what juncture this easing may come about. Wahls's address to the Iowa Judiciary Committee made public in February 2011 was phenomenally influential both immediately and again that year when it went viral for a second time. But Wahls's message was hardly new. The idea that "love makes a family" has long circulated in US society but to much less effect. In 1999, for example, a book called *Love Makes a Family* provided a set of portraits of families with gay, lesbian, bisexual, or transgender members (Kaeser and Gillespie 1999). Yet in February 2011, Wahls's version of this message took hold in the US public imagination and deliberation in a new way. The exact reasons are surely impossible to determine for certain.

In Chapter 4, however, I proposed that the qualities of Wahls as a messenger and the open, problem-solving, and non-blaming framing of his message were largely responsible for his extraordinary reception. Wahls was socially similar to a mainstream audience and offered warm openings and safe entry points for considering the issues. But the timing of his address and happenstance elements of the surrounding circumstances also appear to have played a role. Specifically, Wahls spoke at a time when deliberation on LGBT equality was gaining stronger momentum toward increasing acceptance. This momentum seems to have been driven in part by a series of teen suicides that occurred from late summer through the fall of 2010. As tragic happenstances, these suicides were unpredictable. But they served as precipitating events for further reflection in the public domain. These events made the US public awaken to the potentially deadly consequences of casually or habitually used anti-gay slurs and anti-LGBT aggression. The teen suicides also inspired new cultural forms, such as the social media campaign "It Gets Better," which brought many well-known people to visibly proclaim the value of a life lived as a gay, lesbian, bisexual, or transgender person. The upshot is that while the tools for social reflection and deliberation may exist in a democratic society at any point, serendipitous occurrences and other factors of timing may shape when and how this existing potential takes form as widespread conscious reflection leading to a new collective will or to greater clarity on an existing public will.

Deliberative Democracy As Collective Will Formation: An Open-Ended Process

Theoretically, and also based on the LBGT case study offered in this work, I suggest fourth that deliberative democracy realized through deliberative systems can be seen as an open-ended exercise in collective will formation. This includes the conscious (re)crafting of both the self and society. This process is potentially always ongoing. At the time of this writing, the US majority in favor of LGBT equality is still growing and implementation of these new values and norms continues to unfold. As legal acceptance of same-sex marriage is now the law of the land, the focus of public consideration has shifted to a focus on modes of transgender equality and incorporation. New information, understanding, and inclusion of transgender experience, gender fluidity, and other forms of gender diversity are also reaching new heights and visibility.[29] Attention to intersex identity is still little discussed at the time of this writing, yet it may still become a future focus of public deliberation. Moreover, as the public deliberation evolves, so too do the attitudes of millions. Many who have posed the staunchest opposition to LGBT equality in the past – including numerous evangelical Christians – have already changed their minds on the issue or are considering how to adjust and reconcile their views with the new public consensus.[30] Relatedly some new deliberative entrepreneurs, such as Matthew Vines, are facilitating new reflection among the most resistant segments of the American population.[31] These transformations suggest that a deliberative system may facilitate ongoing deliberation on a complex topic area after a majority public will has been reached.

In addition, the deliberative process of collective will formation may include an almost infinite array of elements that help people to reflect on and, as needed, let go of conflicting belief systems and other tensions within themselves as part of deliberating upon issues of common concern. Examples abound in the LGBT case of relevant events or statements that are seemingly small, but when circulated in a large-scale deliberative system have large consequences. The use of an anti-gay slur in a basketball game and the rejection of a lesbian mother from a role in Cub Scout leadership are examples. But influential too is the visible use of speech and action to provide support and comfort to others who suffer the pain of such rejecting actions. John Amaechi, for example describes the teenage basketball fan who feels crushed by the use of an anti-gay slur by his hero Kobe Bryant. The teenager feels he has no

---

[29] For mainstream coverage of Australian model Ruby Rose coming out as gender fluid in a short film entitled "Break Free," see Rachel McRady, "Ruby Rose Destroys Gender Roles, Transforms From Female Ideal to Male Ideal in a Short Film 'Break Free,'" *US Weekly*, published electronically, June 17, 2015, www .usmagazine.com/celebrity-news/news/ruby-rose-break-free-film-gender-roles-2015176/.

[30] Jim Hinch, "Evangelicals Are Changing Their Minds on Gay Marriage: And the Bible Isn't Getting in Their Way," *Politico Magazine*, published electronically, July 7, 2014, www.politico.com/magazine/story/2014/07/evangelicals-gay-marriage-108608.html#.VZGqcqZQiX0. But also, Michael Paulson, "With Same-Sex Decision, Evangelical Churches Address New Reality," *The New York Times*, published electronically, June 28, 2015, www.nytimes .com/2015/06/29/us/with-same-sex-decision-evangelical-churches-address-new -reality.html.

[31] Religion & Ethics NewsWeekly, "Matthew Vines on God and the Gay Christian," *YouTube*, Video, 05:45, posted on November 7, 2014, www .youtube.com/watch?v=IGWc2ZbjxZY.

voice, and reaches out to John Amaechi for help. Through Amaechi's effort, the boy's story and pain are told not only to Bryant for his reflection, but to the world. Amaechi states:

I think that is what this young man who contacted me from LA wanted. He wanted the antidote [to the anti-gay slur used by his basketball hero Kobe Bryant]. And then he wanted me to spread it around. I was very fortunate to have an education in words from my mother in how to use them therapeutically.

And what you suddenly realize [when you try this] is the amazing power of mindfully used words. Of staying in the moment and using the right words at the right time and you suddenly realize it's kind of magic. And although people can be careless and thoughtless and say those words—those … [hateful words]—but the fact is that we, if we are mindful and in the moment, we can say the right thing that is the antidote to that.

Moreover, Amaechi points out that this is not a rare skill.

We can all do it. Although the results can feel like magic, there is nothing mystical about the skills. We can learn them, we can do them, and half of them is just being there in the moment.[32]

Amaechi's words illustrate the idea that deliberative democratization can take many forms. Moreover, the most important activity of opening up a space of reflection and greater peace for others struggling with matters of common concern is always an option at hand for everyone. The seemingly small everyday activities of mindful attention to the worries of others are, this LGBT case study suggests, just as important in the formation and growth of a deliberative system as the viral topical video, or the work of a deliberative entrepreneur who has a worldwide audience.

No Necessary Outcomes: Deliberative Results Are Matters of Choice and Will

Finally, and as sketched in Chapter 1, there is no guarantee that any specific deliberation will render a just decision or course of action as the collective will. However, observationally, despite many failures,

---

[32] DiversityInc, "John Amaechi: Hate Speech Goes Way Beyond the N- and F-Words," *YouTube*, Video, 31:24, posted on November 15, 2011, www.youtube.com/watch?v=rLteJkaoGnU.

evidence is abundant that, over time, humanity has generally become more peaceful, more caring of others, and more accepting of difference in social life (Pinker 2011). This has been so especially among democratic nations in what has been often called "the democratic peace." It therefore may be true, as Martin Luther King Jr. once quoted, that "the arc of the moral universe is long, but it bends toward justice." [33] If so, then while any single public deliberation might have unjust results, over time humanity appears to be choosing to live in greater peace, justice, and harmony. Nevertheless, as deliberative democracy can be seen as part of a revised – and heretofore failing – Enlightenment project, nothing is certain. Human history confirms moreover that back steps toward injustice and discord often punctuate its long-term movement toward peace and justice.

Moreover, as I stressed in Chapter 4 and previously in this chapter, cognitive obstacles to public deliberation can and will prevail if people do not choose to ultimately acknowledge those obstacles and strive to face and overcome them both individually and collectively. At a bird's-eye view, the process of deliberation and collective will formation sounds fun and easy – talking together to consciously decide which things most benefit the whole and which elements to drop that no longer serve the common good. But at the ground level, deliberation is challenging and may often require looking into the self and society at things that may be uncomfortable to face, much less transform. Cognitive scientists in various fields remind us that conscious thought is "slow effortful work" (Kahneman 2011). Overall, and as already indicated, there is nothing necessary about the emergence of deliberative systems or the outcomes that may be produced through them. Similarly, as a corollary, there is nothing necessary about whether members of any given democratic public will actually choose to do the work – including the work of self-examination – that deliberative systems require of us all.

This is not to suggest, however, that the US deliberation on LGBT equality accomplished via a deliberative system appears to have been a boring, time-consuming grind. On the contrary, the evidence

[33] February 8, 1958, *The Gospel Messenger, Out of the Long Night* by Martin Luther King, Jr., Start Page 3, Quote Page 14, Column 1, Official Organ of the Church of the Brethren, Published weekly by the General Brotherhood Board, Elgin, Illinois. Quote attributed first to Theodore Parker, *Ten Sermons of Religion* (Boston: Crosby, Nichols, and Company, 1853).

presented in the case study suggests that the creative aspects of a deliberative system can make the work of public deliberation fun and comparatively brief, albeit not necessarily easy. It takes, for example, three minutes to listen to Zach Wahls's address, to read a blog, or to view a video of a shooting of a US Black youth by police, or to examine images of an injured child killed or hurt in an armed conflict or refugee crisis elsewhere around the globe.[34] The LGBT case study presented here suggests that at a practical everyday level, the work of the deliberative process can be picked up and put down as needed – and thus straightforwardly integrated into daily life – and yet still produce important results at both individual and collective levels. Nevertheless, the fact remains that there is no guarantee that people will choose to do the cognitive work and self-reflection that deliberative democracy requires of everyone. If they do choose to engage in public deliberation, then they would also need to make at least three nested choices.

The three interconnected choices to be made are: (1) Will people choose to do the work of paying attention in the deliberative process and taking part in it (i.e. *provide conscious engagement*)?, (2) Will people choose to do the sometimes challenging work of grappling with collective problems that may trigger internalized fears, anxieties, and the pain of conflicting inner belief systems, and to be open to personal and collective change in the process of collective deliberation (i.e. *be open to the work of changing society and the self*)?, and (3) Will people choose to let go of the collective illusion that received belief systems are necessary and durable, and thus take the leap of faith that they are created by society in an ongoing basis and therefore can be recreated on different terms by the collective at any time (i.e. *accepting and deploying the central insights of the linguistic turn*)? Overall, the general answer to these questions may be an obvious yes. But at the level of daily activity, the answer to these questions in relation to any specific hot-button issue of common concern that might be democratized is less certain. All three of these choices require active and sometimes painful effort that some people in a democracy may not be willing to exert.

---

[34] "How Omran Daqneesh, 5, Became a Symbol of Aleppo's suffering," www.nytimes.com/2016/08/19/world/middleeast/omran-daqneesh-syria-aleppo.html?_r=0.

Providing Conscious Engagement: It is simpler at some level, and much less work, to continue living through internalized social scripts automatically triggered by what is passing in the moment. The physical system of automaticity is embodied and serves an important purpose – to conserve time and energy. Some estimates are that people are functioning on "autopilot" – literally without conscious awareness, 80 to 90 percent of the time (Banaji and Greenwald 2013, 61). The cost of this habitual use of automaticity is that "choices" made unconsciously may not be the wisest ones for the individual or for the collective. Moreover, as I have argued at length elsewhere, widespread automaticity in moments of discretion at home, at work, or in the street – discretion wielded unconsciously for example by teachers, bankers, or law enforcement personnel – is a moment in which inherited social scripts of social hierarchy and inequity can be reiterated again from moment-to-moment, thereby persisting in time even when the society as a whole endorses and desires greater equality (Barvosa 2008, 207–229). It is through *conscious* activity that people can change these scripts from one moment to the next. But while chronically operating through automaticity has considerable risks, the alternative of conscious engagement is more work. It is conceivable that people will in the future choose on the whole to forego the effort that deliberative systems and deliberative democracy would demand of all members of the society.

Opening to Change in the Self and Society: It is also possible that people will forgo dealing with the harder social questions. For example, on the current topic of police officers involved in shootings of Black men and boys, at the time of this writing, in the US white members of society are far less likely to discuss racial issues on social media than Blacks.[35] This is consistent with the rise of a social movement (e.g. Black Lives Matter) in which conversations are often largely limited to those who identify with and belong to a movement community. But this pattern of limitation is not conducive to the emergence of a large-scale deliberative system on racial disparities in the use of deadly force by police. To grapple with this question in a large-scale deliberation, it would be necessary for many more people to reconsider the problem of

---

[35] Gene Demby, "On Social Media, As In Life, White People Are Always Less Likely to Talk About Race," *NPR*, August 18, 2016. www.npr.org/sections/co deswitch/2016/08/18/490340600/on-social-media-as-in-real-life-white-people-are-way-less-likely-to-talk-about-r.

racial hierarchy that has existed in the US in different ways since before its founding. The race problem in the US, however, activates collective trauma, denial, anger, frustration, anxiety, or pain on all sides. The model of deliberative system formation offered in this work suggests that these anxieties – which are the "inner reflections of outer conflict" – would need to be engaged and resolved as a deliberative system emerged to focus on the problem of racial inequity. As in the LGBT case, a successful deliberation that fostered social change would also involve, and likely require, healing and/or growth in some form within many if not all members of the polity. Will people be willing to further lighten their own load of worn-out belief systems in favor of new ones created and endorsed by the collective? The LGBT case suggests that many may choose to do so, but this is not yet clear on other topics.

Similarly regarding the potential deliberation topic of economic inequality, the negative effects of economic inequality for families are well documented. Yet simultaneously many, if not most, opinion polls show the US public reports that all is well for them financially, and they are optimistic.[36] The disjuncture between these two facts presents a similar kind of "paradox" as the long-term anomalies bifurcating social from legal equality in the LGBT-related Gallup polls. In the case of economic inequality, these contradictory findings may reflect cognitive denial, dissociated anxiety, triggered flight or freeze responses associated with collective or individual trauma, or something else unknown. In addition, recent studies indicate that some segments of the population affected by extreme economic inequality – especially white middle-aged men without higher education – are experiencing rapidly rising death rates from drugs, alcohol, and suicide.[37] These

---

[36] Pew Charitable Trust, "Report: The Precarious State of Family Balance Sheets," January 29, 2015, www.pewtrusts.org/en/research-and-analysis/reports/2015/01/the-precarious-state-of-family-balance-sheets; DeLeire and Lopoo, *Family Structure and the Economic Mobility of Children*; Stilwell, "Ready for a Financial Shock? Most Americans Aren't"; JP Morgan Chase & Co. Institute, "Weathering Volatility." See also Press Release, "Pew Survey Shows Americans' Financial Worries Cloud Optimism," *The PEW Charitable Trusts*, published electronically, March 5, 2015, www.pewtrusts.org/en/about/news-room/press-releases/2015/02/26/pew-survey-shows-americans-financial-worries-cloud-optimism.

[37] Gina Kolata, "Death Rates Rising for Middle-Aged White Americans, Study Finds," www.nytimes.com/2015/11/03/health/death-rates-rising-for-middle-aged-white-americans-study-finds.html.

results are being attributed in part to downward mobility, unattended health problems, and scripts of masculinity that may foreclose reaching out for alternative assistance. Together these elements plausibly suggest that there is a striking tendency among many if not most Americans *not* to acknowledge the problems caused by economic inequality, much less grapple with it usefully in the company of other members of US society. This is a choice, and it may well be the case that members of the US public will continue to choose not to engage in collective will formation on the issue of economic inequality even if it would be possible to do so through the formation of a deliberative system.

Finally, in regard to *Accepting and Deploying the Central Insights of the Linguistic Turn,* the vision of realpolitik in American politics is such that most people – including most political scientists – see the social and political status quo as virtually immovable based on the necessary qualities of life that shape it. The common perspective is that the status quo is necessary: "it is simply the way it is." But the linguistic turn indicates that any and all aspects of a status quo are ultimately established through social conventions. When those conventions shift, so too does the status quo. The idea that prevailing norms and practices are fundamental and necessarily enduring is therefore an illusion (itself the product of a constructed narration). Cultures at all levels are creations of humanity. At the point that humanity chooses to create its cultures differently it may do so at any time. Just like the "reality" TV shows so common in popular television, there is nothing ultimately real about them – the reality they portray is concocted, ever transformable through the creative process of human beings. Yet the portrayal of such faux reality has the power to sustain the illusion of permanence/necessity on an indefinite basis to the extent that people continue to accept and endorse that convention and the illusion of permanence it projects.

The power of the illusion of the permanence and necessity of any social practice perhaps explains why the linguistic turn is so difficult for scholars to embrace beyond a superficial level. Knowledge of the linguistic turn has existed in many different forms and across disciplines since the mid-twentieth century (Barvosa 2008). Yet the implications of this insight for deliberative democracy are still little attended to by scholars of deliberative democracy. Moreover, the insights of the linguistic turn are effectively unheard of to most members of the mainstream public, at least in US society. Yet as Jürgen Habermas has pointed out, the linguistic turn dramatically changes what we understand the process of reasoning to be. Logically, it also transforms how we understand what human beings, individually and collectively, are capable of achieving in social and political life using the instruments of social construction, sustained conscious thought, and their voice. After all, believing that expressions of public opinion are powerless to remake social life is itself a socially constructed belief system that sustains the status quo. As former US Representative Barney Frank (discussed in Chapter 2 as a deliberative entrepreneur) has stated: "As influential as money has become [in American democracy], it can be countered by the effective mobilization of public opinion ... the claim that big money is politically invincible is especially self-defeating" (Frank 2015). If Barney Frank is correct, then there is hope for meaningful public empowerment even under currently strained conditions. Moreover, it may be especially important to release the self-defeating pessimism Frank identifies in light of the potential power of a deliberative system to serve as a vehicle of collective will formation and implementation. As such, whether people will choose to accept and apply the principles and implications of the linguistic turn is an open question. But that question is at the core of whether deliberative systems will become a useful means for establishing the common will and realizing it in material life.

Conclusion

Large-Scale Deliberative Democracy: Possible If Chosen

Even the decentered society cannot do without the reference point provided by the projected unity of an inter-subjectively formed common will.[1]

—*Jürgen Habermas*

Today American democracy has reached a level of polarization and rancor that has left most Americans, many scholars, and other observers around the world feeling concern, and sometimes despair, about the future of American democracy and its global influence. In this context, I have offered in this book a theoretical model and evidence from an illustrative case study that at long last, US democracy could be materially transformed into a deliberative democracy. In such a deliberative democracy, political decision-making centers on the voices and will of a democratic public that is engaged in collective discussion and conscious reflection in order to generate a collective will regarding how they choose to live in common on specific issues.

If the theoretical model and illustrative case study offered here are persuasive, then the developments and opportunities they describe are perhaps most likely to be welcomed by scholars of democracy. For several decades, theorists of deliberative democracy – including especially by Jürgen Habermas, Jane Mansbridge, Seyla Benhabib, Robert Goodin, and many others – have argued that the next potential phase in the evolution of democracy would be the emergence of deliberative democracy. In this possible democratic development, the central work of collective self-governance shifts to making public choice through large-scale communication. Deliberative democracy has been thus envisioned as a conversation-based process in which public reason and reflection facilitate the development of a guiding public will.

---

[1] Jürgen Habermas, "The Unity of Reason in the Diversity of Its Voices," in *Post Metaphysical Thinking: Philosophical Essays*, trans. William Mark Hohengarten (Cambridge: MIT Press, 1992), 141.

Once formed through deliberative practice, this collective will can then be implemented in law and public policy through existing structured means. In addition to theory development, during the decades in which deliberative democracy has been theorized, significant empirical experimental research – such as that by James Fishkin, John Gastil, John Dryzek, John Parkinson, Nicholas Pidgeon, and many others – has been conducted examining diverse deliberative practices and policy deliberation protocols, seeking in their research for the means by which to implement deliberative democracy. While these empirical studies have been very fruitful, they have, with some exceptions, focused primarily on small-scale deliberative practices.

Consequently, thus far in both theory building and in empirical research, the means by which a large-scale, nationwide, public deliberation could be achieved in practice have remained unknown. Over time, many critics of deliberative democracy have understandably concluded – and many of its proponents sometimes despaired – that deliberative democracy is an enticing ideal, but one that can never be realized in practice, particularly on a large scale. In response to this skepticism regarding the problem of scale, a team of democratic theorists recently proposed that large-scale, informal deliberative systems comprised of many elements already within society may offer the solution to this problem of scale (Mansbridge et al. 2012). Although welcomed enthusiastically by many, this proposal is also theoretical in character, and does not featuring a clear path to practical implementation. Acknowledging this, Mansbridge et al. have also called for a template identifying the conditions necessary for a deliberative system to function in everyday life.

In this book, I have responded to this call for a theoretical model of the empirical practices and conditions that could foster the growth and effective function of a large-scale deliberative system as a vehicle for deliberative democracy. In this work, I offered a theoretical model in which I have suggested a range of concepts, relationships, and conditions that appear to be necessary for the effective emergence, growth, and practical operation of a large-scale deliberative system. In addition, based on an exploratory data analysis, I offered an illustrative case study, in which I have proposed that the US public has already succeeded in creating one example of a large, nationwide, deliberative system on the topic of LGBT equality. This deliberative system arose in the form of an informal, self-assembled, nationwide public engagement that was generated through social network–based processes of public communication and reflection observable in the US from early 1987 to at least mid-2015 and beyond. In this time period, changes in the availability and social uptake of new communication technologies and social media platforms visibly accelerated deliberative activity between 2006 and 2015. I have further suggested that through this deliberative system, the US public deliberated on the question: *Should LGBT people be accepted and integrated into mainstream US society on an equal basis, and if so, how?* As described in the introductory chapter, this question, and the case study of public engagement on LGBT equality, is derived from an exploratory theoretical analysis of a qualitative data set of eight thousand pieces of collected material reflecting events, speech acts, discourses, and structural transformations that took place in the 28-year time period of the case study. This collection of research materials is not exhaustive, but rather represents a diverse sampling of elements that reflect the evolution of public thought on LGBT equality in the US over time.

Through this empirical case study of US public engagement on LGBT equality, I have traced and theorized how the US public came to answer "yes" to the question of common concern in the LGBT case, and how it has proceeded to identify and advance the terms and content of LGBT equality. These terms include, but are not limited to, the equal social and legal acceptance of same-sex marriage, the redefinition of conventional family life to incorporate LGBT relationships and family ties, the rejection of religious exceptions to the equal treatment of LGBT in commerce, and slow movement toward the equal incorporation of transgender personnel in the US military. I have proposed that this US deliberative system is still in effect at the time of this writing and continues to facilitate deliberation on interrelated issues of sexual and gender diversity, and to serve as a vehicle for the implementation of the public will on LGBT equality, especially on implementation of equal rights for the US transgender minority. In the remainder of this concluding chapter, I briefly summarize the theoretical model for the empirical emergence, growth, and function of a deliberative system as an instrument of deliberative democracy. In this chapter, I also sketch what this model and accompanying case study of a deliberative system might suggest for future research. Finally, because this research is based on exploratory data analysis, the theory and concepts offered here can be produced, but not yet fully confirmed, using the materials reviewed in this case study. Many open questions thus remain and this concluding chapter closes with a call for additional research.

What Has Been Learned?

This practical model of deliberative system formation includes all of the major functions of deliberative systems – i.e. democratic, epistemic, and moral – theorized by Jane Mansbridge and her colleagues (2012). Yet as also anticipated by Mansbridge et al., these functions are not in themselves sufficient to produce an operative deliberative system. I have proposed in this work that deliberative systems in practice require additional elements and conditions to support their growth and function. Consequently, the theoretical model of deliberative system formation offered here contains a range of diverse components. These components contribute to the system independently, but they are also interrelated and together they comprise the underlying mechanisms, cognitive conditions, and social infrastructure at work in the self-assembly of the deliberative system. These diverse elements are illustrated in the LGBT case study.

Specifically, and as detailed in the case study chapters and the theoretical overview in Chapter 1, the overall constitutive components of deliberative system formation as modeled here include: (1) the inner reflection of individuals, (2) three *deliberative catalysts*, (3) the existing *social networks* through which deliberative materials flow, (4) seven microsteps though which the deliberative social networks are self-assembled by the public, and (5) the communication practices used to aid the circumvention or *overcoming of three cognitive obstacles* including implicit bias, identity threat, and topic-related fears, as well as hidden quandaries of unspoken fears and anxieties that undermine reflection on a given topic. (A fourth potential cognitive obstacle to deliberation of post-traumatic fear arising from collective or individual trauma is also identified in Chapter 1, but is not illustrated or theorized further in the case study provided in this book). Of these five factors, the cognitive obstacles to deliberation are commonplace, but were also demonstrably overcome or circumvented in many instances discussed in the LGBT case study. I have argued in this work therefore, that these cognitive obstacles can be intentionally transcended through processes that – as detailed in case study Chapters 4 and 5 – also often involve personal transformation, growth and healing on the part of members of the public in ways beneficial to all. Nevertheless, and as theorized and illustrated through empirical examples in Chapter 5, the overcoming of common cognitive obstacles to deliberative practice is also conditioned by the vagaries of timing, public readiness, and the influences of happenstance events that may provide impetus to or conversely diminish the momentum of deliberative activity.

A Theoretical Model Illustrated: Underlying Mechanisms of Deliberative System Formation

As already generally observed in this chapter, the model of a deliberative system sketched in this book indicates that in practice deliberate systems emerge as a collectively self-assembled, large-scale, issue-bounded, deliberative system created by the members of the general public themselves. The public contributors involved in this self-assembly process include many that are already visible in society and have been previously identified by other theorists of deliberative systems as likely to take part. These elements include all parties articulating reasons to embrace or abandon specific conventional or proposed norms and practices, including the state at all levels, the media (i.e. mass, niche, and social media), commercial enterprises of market economy, organizations of civil society (e.g. churches, schools, social groups, and so on), sources of independent knowledge production (e.g. universities, think tanks), social movement groups, and various subgroups of the general public including those of the many public domains that represent overlapping or divided subgroups within the general public as a whole. In addition, and as theorized by Robert Goodin, individual reflection – which often occurs in private – is the primary and indispensible underlying process by which public deliberation proceeds. I have argued in preceding chapters that the LGBT case provides empirical insights and support for Goodin's articulation of how individual deliberation within can solve much of the problem of scale so far faced by scholars of deliberative democracy (2003).

Moreover, as illustrated in Chapter 3, the public self-assembly of a deliberative system depends upon existing social networks, and increasingly on the communication technologies and applications (e.g. smartphones and social media platforms) that now permeate many networked societies. Social networks have historically been a basis for public communication, mutual engagement, and collective self-organization. Yet as I have argued in this work, the epochal shift of the information age and the societal change that it has prompted now combine to make large-scale, public deliberation materially possible. Specifically, as many societies have incorporated technological change, communication technologies, and information systems, these elements now dramatically enhance the capacity for existing social networks to serve as the source and infrastructure of large-scale public deliberation. In other words, just as new information technologies have enabled the rise of networked social movements as described by Manuel Castells (2012), these same elements also make possible the rise of networked deliberative systems. Like networked social movements that are self-organized using social media and new communication technologies, deliberative systems too can now emerge in which democratic publics can self-organize to reflect on matters of common concern. As I have argued in this work, however, technological innovation and the presence of social networks alone cannot produce democratic engagement. Rather, other conditions and mechanisms are also required, such as relevant catalysts, distinct social processes of network self-assembly, as well as techniques for the circumvention of specific cognitive obstacles that help participants to willingly become open to possible change in themselves and in society.

Deliberative Catalysts as Mechanisms and Conditions: As sketched in Chapter 1, and further elaborated in Chapter 2, at least three catalysts are needed to initiate the process of deliberative system growth as it has been modeled in this book. I have labeled these: (1) *deliberative entrepreneurs*, (2) *deliberative packages*, and (3) *precipitating events*, the third of which triggers by happenstance new rounds of deliberation. Among these, deliberative entrepreneurs are one of the most important ingredients, but they are also potentially one of the least likely of the catalysts to be readily witnessed. Deliberative entrepreneurs are defined in this work as those who actively invite and facilitate public reflection through their words and actions. In so doing, deliberative entrepreneurs take it upon themselves to raise issues of contestation in open and generative ways that welcome *all* to take part in new reflection without levying judgment on whatever points of view the invitees now hold. Deliberative entrepreneurs generally juxtapose – and thus place into cognitive tension – competing ideas to evoke conscious reflection and deliberation on a given topic. In this, deliberative entrepreneurs do not demand or urge a particular choice upon listeners (although their own views and preferences may be well known). Instead, as illustrated in the LGBT case study, deliberative entrepreneurs explicitly encourage members of the public to *think for themselves* about the competing ideas that they have presented for deliberation. As detailed in Chapter 1, unlike movement advocates who often press their point by challenging their perceived opponents, deliberative entrepreneurs decline to establish an us-versus-them boundary among members of society who disagree, instead regarding all members of a society as an interconnected whole facing a common problem. They thus also avoid statements of blame or shame, accepting all parties while also urging *thoughtful* reconsideration on the matter under public review as a means of collective problem solving.

The materials analyzed here in the LGBT case study affirm that, in general, each deliberative entrepreneur operated largely within a single domain of American social life in which they are already known, and/or had a history of activity and ties. That is, they operated first in the domains in which their life is centered. The influence of deliberative entrepreneurs has been illustrated in this work through stories of the contributions of a range of different individuals in various social domains. Examples of deliberative entrepreneurship narrated in this work include those in electoral politics (Barney Frank), religious groups (Bishops Gene Robinson and John Shelby Spong), the entertainment industry (Ellen DeGeneres and Daniel Karslake), professional basketball (John Amaechi and Rick Welts), and youth organizations (Zach Wahls), among others. In addition, some deliberative entrepreneurs featured in this work have multiple identities and lives that span across often divided social domains. As such, some of these deliberative entrepreneurs operated at the intersection of two or more social domains. As early as 1989, for example, endocrinologist Pernessa Seele bridged the domains of medicine and religion, urging leaders of African American churches in Harlem to deliberate anew on compassionate approaches to the care of those afflicted with AIDS. In time, Seele's deliberative work extended globally to reach denominations worldwide.

In addition to the concept of deliberative entrepreneurs, the second deliberative catalyst described in this proposed model has been that of deliberative packages. Deliberative packages have been defined as cultural products of any kind (e.g. films, songs, interviews, media reports, blog posts, including some relevant personal experiences, etc.) that offer preassembled collections of materials that evenhandedly juxtapose competing ideas, and supply relevant and reliable stories, data, or concepts that can usefully inform deliberation on a topic under public consideration. Examples drawn from the LGBT case include a wide array of materials including the documentary film *For the Bible Tells Me So* written and produced by Daniel Karslake, as well as countless other pieces. As highlighted especially in Chapter 3, deliberative packages often provide personal narratives or scenarios that illustrate how the issue being deliberated already influences – or might come to influence – the daily lives of real people. In the examples in this case study, some deliberative entrepreneurs constructed their own deliberative packages; others used preexisting deliberative packages, or did both in order to prompt public reflection. In all cases, however, and for reasons elaborated at length in Chapter 4, in order to be effective in prompting the conscious reflection necessary to deliberation, deliberative packages must juxtapose competing ideas so as to provide the audience with the opportunity to undergo relevant cognitive load that can help people to sidestep or overcome the three common cognitive obstacles to conscious reflection and deliberation described in Chapter 4.

Lastly, the third deliberative catalyst modeled in this work has been that of precipitating events. Precipitating events are unexpected, happenstance occurrences, including relevant personal experiences, that are related to the issue under public deliberation and that provide new impetus to the activity of personal and/or collective deliberation on that topic. As has been highlighted with examples in Chapters 2 and 3, precipitating events often serve as flashpoints for deliberation by members of the public. In the LGBT case study, examples have included a series of teen suicides among LGBT youth in the summer and fall of 2010, and the removal of a lesbian mother from serving as the den mother for her son's Cub Scout troop in 2012. In addition, significant structural changes such as the passage of relevant state or local laws or major court rulings also serve as precipitating events. In these and other descriptive examples presented in this work, precipitating events triggered new flurries of public discussion. They provided not only examples that offered food for thought but a renewed flow of deliberative materials for public reflection through social networks. As I have theorized throughout this book, stimulating the flow of invitations to deliberate and deliberative materials through existing or emerging social networks is a primary mechanism of the public self-assembly of deliberative systems.

Deliberative System Growth to Large-Scale Through Seven Microsteps and Three Growth Phases: In the model and case study presented in previous chapters, I have proposed that in practice large-scale deliberative systems grow as the influence of deliberative catalysts flows through existing or new social networks. In everyday life, the catalyzing flow of deliberative materials through social networks often occurs hand-to-hand or via social media. As deliberative catalysts circulate, they present individuals and groups with opportunities and ready-made materials for reflection on the matter under consideration in the deliberative system. By extension, in this practical model, deliberative systems emerge and grow only to the extent that seven different microsteps occur widely enough to establish and spread deliberative activity in daily life, including the formation of deliberative social feedback loops. These seven microsteps are thus the ground-level means by which members of the general public self-assemble the deliberative system. That deliberative system is, in effect, a social network of people who are considering a specific public issue using the materials for reflection that are traveling through their self-assembled deliberative networks. The larger the deliberative network grows, the larger the scale of the deliberation. Of the seven microsteps of public self-assembly enumerated in Chapters 1 and 3, step seven is oriented toward the implementation of the public will in law and policy if and when a consensus collective will has been formed using the first six microsteps.

These seven microsteps of deliberative system formation are: (1) the inspiration of new incidents of deliberative entrepreneurship, (2) engagement in creating and/or circulating deliberative packages, (3) the acceptance of invitations to deliberate, and engagement in personal reflection or collective deliberation, (4) passing on news of one's in-progress deliberation in social networks, including describing one's reasoning or the deliberative materials being used, (5) expression of post-deliberation views to others through speech-and decision-consistent *actions*, (6) facilitating the flow of announcements of post-deliberative decisions through social networks, thereby encouraging others to reflect on the matter, and also announce their own considered views, and (7) in the case of the emergence of a consensus public opinion, step seven involves remaining attuned to the issue and acting to express the new (or clarified) public will in ways that can be recognized and applied by policymakers, especially by forcefully issuing public objections to polices that contravene the collective will in a "siegelike manner" that withholds democratic legitimacy from lawmaking that disregards the public will. In this proposed model, these microsteps (particularly the first six) need not happen in linear sequence. On the contrary, millions of people may be at different steps and stages of the deliberation on a topic at different times. Nonetheless, as illustrated in case study Chapters 3 and 4, social network dynamics are such that even seemingly small contributions to deliberative activity in any of these steps can significantly increase the growth and extent of the deliberative system overall.

In addition, as a deliberative system is publicly self-assembled through these seven microsteps of deliberative system formation, the system can grow to a large scale through three growth phases. Growth to the national scale is *not* inevitable and may stall or never begin if the flow of deliberative materials falters or if public practice of the assembly microsteps is limited across social networks. However, the LGBT case illustrates how successful system growth to a large, nationwide, scale can occur. This growth is modeled as having three phases from, (a) *person-centered deliberative networks*, to (b) *bounded domain-specific deliberative networks*, and finally to (c) open deliberative networks that span across various social domains and can reach national (and potentially international) scale. Drawing from social network science, as described in Chapters 1 and 3, person-centered networks begin with a person as a central node in a social network in which they invite and aim to foster deliberation. As I have illustrated with examples from the LGBT case study, such deliberative entrepreneurship often inspires others to engage in similar activity, thereby creating more sources of circulating invitations to deliberation such that deliberative entrepreneurs take up central places (i.e. have the most direct and indirect ties) in self-initiated deliberative social networks.

If the microstep of inspiring new deliberative entrepreneurship reaches sufficient levels, a deliberative system may grow beyond the person-centered network phase to take the form of a large domain-specific bounded network. Within domain-specific bounded networks, the deliberative materials that circulate are suited to the specificities of a given social domain, and in time, the spread of deliberative materials and practice may come to saturate an entire social domain. An example of this amplification and expansion process is illustrated in Chapter 2 with the person-centered social network of Episcopal Bishop V. Gene Robinson. In this instance, deliberation spread from an initial choice on LGBT equality within a local faith community in New Hampshire, to grow exponentially throughout the entire social domain, resulting in time in deliberation on LGBT equality in the entire US Episcopal Church, which ultimately endorsed and implemented LGBT equality in its practices. This domain-specific bounded network, in turn, had deliberative influence internationally, reverberating throughout the worldwide Anglican Communion.

Likewise, in Chapter 3 I have illustrated domain-specific deliberative system growth through an example of the US professional basketball association, the NBA. The NBA represents the special case of a relatively close knit or cohesive social network that can be more impervious to external influence from deliberations in other social domains. In this illustrative example of the model, the convergence of precipitating events, deliberative packages, and deliberative entrepreneurship in 2011 suddenly catalyzed extensive deliberation on the antigay atmosphere within the NBA – which had been until that point closed to the deliberations on LGBT equality that had taken place across US society. As illustrated with the case of the NBA and the Boy Scouts of America, however, if deliberation can be catalyzed from *within* a cohesive social domain itself, then that deliberation is likely to proceed rapidly because the flow of materials is extensive in such densely networked groups.

In the third phase of deliberative system growth, deliberative networks that saturate specific social domains begin to spread across the boundaries of other social domains and may eventually grow into what social network scientists call an open network. In this proposed model of deliberative system formation, this third phase of system growth involves the development of an open deliberative network in which deliberative materials – including the invitations and opportunities offered by deliberative entrepreneurs – flow freely throughout a wide and growing social network that spans across multiple social domains over time. Increasingly as this stage, anyone can join the deliberation from virtually any point in the society. In so doing, they may also link their own social networks into the deliberative system at will. If this process of deliberative network expansion proceeds far enough, then the deliberative system reaches a national scale in the form of network saturation across all social domains. At this large-scale national level, virtually everyone has been exposed to the question under consideration, is familiar at some level with the issues, and the vast majority have considered and formulated their own views based on materials that have flowed their way, or they are in the process of doing so. Based on exploratory data analysis, I have proposed that the US public discussion of LGBT equality is an example of this kind of large-scale, nationwide deliberation, and thus provides an illustrative example of a large-scale, open network, deliberative system in action.

In addition, in the model offered here, I propose that this third phase of large-scale deliberative system growth also opens the potential for a deliberative system to serve as an ongoing instrument of implementation of any collective will that may be formed (or clarified) through the deliberative process. As theorized by Jürgen Habermas, the capacity of a deliberative system to implement the collective will does not arise from the supplanting of governing bureaucracies. Rather, communicative power exists in the intense public pressure that can be applied in a "'siegelike' manner" by the public through its deliberative networks. I have illustrated the practical implementation power of deliberative systems in Chapter 3 with examples drawn from the LGBT case. This is especially visible in the public pressure applied to government agencies that have defied the new public consensus regarding LGBT equality. An illustration featured in Chapter 3 is the 2015 seven-day public siege on the state of Indiana that caused it to revise a religious freedom bill that would have otherwise authorized businesses to deny services to LGBT people on religious grounds.

Overcoming Cognitive Obstacles to Deliberation in Deliberative System Growth: In addition to the role of individual reflection, deliberative catalysts, and social networks, I have suggested in the proposed model that deliberative system formation requires that steps are taken to help circumvent or overcome at least three cognitive obstacles that can block personal reflection and prevent or limit the flow of deliberative materials through existing social networks. These cognitive obstacles exist at the individual level, but when their effects are widespread, they can also shape collective social norms and practices (Barvosa 2008, 208–221). These three cognitive obstacles are: inattention-based *implicit bias* (also known as unconscious bias*), *identity threat* (defined as perceived threat to a treasured sense of self), and the activation of *fear*, including relevant social fears such as fear (conscious or subconscious) of exclusion, marginalization, or loss of social belonging or status. The third of these also includes the special obstacle of post-traumatic fear, which is defined in Chapter 1 but is not further discussed in the case study. Together approaches to overcoming all three of these obstacles are defined and analyzed in detail in Chapters 4 and 5 through the LGBT case study.

Overall, however, all of these cognitive obstacles to deliberative system formation involve some aspect of the inner multiplicity of the self, either in its physical form of various systems of perception (i.e. "autopilot" systems, and emergency self-defense systems that involve automatized activation of encoded scripts) or in the multiplicity of socially imprinted materials that form the substantive content of the self and subjectivity as embodied consciousness. The cognitive obstacles discussed in this model involve those aspects of human embodiment that can, when activated, override the immediate capacity for conscious reasoning in a given moment, and that perform this override function outside of our conscious awareness. In other words, when they are activated, these obstacles are such that systems of automaticity or fear response temporarily foreclose the physical potential for conscious thought and reflection. At these times, conscious thought is *physically impossible*, such that individuals cannot engage in the most necessary activity of deliberative practice – conscious thought – until fear and/or automaticity subside.

As discussed in Chapters 4 and 5, in addition to the physical forms of human multiplicity, the mind of each person also includes a multiplicity of social content that can be in conflict in ways that at times present obstacles to conscious reflection. The diverse content within the self has been absorbed from social life and encoded in the brain as neural pathways. These encodings often include contradictory belief systems, conflicting ideas, and incompatible frames of reference that jumble together in the mind as an unorganized array of social scripts. Each such script may be activated neurally by elements of a passing context to temporarily assume cognitive significance as the frame of reference for thought, feeling, and action in a given moment. As such, overall, the self is comprised of an adaptive, yet also often unruly, multiplicitous internal diversity in form and content that can lead to unreflective, sometimes problematically biased, and even destructive, results. For the purposes of deliberative system formation, among the aspects of self that require most attention are those elements of inner multiplicity that contribute to obstacles to conscious reflection, including deliberation of relevant contradictions among inner belief systems, chronic fears, unfounded perceptions of threat that involve various internalized identities, and other socially encoded content in the mind (Barvosa 2008, 109–139). However, some of the tensions among the multiplicity of identities and social content in the mind are also productive and serve as sources of creativity, social connection, and critical distance on issues. Yet with regard to deliberative system formation and function, as illustrated in Chapters 4 and 5, some of these inner conflicts and tensions can manifest as cognitive obstacles to deliberation.

Specifically, in the context of public deliberation, the three cognitive obstacles identified here can appear in how people address, or inattentively do not address, a topic under public consideration. The cognitive obstacles to deliberation and individual reflection also appear as blind spots, avoidance, denial, or self-affirming interpretations that may seem (subconsciously) to serve self-preservation on one level, while also undermining deliberative democracy on another. Moreover, these cognitive obstacles may be triggered more acutely on genuinely threat-ridden topics, such as climate change. Environmental psychologist Robert Gifford, for example, has recently identified numerous different cognitive obstacles to public reflection on climate change (Gifford 2015). Separately, fellow environmental psychologist Nick Pidgeon has also pointed out that some cognitive obstructions to public reflection on climate change arise from social expectations and fears such that he has cautioned against evoking fear in public communications on the subject.[2] Similarly, I too have suggested in the proposed model that the three cognitive obstacles of inattention-related implicit bias, identity threat, and fear activation (including post-traumatic fear) are important considerations in the formation of deliberative systems that can present obstructions to deliberative system growth *even when other favorable conditions are present.*

As a result, in the model presented in Chapter 1, circumventing – and potentially overcoming – these obstacles in specific public deliberations is a necessary condition for the formation of an effective deliberative system. More specifically, drawing illustration from examples

---

[2] Bristol Natural History Consortium, "Nick Pidgeon (Part 2) – Communicate 2009," Nick Pidgeon address delivered at the *Valuing the Invaluable* Communicate Conference (2009), posted August 2, 2010, www.youtube.com/watch?v=qjdkAdwO0rc 0:00–7:13.

in the LGBT case study, I have offered theoretical observations on at least six practices that appear in the LGBT case to have helped deliberators sidestep and/or overcome these three cognitive obstacles. These practices are discussed throughout the case study chapters as defining characteristics of deliberative packages and deliberative entrepreneurship. They are also illustrated in Chapter 4 through the example of the deliberative debut of Zach Wahls. These practices have been identified as communication strategies and actions that provide deliberative materials and opportunities in specific ways that help participants overcome cognitive hurdles to deliberation. These practices are ones that: (a) place listeners under relevant cognitive load through narrative messages and comparative strategies, (b) activate a sense of social similarity that can foster feelings of safety and ease of familiarity, (c) affirm listener identities, and/or highlight a basis for common identification with those entrepreneurs offering competing points of view, (d) create open invitations to deliberation by declining to frame topics though us-versus-them narratives, or shaming or blaming discourses that can trigger public fear or avoidance, (e) ease potential or apparent fears of would-be deliberators by reframing or reconstructing underlying social narratives that excite trepidation, and (f) reframe troubling social contradictions and/or socially reconstruct obstructive belief systems in ways that resolve social contradictions and tensions (both known or present as hidden quandaries) that can block consideration and/or reconsideration of the matter at hand.

These practices are illustrated with examples throughout the four chapters of the LGBT case study. For instance, examples of the effective use of these tools have been provided in Chapter 4 with reference to NBA administrator Rick Welts and retired NBA player John Amaechi.These various practices can help to overcome the cognitive obstacles to deliberation of implicit bias, perceived identity threat, and activated fears, but they do have limitations. Use of these tools alone cannot ultimately succeed without the active willingness of groups and individuals to confront and resolve these obstacles as needed as part of participation in a growing deliberative system. As discussed in the next to the last section of this concluding chapter, a pressing question yet remains as to whether people would again choose to do the work of overcoming cognitive obstacles to deliberation on topics other than LGBT equality. The formation of other deliberative systems would require such active willingness on the part of most, if not all, members of US society.

Five General Characteristics of Deliberative Systems in Practice

The theoretical concepts and relationships just listed are proposed in this work as underlying mechanisms and necessary conditions for the self-assembly of deliberative systems. They have also been the basis for the suggestion of five other general characteristics of a deliberative system in everyday practice.

Deliberative Systems Distinct from Social Movements: As elaborated in Chapter 1, deliberative systems are distinct from social movements in a key way that is also definitive of deliberative systems in practice as modeled in this book. In sum, as Manuel Castells has argued (2012), the networked social movements that prevail in the current stage of the information age commonly deploy us-versus-them framings in order to create movement communities. The formation of movement communities serves the vital purpose of encouraging people who have been marginalized to let go of any fear or apathy that they may have regarding transforming their circumstances, and within the company of a movement community, gain the courage to speak out and act on their own behalf in concert with others. While social movements thus serve an essential purpose by raising points of societal concern and empowering groups that have had little voice, they can also have divisive effects as a result of using us-versus-them perspectives and discourses in order to build a movement community.

In contrast, deliberative systems are marked by careful avoidance of us-versus-them framings and discourses of blame or shame. Instead, they utilize open and capacious framings of "us" and "we" to designate a problem or question as one of common concern that is ideally to be reflected upon and addressed by all members of the society as each considers the question at hand. Deliberative systems also resolutely endorse the free will of everyone by not pressing any particular choice or perspective on any deliberator, but instead extending respect to all no matter how they ultimately decide on the issue. In other words, consistent with Habermas's original theorization, the modus operandi of a deliberative system in practice is to foster independent reflection by all *regardless of the outcome of the deliberation.* The role of a social movement, in contrast, is to press the importance of a particular issue, bring attention to its impact on particular people, and to advocate for a particular resolution of the problem on the basis of its expressed virtues as understood from the perspective of the movement.

Issue Specificity: Deliberative systems have been theorized in this work as likely to rise on an issue-specific basis as it did in the US public engagement on LGBT equality. As was elaborated in Chapter 5, democratic societies may not always be ready to address certain topics. In those instances, obstacles to a topical deliberation will prevail over the impetus to engage in collective reflection and will formation on those issues. As a result, deliberative systems are more likely to emerge on topics about which at least some significant segment of the society is willing to grapple, and/or one upon which deliberative entrepreneurs and/or social movements emerge and persist in placing a difficult issue on the social and political agenda. In such cases, a deliberative system may form on that specific topic as it did in the case of LGBT equality.

Reason Giving and Deliberative Practices Take Many Forms: Western discourses of public reason have been criticized by many scholars as too frequently privileging linear logic to the exclusion of other foundations of wise judgment such as aesthetics, affective or emotional judgments, intuition, moral preferences, and (in recently emerging post-secular discourse) spiritual perspectives that can be articulated ecumenically and across secular/spiritual divides (Habermas et al. 2010). Through illustrative case study examples, I have suggested that the exchange of reasons in a deliberative system may include not only simply logic, but may also involve a successful exchange of ideas and arguments that involve many forms of attentive reasoning, including aesthetics, spiritual perspectives, social storytelling, and emotionally based judgments, such as those expressing love and acceptance of all human beings.

Moreover, based on the evidence reviewed in this work, I have proposed in this model of deliberative system formation that the empirical practices and modes of deliberative reasoning also take an infinite array of forms from art and chitchat, to song and silence. Thus the *form* of reasoning exchange is inclusive and a deliberative system may encompass a broad array of elements in any given instance.

Microsteps of Deliberative Network Formation are Nonlinear but Synergistic: In this proposed model of deliberative system formation, seven contingent and interrelated small steps and activities serve as the practical means by which the public self assembles the deliberative system. It is, I suggest, by these small but critical steps that deliberative systems appear to either grow or stall (these microsteps are distinct from the larger phases of system growth from person-centered networks to bounded then open networks). These microsteps include accepting invitations to reflection, inspiring others to engage in reflection, circulating publicly the results of one's own personal reflection, and so on. However, participants individually need not complete all of these steps in a linear sequence for the whole deliberative system to grow. Rather, various steps of the process may be happening simultaneously with many people taking different steps at any given time. In addition some participants might skip steps or circle back to undertake steps again on other aspects of the topic as occurred in the US public deliberation on LGBT equality.

While the movement of deliberative system growth thus does not require everyone to be on the same step, the flow of activity in the deliberative system (and by extension the system's growth or contraction) depends on how much overall activity is taking place in the system at any given time. The patterns I reviewed in the LGBT case study suggest that there is likely to be an ebb and flow in deliberative activity in which specific catalysts trigger flurries of deliberation that are punctuated by periods of relative calm. Moreover, as highlighted below, the growth and activity of the deliberative system involves the flow of deliberative material through social networks. In those networks, peaks and valleys in activity appear synergistic – the more people take part, the more the flow of activity increases, and in turn, the more people take part. Conversely, as the flow of deliberative materials tapers off, activity in the system flags as well.

No Necessary Outcomes But Potential for Justice Over Time: Deliberative democracy – of which deliberative systems are a part – is looked upon philosophically as the next possible evolutionary stage of democracy, as well as an aspect of reviving the Enlightenment project of pursing peace through conscious reasoning. The practice of deliberative democracy as an aspect of the Enlightenment project also respects the free will of both individuals and the collective. There is thus no guarantee that a particular public deliberation would render a just decision or course of action as the collective will. However, there is documented evidence that over time, humanity as a whole has become less violent, less intolerant, less hateful, and less willing to take advantage of, or to otherwise harm, fellow human beings (Pinker 2011). Clergyman Theodore Parker inspired Dr. Martin Luther King, Jr. who famously quoted him saying, "the arc of the moral universe is long, but it bends toward justice."[3] If these long-term trends and insights contain wisdom, then it stands to reason that while the process may not be linear, deliberative democracy can and would produce outcomes characterized by justice most of the time and would do so ultimately over time.

Does Building Deliberative Systems Issue-by-Issue Reintroduce the Problem of Scale?

Finally, if deliberative democracy operates only when a public creates its own issue-specific deliberative system, then this raises the question of whether this mechanism of public deliberation simply reintroduces the problem of scale. Is it possible to create so many deliberative systems to address the many collective problems and questions that societies face or are likely to face in the future? What if hidden quandaries – unspoken collective fears and anxieties – that can block the emergence of a particular deliberative system cannot be located or overcome on particular topics? Would deliberative system growth become impossible on those topics? Does the intersection of many difficult issues make the emergence of some issues-specific deliberative systems less likely? Can fatigue or a feeling of being overwhelmed by various issues among the public stymie deliberative system growth if many individual systems must be constructed? If only one full, national-scale, deliberative system has emerged so far, is it unlikely that other systems will also emerge in future?

The theory-based answer I can offer to these questions is both yes and no. Yes, the daunting practical challenge of the self-assembly of numerous deliberative systems on different topics is a meaningful obstacle that could have significant obstructive impact. Yet this obstacle need not be decisive in blocking the growth of future deliberative systems over time. I propose speculatively that at least two factors set the stage for: (a) more deliberative systems to emerge over time, and (b) the potential that different deliberative systems could merge, eventually converging into one overarching system through which a democratic

---

[3] February 8, 1958, "The Gospel Messenger, Out of the Long Night," by Martin Luther King, Jr., Start Page 3, Quote Page 14, Column 1, Official Organ of the Church of the Brethren, published weekly by the General Brotherhood Board, Elgin, Illinois. Quote attributed first to Theodore Parker, *Ten Sermons of Religion* (Boston: Crosby, Nichols, and Company, 1853).

public routinely and confidently addresses the issues that it faces. These two factors are first, the interrelatedness of all people and their problems, and second, the comparative relief and even pleasure that emerges from resolving a common problem, especially in contrast to the ongoing rancor and unease of maintaining societal difficulties and conflicts. In the US for instance, there is currently so much frustration and unease across the political spectrum that whatever demands they place on us, deliberative processes for democratic resolution may provide welcome hope and viable alternatives that will have considerable appeal in contrast to the status quo.

If, therefore, public awareness can grow regarding the practical possibility of deliberative democracy, and if public proficiency can spread in the practices and requirements of deliberative system formation, then it is possible that a widespread impetus already exists among the US public – born of frustration and discontent – for members of US society (and perhaps other nations), to take up the tools of deliberative practice in order to create public-centered, deliberation-based democracy for themselves. If so, then theoretically at least, public familiarity and confidence with deliberative practice might soon combine with current discontent to foster the growth of the numerous different deliberative systems that are needed. Moreover, if issue-specific deliberative systems were to become increasingly commonplace or even ubiquitous, eventually those many deliberative systems might, theoretically at least, functionally morph into one common deliberative system that serves as the vehicle for the practice of consciously engaged and ever-ongoing collective will formation.

Relatedly, in terms of the intersection of many difficult problems acting as a stumbling block to deliberative systems formation, it is true that the interrelatedness of hot-button topics and problems could block the emergence of new deliberative systems. For example, the problem of enduring racial hierarchies in the US, including the mass incarceration of Blacks that plagues American society, intersects with large-scale economic inequalities, urban resource disparities, unique regional histories, and stubbornly problematic patterns of institutional influence involving policing and patterns of school and residential segregation (Alexander 2012). All of these intersecting elements likewise invoke gendered factors, and in some cases nativity and other dimensions of social diversity, as well as other collective social problems such as disparities in healthcare access, educational access, and patterns of collective trauma in various communities. A consensus already exists in the US that racism is unacceptable. Yet racial disparities persist. Given the complexity of enduring racial inequality in the US, attempts to address the matter invokes so many intersecting issues that it may seem impossible to deliberate on this problem, much less dismantle it.

Yet, theoretically at least, intersectionality in this context cuts both ways. Yes, the complexity of intersecting issues could serve as a barrier to deliberative system formation. This might be especially so if each intersecting factor has its own hidden quandaries – i.e. sets of unspoken fears and anxieties – that could cause people to avoid the issue or remain attached to a set of self-affirming biases or blind spots (Chapter 5). Conversely, however, if those hidden fears and anxieties began to shift and diminish as obstacles to personal reflection and contemplation, then the intersectionality of complex issues might sustain, and even add speed to the formation of a topically encompassing deliberative system. Intersectionality can foster deliberative system formation because the condition of interconnected issues automatically links many diverse people into a relationship of common concern *and* also differing experience related to the complex topic at hand. With many diverse people already linked together by common concern – yet with each bringing diverse perspectives as well as linkages to their own social networks – the necessary growth and amplification from small person-centered deliberative networks founded by deliberative entrepreneurs, to larger social-domain saturating networks, to even larger-scale open deliberative networks may occur more easily and more quickly as people from many different social domains are drawn to joining in the deliberation in part because of their varied ties to the intersectional aspects of the problem at hand.

Likewise, while a set of deep fears, anxieties, stereotypes, and animosities may inhibit communication across different social networks, once groups are linked into an even fledgling dialogue on a complex topic of common concern, shifting perceptions and new actions that may emerge in the course of deliberation may begin to cross the boundaries of many different social domains. Like a house of cards, existing systems of false beliefs, mutual fears and anxieties, stereotypical misconceptions – all of which are inherited from hierarchical social life and often sustained by isolation in homogeneous social networks – may begin to fall away and transform for those individuals engaged in deliberation. In turn, such shifting views and new awareness gained through deliberative interactions could then pick up social momentum, increasingly circulating through many diverse and divided social networks that are converging topically due to the intersecting aspects of the complex issue under deliberation. In such a potential scenario, the intersecting complexities of difficult problem raise the theoretical possibility that widespread misperceptions and errors could be faced and remedied on a wider basis *more* quickly than when deliberative systems face more isolated issues, *if* the initial activation barriers can be overcome. Overall, if a deliberative system could be created on the issue of LGBT equality, which was an issue of longstanding bias and subordination, then there is valid reason to hope that other deliberative systems could be created on other topics, including the complex topics that face US society today, many of which are also faced by other societies around the globe.

Implications for the Original Conundrum of Peace and Public Reason

This general observation on the prospects for deliberative system formation brings this study of deliberative democracy full circle back to where this project began. It returns to contemplation of the original intellectual context and purpose for which Jürgen Habermas first developed his theory and concepts of discourse ethics, concepts that inspired the idea of deliberative democracy. Habermas's motivation was to explore the potential for a new form of reasoning – collective communicative reasoning – that could potentially correct the failures of the Enlightenment project and restore its pursuit of peace and justice through human reason. Recall from the Introduction that Jürgen Habermas conceived of the ideal of deliberative democracy as part of his project of rethinking reason itself (1992). He meant his revised idea of collective reasoning to be an instrument by which humanity could restore the promise of the Enlightenment by fostering peace and justice through public reasoning against the historical prevalence of religious intolerance and violence (145).

On the whole, the model of deliberative system formation that I have offered in this book, and the related case study of US public engagement on LGBT equality, both reflect Habermasian expectations. Specifically, the practical prototype and illustrative case study provided here express and illustrate Habermas's view that the practice of deliberative democracy could not be produced by deliberate design. Rather it had to arise from society as a form of self-organization. Moreover, it could also arise under conditions of dominion yet not be thwarted or distorted by that condition (Habermas 1990c, 364; 1990b, 315; 1992, 146). The LGBT case study detailed in Chapters 2 through 5 demonstrate this pattern. The deliberative system on LGBT equality emerged from civil society, aided eventually by new communication technologies, and it sprang up because of the subordination of the US LGBT minority. Just as Habermas theorized, problems of social domination were not overwhelming obstacles to widespread deliberation, but instead the principal occasions for deliberative democracy to form (Habermas 1990b, 315).

Given these developments, what, if anything, do these parallels suggest regarding Habermas's further goal of refashioning and redeeming the Enlightenment project through communicative reason and deliberative democracy? I suggest that, on the whole, this study proposes and illuminates, after all, just what Habermas originally envisioned. Across the preceding five chapters, I have proposed, based on exploratory data analysis, that public deliberation is at last a realistic tool by which humanity – if it chooses to undertake the work – can *consciously* determine its own collective will in a movement toward peace and justice, and that in at least one recent US case, it has already done so. Humanity can thus use the tools and practices of deliberative systems (i.e. communicative reason) to determine what it values as true and right. In this sense, the Enlightenment project of pursuing peace through large-scale public reason appears to be materially possible. But I have also proposed additional elements to this Habermasian revision of the Enlightenment project that borrow insights not from Habermas, but rather from his forebears in the Frankfurt School, Max Horkheimer and Theodor Adorno, who argued that the non-unitary multiplicity of the self must be considered in the redemption and remaking of the Enlightenment project.

Central in this connection between Enlightenment reason and the multiplicity of the self, is the linguistic turn, i.e. the knowledge that all of social life is formed through social conventions that are produced by humanity itself in an ongoing basis using language-mediated processes that we can refer to simply as processes of social construction. As Habermas himself has noted, the central insights of the linguistic turn irrevocably change our understanding of reason. Our understanding of reason changes because the frames of reference that we inherit and use to reason are themselves simply human creations that may or may not produce accurate or desirable reflections. But the linguistic turn does not remove the possibility of reasoning altogether. Moreover, as I have argued in this work and elsewhere, the insights of the linguist turn are inextricably linked to generating the messy multiplicity of the self, hailed by Horkheimer and Adorno as important to understanding the long-term prospects for peace (Barvosa 2008, 5). The significance of the multiplicity of the self in the pursuit of peace through public reason exists in how the complexity of the self is both a societal mirror *and* a transformative vehicle where conscious reasoning and the practical potential for social change converge. The socially constructed content of the multiplicity of the self (i.e. its multiple identities, conflicting belief systems, crosscutting fears and anxieties, disavowed fragments, and denied inner shadows) and the diverse socially constructed content of social life are both at once the source *and* the effect/reflection of the other. On one hand, the socially constructed content of social life imprints the self (as internalized messages and neural encodings), thus forming the multiplicity of scripts encoded within the self. On the other hand, the socially imprinted and absorbed contents within the self serve, in turn, as the internalized scripts through which people individually and collectively construct social life each moment of every day through their speech and actions both large and small. When people consciously choose – or more often on autopilot subconsciously default to – living the same internalized social scripts over and over, then social life and the status quo remain as they have been. Alternatively, if and when those social scripts are abandoned or transformed, then social change takes place (Wittgenstein 1968; Foucault 1990, 1991; Butler 1990, 1993).

Boiled down, the processes of social construction in relation to peaceful deliberative democratic change *and* the evolving multiplicity of the self involve only this: the ever-ongoing process of individuals and groups choosing either to reiterate the same inherited scripts *in themselves* and in social life, or alternatively of choosing instead to change those scripts and to thereby create new social and political possibilities. The internally multiple and contradictory self is a focal point for this process of choice and change. Throughout the LGBT case study offered in this book, people such as Robin Voss can be seen taking up the project of contemplating (often painfully) two competing inherited ideas about LGBT equality that existed in tension within themselves. In this experience, social conflict is imprinted and mirrored within the multiplicity of one's own self (Chapter 3). Once engaged with this inner conflict, many deliberators employed conscious reflection and ultimately chose to transform (or regularize) their allegiances and commitments by deciding to live by one ideal, while *still physically containing, but not living according* to the other. In turn, this choice and the action of living consistently by it contributed materially to the larger societal transformation. Such an encounter with the inherited multiplicity of the self – which frequently mirrors ongoing social conflicts – thus becomes a proving ground upon which deliberative democratic practice can provide the necessary tools and occasions through which reflective transformation of the self and society can take place.

Key to this transformative potential, however, is the elastic multiplicity of the self to contain opposites, while also affording the choice to attentively select (and even automatize) patterns of *consciously* chosen practice from among that messy multitude within. As expressed in Chapter 5 using Kenneth Gergen's concept of *multi-being*, every saint also as has inherited scripts of cruelty within her. The only difference between such a saint and those who engage in casual or determined cruelty as lived inheritance is that the would-be saint self-identifies with kindness and chooses to stay attentive enough to her daily choices to opt consistently (although imperfectly) for kindness until the impulse to cruelty becomes so faint, so marginal, within her multiplicitous psyche, as to be effectively non-existent. Over time, what determines the likelihood that an inherited social script of kindness, rather than one of cruelty, comes unbidden to mind for the saint – or for any of us – is how strongly we identify with the script of kindness and how often we use it (Barvosa 2008, 74–75). In turn, the ubiquitous mechanisms of social construction dictate that when those who choose kindness express their choice in speech and action in the everyday world, then the world becomes a kinder place. This central insight is not merely high theory; it is what is meant in the popular culture phrase: Be the change that you wish to see. The multiplicity of oneself, with our capacious ability to house opposites and *to attentively* diminish the social expression of unwanted social scripts, makes the multiplicity of oneself not only a mirror of social conflict and a proving ground for newly emerging democratic ideals and reflections, but also the self-reflexive creative vehicle for rendering any individual or collective democratic choice that emerges over time into a practical reality in daily life. In this, the Enlightenment project of seeking peace through reason, and the multiplicitousness and self-making capacities and practices of the self converge as one project.

Overall, the linguistic turn reveals that the practices for forming and transforming the status quo and for crafting the lived multiplicity of the self are the same. The specific content of each unique person may vary, but the *process* of change itself is consistent. By extension, the inner multiplicity of the self is potentially infinite in part because the creative capacity of humanity is also infinite. Consequently, while the multiplicity of the self can be a source of implicit bias, it is not itself a problem that obstructs the formation of deliberative democracy. Ignored or mismanaged contradictions within the self can become the source of major social and political problems when societies fail to walk the talk of their avowed social and political principles as a reflection of the enduring contradictions among competing inherited ideas within both individuals and collectives (Barvosa 2008, 131–139, 207–222). But this hazard also reveals that the multiplicity of the self is likewise intrinsic to the opportunity of creating transformative democratic deliberation and change in which consciously chosen principles are observed. This is because it is only by grappling with opposing ideas (both those encountered within the self and those encountered in society, which are frequently the same) that the conditions and materials for *conscious* judgment and discernment on the part of the socially constructed self arise (175–206). Without this contrast and tension between alternatives, it is impossible to detect whether a reasoner has chosen freely a principle or simply proceeded on the basis of an activated internalized script (83–108). This is the reason why the theoretical concept of deliberative packages proposed in this work must, by definition, offer a juxtaposition of competing ideas (Chapter 1). In other words, because all of the frames of reference for reasoning within the socially constructed self come into the self as a social inheritance, a juxtaposition is required to create the opportunity for individual *conscious* choice, which can only be witnessed as an active judgment among divergent alternatives or as a hybrid response fashioned from the material of competing options.

Seen now through this detour into the linguistic turn and the related multiplicity of the self, deliberative systems – and deliberative democracy more generally – emerge as a vehicle by which democratic societies can use individual and collective reason to judge collectively which socially constructed and inherited aspects of the self and society to abandon because they no longer serve the common good. In so doing, a democratic public can use a deliberative system as the means to distinguish what *it chooses to accept as right* from the flotsam and jetsam of inherited biases, random beliefs, fears, and other notions that are the detritus of a long human history of inequitable power relations, violence, and cruelty. That detritus has, however, left its social traces as encodings in the brains and bodies of virtually everyone in every society. These encodings remain in the self and society despite the fact that these lingering scripts may have long outlived any positive purpose they might once have served. Deliberative systems, I have proposed in this book, are emerging now as a means by which collectives may choose together which of their socially inherited scripts they wish to let fade away through dis-identification and disuse.

Overall, deliberative democracy – considered alone or as part of a revised Enlightenment project – can be seen as a practice of individual and collective self-making. By adopting practices of deliberative democracy, a democratic public can select collectively and consciously from what has been historically given by deciding through communicative reason what they will retain and what they will let go of from the social inheritance that *is within each person* as an embodied multiplicitous self, and also *among them* in the fabric of any long-standing society. In this sense, deliberative democracy is a vehicle fit for the pursuit of long-term peace and justice through the social reconstruction of social and political life in a manner that is collectively and democratically chosen by members of a society. Through the self-assembly of deliberative systems therefore, a democratic people may gains the tools it needs to form its collective will, and to live in common in keeping with the values and principles upon which it can collectively agree.

From Problems of Scale to Questions of Will

If the practical prototype of deliberative system formation that has been presented in this work is plausible and ultimately confirmed as valid, then the question now before scholars is less *can* societies realize deliberative democracy, but instead will people choose to do so given what it demands of them? In the form of deliberative systems, deliberative democracy asks quite a lot. It demands effort and attention, and a willingness to be open to potential change (and healing) in the self and society. As previously stressed, in this it also demands the work of contemplating the imprints that social life has left within ourselves, including inherited biases, blind spots, and any contradictory belief systems and ideas within the self.

The willingness to face and release these less-than-positive aspects of the self is important. For as philosophy and scientific understandings of the multiplicity of the self reveal, when human beings are – individually or collectively – shortsighted, hateful, harmful, selfish, violent, or cruel, the immediate source of this often exists in the influence of the unsorted jumble of intrapsychic debris within the human mind that distracts people – individually and collectively – from living through the better part of ourselves.[4] Often the momentum and durability of such habits of injustice are increased by related structural factors, the social construction of formal systems, subcultures, and self-affirming narratives that affirm and thereby sustain cultural patterns of hostility, rigidity, or greed from which the enduring problems of humanity ultimately emanate.[5] This state of affairs is socially generated and therefore always subject to being socially transformed. But facing these realities is hard and, at times, painful and unsettling work.

In the case of US public deliberation on LGBT equality examined in this work, millions of members of the US public courageously faced – and some continue to face – various unpleasant aspects of the self and society related to the issues involved in the journey toward recognizing LGBT equality. But it remains an open question whether this courage will also prevail on other questions of how to live in common that might be democratized. In the US context, such possible questions include issues associated with economic inequality, enduring gender inequity, and racial inequality, including the disparate racial impact of the use of deadly force by police.

Yet the LGBT case study that has been presented as the centerpiece of this book suggests that in the event that other deliberative systems become a reality in the US context, it is possible that many people

---

[4] See Rita Carter, *Multiplicity: The New Science of Personality, Identity, and the Self* (New York: Little, Brown & Co., 2008); Barvosa, *Wealth of Selves*, 2008; Benaji and Greenwald, *Blind Spot: The Hidden Biases of Good People*, 2013.

[5] Alex Gibney et al., *Enron:The Smartest Guys in the Room*. DVD. 110 mins. Los Angeles: Magnolia Home Entertainment, 2005.

would step forward to encourage and help fellow members of the US public to take part in deliberative practice. Once again, perhaps, deliberative entrepreneurs would rise up and take it upon themselves to provide the means and the support for people to think for themselves using the better parts of who they are as individuals and as members of collectives. When Ellen DeGeneres urged people to "be kind to one another," when Zach Wahls suggested that people observe their principles and engage in "basic fairness," neither was denying the problems in the world. Instead both urged people to think for themselves and reminded them to do so through the kind and fair parts of who they are. Likewise, when Bishop V. Gene Robinson said of those who hated him, "I love them anyway," and when Daniel Karslake said "maybe perhaps" there is another way to think about this apparent problem, when Rick Welts and John Amaechi said effectively, "well things are bad, but they can be made better," all of these deliberative entrepreneurs prompted people not only to consciously think and reason, but also to privilege the kinder parts of themselves as frames of reference when doing so.

Moreover, as these and other examples presented in this work have attested, one person can make an enormous and pivotal difference in whether and how others come to critically reflect on a matter of common concern. As indicated in Chapter 5 through the words of John Amaechi, anyone and everyone can learn the skills by which to help others experience an antidote to the pain of social conflict. Anyone and everyone can learn, like Zach Wahls, to ignite the courage in others to overcome inattention and fear, and to take part in conscious reflection on issues of importance to all. Overall, even if the prevalence of the will to engage in deliberative system building is uncertain, the research that has been presented here suggests that there are likely to be many individuals in US society who are willing to help create deliberative systems by encouraging others to engage in deliberative practice and to bring their better selves to the process. Only time will tell, however, what the next step in the evolution of democracy will bring.

A Call for Further Research

In the meanwhile, scholars of deliberative democracy – theorists and empiricists alike – still have much to consider, create, and contribute toward a deeper understanding of deliberative practice on large and small scales. Many open research questions remain and some new ones will be raised by the theoretical concepts, relationships, and hypotheses that have been offered in this book. First, confirmation of this theoretical model of deliberative systems is still needed, including any required modifications and refinements. Given that the theoretical template presented here is based on exploratory data analysis and thus cannot be validated using the same qualitative data collected for this study, methodologically speaking, confirmation would require additional research into the concepts, processes, and hypotheses proposed as part of the practical prototype presented in this work (Stebbins 2001; Tukey 1984, 181).

Second, as I described in Chapter 1, the theoretical template presented in this work raises other immediate questions that could also be addressed through further exploratory data analysis. This includes the search for other possible deliberative systems that may be in the early stages of formation, such as nascent deliberative systems on US economic inequality, gender equity, and the disparate racial impacts of suppressive policing practices on Black and Latino men and boys. Other topics of immediate focus could include exploration of individual and collective trauma as a cognitive obstacle to public deliberation (Erikson 1994). Can trauma and collective trauma be reliably detected as a disruptor of the growth of public deliberation? In addition, given the prevalence of cognitive obstacles to the emergence of large-scale informal deliberative systems on difficult topics, it is still very worthwhile to ask: Can formal institutional protocols be found to create deliberative practice on a large scale?

Third, many open research questions remain regarding facets of deliberative systems. Further theorizing, as well as big data research with both quantitative and qualitative empirical study, could shed further light on many remaining questions regarding the ongoing US deliberation of LGBT equality. By the time of this publication, US consensus favoring LGBT equality had reached 63 percent. Has the emergence of this new consensus followed the common path of the "diffusion of innovation" model, in which change in public opinion is now in the "late-majority" phase (Rogers 2003)? If so, in terms of conscious reflection, do late adopters of the new consensus still deliberate and reflect, or do some follow the trends begun by early adopters? Some qualitative self-descriptions among religious conservatives cited in Chapter 4 suggest that the answer to this question is yes, deliberation continues, but more research would be required to know with certainty.

Other questions involving technology and measurement also remain. For example, at what specific numerical threshold might the zeitgeist of a proclaimed "national conversation" actually be said to tip into a discernable deliberative system on a given topic? Or at what threshold could a deliberative system be said to exist in a given social domain and/ or across a number of social domains, or in a nation at large? What role can the design of online discussion spaces (Wright and Street 2007) play in fostering deliberative systems, or alternatively in triggering cognitive obstacles to deliberation? What role might personal experiences of being overwhelmed by hyper-connectivity (Turkle 2011) play in the success or failure of informal deliberative systems? Likewise, more inquiry is needed on the powers of implementation of a large-scale deliberative system. What, if any, new institutional designs are needed for integrating large-scale deliberative systems into regular cycles of policymaking and policy, especially in light of current understandings of evidence-based policymaking (Hajer and Wagenaar 2003; DeLeon 1997; Moran, Rein, and Goodin 2006; Greenwood 2014)? On the issue of implementation only one thing seems to be certain, that the integration of a collective will formed through deliberative practice into policymaking is likely to be iterative (Fung 2006).

In addition, further scholarly attention to the cognitive obstacles of implicit bias, perceived identity threats, and topic-related fears is also worthwhile. The analysis offered in this work suggests that, theoretically at least, identifying and understanding the influence of cognitive obstacles in large-scale deliberative systems requires focusing not only on what is being said overtly in the public domain, but also on what is unspoken and may be revealed only in discrepancies between words and deeds, or by outlying data points in empirical findings, which suggest that what appears on the social surface may not be the whole story. Continued focus on cognitive obstacles to large-scale deliberation would also involve sustained attention to the multiplicity of the self as chronic injustices often stem in large part from the fact that the self is not a perpetually rational and unitary force, as it is sometimes still viewed (Banaji and Greenwald 2013; Kahneman 2011; Barvosa 2008).

Finally, research cultures across disciplines are diverse and often difficult to shift (Knorr-Cetina 1999). But in light of the diverse qualities of publicly self-assembled deliberative systems as theorized here, future research could likely benefit from the application of an interdisciplinary sensibility. Moreover, given the important success of recent contributions of research teams working on deliberative democracy (e.g. Mansbridge et al. 2012; Nabatchi et al. 2012), teams of researchers might more easily bring the variety of disciplinary perspectives needed to tackle remaining questions, including detailed historical knowledge, insights from cultural studies and social psychology, expertise in social network science, and scholarly outlooks on democratic theory and practice from within political science, social psychology, and science and technology studies.

In whatever manner new research on deliberative democracy unfolds, it appears that the elusive dream of deliberative democracy might now become an empirical reality. At last it appears possible that if and when human beings face challenging issues – especially issues upon which they had engaged in a destructive manner in the past – that those problems can be considered collectively, and potentially resolved, through the development of informal deliberative systems as part of deliberative democracy. A publicly self-assembled, issue-specific, system of public reflection need not wait for electoral politics to set the agenda. Rather, the work of collective will formation and problem solving can be undertaken proactively by a public through large-scale deliberative systems as described by Mansbridge et al., through individual reflection, as emphasized by Robert Goodin (2003), and on the practical model outlined in this book.

Based on exploratory data analysis and the formulation of a practical prototype of deliberative system formation, I have proposed in this work that at least one such national-scale deliberative system – one focused on LGBT equality – has already emerged in the US with important nationwide results. Other such deliberative systems may also exist in other societies, or might be emerging now in the US or elsewhere on other topics. If other deliberative systems are emerging in the US or elsewhere, then these emerging deliberative systems should be recognized as powerful and capable of centering true political power in the hands of a democratic public. Despite the remarkable political turbulence of our times, there is practical reason to believe that now more than ever before, deliberative democracy is not simply a compelling theory. It is a practical mechanism by which a democratic people can arrive at its own collective will, work to resolve its enduring problems, and renew the Enlightenment project of collective self-governance through conscious reasoning as a means of movement toward greater peace, and the realization of humanity's highest values.

Bibliography

Ackerman, Bruce A. and James S. Fishkin. 2004. *Deliberation Day*. New Haven: Yale University Press.

Adams, Henry, Lester Wright, and Bethany Lohr. 1996. "Is Homophobia Associated with Homosexual Arousal?" *Journal of Abnormal Psychology* 105 (3): 440–445.

Alexander, Michelle. 2012. *The New Jim Crow: Mass Incarceration in the Age of Colorblindness*. New York: Perseus Distribution.

Alston, Macky. 2012. *Love Free or Die*. DVD. New York: Kino Lorber Inc.

Amaechi, John and Chris Bull. 2007. *Man in the Middle*. New York: ESPN Books.

Anzaldúa, Gloria, E. and AnaLouise Keating. 2000. *Interviews – Entrevistas*. New York: Routledge.

Apostolidis, Paul. 2000. *Stations of the Cross: Adorno and Christian Right Radio*. Durham: Duke University Press.

Banaji, Mahzarin, R. and Anthony G. Greenwald. 2013. *Blind Spot: Hidden Biases of Good People*. New York: Delacorte Press.

Barabási, Albert-László. 2002. *Linked: The New Science of Networks*. Cambridge: Perseus Publishers.

Bargh, John A. and Tanya L. Chartrand. 1999. "The Unbearable Automaticity of Being." *American Psychologist* 54 (7): 462–479.

Bartels, Larry M. 2008. *Unequal Democracy: The Political Economy of the New Gilded Age*. New York: Russell Sage Foundation.

Barth, Fredrik, ed. 1969. *Ethnic Groups and Boundaries: The Social Organization of Culture Difference*. Boston: Little, Brown, and Company.

Barvosa, Edwina. 2015. "Mapping Public Ambivalence in the Public Engagement with Science: Implications for Democratizing the Governance of Fracking Technologies in the USA," *Journal of Environmental Sciences and Studies*, 5 (4): 497–507.

   2014. "Unconscious Bias in the Suppression Policing of Black and Latino Men and Boys: Neuroscience, Borderlands Theory, and the Policymaking Quest for Just Policing," *Politics, Groups, and Identities* 2 (2): 260–283.

2011. "Inner Contradiction to Immigration Quagmire: A Response to Rogers Smith." *Perspectives on Politics* 9 (3): 559–562.

2011a. "Mestiza Consciousness in Relation to Sustained Political Solidarity: A Chicana Feminist Interpretation of the Farmworker Movement." *Aztlán: A Journal of Chicano Studies* 36 (2): 121–154.

2008. *Wealth of Selves: Multiple Identities, Mestiza Consciousness, and the Subject of Politics.* College Station: Texas A & M University Press.

Bauer, M. W., ed. 2014. "Special Issue: Public Engagement in Science." *Public Understanding of Science* 23 (1): 1–120.

Baumeister, Roy, F., ed. 1999. *The Self in Social Psychology.* Philadelphia: Psychology Press.

Bazerman, Max, H. and Ann Tenbrunsel, E. 2011. *Blind Spots: Why We Fail To Do What's Right and What to Do About It.* Princeton: Princeton University Press.

Behrens, J. T. and M. L. Smith. 1996. "Data and Data Analysis," in *Handbook of Educational Psychology*, D. C. Berliner and R. C. Calfee, eds. New York: Macmillan, 949–989.

Behrens, John T. and Wayne Rowe. 1997. "Measuring White Racial Identity: A Reply to Helms." *Journal of Counseling Psychology* 44 (1): 17–19.

Beltrán, Cristina. 2010. *The Trouble with Unity: Latino Politics and the Creation of Identity.* New York: Oxford University Press

Benford, Robert D. and David A. Snow. 2000. "Framing Processes and Social Movements: An Overview and Assessment." *Annual Review of Sociology*, 26: 611–639.

Benhabib, Seyla. 2002. *The Claims of Culture: Equality and Diversity in the Global Era.* Princeton: Princeton University Press.

1996. "Toward a Deliberative Model of Democratic Legitimacy," in *Democracy and Difference: Contesting the Boundaries of the Political*, Seyla Benhabib, ed. Princeton: Princeton University Press, 67–94.

Berger, Ben. 2011. *Attention Deficit Democracy: The Paradox of Civic Engagement.* Princeton: Princeton University Press.

Berkowitz, Bill. 2001. "Studying the Outcomes of Community-Based Coalitions." *American Journal of Community Psychology* 29 (2): 213–227.

Bessette, Joseph M. 1994. *The Mild Voice of Reason: Deliberative Democracy and American National Government.* Chicago: University of Chicago Press.

1978. "Deliberation in Congress a Preliminary Investigation." Ph.D. Diss. University of Chicago.

Bevir, Mark. 2010. *Democratic Governance.* Princeton: Princeton University Press.

Blee, Kathleen M., and Kimberly A. Creasap. 2010. "Conservative and Right-Wing Movements." *Annual Review of Sociology* 36: 269–286.

Bronski, Michael. 2011. *A Queer History of the United States*. Boston: Beacon Press.

Brown, Mark B. 2009. *Science in Democracy: Expertise, Institutions, and Representation*. Cambridge: MIT Press.

Burack, Cynthia. 2008. *Sin, Sex, and Democracy: Antigay Rhetoric and the Christian Right*. Albany: State University of New York Press.

Butler, Catherine, Karen Parkhill, and Nicholas Pidgeon, F. 2013. *Deliberating Energy Transitions in the UK—Transforming the UK Energy System: Public Values, Attitudes and Acceptability*. London: UKERC.

Butler, C, C. Demski, N. Pidgeon, K. Parkhill, and A. Spence. 2014. *"Public Values for Energy Futures: Framing, Indeterminacy and Policy Making."* Working Paper London: UK Energy Research Centre.

Butler, Judith. 1990. *Gender Trouble: Feminism and the Subversion of Identity*. New York: Routledge.

    1993. *Bodies That Matter: On the Discursive Limits of "Sex."* New York: Routledge.

Carter, Rita. 2008. *Multiplicity: The New Science of Personality, Identity, and the Self*. New York: Little, Brown & Co.

Cavalier, Robert. ed. 2011. *Approaching Deliberative Democracy: Theory and Practice*. Pittsburgh: Carnegie Mellon University Press.

Castells, Manuel. 2015. *Networks of Outrage and Hope: Social Movements in the Internet Age*. 2nd edition. Cambridge, UK: Polity.

    2012. *Networks of Outrage and Hope: Social Movements in the Internet Age*. Cambridge, UK: Polity.

    1998. *The Information Age: Economy, Society and Culture – End of Millennium*. Vol. 3. Oxford: Blackwell.

    1997. *The Information Age: Economy, Society and Culture – The Power of Identity*. Vol. 2. Oxford: Blackwell.

    1996. *The Information Age: Economy, Society and Culture – The Rise of the Network Society*. Vol. 1. Oxford: Blackwell.

Chambers, Simone. 2003. "Deliberative Democratic Theory." *Annual Review of Political Science* 6 (1): 307–326.

Charmaz, Kathy. 2006. *Constructing Grounded Theory: A Practical Guide Through Qualitative Analysis*. London: Sage Publications.

Clark, Susan and Woden Teachout. 2012. *Slow Democracy: Rediscovering Community, Bringing Decision Making Back Home*. White River Junction: Chelsea Green Publishing.

Cohen, Anthony, P. 1985. *The Symbolic Construction of Community*. Chichester: Ellis Horwood Limited.

Cole, Kathleen, D. 2013. "Thinking Through Race: Social Construction, Social Cognition, and the Unconscious Maintenance of Racial Hierarchy." Ph. D., Political Science, University of California, Santa Barbara.

Coleman, Stephen and Jay G. Blumler. 2009. *The Internet and Democratic Citizenship: Theory, Practice and Policy*. Cambridge: Cambridge University Press.

Cooley, Charles Horton. 1909. *Social Organization*. New York: Charles Scribner's Sons.

Cramer, Duncan. 2003. *Advanced Quantitative Data Analysis*. Maidenhead, Berkshire, England: Open University Press.

Currah, Paisley, Richard M. Juang, and Shannon Minter. 2006. *Transgender Rights*. Minneapolis: University of Minnesota Press.

Dahl, Robert, A. 2002. *How Democratic is the American Constitution?* New Haven: Yale University Press.

Dahlgren, Peter. 2009. *Media and Political Engagement: Citizens, Communication, and Democracy*. Cambridge: Cambridge University Press.

Davies, Gail. 2006. "The Sacred and the Profane: Biotechnology, Rationality, and Public Debate." *Environment & Planning A*. 38 (3): 423–443.

DeGeneres, Ellen. 2011. *Seriously ... I'm Kidding*. New York: Grand Central Publishing.

DeLeon, Peter. 1997. *Democracy and the Policy Sciences*. Albany: State University of New York Press.

Delgado, Ana, Kamilla Lein Kjølberg, and Fern Wickson. 2011. "Public Engagement Coming of Age: From Theory to Practice in STS Encounters with Nanotechnology." *Public Understanding of Science* 20 (6): 826–845.

Demski, Christina, Alexa Spence, and Nicholas F. Pidgeon. 2013. *Summary Findings of a Survey Conducted in August 2012—Transforming the UK Energy System: Public Values, Attitudes and Acceptability*. London: UK Energy Research Centre.

Denison, Erik and Alistair Kitchen. 2015. *Out On The Fields: The First International Study On Homophobia in Sports*. Sydney: Bingham Cup Sydney 2014.

Dias, Brian, G. and Kerry J. Ressler. 2013. "Parental Olfactory Experience Influences Behavior and Neural Structure in Subsequent Generations." *Nature Neuroscience* 17 (1): 89–98.

Dietz, Thomas. 2013. "Bringing Values and Deliberation to Science Communication." *Proceedings of the National Academy of Sciences of the United States of America*. 110 (3): 14081–14087.

Dietz, Thomas, and Paul C. Stern. 2008. *Public Participation in Environmental Assessment and Decision Making*. Washington DC: National Academies Press.

Doidge, Norman. 2007. *The Brain That Changes Itself: Stories of Personal Triumph from the Frontiers of Brain Science*. New York: Penguin Books.

Dryzek, John, S. 2007. "Theory, Evidence, and the Tasks of Deliberation," in *Can The People Govern? Deliberation, Participation and Democracy*, Shawn Rosenberg, ed., Basingstoke: Palgrave Macmillian, 237–250.

2001. "Legitimacy and Economy in Deliberative Democracy," *Political Theory* 29 (5): 651–669.

2000. *Deliberative Democracy and Beyond: Liberals, Critics, Contestations*. Oxford: Oxford University Press.

1990. *Discursive Democracy: Politics, Policy and Political Science*. Cambridge: Cambridge University Press.

Dryzek, John, S., Bonnie Honig, and Anne Phillips. 2009. "Overview of Political Theory," in *The Oxford Handbook of Political Science*, Robert E. Goodin, ed. Oxford: Oxford University Press, 61–88.

Dryzek, John S. and Simon Niemeyer. 2010. *Foundations and Frontiers of Deliberative Governance*. Oxford: Oxford University Press.

Elledge, Jim. 2010. *Queers in American Popular Culture*. Vol. 1. Film and Television. Santa Barbara: Praeger.

2010a. *Queers in American Popular Culture*. Vol. 2. Literature, Pop Art, and Performance. Santa Barbara: Praeger.

2010b. *Queers in American Popular Culture*. Vol. 3. Sports, Leisure, and Lifestyle. Santa Barbara: Praeger.

Erikson, Kai. 1994. *A New Species of Trouble: Explorations in Disaster, Trauma, and Community*. New York: W.W. Norton & Co.

1994a. "Hiroshima: Of Accidental Judgments and Casual Slaughters," in *A New Species of Trouble: the Human Experience of Modern Disasters*. New York: W.W. Norton & Co., 185–202.

Eskridge, William N., Jr. 2008. *Dishonorable Passions: Sodomy Laws in America, 1861–2003*. New York: Viking.

Evans, Jonathan, St. B.T. 2008. "Dual-Processing Accounts of Reasoning, Judgment, and Social Cognition." *The Annual Review of Psychology* 59: 255–278.

Evans, Jonathan, St. B.T., and Keith Stanovich, E. 2013. "Dual-Process Theories of Higher Cognition: Advancing the Debate." *Perspectives on Psychological Science* 8 (3): 223–241.

Fiorino, Daniel J. 1990. "Citizen Participation and Environmental Risk: A Survey of Institutional Mechanisms." *Science, Technology, & Human Values* 15 (2): 226–243.

Fishkin, James, S. 1995. *The Voice of the People: Public Opinion and Democracy.* New Haven: Yale University Press.

Forester, John. 1999. *The Deliberative Practitioner: Encouraging Participatory Planning Processes.* Cambridge: MIT Press.

Foucault, Michel. 1979. *Discipline and Punish: The Birth of the Prison.* New York: Vintage Books.

    1990. *The History of Sexuality: An Introduction.* Translated by Robert Hurley. Vol. 1. New York: Vintage Books.

Frank, Barney, 2015. *Frank: A Life in Politics from the Great Society to Same-Sex Marriage.* New York: Farrar, Straus and Giroux.

Friedkin, Noah. 1998. *A Structural Theory of Social Influence.* Cambridge: Cambridge University Press.

Fung, Arjun. 2006. "Democratizing the Policy Process," in *The Oxford Handbook of Public Policy*, Michael Moran, Martin Rein, and Robert E. Goodin, eds. Oxford: Oxford University Press.

Gastil, John. 2000. *By Popular Demand Revitalizing Representative Democracy Through Deliberative Elections.* Berkeley: University of California Press.

Gergen, Kenneth, J. 2009. *Relational Being: Beyond Self and Community.* Oxford: Oxford University Press.

    1999. *An Invitation to Social Construction.* London: Sage.

Gerring, John. 2007. *Case Study Research: Principles and Practice.* New York: Cambridge University Press.

Gerstmann, Evan. 2008. *Same-Sex Marriage and the Constitution.* 2nd edition. Cambridge: Cambridge University Press.

Gibney, Alex, 2005. *Enron: The Smartest Guys in the Room.* DVD. Los Angeles: Magnolia Home Entertainment.

Gifford, Robert. 2015. "The Road to Climate Hell." *New Scientist* 227 (3029): 28–33.

Gladwell, Malcolm. 2008. *Outliers: The Story of Success.* New York: Little, Brown & Co.

    2000. *The Tipping Point: How Little Things Can Make a Big Difference.* Boston: Little, Brown.

Glaser, Barney G. 1992. *Emergence vs Forcing: Basics of Grounded Theory Analysis.* Mill Valley: Sociology Press.

Glaser, Barney G., and Anselm L. Strauss. 1967. *The Discovery of Grounded Theory: Strategies for Qualitative Research.* Chicago: Aldine Publishing. Co.

Goodin, Robert, E. 2008. *Innovating Democracy: Democratic Theory and Practice After the Deliberative Turn.* Oxford: Oxford University Press.

    2003. *Reflective Democracy.* Oxford: Oxford University Press.

Gould, Deborah. 2009. *Moving Politics: Emotion and ACT UP's Fight Against AIDS*. Chicago: University of Chicago Press.

Granovetter, Mark. 1973. "The Strength of Weak Ties." *American Journal of Sociology*, 87 (6): 1360–1380.

Gregory, R., T. Satterfield, and A. Hasell. 2016. "Using Decision Pathway Surveys to Inform Climate Engineering Policy Choices," *PNAS* 113 (3): 560–565.

Greenwood, Peter W. 2014. *Evidence-Based Practice in Juvenile Justice: Progress, Challenges, and Opportunities*. New York: Springer Briefs in Criminology.

Griswold del Castillo, Richard and Richard García. 2008. "Co-leadership: The Strength of Dolores Huerta," in *A Dolores Huerta Reader*, Mario T. García, ed. Albuquerque: University of New Mexico Press, 23–37.

Habermas, Jürgen. 1996. *Between Facts and Norms: Contributions to a Discourse Theory of Law and Democracy*. Cambridge: MIT Press.

   1993. "Further Reflections on the Public Sphere," in *Habermas and the Public Sphere*, Craig Calhoun, ed. Cambridge: MIT Press, 421–461.

   1993a. "Concluding Remarks," in *Habermas and the Public Sphere*, Craig Calhoun, ed. Cambridge: MIT Press, 462–479.

   1992. "The Unity of Reason in the Diversity of Its Voices," in *Postmetaphysical Thinking, Philosophical Essays*, trans. William Mark Hohengarten. Cambridge: MIT Press, 115–148.

   1990. "The Critique of Reason as an Unmasking of the Human Sciences: Michel Foucault," in *The Philosophical Discourse of Modernity: Twelve Lectures*, trans. Frederick G. Lawrence. Cambridge: MIT Press, 238–265.

   1990a. "Some Questions Concerning the Theory of Power: Foucault Again," in *The Philosophical Discourse of Modernity: Twelve Lectures*, trans. Frederick G. Lawrence. Cambridge: MIT Press, 266–293.

   1990b. "An Alternative Way Out of the Philosophy of the Subject: Communicative versus Subject-Centered Reason," in *The Philosophical Discourse of Modernity: Twelve Lectures*, trans. Frederick G. Lawrence. Cambridge: MIT Press, 294–326.

   1990c. "The Normative Content of Modernity," in *The Philosophical Discourse of Modernity: Twelve Lectures*, trans. Frederick G. Lawrence. Cambridge: MIT Press, 337–367.

   1990d. "Discourse Ethics: Notes on a Program of Philosophical Justification," in *The Communicative Ethics Controversy*, Seyla Benhabib and Fred Dallmayr, eds. Boston: The MIT Press, 60–110.

1989. *The Structural Transformation of the Public Sphere: An Inquiry into a Category of Bourgeois Society*, trans. Thomas Burger. Cambridge: MIT Press.

1989a. "Towards a Communication-Concept of Rational Collective-Will Formation. A Thought Experiment." *Ratio Juris* 2 (2): 144–154.

1984. *The Theory of Communicative Action*, trans. Thomas McCarthy. Vol. 1. Boston: Beacon Press.

1984a. *The Theory of Communicative Action*, trans. Thomas McCarthy. Vol. 2. Boston: Beacon Press.

1979. *Communication and the Evolution of Society*, trans. Thomas McCarthy. Boston: Beacon Press.

Habermas, Jürgen et al. 2010. *An Awareness of What is Missing: Faith and Reason in a Post-Secular Age*. Ciaran Cronin, trans. Cambridge: Polity Press.

Hacker, Jacob S. and Paul Pierson. 2010. *Winner-Take-All Politics: How Washington Made the Rich Richer and Turned its Back on the Middle Class*. New York: Simon & Schuster.

Hagendijk, Rob and Alan Irwin. 2006. "Public Deliberation and Governance: Engaging with Science and Technology in Contemporary Europe." *Minerva*, 44 (2): 167–184.

Hajer, Maarten A. and H. Wagenaar. 2003. *Deliberative Policy Analysis: Understanding Governance in the Network Society*. Cambridge: Cambridge University Press.

Hamilton, David, L., ed. 2005. *Social Cognition: Key Readings*. New York: Psychology Press.

Hammerback, John C., and Richard J. Jensen. 1998. *The Rhetorical Career of César Chávez*. College Station: Texas A & M University Press.

Harthorn, B., Herr, C. Shearer, and J. Rogers. 2011. "Exploring Ambivalence: Techno-Enthusiasm and Skepticism in Nanotech Deliberations," in *Quantum Engagements: Social Reflections of Nanoscience and Emerging Technologies*. T.B. Zülsdorf, C. Coenen, A. Ferrari, U. Fiedeler, C. Milburn, and Matthias Wienroth, eds. IOS Press, Amsterdam, 75–88.

Held, David. 1996. *Models of Democracy*. Stanford: Stanford University Press.

Hertz, Noreena. 2001. *The Silent Takeover: Global Capitalism and the Death of Democracy*. New York: Free Press.

Hoaglin, David C., Frederick Mosteller, and John W. Tukey. 1983. *Understanding Robust and Exploratory Data Analysis*. New York: Wiley.

Horkheimer, Max and Theodor W. Adorno. 1991. *Dialectic of Enlightenment*. New York: Continuum.

House of Lords. 2006. *Science and Technology*—Third Report. House of Lords, London

Huntington, Samuel P. 2004. *Who Are We?: The Challenges to America's National Identity*. New York: Simon & Schuster.

1996. *The Clash of Civilizations and the Remaking of World Order*. New York: Simon & Schuster.

Irwin, Alan. 2006. "The Politics of Talk: Coming to Terms with the "New" Scientific Governance." *Social Studies of Science* 36 (2): 299–320.

Jacquet, Jennifer. 2015. *Is Shame Necessary?: New Uses for an Old Tool*. New York: Pantheon.

Jasanoff, Sheila. 2005. *Designs on Nature: Science and Democracy in Europe and the United States*. Princeton: Princeton University Press.

Kadushin, Charles. 2012. *Understanding Social Networks: Theories, Concepts, and Findings*. New York: Oxford University Press.

Kaeser, Gigi and Peggy Gillespie. 1999. *Love Makes a Family: Portraits of Lesbian, Gay, Bisexual, and Transgender Parents and Their Families*. Amherst: University of Massachusetts Press.

Kahane, David, Daniel Weinstock, Dominique Leydet, and Melissa Williams. 2010. *Deliberative Democracy in Practice*. Vancouver: University of British Columbia Press.

Kahneman, Daniel. 2011. *Thinking, Fast and Slow*. New York: Farrar, Straus, and Giroux.

Kahneman, Daniel, Paul Slovic, and Amos Tversky. 1982. *Judgment Under Uncertainty: Heuristics and Biases*. Cambridge: Cambridge University Press.

Karpf, David. 2012. *The MoveOn Effect: The Unexpected Transformation of American Political Advocacy*. New York: Oxford University Press.

Karr-Morse, Robin, and Meredith S. Wiley. 2012. *Scared Sick: The Role of Childhood Trauma in Adult Disease*. New York: Basic Books.

Karslake, Daniel. 2007. *For the Bible Tells Me So*. DVD. New York: First Run Features.

Kelly, Jamie Terence. 2012. *Framing Democracy: A Behavioral Approach to Democratic Theory*. Princeton: Princeton University Press.

Kinsey, Alfred, C., Wardell Baxter Pomeroy, and Clyde E. Martin. 1948. *Sexual Behavior in the Human Male*. Philadelphia: W.B. Saunders Co.

Kinsey, Alfred, C. 1953. *Sexual Behavior in the Human Female*. Philadelphia: W.B. Saunders Co.

Knorr-Cetina, Karin. 1999. *Epistemic Cultures: How the Sciences Make Knowledge*. Cambridge: Harvard University Press.

Lawrence, William. 1946. *Dawn Over Zero: The Story of the Atomic Bomb*. New York: Knopf.

LeDoux, Joseph, E. 2002. *Synaptic Self: How Our Brains Become Who We Are*. New York: Viking.

1996. *The Emotional Brain: The Mysterious Underpinnings of Emotional Life*. New York: Simon & Schuster.

Leighninger, Matt. 2012. "Mapping Deliberative Civic Engagement: Pictures from a (R)evolution," in *Democracy in Motion: Evaluating the Practice and Impact of Deliberative Civic Engagement*, T. Nabatchi et al., eds. Oxford: Oxford University Press, 32–37.

Lichtenstein, Sarah and Paul Slovic. 2006. *The Construction of Preference*. Cambridge: Cambridge University Press.

Lyon, Arabella. 2013. *Deliberative Acts: Democracy, Rhetoric, and Rights*. University Park: Pennsylvania State University Press.

Maia, Rousiley C. M. 2012. *Deliberation, the Media and Political Talk*. New York: Hampton Press.

Manjoo, Farhad. 2008. *True Enough: Learning to Live in a Post-Fact Society*. Hoboken: John Wiley and Sons.

Mann, Thomas E., and Norman J. Ornstein. 2012. *It's Even Worse Than it Looks: How the American Constitutional System Collided with the New Politics of Extremism*. New York: Basic Books.

Mansbridge, Jane, 1999. "Everyday Talk in the Deliberative System." in *Deliberative Politics*, S. Macedo, Ed. Oxford University Press, 211–239.

Mansbridge, Jane, James Bohman, Simone Chambers, Thomas Christiano, Archon Fung, John Parkinson, Dennis Thompson, F., and Mark Warren, E. 2012. "A Systemic Approach to Deliberative Democracy," in *Deliberative Systems: Deliberative Democracy at the Large Scale*, John Parkinson and Jane Mansbridge, eds. New York: Cambridge University Press.

McNabb, David. 2004. *Research Methods for Political Science: Quantitative and Qualitative Methods*. Armonk: M.E. Sharpe, 384–385.

Mendelberg, Tali. 2001. *The Race Card: Campaign Strategy, Implicit Messages, and the Norm of Equality*. Princeton: Princeton University Press.

Middlebrook, Diane Wood. 1998. *Suits Me: The Double Life of Billy Tipton*. Boston: Houghton Mifflin.

Milgram, Stanley. 1974. *Obedience to Authority: An Experimental View*. New York: Harper & Row.

Mol, Annemarie. 2002. *The Body Multiple: Ontology in Medical Practice*. Durham: Duke University Press.

Moran, Michael, Martin Rein, and Robert E. Goodin. 2006. *The Oxford Handbook of Public Policy*. Oxford: Oxford University Press.

Mosteller, Frederick, and John W. Tukey. 1977. *Data Analysis and Regression: A Second Course in Statistics.* Reading: Addison-Wesley Publishing. Co.

Muthu, Sankar. 2003. *Enlightenment Against Empire.* Princeton: Princeton University Press.

Nabatchi, Tina, John Gastil, Michael Weiksner, G., and Matt Leighninger, eds. 2012. *Democracy in Motion: Evaluating the Practice and Impact of Deliberative Civic Engagement.* New York: Oxford University Press.

Nanda, Serena 1999. *Gender Diversity: Crosscultural Variations,* Long Grove, IL: Waveland Press.

Neblo, Michael. 2005. "Thinking through Democracy: Between the Theory and Practice of Deliberative Politics." *Acta Politica* 40 (2): 169–181.

Omi, Michael, and Howard Winant. 1994. *Racial Formation in the United States: From the 1960s to the 1990s.* New York: Routledge.

Oreskes, Naomi and Erik M. Conway. 2010. *Merchants of Doubt: How a Handful of Scientists Obscured the Truth on Issues from Tobacco Smoke to Global Warming.* New York: Bloomsbury Press.

Owen R., J. Stilgoe, and P. Macnaghten. 2012. "Responsible Research and Innovation: From Science in Society to Science for Society, with Society." *Science and Public Policy* 39 (6): 751–760.

Owen, Richard, John Bessant, and Maggy Heintz. 2013. *Responsible Innovation: Managing the Responsible Emergence of Science and Innovation in Society.* Wiley. http://lib.myilibrary.com?id=477769.

Palmer, Parker J. 2011. *Healing the Heart of Democracy: The Courage to Create a Politics Worthy of the Human Spirit.* San Francisco: Jossey-Bass.

Parekh, Bhikhu C. 2000. *Rethinking Multiculturalism: Cultural Diversity and Political Theory.* Cambridge: Harvard University Press.

Parkhill, Karen, Nick Pidgeon, Adam Corner, and Naomi Vaughan. 2013. "Deliberation and Responsible Innovation: A Geoengineering Case Study," in *Responsible Innovation: Managing the Responsible Emergence of Science and Innovation in Society,* Richard Owen, Richard, John Bessant, and Maggy Heintz, eds. New York: Wiley.

Parkhill, Karen, A., Christina Demski, Catherine Butler, Alexa Spence, and Nicholas F. Pidgeon. 2013. *Transforming the UK Energy System: Public Values, Attitudes and Acceptability – Synthesis Report.* London: UK Energy Research Centre.

Parkinson, John. 2006. *Deliberating in the Real World: Problems of Legitimacy in Deliberative Democracy.* Oxford: Oxford University Press.

Parkinson, John and Jane J. Mansbridge. 2012. *Deliberative Systems: Deliberative Democracy at the Large Scale.* Cambridge, UK: Cambridge University Press.

PEW Charitable Trusts. 2015. *The Precarious State of Family Balance Sheets.* Washington DC: The PEW Charitable Trusts.

PEW Research Center. 2013. *A Survey of LGBT Americans: Attitudes, Experiences and Values in Changing Times, in LGBT in Changing Times.* Washington DC: PEW Research Center.

2013a. *In Gay Marriage Debate, Both Supporters and Opponents See Legal Recognition as "Inevitable,"* Washington DC: The PEW Research Center for the People & The Press, 8–17.

2012. *The Rise of Residential Segregation by Income.* Social & Demographic Trends. Washington DC: PEW Research Center.

Pidgeon, Nicholas, F., Christina Demski, Catherine Butler, Karen Parkhill, and Alexa Spence. 2014. "Creating a National Citizen Engagement Process for Energy Policy." *PNAS* 111 (4): 13606–13613.

Pidgeon, Nicholas, F. and Baruch Fischhoff. 2011. "The Role of Social and Decision Sciences in Communicating Uncertain Climate Risks." *Nature Climate Change* 1 (1): 35–41.

Pidgeon, Nick. 1998. "Risk Assessment, Risk Values and the Social Science Programme: Why We Do Need Risk Perception Research." *Reliability Engineering & System Safety* 59 (1): 5–15.

Pinker, Steven. 2011. *The Better Angels of Our Nature: Why Violence Has Declined.* New York: Penguin Books.

Putnam, Robert D. 2000. *Bowling Alone: the Collapse and Revival of American Community.* New York: Simon & Schuster.

Renn, Ortwin, Thomas Webler, and Peter M. Wiedemann. 1995. *Fairness and Competence in Citizen Participation: Evaluating Models for Environmental Discourse.* Dordrecht: Kluwer Academic.

Rhee, Nari and Ilana Boivie. 2015. *"The Continuing Retirement Savings Crisis."* Washington DC: National Institute on Retirement Security.

Robinson, Gene. 2012. *God Believes in Love: Straight Talk About Gay Marriage.* New York: Knopf.

2008. *In the Eye of the Storm: Swept to the Center by God.* New York: Seabury Books.

Robson, Colin. 2002. *Real World Research: A Resource for Social Scientists and Practitioner-Researchers.* Oxford, UK: Blackwell Publishers.

Rocco, Raymond. 2014. *Transforming Citizenship: Democracy, Membership, and Belonging in Latino Communities.* East Lansing: Michigan State University Press.

Rogers, Everett, M. 2003. *Diffusion of Innovations.* New York: Free Press.

Roscoe, Will. 2000. *Changing Ones: Third and Fourth Genders in Native North America*. New York: St. Martin's Griffin.

Rosenberg, Shawn W. 2007. *Deliberation, Participation and Democracy: Can the People Govern?* Basingstoke: Palgrave Macmillan.

Roughgarden, Joan. 2009. *Evolution's Rainbow: Diversity, Gender, and Sexuality in Nature and People*. Berkeley: University of California Press.

Rudacille, Deborah. 2005. *The Riddle of Gender: Science, Activism, and Transgender Rights*. New York: Pantheon Books.

Rupp, Leila J. 2009. *Sapphistries: A Global History of Love Between Women*. New York: New York University Press.

Savage, Dan and Terry Miller. 2012. *It Gets Better: Coming Out, Overcoming Bullying, and Creating a Life Worth Living*. New York: Penguin Books

Scaer, Robert, C. 2014. *The Body Bears The Burden: Trauma, Dissociation, and Disease*. New York: Routledge.

2005. *The Trauma Spectrum: Hidden Wounds and Human Resiliency*. New York: W. W. Norton & Company.

Sen, Rinku. *The Accidental American: Immigration and Citizenship in the Age of Globalization*. San Francisco: Berrett-Koehler.

Shapiro, Ian and Michael J. Graetz. 2006. *Death by a Thousand Cuts: The Fight Over Taxing Inherited Wealth*. Princeton: Princeton University Press.

Shilts, Randy. 1987. *And the Band Played On: Politics, People, and the AIDS Epidemic*. New York: St. Martin's Press.

Smelser, Neil, J. 2004. "Psychological Trauma and Cultural Trauma," in *Cultural Trauma and Collective Identity*, Jeffrey C. Alexander, ed. Berkeley: University of California Press.

Smith, Graham. 2009. *Democratic Innovations: Designing Institutions for Citizen Participation*. Robert E. Goodin, ed. *Theories of Institutional Design*. Cambridge: Cambridge University Press.

Stebbins, Robert A. 2001. *Exploratory Research in the Social Sciences*. Thousand Oaks: Sage Publications.

Stiglitz, Joseph E. 2012. *The Price of Inequality: How Today's Divided Society Endangers our Future*. New York: W.W. Norton & Co.

Stilgoe, Jack, Simon J. Lock, and James Wilsdon. 2014. "Why Should We Promote Public Engagement with Science?" *Public Understanding of Science* 23 (1): 4–15.

Stilgoe, Jack, Matthew Watson, and Kirsty Kuo. 2013. "Public Engagement with Biotechnologies Offers Lessons for the Governance of Geoengineering Research and Beyond." *PLoS Biology* 11 (11): e1001707.

Stirling, Andy. 2010. "Keep It Complex." *Nature* 468 (7327): 1029–1031.

Thompson, Dennis. 2008. "Deliberative Democratic Theory and Empirical Political Science." *Annual Review of Political Science* 11 (1): 497–520.

Tsvetovat, Maksim and Alexander Kouznetsov. 2011. *Social Network Analysis for Startups*. Sebastopol: O'Reilly.

Tukey, John W. 1984. "We Need Both Exploratory and Confirmatory," in *The Collected Works of John W. Tukey*, Lyle V. Jones, ed. Belmont: Wadsworth Advanced Books & Software. Vol. 4, 811–817.

Turkle, Sherry. 2011. *Alone Together: Why We Expect More from Technology and Less from Each Other*. New York: Basic Books.

Van der Kolk, Bessel A., Alexander C. McFarlane, and Lars Weisaeth, eds. 1996. *Traumatic Stress: The Effects of Overwhelming Experience on Mind, Body, and Society*. New York: The Guilford Press.

Wahls, Zach and Bruce Littlefield. 2012. *My Two Moms: Lessons of Love, Strength, and What Makes A Family*. New York: Gotham Books.

Wasik, Bill. 2009. *And Then There's This: How Stories Live and Die in Viral Culture*. New York: Viking.

Wiggershaus, Rolf. 1994. *The Frankfurt School: Its History, Theories, and Political Significance*. Cambridge: MIT Press.

Wilsdon, James and Rebecca Willis. 2004. *See-Through Science: Why Public Engagement Needs to Move Upstream*. London: Demos.

Wittgenstein, Ludwig. 1968. *Philosophical Investigations*. Translated by G. E. M. Anscombe. 3rd edition. New York: Macmillian Publishing Company.

Wolin, Sheldon, S. 2008. *Democracy Incorporated: Managed Democracy and the Specter of Inverted Totalitarianism*. Princeton: Princeton University Press.

Wright, Scott and John Street. 2007. "Democracy, Deliberation and Design: the Case of Online Discussion Forums." *New Media & Society* 9 (5): 849–869.

Wynne, Brian. 2006. "Public Engagement as a Means of Restoring Public Trust in Science – Hitting the Notes, but Missing the Music?" *Community Genetics* 9 (3): 211–220.

Yarbo-Bejarano, Yvonne. 2006. "Gloria Anzaldúa's *Borderlands/La Frontera: Cultural Studies, 'Difference,' and the Non-Unitary Subject*." in *The Chicana/o Cultural Studies Reader*, Angie Chabram-Dernersesian, ed. New York: Routledge, 81–92.

Yin, Robert. 2003. *Case Study Research, Design and Methods*, 3rd edition. Newbury Park: Sage Publications.

Zimbardo, Philip. 2008. *The Lucifer Effect: Understanding How Good People Turn Evil*, New York: Random House.

Index

abomination, meaning of, 110
Acquired Immune Deficiency
  Syndrome. *See* AIDS crisis
activism and advocacy, 34, 126,
  126n13
Adorno, Theodor, 7, 8, 176, 215,
  267–68
advocacy and deliberative
  entrepreneurs, 126n13
Age of Reason. *See* the Enlightenment
AIDS crisis, 79–81, 83–84
Amaechi, John: attitudes toward, 134;
  on Bryant slur, 141–42, 145; as
  deliberative entrepreneur, 102–5,
  144; on mindful communication and
  healing, 237–38; Welts compared to,
  136, 142
ambivalence, role of, 223n15
American Family Association,
  198n23
Andresen, Ryan, 91–92, 153
Anzaldúa, Gloria, 207
autopilot, cognitive. *See* cognitive
  autopilot

Benjamin, Jody, 154
bias, implicit. *See* implicit bias
biological essentialism, 233
Black Church Week of Prayer, 84
Black Lives Matter, 241
Blankenhorn, David, 204–5, 210
border crossers, 207–8
"born this way" discourse, 227–29
bounded domain specific networks,
  254–55
Boy Scouts of America (BSA): and,
  152–53; communication in, 156–57;
  exclusionary practices of, 148–49;
  leaders, 151; LGBT scout leaders in,
  156; social network cohesion in, 118,

147, 154–55; Wahls relations with,
  149–50
Boy Scouts of America Equal Access
  Act, 148n66
Boy Scouts of America v. Dale, 149
Brown, Mark, 231
Bruce, Ashlee, 165
Bryant, Kobe, 135, 139–43
Bully (film), 94

Cable News Network (CNN), 154, 159
California, Proposition 8 in, 204–5
case study, LGBT. *See* LGBT case study
Castells, Manual: on the networked
  society, 119n5, 127; networked
  systems in relation to, 250; *Networks
  of Outrage and Hope*,
  64–67; on social movements, 116; on
  us-versus-them narrative, 260
catalysts, deliberative. *See* deliberative
  catalysts
centrality, network, 179–81, 207
Chapin, Sean, 133n27
Cheney family, 208
children, impact of same sex marriage
  on, 191–92
Children and the Law blog, 130
civility and incivility, 73n75, 210
CNN (Cable News Network), 154
cognitive autopilot, 53–60, 106,
  177–78, 185–86, 241
cognitive load, 184–85, 259
cognitive obstacles: bias, 171–72,
  184–85; circumventing, 53–60, 197,
  230–35, 258–59; enumerated, 52;
  fear, 185–86; hidden, 60–62; identity
  threat, 187–94; remedies for, *194*;
  research on, 275; role and nature of,
  256–57; the self in relation to, 217;
  trauma, 62–64, 274; types of, 173;